DEATH AND DYING IN IRELAND, BRITAIN AND EUROPE

Historical Perspectives

Edited by

JAMES KELLY
MARY ANN LYONS

First published in 2013 by Irish Academic Press
8 Chapel Lane
Sallins
Co. Kildare, Ireland

This edition © 2013 Irish Academic Press
Individual chapters © contributors

British Library Cataloguing in Publication Data
An entry can be found on request

ISBN: 978 0 7165 3188 3 (cloth)
ISBN: 978 0 7165 3191 3 (paper)
ISBN: 978 0 7165 3192 0 (ebook)

Library of Congress Cataloging-in-Publication Data
An entry can be found on request

Printed in Ireland by Sprintprint Ltd.

CONTENTS

ACKNOWLEDGMENTS

Though there have been a welcome number of engagements with aspects of the phenomenon, the subject of death and dying has largely been accorded a peripheral space in the narrative of Irish history. This is less obviously true of Irish archaeology because of the centrality of divers places of interment (tombs, graves, cists, barrows and so on) and the grave goods often found therein to the generation of the narrative of prehistory. But as approaches to the evidential record – to which scholars in both disciplines appeal in order to reconstruct and to understand the past – evolve and expand, the realization (more advanced in archaeology than in history) that the study of death in history involves more than establishing how the living commemorated or remembered their dead has promoted a more expansive engagement with the subject. Death is a multi-dimensional, multi-faceted phenomenon, virtually as diverse as life itself. It can, as a result, be approached, interrogated, viewed, and reconstructed in a great variety of ways and from a multiplicity of perspectives in order to illuminate and amplify a myriad of social, economic and political trends and tendencies. A single volume cannot, and the essays in this volume on death in Ireland, England and Europe across several millennia do not, aspire to engage with more than a sample of these. However, the contributions are offered in the anticipation not only that they offer new perspectives, but also that they demonstrate the capacity of the subject to illuminate long-established themes such as the emergence of Christianity, the use of the hunger strike, and casualties incurred during strife. They also expand our understanding of what it meant to live (as well as to die) during the prehistoric and historic eras.

The thirtieth biennial Irish Conference of Historians, from which all but one of the fourteen essays presented in this volume derive, had 'death and dying' as its theme. It was the occasion for a gathering of scholars who were at one in the belief that an exploration of how death and dying were experienced, responded to, and interpreted has much to relate about past attitudes and past societies. Each has made an important contribution to locating death more securely and centrally within the narrative of the past. As with any collective endeavour, the editors of this volume have incurred considerable intellectual, personal, organizational and institutional debts during its preparation. It is our pleasure to thank the contributors who have made the book possible, first by responding positively to the invitation to participate in the conference which was hosted jointly by the National University of Ireland Maynooth and St Patrick's College, Drumcondra, and which took place at NUI, Maynooth (19–21 June 2011). The editors would like particularly to thank thank Ann Donoghue, Mel Farrell, and Catherine Bergin who assisted in the organization of the event. We wish also to thank those who chaired sessions. Particular thanks are due to Professor David Dickson who delivered Professor Ó Grada's paper. As editors we thank the authors for the for the professionalism and personal courtesy with which they responded to our communications, and more generally for their support and co-operation at all stages in this endeavour. We are very grateful to our colleagues on the Royal Irish Academy Committee for Historical Sciences, under whose aegis both the conference and the conference proceedings are organized; to An Foras Feasa: the institute for research in Irish historical and cultural traditions at NUI, Maynooth; the History Department, St Patrick's College, Dublin City University, and the History Department at NUI, Maynooth for institutional and practical support. Thanks are due also to the Research Committee at St Patrick's College for financial support, which has facilitated the publication.

More broadly, it is with gratitude that the editors acknowledge the archives, archivists, trustees, custodians and copyright holders of the manuscripts, rare books and newspapers and other sources consulted by the authors of essays in the volume. Finally, we extend our thanks to Lisa Hyde and all at Irish Academic Press for their belief in the project, and their enduring commitment to the publication of history.

JK; MAL
November 2012

FIGURES, MAPS, TABLES

Figures

Maps

Tables

ABBREVIATIONS

AN	Archives Nationales
b.	born
BL	British Library
BMH	Bureau of Military History
c.	*circa*
CAI	Cork Archives Institute
cal.	calibration/calibrated
CPM	Cork Public Museum
d.	died
DDA	Dublin Diocesan Archives
DIB	*Dictionary of Irish Biography* edited by J. McGuire and J. Quinn (9 volumes, 2009)
ed./eds	editor/editors
edn.	edition
EHR	*English Historical Review*
IHS	*Irish Historical Studies*
LMA	London Metropolitan Archives
MAI	Military Archives of Ireland
MNI	Minimum number of individuals
MS(S)	Manuscript(s)
NAI	National Archives of Ireland
NFC	National Folklore Collection
NLI	National Library of Ireland
n.d.	no date
new ser.	new series
no./nos	number/numbers
NUIG	National University of Ireland, Galway
NUIM	National University of Ireland, Maynooth

PRONI	Public Record Office of Northern Ireland
QUB	Queen's University, Belfast
rept.	Reprinted
RIA	Royal Irish Academy
RIA proc.	*Proceedings of the Royal Irish Academy*
RSAI Jnl.	*Journal of the Royal Society of Antiquaries of Ireland*
TCD	Trinity College, Dublin
TNA	The National Archives, Public Record Office
trans.	translation
UCC	University College, Cork
UCD	University College, Dublin

THE CONTRIBUTORS

GUY BEINER is a senior lecturer in modern history at Ben-Gurion University of the Negev, Israel. He was a Government of Ireland scholar at University College Dublin, Government of Ireland Research Fellow at Trinity College Dublin, and National Endowment for the Humanities Fellow at the Keough-Naughton Center for Irish Studies in the University of Notre Dame. His book *Remembering the Year of the French: Irish Folk History and Social Memory* (2007) has won numerous international awards.

EDEL BHREATHNACH is CEO of the Discovery Programme, an Irish archaeological, historical and geo-surveying research body funded by the Heritage Council. She is a medievalist who has worked on inter-disciplinary projects relating to the Hill of Tara and other historical Irish landscapes, monasticism and mendicantism in medieval Ireland, the history of the Irish Franciscans, and the intellectual culture of medieval Ireland.

CIARA BREATHNACH lectures in history at the University of Limerick. Her research focuses on the social, economic and cultural history of nineteenth-century Ireland. She is the author of *The Congested Districts Board of Ireland, 1891-1923: Poverty and Development in the West of Ireland* (2005) and (with Aoife Bhreatnach) *Portraying Irish Travellers: Histories and Representations* (2007); and editor of *Visual, Material and Print Culture in Nineteenth-Century Ireland* (2010). She is currently working on the social history of medicalization and corporeal care in Ireland 1860-1922.

DAVID BUTLER is a part-time lecturer in the School of Geography and Archaeology in University College Cork where he is academic coordinator of the NUI Diploma in Local and Regional Studies. He previously taught in the Department of History, University of Limerick, 2007–09. He is the author of *South Tipperary, 1570–1841: Religion, Land and Rivalry* (2005). He has, since 2000, served as a board member of The Butler Society, and was, in 2006, appointed editor of *Journal of the Butler Society*.

JOSEPH CLARKE is lecturer in Modern European History in Trinity College Dublin. He is the author of *Commemorating the Dead in Revolutionary France: Revolution and Remembrance, 1789–1799* (2007 and 2011). The main focus of his current research, entitled 'Revolution, revival and reaction: the culture and politics of religion in France from Republic to Restoration', is to chart the impact of revolutionary dechristianization upon the cultural values and political identities of the generation that came of age in France during the 1790s.

GABRIEL COONEY, MRIA, is Professor of Celtic Archaeology at UCD and a member of the RIA Committee for Archaeology. A specialist in the Neolithic era, he is founding editor of *Archaeology-Ireland*, a member of the editorial board of *World Archaeology*, and chairman of the Historical Monuments Council of Northern Ireland. He is author (with Eoin Grogan) of *Irish Prehistory: a Social Perspective* (1994); *Landscapes of Neolithic Ireland* (2000), and *Key Recommendations from the Royal Irish Academy Forum: Archaeology in Ireland: a Vision for the Future* (2007). He is currently completing a book on death in prehistoric Ireland.

VANESSA HARDING is Professor of London History at Birkbeck, University of London. Her research combines demography, environmental history, and topography, as well as social history and the history of material culture, to reconstruct social interactions and networks in the expanding metropolis. She has published numerous articles and essays on aspects of this topic, and advised on archaeological publication programmes; her book *The Dead and the Living in London and Paris, 1500–1670* was published in 2002.

JAMES KELLY, MRIA, is Cregan Professor of History, and Head of the History Department at St Patrick's College, Dublin City University. His publications include *That Damn'd Thing Called Honour: Duelling in Ireland, 1750–1860* (1995); *Poynings' Law and the Making of Law in Ireland, 1660–1800* (2007); *The Proceedings of the House of Lords, 1771–1800* (3 Volumes, 2008); *Sir Richard Musgrave, 1746–1818: Ultra Protestant Ideologue* (2009), and *Clubs and Societies in Eighteenth-Century Ireland* (edited with Martyn Powell) (2010).

DAVID LEDERER is a senior lecturer in history at NUI, Maynooth. He has published widely on the history of suicide. His monograph, *Madness, Religion and the State in Early Modern Europe: a Bavarian Beacon* (2006) won the Gerald Strauss prize from the Sixteenth-Century Society for best book in Reformation history. He has held various fellowships (Alexander-von-Humboldt Foundation, the IRCHSS, the Fulbright Foundation and the German Academic Exchange Service) and has served as visiting professor to the Catholic University of America, the Chinese University of Hong Kong and the Ludwigs-Maximilian University in Munich.

MARY ANN LYONS is Professor of History and Head of department at NUI, Maynooth. Her publications include *Church and Society in County Kildare, c. 1470–1547* (2000), *Franco-Irish Relations, 1500–1610* (2003), and (with Thomas O'Connor) *Strangers to Citizens: the Irish in Europe, 1600–1800* (2008). As co-director of the Irish in Europe project she has edited *Irish Communities in Early Modern Europe* (2006) and *The Ulster Earls and Baroque Europe: Refashioning Irish Identities, 1600–1800* (2010).

WILLIAM MURPHY is a lecturer in Irish Studies at the Mater Dei Institute of Education, Dublin City University. He is co-editor of *The Gaelic Athletic Association, 1884–2009* (2009), which was awarded the Best Sports History Edited Collection published in English in 2009 by the North American Society for Sport History. His primary interest is in the history of the Irish revolution, and his research is currently focused on political imprisonment during that period. His monograph *Political Imprisonment and the Irish, 1910–1921* will be published in 2013.

ELIZABETH O'BRIEN is a Research Fellow with the UCD Mícheál Ó Cléirigh Institute. An archaeologist and historian, she has worked for many years on burials and burial practices in late prehistoric and early medieval Ireland and Britain. She has published widely on the subject and is the primary researcher for the Heritage Council INSTAR 'Mapping Death' project. She has excavated Dundrum Castle, County Dublin; Durrow, County Offaly; Ballyman, County Dublin; and Ballymacaward, County Donegal.

CORMAC Ó GRÁDA, MRIA, is Professor emeritus of Economics at UCD. His recent books include *Famine: a Short History* (2009); *Ireland's Great Famine: Interdisciplinary Perspectives* (2006); and *Jewish Ireland in the Age of Joyce: a Social Science History* (2006). His current research (with Morgan Kelly) is focussed on the economic history of England before the Industrial Revolution.

EUNAN O'HALPIN, MRIA, is Bank of Ireland Professor of Contemporary Irish History at Trinity College Dublin. He has written widely on aspects of twentieth-century Irish and British history and politics. He is a joint editor of the Royal Irish Academy Documents on Irish Foreign Policy series. His next book (with Daithí Ó Corráin), *The Dead of the Irish Revolution*, is being prepared for publication. He is currently preparing two monographs: *Diplomacy, Security and the Northern Ireland Crisis, 1965–1998* and *Between Two Evils: Afghanistan and the Belligerent Powers in the Second World War*.

CLODAGH TAIT lectures in the Department of History, Mary Immaculate College, Limerick. Author of *Death, Burial and Commemoration in Ireland, c.1550–1650* (2002) and co-editor of *Age of Atrocity: Violence and Political Conflict in Early Modern Ireland* (2007), she has published articles on childbirth, baptism, naming, Catholic religious devotion, commemoration, martyrdom, and riot and protest. She is currently completing a survey of the cultural and social history of the British and Irish Isles in the sixteenth and seventeenth centuries.

SARAH TARLOW is Professor of Archaeology and Director of the Centre for Historical Archaeology at the University of Leicester. Editor (with Fokke Gerritsen and Michael Dietler) of *Archaeological Dialogues*, her publications include *Bereavement and Commemoration: An Archaeology of Mortality* (1999); *The Archaeology of Improvement in Britain, 1750–1850* (2007); *Ritual, Belief and the Dead Body in Early Modern Britain and Ireland* (2011) and (with Annia Cherryson and Zoe Crossland) *A Fine and Private Place: The Archaeology of Death and Burial in Post-Medieval Britain and Ireland* (2012).

JOHN WOLFFE is Professor of Religious History at the Open University. His publications include *The Protestant Crusade in Great Britain, 1829–1860* (1991); *God and Greater Britain: Religion and National Life in Britain and Ireland, 1843–1945* (1994); *Great Deaths: Grieving, Religion and Nationhood in Victorian and Edwardian Britain* (2000), and *The Expansion of Evangelicalism: The Age of Wilberforce, More, Chalmers and Finney* (2006). He currently holds a fellowship funded under the UK Research Council's Global Uncertainties programme for a project on 'Protestant–Catholic Conflict: Historical Legacies and Contemporary Realities', which, among other things, seeks to set new work on Northern Ireland sectarian tensions in a broad historical and comparative framework.

INTRODUCTION

Death cannot be regarded as one of those historical topics that historians and archaeologists have overlooked. Its ubiquity, inevitability, and enduring capacity to intrude, often dramatically, and, by definition, decisively, have guaranteed it a place of prominence in most narratives. Yet until the 1970s it was hardly deemed worthy of study in its own right. As one of the ineluctable facts of the human condition, its very omnipresence paradoxically facilitated its elision from the historical narrative other than as a collateral consequence of the struggle for survival in times of famine, disease and war, when the preoccupation was essentially with numbers, rather than the experience, its register and impact. Death was also manifestly unavoidable in grand narratives of the rise and fall of civilizations and great powers, and arguably still more so in the struggle of smaller polities and identities for survival.[1] It was integral to the relationship of man and nature – one of the primary vectors of history.[2] Furthermore, it was, and is, intrinsic to the striking demographic growth of the species – the significance of which for human conduct and behaviour is arguably still not sufficiently factored into the explanations proffered for the major transformations that punctuate the grand narrative of human history, both in the far past and in more recent times, when the existence of statistical data (in however raw a form) permits some informed numerative perspectives.[3] Even demographers, who have aspired to reconstruct and, thereby, to explain the varying fortunes of the human population, for whom death is a constant, have accorded the subject less attention than might be anticipated.[4]

This is not to suggest that death and the manner in which it has been represented has been completely overlooked. The usefulness of monumental features (tombs and allied architectural phenomena) as a means of accessing the culture and history of pre-literate civilizations

1

requires little elaboration; it has permitted archaeologists not only to construct a credible sequence of civilizations across the globe, but also to access the cultural worlds of successive prehistoric communities. In the historical era, monuments to the dead have likewise provided a rich route into contemporary thinking for a great variety of eras up to and including that named after Queen Victoria of England (1837–1901), although the preoccupation with graves and memorials constructed in that, and earlier, eras was less about death than the memorialization of the dead. In other words, more attention was paid to the design and style of the mausolea, memorials and other graveyard furniture than to the manner in which people died, or to the meaning and impact of death for and upon those who were bereaved.[5] Indicatively, one can readily locate institutional histories of graveyards from the nineteenth and twentieth centuries, which engage informatively with the politics of interment, with matters such as body-snatching and other anti-social practices, with the lives of the 'great (men)' who were laid to rest within their walls but not with the phenomenon or experience of death.[6] Even medical historians have not distinguished themselves in this respect, preferring to focus on the emergence of the hospital, on the development of different medical specialisms, and on the science of medication rather than on either the manner of dying or the reality of death. Indeed, as many studies (not least Vanessa Harding's exploration of the experience of death in early modern London in this volume) have demonstrated, medicine, medical treatment, and the medical profession in its various manifestations were not integral to the 'good death' that the dying and their families aspired to achieve until the modern era.[7] Doctors, it has often been observed, are interested in the ill body only so long as they entertain the prospect of effecting a cure; as a result, they long perceived the death bed as no place for them. This was emphatically the case in the early modern era when, in the words of Roy Porter: 'pre-modern physicians ... believed their job was to make a prognosis, informing the dead of their imminent fate. The physician would then withdraw, leaving the dying person to compose his mind and his will, and make peace with God and his family.'[8] The medicalization of death transformed this relationship, and resulted in nineteenth-century doctors and nurses assuming responsibility for the management of death, and a corresponding reduction in the control previously exercised by the dying and their families. Despite that change, however, the interpretative template adopted by historians of medicine long remained firmly anchored in an institutional and 'great men' framework which presented death as an incidental corollary that, like breathing and eating, seemed hardly deserving of particular attention when there were so many other, evidently more compelling, matters to be addressed.[9]

This situation persisted until the 1970s when, as a result of 'the rediscovery of death', which Michel Vovelle locates in the 1960s, scholars and commentators anchored in a range of disciplines began to take a new interest in the subject.[10] In history, the premier voice was that of Philippe Ariès. Having achieved renown internationally for his classic, and disputed, history of childhood, Ariès published two texts in the 1970s that provided an interpretative framework within which death might be comprehended historically. The combined impact of *Western Attitudes Towards Death*, the published text of a series of lectures delivered at Johns Hopkins University in 1973, and the more substantial *L'homme Devant la Mort*, published in French in 1977, and in English translation as *The Hour of Our Death* in 1981, galvanized interest in the subject. It may well be, as Roy Porter observed in a considered assessment of the impact and significance of both works published in 1999, that Ariès' approach is flawed conceptually and historically because the author was guided in his interpretations by 'his Catholicism, his reactionary politics (he came from an ultra-royalist family), and his luddism',[11] but it was also flawed methodologically:

> One problem posed by Ariès' approach is that he did not offer a simple linear periodization, but a *mélanqe* [sic] of the synchronic and the diachronic. While *mentalités* change, old beliefs, Ariès presumes, are not wholly superseded, and sometimes he seems to subscribe to dated notions respecting the timelessness of folk wisdom.[12]

It is broadly acknowledged that Ariès' limitations are most evident in relation to the early modern and modern eras with which he entertained the sharpest personal, philosophical, political and religious unease. He failed also, as Porter has cogently argued, to take 'adequate account of death as theorized by medicine and science'.[13] But the limitations of his approach notwithstanding, the impact of his intervention was dramatic and immediate. Though scholars like François Lebrun and Michel Vovelle were already embarked on important local studies, Ariès' publications paved the way for a flurry of focussed enquiries that incrementally modified, refined and improved on his finding and method.[14] They also facilitated the publication during the 1980s and 1990s of several path-breaking studies of death that were both more conceptually robust, and more specific and penetrating in their reconstructions and conclusions.[15] For geographical and cultural reasons the various approaches pursued by Clare Gittings, Ralph Houlbrooke, David Cressy, Julian Litten, and Vanessa Harding may echo more obviously with Irish scholars, and most readers of this collection, than the interventions of Paul Binski, François Lebrun, Michel Vovelle, Pierre Chaunu, R.A. Etlin, and John McManners, who have advanced understanding of the history of death in France and Europe.[16] But as Joseph Clarke's references to, and amplification of, the works of Vovelle, Etlin, Chaunu and McManners demonstrates (Chapter 6), even though it has been more thoroughly explored there than in most jurisdictions, there is still much about the subject of death in France that remains unclear, or incomplete, and deserving of further close enquiry. In endeavouring to advance this field of scholarship, albeit with particular reference to Ireland, this collection implicitly favours a multi-valent approach by engaging with death and dying from a range of perspectives and by employing a variety of approaches, which highlight not only that attitudes towards death and dying changed over time, but also that there were different modes of dying. By extension, the meaning, way, and impact of death can advantageously be amplified within particular contexts as well as across whole social systems in the manner of Ariès and Vovelle.

As Susan Leigh Fry's pioneering examination of the medieval era, and Clodagh Tait's account of death, burial and commemoration in early modern Ireland illustrate, Irish burial practices bear closer comparison with those of early modern England than they do with France.[17] This notwithstanding, because of the importance of Christianity in shaping attitudes and guiding practices before the Reformation, and the significance of confessional identity in the aftermath both of the Reformation and the Counter Reformation, one must also recognize that Ireland was not cut off from the Continent, that European Catholic religious norms continued to influence and guide attitudes to death and dying, and that these can be identified in the manner in which the dead were dealt with. In addition, there was an identifiable indigenous tradition relayed through prehistory and the early Middle Ages (addressed here by Gabriel Cooney (Chapter 1) and by Elizabeth O'Brien and Edel Bhreathnach (Chapter 2)) that justifies when it does not demand a more geographically localized approach than that employed by Ariès, or by Vovelle in his 'epic' account of 'death in the western world'.[18]

The suggestion that enquiry into death and dying can better be pursued through locally focussed and temporally shorter studies is one implication of the approach taken by those that have followed in the footsteps of Ariès and Vovelle. It certainly informs the engagement with death and dying in the different contexts and jurisdictions featured in this collection. But these essays also seek to engage broadly with multiple dimensions of the phenomena, both by ranging across thousands of years of human activity and by sustaining a less schematic approach than that pioneered by Ariès.[19] Thus, as well as pursuing political death from a number of perspectives – specifically the phenomenon of hunger strike in Ireland (Chapter 12) and how the ideal of dying for one country had a different register in Ireland than it had in England during the nineteenth and twentieth centuries (Chapter 14) – there remains the thorny question of who, how and why people were killed during the War of Independence that secured the country's autonomy from Great Britain (Chapter 13). Significantly, this continues to prompt a sharply divided response that echoes long established confessional and ideological attitudes.[20] For that reason, detailed forensic enquiry is essential if the subject of political death, in particular, is not to remain mired in personal or ideological (as opposed to evidential) disputes, though one cannot, of course, assume that the interrogation of historical evidence alone will produce an agreed conclusion. On the contrary, one can readily conceive of a situation in which religious or philosophical rather than political conviction could present an obstacle in a full comprehension of infanticide or suicide, for example. That is not a reason for failing to engage with such disputed forms of death, but it does present an additional challenge. The conspiracy of silence that shrouded infanticide,[21] suicide, and other culturally disapproved death in Ireland and elsewhere long functioned as a barrier to their scholarly investigation. This is no longer the case: James Kelly's analysis of suicide in eighteenth-century Ireland (Chapter 5) and David Lederer's reconstruction of the circumstances in which suicidology emerged in the nineteenth century (Chapter 9) are indicative of a readiness to engage maturely in explorations of the history of the phenomenon from a variety of perspectives in an attempt to give it meaning. There are unmistakable signs, certainly, that scholars, and by extension society at large, are less prepared to defer to traditional sensitivities, whether the subject is the treatment of the bodies of heroes or villains (as instanced by the intriguing comparison between the fate of Oliver Cromwell's head and that of Oliver Plunkett (Chapter 3)), cannibalism and famine (Chapter 8), the contested memory of the 1798 Rebellion (Chapter 7), or the sectarianism evident in the folklore that informed popular conviction about death (Chapter 11).

The fact that it is now possible to pursue such a range of diverse approaches in order to locate death and dying in their wider social, temporal and geographical contexts is a product of the quiet revolution in the study and understanding of death that has been taking place in Ireland over the past decade. This could hardly have occurred but for the pioneering endeavour of Ariès, Vovelle, Gittings, Houlbrooke, and others; their prominent presence in the bibliographies of books and apparatus of articles on the subject in Irish history is ample testament to their formative influence.[22] But the increased preparedness to engage with death is also possessed of an important indigenous dimension, which is particularly visible at the intersection of archaeology, architecture, history of art and history, and manifest in the interest in tombs, sepulchra, mausolea, and other locations in which the dead were laid to rest, either complete or, as was common in prehistory, in cremated form. The literature on archaeological funerary monuments is enormous, in keeping with their importance to the ongoing task of deciphering the prehistoric record.[23] By comparison, the corpus of descriptive and interpretative work dating from the historic era is more compact, but important contributions by John Hunt, John Bradley, Raymond Gillespie and Rolf Loeber (among others) are illustrative of its vibrancy, and its capacity to inform way beyond the iconography of the memorials.[24] However, death (if not dying) is a subject in which history and archaeology can each inform the other, as the recent edited collection by Corlett and Potterton on death in the Middle Ages well attests.[25]

By combining the results of rich discoveries in the archaeological and architectural record, and marrying these with the expanding corpus of archival evidence that is slowly being uncovered, it should be possible to construct an integrated picture of death in the prehistoric and historic eras. This task must benefit from a number of ongoing projects, two of which – the 'Mapping Death' project, based at University College Dublin, which focuses on burial practices in early medieval Ireland, and 'Death and Funerary Practices, 1829–1901', which is based at the University of Limerick – feature in this collection (Chapters 2 and 10). It will also be necessary to build on other individual initiatives which have employed more familiar approaches, among which Nina Witoszek and Pat Sheeran's study of 'funerary traditions' during the nineteenth century, and Anne Ridge's account of 'death customs' in Connaught during the twentieth century point the way forward.[26] Together and individually, these and other works attests to the fact that death offers an important conduit into a society and the people in it. Furthermore, it is an intrinsically interesting phenomenon, and as the parameters of social history and the history of the quotidian continue to expand, so too do the potentiality and possibilities of studying death, in all its dimensions.

In keeping with the varieties of approach that the subject facilitates, this collection aspires to offer new perspectives on death and dying in Ireland, Britain and Europe. In addition, it endeavours to encompass the full span of human settlement by embracing prehistory as well as history, and by commencing with an examination of the changing relationship of living and the dead across the course of Irish prehistory. Drawing upon the wealth of data derived from development-led archaeological work and the recognition of the need to reconsider established orthodoxies about mortuary practice over the span of Irish prehistory (8000 BC – 500 AD), Gabriel Cooney (Chapter 1) explores the broad patterns and trends in the mortuary record over this extended period. Challenging the validity of social models of death and dying which tend to generalize and to see prehistoric mortuary practice as normative and unchanging, Cooney's detailed consideration of the archaeological record from an anthropological perspective highlights very considerable diversity in mortuary practice within cultural traditions at specific times in Irish prehistory, depending on the social role and standing of the deceased. The implications of the visitation, adaptation, alteration and veneration of sites of human burial are addressed, primarily with a view to establishing clear indications of important changes over time in the relationship between the living and the dead, as well as in the social construction of the past. Mortuary rites are shown to have been used by the living to express links with and differences from other communities, and also to distinguish those people within the communities whose remains were deposited in selected sacred places. Cooney emphasizes the significance of cemeteries as material reminders of people's shared history owing to the presence of their ancestral dead and their treatment of the dead in activities that reflect a set of common values. His essay shows clearly that the post-mortem treatment of the socially significant deceased was both complex and dynamic, with the dead continuing to shape the narrative of Irish prehistory.

In their complementary and probing essay on burial in early medieval Ireland, Edel Bhreathnach and Elizabeth O'Brien present a multi-dimensional interpretation of burial practices in Ireland, which are variously viewed as indicators of social practices, social hierarchies, cultural intrusions, territorial boundary markers, the taking of territory, the establishment of dynasties, religious conversion and external relationships. These fresh insights are among the first fruits of the 'Mapping Death' project which involves archaeologists, historians, anthropologists, geneticists, neurologists and osteo-archaeologists, and which is permitting a more detailed and grounded understanding of the composition and cultural and medical profile of the Irish population during the period from the first to the eighth centuries AD through an analysis of burial evidence. Archaeological, anthropological, historical, literary, and scientific evidence is combined to construct an increasingly sophisticated image of daily life in Ireland, of social hierarchy and of important changes such as the conversion to Christianity. In particular, ancestral burial mounds (*ferta*) situated on boundaries are shown to have played an important role in early Irish law, especially when a claim to territory was at stake. Bhreathnach and O'Brien explore the stages in the process whereby the church authorities exerted control over burial practices, inducing people to abandon burial among their ancestors in *ferta* in favour of church cemeteries. Yet they emphasize that archaeological and scientific evidence, revealed by the 'Mapping Death' project, indicates that these changes did not in fact occur until about three centuries after the introduction of Christianity to Ireland.

Moving forward to the early modern era, Sarah Tarlow explores the actual and figurative journeys of the bodies, and more specifically the heads, of two major figures in seventeenth-century Irish history – Oliver Cromwell and Oliver Plunkett, the Roman Catholic Archbishop of Armagh – between their execution and the present, and highlights the marked contrast and changes in their treatments over time. As Tarlow demonstrates, Oliver Plunkett died the worst death of a criminal, but, having escaped bodily annihilation, he ultimately became an object of veneration whereas Cromwell was given a state funeral and buried with honour, only to be subsequently 'disinterred, dismembered and degraded as an object of vilification or curiosity'. This leads Tarlow to contend that a dead body or body part is not merely a blank sheet on which society can inscribe its categorization of the worth of the deceased; rather, it is 'actively involved in the creation of character, memory and historical legacy', and in that context, figures such as Cromwell and Plunkett will continue to structure their own historical meanings into the future.

Still in the early modern era, but broadening the focus from individuals to 'the fairly public business of dying' as it took place in London, Vanessa Harding explores the various ways in which the city's community survived the practical and psychic impact of enormously high mortality (it is estimated that a million and a half people died in the city between the early sixteenth and the late seventeenth centuries). Having provided a profile of those who died and the main reasons for their deaths, levels of spiritual preparation and psychological preparedness for death are assessed based on a probing and generously illustrated investigation of will-making. Through an analysis of the experience of dying in the contexts of civic space, social order and the dynamics of family and household, Harding shows that in early modern London, death normally took place in a domestic setting, that it was usually low-key, was as likely to be attended by neighbours as by family, and was often a site of intrigue and calculation in which greed and self-interest were rarely far distant.

Shifting the focus back to Ireland, James Kelly draws upon a sample of 675 cases of suicide and parasuicide reported in Ireland to provide an outline of the main features of suicide, and to explore evolving responses to the phenomenon, including those of the public across the eighteenth century. The aim is to locate suicide within the penumbra of death and dying in Ireland during this period. Kelly's inquiry identifies the 1760s as a significant decade when the combined impact of the increased number of reported suicides and the emergence of a more news-orientated press paved the way for a fuller engagement with the subject. Moreover, self-inflicted death may have become increasingly normalized in public discourse during the last quarter of the eighteenth century as a consequence of the greater coverage afforded the suicide of known public figures. This notwithstanding, the most striking observation to emerge from an examination of suicide in eighteenth-century Ireland was not 'the growth of leniency' but the enduring hostility towards 'self-murder'. This was determined by a combination of religiously-inspired interdicts, legal proscriptions and popular sanctions, which ensured that entrenched attitudes changed slowly, and, by extension, that only a fragile case can be ventured, using the Irish experience, for the secularization of suicide.

In the midst of the Terror, the everyday experience of death and dying was transformed in towns and villages throughout France. As the Revolutionary Republic embarked on a crusade to dechristianize every aspect of French life in 1793, the customs and ceremonies that had defined the business of death and dying for generations were replaced by a radically new ritual of death. As church bells fell silent and the conduct of the last rites was transferred from the cleric to the civil servant, the cemetery became a secular, and deeply contested, space in communities across France. Drawing on published and unpublished sources from archives across France, Joseph Clarke's essay explores how the Republic's dechristianization of death emerged as one of the defining cultural conflicts of the 1790s, challenges many assumption underpinning existing scholarship in this field, and addresses the question – what was its legacy in the years that followed the Terror? Clarke explores the new rites the Republic attempted to impose throughout the 1790s and the political, cultural and sometimes violent conflicts they gave rise to on streets and in churchyards throughout the Republic. The various stances adopted by the dramatically reduced cohort of Catholic clergy are afforded particular attention and Clarke assesses 'dechristianization's catastrophic effect on the ecclesiastical demography of France', which he argues represented a 'seismic shift in the spiritual economy of entire communities'. As communities across France repudiated the Republic's new rituals in the name of customary culture, the cemetery emerged as a frontline of France's 'culture wars' – a space characterized by controversy, conflict and often bloody confrontation.

In his essay titled 'Forgetting to remember Orr', Guy Beiner focuses on the remembrance of William Orr, 'the proto–martyr of Irish republicanism' who was executed in 1797, to illustrate how we have engaged in 'restorative re-telling of memory' or 'reparative remembering' from the 1790s to the present. Beiner identifies the manner in which the 1798 Rebellion is remembered in counties Antrim and Down as a manifestation of 'collective amnesia' *par excellence*. In a further instance of this amnesia, he references the Presbyterian communities, strongly implicated in a failed republican rebellion against the crown, who subsequently realigned their political allegiances towards unionism, loyalism and Orangeism, and deliberately censored public recollections of insurgency. Drawing upon recent research, Beiner acknowledges that in the immediate aftermath of the rebellion such acts of *damnation memoriae* may not in fact have been as complete as once thought, and that therefore the 'time of death' of memory should be post-dated into the early nineteenth century. However, in a penetrating analysis of memory and forgetting, he uncovers evidence which suggests that the troubled legacy of the past did not simply pass away, and highlights how attempts to proscribe problematic memories tend to instigate complex practices of recalcitrant remembrance, which are often masked as forms of sham forgetfulness. Far from being forgotten, the dead of 1798 are shown to have weighed heavily on social memory in Ulster. Citing local traditions – repeatedly reformulated in popular culture and documented over two centuries in private correspondence, antiquarian studies, local histories, folklore collections, historical fiction, drama, poetry, song books, provincial newspapers, journals, travel guides, and museum collections – Beiner reveals how communities and individuals in the north of Ireland professed to forget, yet found myriad ways to recall, commemorate, reconstruct, and reinterpret memories of the dead. He demonstrates how the resourceful inspection of these repositories of vernacular historiography can yield unique, subtle and revelatory insights into the ambiguous nature of social forgetting, which in Ulster oscillated between recurrent efforts to bury recollections of past embarrassments and the resurrection of tenacious counter-memories.

Cormac Ó Gráda's exploration of varieties of Irish famine death (Chapter 8) presents a comparative perspective on two aspects of mortality during past Irish famines. Firstly, the causes of death during Ireland's 'other great famine', that of 1740–41, are examined. Commencing with a brief commentary on John Rutty's *Chronological*

History (1770), the best-known text on the causes of death during that famine, he proceeds to consider a previously overlooked contemporary medical treatise, *Observationes Medicales*, which was published in Dublin in 1746. Penned by a Cork-born medic, Maurice O'Connell, it features commentary on various diseases and their treatments, which amplifies and expands our understanding of famine death in the eighteenth century, and of the 1740–41 famine in particular. The second aspect of famine mortality explored is cannibalism in Ireland. There is no evidence of murder-cannibalism in Ireland during the 1840s (not even in folk memory), and Ó Gráda poses searching questions as to why this might be, given 'the massive and horrific scale of the Great Famine … and the extent of excess mortality over such a long period'.

The nineteenth-century association of Protestantism with modernity originated with the works of first-generation sociologists in the new nation of Germany. By embedding the modernity thesis within the framework of Prussian-led evangelical nationalism, the sociological discipline strengthened its claim to scientific legitimacy. Most leading German academic sociologists (Joseph Schumpeter, Werner Sombart, Ernst Troeltsch, Max Weber) discoursed on the modernizing importance of the Protestant Reformation for capital formation, social individualization, and the rise of the modern state. Meanwhile, Émile Durkheim's *Le Suicide* (1897), a fundamental treatise on the scientific nature of sociological statistics, helped to establish what gradually became known as 'Sociology's One Law', that is, Protestant's kill themselves more often than Catholics. As a result, it became axiomatic to link the three phenomena – suicide, Protestantism and modernity – in a complementary tautology. Suicide rates appeared to rise in modern societies and Protestant societies exhibited enhanced features of modernity, such as higher suicide rates. David Lederer's essay, titled 'Suicide statistics as moral statistics: suicide, sociology and the state' (Chapter 9), shows that Durkheim's results were largely derived from earlier nineteenth-century moral statisticians, notably the German national economist Adolf Wagner; the evangelical theologian Alexander von Oettingen; and the Italian psychiatrist, Enrico Morselli. All three were fervent nationalists, practitioners of sociological fatalism and, especially in Morselli's case, converts to social Darwinism. Lederer highlights how in their argumentation, high suicide rates among Protestants were presented simultaneously as a social malaise and a badge of modernity in Protestant social bodies that contained inherent automatic eugenic mechanisms for cleansing themselves of degenerate elements. This essay explores the influence of Protestant nationalism on the interpretation of suicide within the nascent discipline of sociology.

11

Death notices and obituaries printed in provincial Irish newspapers during the period 1820–1900 are the subject of Ciara Breathnach and David Butler's contribution (Chapter 10). Based on an analysis of the nature and function of over 157,000 notices, two striking features emerge: first, that the growing popularity of the death notice in the nineteenth century was an expression of rising middle-class Catholic aspirations, and second, that it assisted the Catholic Church to exert greater control over funerary culture. The introduction of this new element into the funerary ritual certainly served to memorialize the middle-class dead in a way that set them apart from the peasantry. As such, it can be identified as a significant departure from customary practices since, for the majority of Irish people, funeral customs were traditionally deeply rooted in the vernacular and in a cultural tradition that was mainly oral. Drawing upon the work of anthropologist Lawrence Taylor, Breathnach and Butler emphasize that in nineteenth-century Ireland, death was 'an opportunity for furthering social, cultural, and political ends', and they observe, 'nowhere are family ambitions made clearer than in the pageantry of funerary customs'.

Graveyards and those buried within them were the subject of frequent comment in Irish folk tradition. The presence of the bodies of those reputed as saints and martyrs excited local pride, and physical remains reputed to be those of holy people were often deemed to possess curative and magical properties. The graveyard itself was sacred, and insults might be revenged by its ghostly occupants. Though serving as a resource for the community in devotional and practical terms, graveyards and the bodies within them could also be a focus of conflict and competition. While the co-interment of Protestants and Catholics was not uncommon, tension was not unusual. Tales of the separation of Protestant and Catholic burials, and of churchyards rejecting the bodies of Protestants and even leaving their original sites in protest when Protestants were buried there, can be found throughout Ireland, and are evidence of complex inter-denominational relationships at local level. Clodagh Tait's essay relays stories told about the dead and their burial places that are quite implausible but which provide revealing glimpses of the dynamics underpinning community relations. Recognizing that oral tradition not only reflects how communities engaged with their own pasts, but also actively shaped human actions and interactions in various presents, Tait highlights folklore's potential as 'an imaginative resource'. Through her sensitive engagement with stories about wandering graveyards, jumping churches, and rogue corpses, she excavates the *mentalité* of early modern Protestants and Catholics, revealing instances of toleration as well as conflict. Specifically, she shows how tales told about graveyards both assisted in the construction of local and confessional identities and impressed on sacred spaces the map of human relationships within parishes during the early modern period and beyond.

Between August and November 1920, during the War of Independence in Ireland, three Irish men, Terence MacSwiney, Michael Fitzgerald and Joseph Murphy, died as a result of two linked hunger strikes at Brixton and Cork prisons. These hunger strikes were the first in modern Irish history to result in death due to *prolonged* self-starvation. Drawing on Drew Gilpin Faust's study of death and the American Civil War, William Murphy sets the context for the hunger strikes, focussing in particular on the prior use of the hunger strike, on the realization of government that if it gave in, it negated the purpose of imprisonment, and showing how, once it was apparent that this was the government's fixed position, those on strike, and their families, contrived to ensure that they experienced what was deemed a 'good death'. Murphy's exploration of the episode is revealing of the implications of prisoner deaths for those charged with the day-to-day management of the strikers (prison staff, particularly prison medical officers) as well as for those at more senior levels in administration and politics. Furthermore, in his exploration of the controversy stirred by the duration of the strike, and the suggestion that the men may have been fed, Murphy presents strong evidence of the determination on the part of the hunger strikers and their families, the MacSwineys especially, to resist the attempts of the authorities to diminish the prisoners' heroic, patriotic, and fatal protest. The manner in which the memory of those who died was moulded, beginning with the immediate reaction to their death, the conduct of their funerals, and commemoration thereafter, provides a revealing case study both of the enduring power of death among the living, and of the construction of memory. The reason why MacSwiney is remembered to the exclusion of the other two strikers is plainly stated: it was the result of 'unmistakably successful efforts made by him, those around him at the time, and others since, to use these circumstances to create a martyr'.

IRA killings of alleged civilian spies and informers during the War of Independence (1919–21) in Ireland and its aftermath is the subject of Eunan O'Halpin's essay (Chapter 13). Based upon data gathered in the course of the *Dead of the Irish Revolution* project, which seeks to establish who died, when, where, why and by whose hand during the Irish revolutionary period, O'Halpin explores both the value and the limitations of focussing on fatalities as a measure of political violence and unrest during the War of Independence. Two main categories of fatalities are discussed: people killed while allegedly attempting to escape from arrest or to avoid capture – deaths almost always inflicted by the security forces; and people killed as alleged informers, 'spies' or agents – deaths almost always inflicted by separatists or others purporting to be such. The meaning and utility of these two explanatory categories are explored, both in terms of how such deaths were understood at the time, and of how more recent scholarship has addressed them and the underlying patterns of largely arbitrary killing which they disclose. In a revealing commentary on the particular challenges associated with attempting to explain such deaths individually, O'Halpin identifies limitations imposed on researchers in instances where official records may be brief and non-committal, together with other forms of memory, recollection and explanation that can also prove problematic when one engages with this especially sensitive dimension of the War.

In the final essay in this volume, 'The mutations of martyrdom in Britain and Ireland, c.1850–2005', John Wolffe subjects the powerfully emotive constructions placed on political and religious martyrdom between the mid-nineteenth century and the early twentieth to critical examination. He reveals how the language and rhetoric of martyrdom, with its Christian roots, was utilized by Protestants and Catholics during the mid-nineteenth century on both sides of the Irish Sea. He shows how, among Protestants, the republication of Foxe's *Acts and Monuments* and the commemoration of the Marian Martyrs served both as a source of spiritual legitimacy and fuel for the fires of anti-Roman polemic, while among Catholics, at a slightly later date, there was a comparable emphasis upon Elizabethan and seventeenth-century martyrs such as Edmund Campion, Margaret Clitherow, Philip Howard and Oliver Plunkett, culminating in the works of the martyrologist Dom Bede Camm at the turn of the twentieth century. In the meantime, in Britain the notion of martyrdom assumed more secular and nationalistic connotations through its association with Christian military heroes such as Hedley Vicars and General Gordon, and in Ireland through the cult of the Fenians executed in Manchester (1867). Wolffe traces this trend through to its climax in the era of the Great War, highlighting how the language of martyrdom was readily applied to the war dead, and in Ireland, to the leaders of the Easter Rising. He claims that the Second World War dead were not viewed as martyrs in the same way as those who died in the Great War, but notes the recurrence of the *motif* in relation to the IRA hunger strikers, and its denial when invoked with reference to contemporary suicide bombers. He clearly demonstrates that the '"terrible beauty" of martyrdom in all its permutations merits more attention than it has yet received from historians'.

The fact that this collection concludes with an essay that engages, however briefly, with death in the present is an earnest of its aspiration to stimulate an engagement with the subject across time. Inevitably, this collection offers no more than a series of snapshots, the majority focussed on Ireland. However, rather than this being a limitation, it is hoped that it offers an illustration not only of what has been achieved but also of what can be accomplished. If the collection encourages others to query the conceptual, attitudinal and evidential barriers that sometimes have discouraged a full and open engagement with the themes of death and dying in their various manifestations and contexts, it will have been worthwhile.

NOTES

1   There are any number of accounts, for example, see Paul Kennedy, *The Rise And Fall of the Great Powers: Economic Change and Military Conflict from 1500 to 2000* (London: Unwin Hyman, 1988); Norman Davies, *Vanished Kingdoms: The Rise and Fall of States and Nations* (New York: Viking, 2012).

2   For example, see the Keith Thomas classic, *Man and the Natural World: Changing Attitudes in England, 1500–1800* (London: Allen Lane, 1983).

3   However, see James Belich, *Replenishing the Earth: The Settler Revolution and the Rise of the Anglo-World, 1783–1939* (Oxford: Oxford University Press, 2009), for an engagement which takes this subject into account.

4   Livi-Bacci Massimo, *A Concise History of World Population* (Cambridge, MA: Blackwells, 1992); Thomas MacKeown, *The Modern Rise of Population* (London: Edward Arnold, 1976); E.A. Wrigley and R.S. Schofield, *The Population History of England, 1541–1871* (Cambridge: Cambridge University Press, 1989); Mary Dobson, *Contours of Death and Disease in Early Modern England* (Cambridge: Cambridge University Press, 1997).

5   For an excellent example see David Charles Sloane, *The Last Great Necessity: Cemeteries in American History* (Baltimore: Johns Hopkins, 1995); J.S. Curl, *The Victorian Celebration of Death* (Newton Abbot: David and Charles, 1972).

6   W.J. Fitzpatrick, *History of the Dublin Catholic Cemeteries* (Dublin: W.J. Fitzpatrick, 1900).

7   See Chapter 4.

8   Ray Porter, 'Death and the Doctors in Georgian England', in Ralph Houlbrooke (ed.), *Death, Ritual, and Bereavement* (London: Routledge, 1989), pp.77–94; idem, 'The hour of Philippe Ariès', *Mortality: Promoting the Interdisciplinary Study of Death and Dying*, 4:1 (1999), pp.83–90, at pp.87–8.

9   For an analysis of the impact of this on the history of medicine in Ireland see Greta Jones and Elizabeth Malcolm, 'Introduction: an Anatomy of Irish Medical History', in eadem (eds), *Medicine, Disease and the State in Ireland, 1650–1940* (Cork: Cork University Press, 1999), pp.21–39; James Kelly with Fiona Clark, 'Introduction', in idem (eds), *Ireland and Medicine in the Seventeenth and Eighteenth Centuries* (Farnham: Ashgate, 2010), pp.1–15.

10 Michel Vovelle, 'Rediscovery of Death Since 1960', *Annals of the American Academy of Political and Social Science*, 447 (Jan. 1980), pp.89–99.

11 Porter, 'The Hour of Philippe Ariès', p.85; see P.H. Hutton, 'The Post War Politics of Philippe Ariès', *Journal of Contemporary History*, 34:3 (1999), pp.365–81; idem, *Philippe Ariès and the Politics of French Cultural History* (Amherst: University of Massachusetts Press, 2004).

12 Porter, 'The Hour of Philippe Ariès', p.83.

13 Ibid., pp.86–8.

14 François Lebrun, *Les Hommes et la Mort en Anjou aux XVIIe et XVIIIe Siècles: Essai de Démographie et de Psychologie Historique* (Paris: La Haye, Mouton and Co., 1971); Michel Vovelle and Gaby Vovelle, *Vision de la Mort et de l'au-dela en Provence du XV au XX Siècle d'après les Autels des Âmes du Purgatoire* (Paris: A. Colin, 1970); Michel Vovelle, *Piété Baroque et Déchristianisation en Provence au XVIIIe Siècle: les Attitudes Devant la Mort d'après les Clauses des Testaments* (Paris: Plon, 1973).

15 For a considered analysis of Vovelle's work, which has fairly been described as 'more complex and more nuanced' than that of Ariès, see Thomas Kselman, 'Death in the Western World: Michel Vovelle's Ambivalent Epic *La Mort et l'Occident, de 1300 à nos jours*', *Mortality*, 9:2 (2004), pp.168–76.

16 Clare Gittings, *Death, Burial and the Individual in Early Modern England* (London: Routledge, 1988); Ralph Houlbrooke, *Death, Religion, and the Family in England, 1489–1750* (Oxford: Clarendon Press, 1998); David Cressy, *Birth, Marriage and Death: Ritual, Religion and the Life Cycle in Tudor and Stuart England* (Oxford: Oxford University Press, 1997); Julian Litten, *The English Way of Death: The Common Funeral Since 1450* (London: R. Hale, 1991); Vanessa Harding, *The Dead and the Living in Paris and London, 1500–1670* (Cambridge: Cambridge University Press, 2002); Paul Binski, *Medieval Death: Ritual and Representation* (London: British Museum, 1996); Michel Vovelle, *La Mort et l'Occident, de 1300 à nos jours* (Paris: Gallimard, 1983); Pierre Chaunu, *La Mort à Paris, 16e, 17e et 18e Siècles* (Paris: Fayard, 1978); R.A. Etlin, *The Architecture of Death: The Transformation of the Cemetery in Eighteenth-Century Paris* (Cambridge, MA: MIT Press, 1984); John McManners, *Death and The Enlightenment: Changing Attitudes to Death Among Christians and Unbelievers in Eighteenth-Century France* (Oxford: Oxford University Press, 1985).

17 Susan Leigh Fry, *Burial in Medieval Ireland, 900–1500; a Review of the Written Sources* (Dublin: Four Courts Press, 1999); Clodagh Tait, *Death, Burial and Commemoration in Ireland, 1550–1650* (Basingstoke: Palgrave, 2002).

18 See Kselman, 'Michel Vovelle's ambivalent epic', pp.168–76.

19 This was one of Vovelle's reservations with Ariès' method: see Kselman, 'Michel Vovelle's ambivalent epic', p.169.

20 See John Regan, 'Irish Public Histories as an Historiographical Problem', *IHS*, 37 (2011), pp.265–92; idem, 'The "Bandon Valley Massacre" as a Historical Problem', *History*, 97:1 (Jan. 2012), pp.70–98; Niall Meehan, review of *Terror in Ireland, 1916–1923*, David Fitzpatrick (ed.) (Dublin: Lilliput Press, 2012) and reply, *Institute of Historical Research: Reviews in History* [Online], August 2012. Available from: www.history.ac.uk/reviews/review/1303 [accessed 29 November 2012].

21 A conspiracy that no longer has purchase: see James Kelly, 'Infanticide in Eighteenth-Century Ireland', *Irish Economic and Social History*, 19 (1992), pp.5–26; Elaine Farrell, *Infanticide in the Irish Crown Files at Assizes* (Dublin: Irish Manuscripts Commission, 2012); eadem, *'A Most Diabolical Deed': Infanticide and Irish Society, 1850–1900* (Manchester: Manchester University Press, 2013); Cliona Rattigan, *'What Else Could I do?': Single Mothers and Infanticide, Ireland, 1900–1950* (Dublin: Irish Academic Press, 2011).

22 See, Tait and Fry, for example; as note 17.

23 One may simply instance the megalithic tomb phenomenon, which comprises court tombs, passage tombs, portal tombs and wedge tombs, each of which has a substantial literature: see Gabriel Cooney, *Landscapes of Neolithic Ireland* (London: Routledge, 2000); M.J. O'Kelly, 'Neolithic Ireland' in Dáibhí Ó Cróinín (ed.), *A New History of Ireland, Vol. I, Prehistoric and Early Ireland* (Oxford: Oxford University Press, 2005), pp.69–97.

24 John Hunt, *Irish Medieval Figure Sculpture, 1200–1600: A Study of Irish Tombs with Notes on Costume and Armour* (2 Volumes, Shannon: Irish University Press, 1974); John Bradley, 'Anglo-Norman Sarcophagi from Ireland', in Gearóid MacNiocaill and Pat Wallace (eds), *Keimelia: Studies in Medieval Archaeology and History* (Galway: Galway University Press, 1988); Raymond Gillespie, 'Irish Funeral Monuments and Social Change, 1500–1700 – Perceptions of Death', in idem and B.P. Kennedy (eds), *Ireland: Art into History* (Dublin: Town House, 1994), pp.155–68; idem, 'Funerals and Society in Early Seventeenth-Century Ireland', *RSAI Jnl.*, 115 (1985), pp.86–91; Rolf Loeber, 'Sculptured Memorials to the Dead in Early Seventeenth-Century Ireland: A Survey from *Monumenta Eblanae* and Other Sources', *RIA proc.*, 81C (1981), pp.267–93.

25 Christiaan Corlett and Michael Potterton (eds), *Death and Burial in Early Medieval Ireland* (Dublin: Wordwell, 2010).

26 Nina Witoszek and Pat Sheeran, *Talking to the Dead: A Study of Irish Funerary Traditions* (Amsterdam: Rodophi, 1998); Anne Ridge, *Death Customs in Rural Ireland* (Galway: Arlen House, 2008).

ENGAGING WITH PREHISTORIC LIFE AND DEATH: THE CHANGING RELATIONSHIP OF THE LIVING AND THE DEAD OVER THE COURSE OF IRISH PREHISTORY

GABRIEL COONEY

Introduction: Bringing the Dead to Life

In many treatments of the past in Ireland, the first eight thousand years get very short shrift.[1] Archaeologists would argue that in taking this approach we are missing out on the long-term significance of prehistory for understanding Irish cultural identities and landscapes. Prehistory extends over three-quarters of all the time that people have lived on the island. Human presence and impact upon the landscape from 8,000 BC to the early centuries of the first millennium AD was very widespread and varied. Indeed, as Kirch has pointed out, the problem may be with the term prehistory itself, implying as it does some qualitative difference between document-based history and a history which privileges the archaeological record of human material culture; this unwritten text consists of 'diachronically meaningful variation and patterning in the world at large' and draws on collaborative evidence from a range of different disciplines.[2] In prehistory then, the reconstruction and interpretation of personal and social lives relies on physical remains, both of people themselves and their material culture. As the most direct record of prehistoric people – their own (predominantly skeletal) physical remains – confront the archaeologist, they necessitate inquiry into life and death issues. Hence mortuary practice is a central concern of prehistoric research.[3]

Normally the way archaeologists deal with and write about prehistory is to divide it into periods that represent and follow internationally-recognized classifications. These correspond both to blocks of time and to significant social and technological patterns of life.[4] While this chronological approach to prehistory in Ireland is useful, other perspectives are also revealing. For example, the burial record poses questions that require us to think across these established time divisions, as well as to explore closely the record within them. Many locations were used, and re-used, as cemeteries over long periods. The implications of the visitation, adaptation, alteration and veneration of places of human burial will be addressed in this essay, the primary thrust of which is the identification of the main trends in the archaeological record. The chronological range extends from the beginnings of human settlement in the ninth millennium to the first millennium BC. Burial traditions at the end of prehistory are considered by Bhreathnach and O'Brien in the context of their examination of the complex changes to mortuary rites that followed the transition to Christianity (Chapter 2).

People and Death in Prehistory

The People of Prehistoric Ireland INSTAR (Irish National Strategic Archaeological Research Programme) project has estimated that there are at a minimum about 3,000 individuals represented in the full corpus of human remains dating from prehistory.[5] Remembering that this figure is drawn from a span of time extending over 8,000 years, the evidence clearly cannot be used to estimate the size of the population at any stage in prehistory. It is apparent also that the burial record is dominated by the remains of the minority of the population who were treated, and remembered, in particular ways after death. Sex and age are the mostly widely used axes of social differentiation, in life and in death, in all societies ranging from those that are egalitarian to those defined by social ranking. In the traditional, small-scale societies that characterized Ireland in prehistoric times, both the birth and death rate of children would have been high. But there is a consistent under-representation of children compared to adults in the burial record across the whole of prehistory. It is not as easy to generalize about distinctions based on sex, but the evidence from some periods suggests that adult males were more prominent in formal burial rites than females. Since the contemporary living populations would have sustained a rough balance between men and women, it would appear that men and women were treated differently in death.[6]

After death, the place of the deceased in society is marked and remembered by the living. Hence it is useful to think about identity and status in prehistory in terms of the relationships between people. Ingold has argued that there are two ways of constructing identity in small-scale societies. Firstly, there is genealogical identity; here, origins provide the basis for who people think they are. Secondly, there is relational identity, which is the construction and maintenance of links between persons and things that are at the heart of people's sense of who and what they are.[7] Helms has pointed out that such societies are always concerned to a greater or lesser extent both with ancestral origins and how the ongoing activities of the living, including the treatment of the dead, fit with the past. The treatment of the dead in itself is a way of marking, re-marking, and remembering the long-term nature of the group – a critical characteristic in societies where authority is perceived to be handed on from the past. Helms argues that the key to understanding the emergence of leading groups in traditional societies is to identify the ways in which they establish links with the past, through the physical remains of the dead, to the ancestors and the origins of the society in which they occur. What can be tracked over time are changes in the ways in which the living related to the dead and hence in the social construction and remembrance of the past.[8]

Hunter-Gatherer Mortuary Rites

One of the most dramatic examples of how recent research has changed our understanding of mortuary practice in prehistory is Hermitage near Castleconnell, County Limerick (Fig. 1.1). The oldest burial, radiocarbon-dated (c14) to between 7530–7320 BC, contained the cremated remains of an adult, probably a male. The body had been cremated and then virtually all the burnt bone, almost 2,000 grams, was collected and placed in a pit, apparently around a wooden post, acting as a visible grave marker. Two burnt microliths and a burnt shale axehead were placed over the cremated bones. These objects were with the individual when the cremation took place and they were carefully collected from the pyre to be placed with the bones in the pit. There were two other pits nearby with fragments of cremated bone suggesting deposition of human bone between c. 7000 and 6600–6400 BC.[9]

Hermitage is an important addition to our understanding of the mortuary rites of the earliest inhabitants of Ireland, Mesolithic (8000–4000 BC) hunter-gatherers, for a number of reasons. Accepting the time gap between the dates of the bones of those buried here, people appear to have returned to bury individuals on at least two occasions. In short, the concept of a cemetery may already have been established. The rite was cremation and, while inhumation has tended to dominate general discussion of Mesolithic burials and deposition of human bone, the widespread use of cremation in Europe has been recognized over the last decade. The oldest burial at Hermitage seems to have been deliberately marked and commemorated by the living with a timber post. This makes it one of the few avowedly ceremonial structures that we can date to the Mesolithic in Ireland, or Britain. The partial collection and placement of cremated bone in the case of the later burials also suggest careful, deliberate acts and variety in the treatment of the dead.[10]

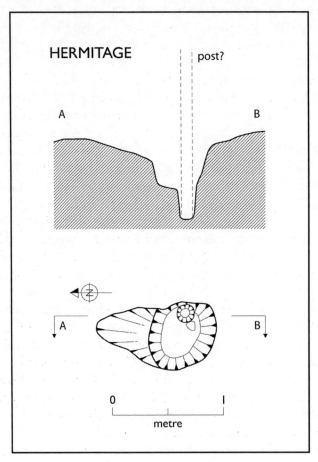

Fig. 1.1 The early Mesolithic burial at Hermitage, County Limerick (after Collins and Coyne[11])

The hilltop cave site at Killuragh in east County Limerick is the only other Irish site that has produced human bone evidence dating to before 5000 BC. Excavation provided evidence for the placement of disarticulated human bone and microliths around 7000 BC. This was the first of a number of episodes in which Killuragh cave was used for the deposition of human bone. A human jaw gave a date of between 4450–4220 BC. Dowd has pointed out that the adult human femur from Sramore Cave, County Leitrim (one of three human bones from this cave), dates to 4217–3967 BC. A second bone from the site has now been shown to date to the same period. This represents hunter-gatherer depositional activity in this cave during the last centuries of the Mesolithic period. The use of caves for the deposition of human bone is also a feature of the Mesolithic in Britain.[12]

A piece of adult human femur was found in a midden at Rockmarshall, County Louth, dated to 4720–4360 BC. It is an isolated piece of human bone on a site that is otherwise dominated by subsistence activities. In this sense, the Rockmarshall discovery can be compared with the recovery of the scattered remains of at least one mature adult in his/her late 20s or early 30s from Ferriter's Cove on the Dingle Peninsula. The human bones came from the central area of the excavation where there were other deposits, including the earliest dated domesticated cattle bone in Ireland or Britain. The human remains consisted of several fragments, mainly lower limbs, and seven teeth that were found close together, dated to between 4530–4310 BC.[13]

At first glance it would seem that Hermitage, Killuragh and Sramore tell a very different story about Mesolithic people's treatment of their dead than Rockmarshall and Ferriter's Cove, but there are significant similarities when we consider the evidence in the context of the framework of cosmological belief. The discovery of isolated human bone or the partial inhumed remains of a person on these coastal sites may appear casual, but its occurrence at what are ostensibly places where people were living, eating and sleeping supports the idea that the boundary between the living and the dead may have been porous. Evidence of human occupation at Ferriter's Cove and Rockmarshall attests to Mesolithic people's knowledge of the richness of the coastal zone as a source of food. Like caves, the coast was a boundary and a point of contact between different zones in the hunter-gatherer cosmos. In both north-west Europe and north-east America, hunter-gatherer cemeteries were most frequently placed in the coastal zone, sometimes on off-shore islands that emphasize the interplay of the land and the sea, the living and the dead. This may be viewed in the context of the belief in present-day, small-scale, traditional coastal societies in other parts of the world that on death, the spirits of the dead travel to off-shore islands, where they reunite with other spirits and are revitalized.

It is difficult to present a coherent narrative for Irish Mesolithic mortuary practices because the number of sites with relevant evidence

21

is small, spread across a time span of more than three thousand years, and varied. But what evidence there is can helpfully be placed in the wider context of Mesolithic mortuary practice in Europe. The existence of Mesolithic cemeteries had been connected to increasing population, greater social complexity and sedentism in the later part of the Mesolithic. The lack of equivalent evidence from the Irish late Mesolithic could be read as supporting the notion of a particular, insular cultural identity that sets it apart from the broader social pattern then developing in north-west Europe. But it is now clear that some European cemeteries, including Hermitage, predate this phase. Does this mean that the cultural innovation, creativity, and differentiation between individuals that cemeteries are seen as marking, emerged earlier than is generally acknowledged?[14]

Monumentality and Death Among Early Farmers

At Millin Bay, County Down, on the east coast of Ireland and on a ridge overlooking the Irish Sea stands a monument dating to the second half of the fourth millennium BC. A collective deposit of the disarticulated bones of children and adolescents was placed at the southern end of a long cist set in a pit. This was matched by what appeared to be a broadly contemporary series of deposits of single adult cremations in small cists outside the mound that covered the cist. It could be argued that the site illustrates a wider distinction in the treatment afforded adults and children in death in Ireland during the Neolithic (4000–2500 BC), particularly in the passage tomb tradition of the later fourth millennium BC. There appear to have been recognizable, recurring patterns of mortuary activity that linked children with inhumation, and adults with a greater emphasis on cremation and the provision of accompanying artefacts. The locations where children's remains were often placed may also imply that it was the practice to treat them in a different way after death.[15]

In keeping with the situation just described for Ireland, comparably distinctive and varying patterns of burial practice have been identified in the archaeological record of the broader Neolithic. Bradley, for example, has argued that in contrast to southern Britain where inhumed remains are common, cremation was the dominant rite in earlier Neolithic burial monuments (court tombs) in Ireland and western Scotland and that these differences illustrated important contrasts in social practice, focused on the character of domestic life and the circulation of unburnt bone as relics. These broad conclusions suggest that there is a very strong link between the way we construct notions of the individual and social bodies in the Irish Neolithic, based upon what we know of the character of mortuary rituals, and the distinctions that can be drawn between the use of inhumation and cremation.[16] But they are also worth exploring further for a number of reasons.

Firstly, the reality is that there are significant variations in mortuary practices *within* cultural traditions that are occluded by these general statements. Secondly, there is evidence for the contemporaneousness and combined use of the practices of inhumation and cremation. This is indicated, for example, by the occurrence of unburnt bone with cremation deposits in passage tomb mortuary deposits. Hence any discussion of how the body was transformed at death need to consider that these practices were potentially used in tandem. Indeed, as a third point, it must be emphasized that human bone in Neolithic monuments is not always evidence of burial practices; it can point to the active use of human bone in ancestral rites, and shows that in some cases, there were prolonged stages in the post-mortem treatment and deposition of human remains.[17] Helms has pointed out that people often acknowledge and sometimes combine the two types of ancestors. Thus the recently deceased may have a relatively short shelf-life as ancestral beings or, over time, they may be remembered collectively as the creator ancestors. For early agricultural groups, those whom Helms calls the 'distinguished dead' would have been important in demonstrating the durability of the group and the link between the present and previous generations of the group.[18] For people living in Ireland during the Neolithic, the challenge was how to create ancestors who would continue to be present and 'alive', although physically deceased, to help the living. The dichotomy between the decomposition of the body on death and the notion of the ancestors as an active, immortal and pure presence had to be confronted.

To illustrate this, I want to compare and contrast the mortuary practices that characterize the court tomb and passage tomb traditions. These are two of the four major megalithic tomb or monumental traditions of the Irish Neolithic – with some 390 sites classified as court tombs, and 230 as passage tombs. The construction and initial use of court tombs was during the period 3715–3530 BC. The start date for the construction of passage tombs in Ireland is contested, but it is suggested that it was within the period 3495–3285 BC (the third quarter of the fourth millennium BC) with their first use ending in 2860–2795 BC. Thus the court tradition in Ireland belongs to the earlier Neolithic, and the main use of passage tombs to the middle and later phases of this period.[19]

Two recently excavated sites illustrate the variety that seems to characterize court tomb mortuary rituals. At Creggandevesky in County

Tyrone, a gallery of three chambers opened onto a semicircular court. It produced cremated human remains of a minimum of twenty-one individuals (MNI); twelve adults, one adolescent, and eight individuals of unidentifiable age were found in a number of locations but especially around the entrance and in front of the burial gallery. At Parknabinnia, County Clare, a two-chamber gallery was fronted by a narrow 'court' feature. In the chamber, there were the fragmented remains of a MNI of at least twenty; the majority were adults (an adolescent, and two young children were also represented). The character of the inhumed bone, and the patterns in which it was deposited, have been interpreted by Beckett as primary inhumations disturbed in the course of successive interments. The piling up of bones in the front chamber against the blocking slabs separating it from the back chamber indicated that the back chamber passed out of use first. In both chambers the bottom layer of stone and bone seemed to stabilize the upright slabs and thus to have been part of the original construction. At the two sites, cremation and inhumation were used as alternative strategies to create the remembered dead who were literally built into the past and future. This supports Powell's argument that the architecture of the court tombs was combined with depositional practices to create a sense of social history that stressed lineage and descent.[20]

In the case of the passage tomb tradition, cremation is regarded as the primary treatment of the body after death. The deposits found in passage tombs are frequently described as clean, communal deposits consisting of the remains of several individuals. Some tombs, such as Tara and Knowth, with successive deposits of this character have evidence for the deposition of the remains of large numbers of people. It is tempting to read into this that what we are seeing in these deposits is the creation of selected, collective, communal ancestors from the remains of the dead and that the remembered dead served in this way to foster a particular sense of social identity. But elements of these communal deposits also indicate the complexity and sequence of the treatment of the body at death. The fact that they are communal deposits points to the mingling of the remains of different individuals, who are unlikely to have died at the same time. This raises the issue of whether they were cremated at different times and locations, and then brought together or cremated communally. The frequent occurrence of unburnt bone, skull and long bones in these deposits also raises questions as to whether there was a primary stage in the post-mortem treatment of bodies when the soft tissue was allowed or facilitated to decompose and whether at some point before cremation, selected bones were used for other purposes.[21]

Alternatively, people may have been treated differently after death. Given the potency of the skull as a marker of identity, it is not surprising to find that it is often used in ancestral rites. In some instances, unburnt skulls are found with cremation deposits. At the passage tomb at Fourknocks I (Fig. 1.2), the formal deposition of the clean cremation deposits above stone flags and sealing by further stones in the burial chambers is matched by a series of deposits in the entrance passage which appear to extend from the construction of the site to its closure. In the passage, the bones were placed between rough stone sealing layers, which created a link back to the original floor of the passage, and echoed the character of the deposits in the chambers. At the entrance, on a paved floor, a human skull was set in a spread of cremated bone and partially protected by a setting of stones. At a higher level in the fill of the passage, two adult skulls were found side by side facing outwards, and there were long bones near the skulls with cremated bone.

Fourknocks provides strong evidence that the cremation process involved the burning of disarticulated bone. At Fourknocks II (Fig. 1.2), about 50m from the passage tomb in what was described as a cremation trench, there were four hollows or pits with cremated remains; three appeared to represent single adults burnt *in situ*. The excavator suggested that these represented the latest cremations, the inference being that the bone from earlier episodes of cremation had been collected from the trench, cleaned of pyre material and then placed in the tomb nearby. The cremation trench was covered by a pastiche passage tomb passage under a mound, with accompanying deposits of human bone, thereby creating a 'twin' for the passage tomb.[22]

This interplay between the construction and use of the monuments at Fourknocks and the treatment and deposition of human remains indicates that the dead were not just placed in monuments. As they were transformed after death they became a central part of how monuments were created and understood. The treatment of the body after death was integral to the way in which a sense of social identity was created through the construction and use of these monuments. As well as seeing the selected remains of the dead placed within passage tombs, the 'portability' of cremated bone facilitates the physical incorporation of human remains into the structure of the monuments. Thus at Fourknocks, the deposition of human remains was integral to the transformation of the original cremation area into a quasi-passage tomb, to match the traditional passage tomb beside it. The remains of the remembered dead became permanent, eternal, etched into the very fabric of passage tombs.

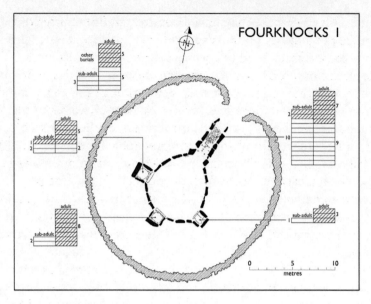

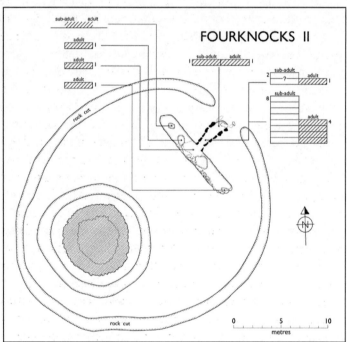

Fig. 1.2 Plans of Fourknocks I and II (based on Hartnett[23])

The Place of the Dead in Early Metal-Using Societies

The period in Ireland from about 2500 BC to the centuries after 2000 BC, down to about 1500 BC, was not only a time of technological change and innovation arising from the introduction of metallurgy, but also of striking diversity of mortuary practice. There were two major and, ostensibly, quite different traditions of burial rite, which overlapped in practice. Firstly, there are the last of the major series of megalithic tombs in Ireland – the wedge tombs. These tombs were constructed and first used in the period 2450–2050 BC. Wedge tombs are an interesting aspect of this innovative period in that, as Carlin has put it, they represent a notable reinvention of the megalithic tradition at the end of the Neolithic. It is clear, indeed, that links with the broader megalithic tradition and the past were strong in this period since it witnessed the placement of human remains in monuments such as court tombs and portal tombs that may have been up to a thousand years old. At the same time, at least some of the communities building wedge tombs used Beaker pottery, an international style of pottery widely associated with the new copper technology which occurs in a range of contexts in Ireland. Hence wedge tombs were part of this transitional time when Ireland was clearly linked with a wider European world.[24]

Secondly, there are what are commonly referred to as Early Bronze Age cemeteries. These began in the period when wedge tombs were constructed, and developed in the centuries around 2000 BC. In many cases, their use persisted well beyond 1500 BC. There are a variety of events and structures associated with them, but the core element is a varying number of cist and pit graves, most containing the burial of a single individual. Since some do not have any visible marker, the term flat cemetery is used. In other cases, the burials are placed either in an existing monument or in a purposely built one; in these cases, the term cairn or mound cemetery is employed. In the later stages of the period it became increasingly common also to mark the location of certain graves by covering them with a small round mound or barrow. The material for this covering monument was derived from a ditch that also served to encircle and define the grave. These cemetery types occur in great numbers across the country; in excess of 600 are known, with a somewhat restricted occurrence in the south-west. Their number raises interesting questions both about the extent of contemporary settlement and the relationships between these cemeteries and communities of the living.[25]

The complementary distribution of wedge tombs and cemeteries has long been remarked on, as have the differences between the ceramics found with human remains in these two contexts. As noted above, a widely occurring international style of pottery known as Beaker is known from wedge tombs as well as other contexts in Ireland. The graves in the Bronze Age cemeteries feature a range of successively developed ceramic styles known as Food Vessels (generally placed with the burials) and Urns (covering cremations as this rite became the dominant one). The use of the earliest style, the Bowl Food Vessel, overlaps with that of the Beaker in wedge tombs. It has been suggested that this was part of a growing regionalization of both burial practice and the Beaker tradition across Britain and Ireland during the period after 2200 BC. Until recently, it has been common practice in the archaeological literature to see these two sets of archaeological data – wedge tombs and the cemeteries – as representing two different and distinct cultural and ethnic identities. In some discussions they have even been regarded as representing two different peoples.[26]

However, cultural identity is likely to have been more open and fluid than our division of the burial record into two major blocks suggests. In both wedge tombs and the cemetery tradition, cremation and inhumation were regarded as appropriate post-mortem treatments of the dead, and there was a focus on particular individuals and on family or corporate groups. Mortuary rites were actively used by the living to express links with and differences from other communities, and to differentiate the people within communities whose remains were deposited in these sacred places.

One of the striking features of excavated wedge tombs is the number of them used as Bronze Age cemeteries. In effect, they can in some cases be seen as the first phase of such cemeteries. In exploring the relationships between wedge tombs and cemeteries, the site of Kilmashogue, County Dublin is often referred to (Fig. 1.3). Here, local people built, used and then partially dismantled a wedge tomb to provide an appropriate context for a small cemetery. The earlier burials in the cemetery accompanied by Bowl Food Vessels are in cists, placed in the cairn of the wedge tomb on the southern side of the chamber. The most impressive is covered by a capstone that was originally one of the roof stones of the wedge tomb. The tomb cairn was modified on this southern side and all that would have been visible on the surface were small circular cairns covering individual cists. Later a pit was dug into the entrance area of the wedge tomb and a cremation covered by a Vase Urn was placed there. In the eastern part of the Burren in County Clare in a small cairn at Coolnatullagh, there was a central cist with the inhumed bones of an adult, a deposit of cremated human bone and

KILMASHOGUE

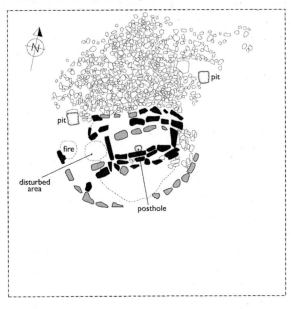

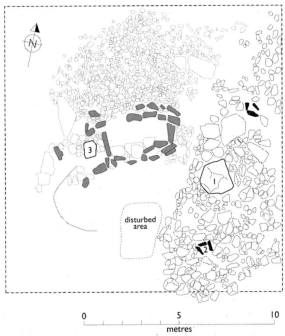

Fig. 1.3 Phases in the use of the Kilmashogue wedge tomb
(based on Kilbride-Jones[27])

a bone from an infant. The unburnt bones yielded a date of 2460–2140 BC. The inhumed remains of a 13–14-year-old in a pit was dated to 1880–1610 BC. There were deposits of both cremated and unburnt bone within the cairn. In the same townland, just over 500m north of this site and overlooking it, there is a wedge tomb.[28]

Taking into account the temporal and spatial closeness of sites in areas where the two traditions overlap, it should not come as a surprise that we see parallels and resonances in the mortuary practices employed in wedge tombs and in cemeteries. In both wedge tombs and cemeteries there are inhumed burials and deposits; in other cases, people were cremated and burnt bone deposited. Deposition of the bone occurred sometimes immediately after cremation, but in other instances a long time may have elapsed between the two events. Both complete and token cremations are represented in wedge tombs and the cemeteries. The placement of human bone also seems to chart relationships between people, and between particular individuals and others. Where the mortuary rite focused on a particular individual, there is often the deliberate placement of bone from another person, sometimes a child. In other cases, the contrast is between the burial of one individual in a grave context and the deliberate juxtaposition of the remains of several people in another. It might be said that this misses an essential difference in terms of monumentality; the wedge tomb provided a sacred space as well as a grave. But there is great variety in the scale of wedge tombs, and in the scale of cists; some of the latter are described as sub-megalithic but the manner of their construction indicates that they were conceived as monuments in their own right. This complexity and variety of ritual indicates that mortuary practice was constructed within a framework of rite and beliefs that was shared and understood by people who used both wedge tombs and cemeteries.

How did these traditions emerge? It is convention to locate the cemeteries in a wider north-west European movement towards single burial, which dates from the beginning of the Bronze Age, and to characterize wedge tombs as the last stage in the megalithic tomb tradition in Ireland. But in the context of individual sites, how communities interpreted their own past, and why and where they built wedge tombs and used cemeteries is also very variable, which supports the conclusion that the framing of life and death in local, active frames of meaning was what was most significant. In some cases, it is as if history began with the cemetery or wedge tomb; there is no immediate link in that locale to the past. In other cases, it would seem that a connection and linkage to the past was deliberately sought. Hence, we see the frequent location of wedge tombs close to older megalithic tombs in some parts of the country – in the Dublin mountains, for example, where they seem to be juxtaposed to passage tombs on the hilltops and portal tombs in more low-lying locations. The people who placed their dead in cists and pits also wanted to create a direct, physical link to the past – specifically, and immediately, to previous graves and, more broadly, to the wedge tombs and other, older, megalithic tombs, through the placement of such burials in the cairns of such tombs and the adaptation of such cairns and mounds as cemetery mounds. Here our division of the past into time periods may hide an important continuity of tradition and practice.[29]

What we can say is that within these traditions a sense of history was created by the presence of the ancestral dead, and the treatment of the dead by activities that reflect a set of common values. At the beginning of the period, those values were encapsulated and visible in wedge tombs; by its end, they were focused on the mortuary rites and graves of selected individuals. The people who espoused these values were probably rooted in oral narratives, and the cemeteries in which they were buried served as material reminders of a shared history and provided part of the moral framework that determined current behaviour.

Lines Across the Landscape: The Narrative of Barrow Cemeteries

Mortuary practice in Ireland in the period after 1600 BC manifests continuity in the use of and respect for previously used sites, but in other ways mortuary practice changed dramatically. The treatment of cremated bone suggests that elements of funerary practice may have continued to be elaborate, at least for some individuals, but in many communities there was a move away from the actual burial of people.[30]

Evidence for these changes in practice is provided in the form of cremated human bone, which has been discovered, often in token amounts, on a wide range of sites. Cremations are most commonly found in pits, frequently mixed with charcoal and soil. They are very often accompanied by coarse pottery as sherds or complete vessels. The pits can either occur as single, isolated features, or, more usually, they form part of clusters. This suggests that there were places set aside for burial. In some cases, these pit clusters/cemeteries do not appear to have had any surface definition or enclosing element. In other cases, it would seem that pits were enclosed within circular ring-ditches.[31]

Many of these sites were originally covered by barrows or related features. What has also become apparent is that barrows and ring-ditches were current in Ireland from at least the middle of the second millennium BC until the seventh century AD, well after the process of Christianization had begun. Hence the development of this barrow tradition was an important component of the way in which the dead and the ancestors were treated at death and how they were regarded after death. In this context, barrow cemeteries provide a very important focus for discussion of the social significance of the dead, tradition and memory in later prehistoric Ireland.[32]

In the middle of the second millennium BC, there were two linked developments. Firstly the graves of particular individuals were defined and marked by being located within a ring-ditch or barrow and, secondly, people placed such monuments in proximity to others, which lead to the development of what are called barrow cemeteries. Viewed from the perspective of the Early Bronze Age when burial was reserved for select members of communities, one of the ways in which these individuals were commemorated was to mark their grave as separate, and therefore special. What happened in the course of the first half of the second millennium BC was that the concept of marking a grave as a monument became a more important feature of the funerary rite. Barrows were built and remodelled, memory charged or changed, through and by the activities at the sites (Fig. 1.4). Just as the history of specific sites is varied, so is the pattern of spatial distribution of barrows. If we can see the sequence of events at individual sites as the working out of links with past lives and ancestors, can the arrangement of barrows inform us in a complementary manner about social history and the creation of links between the living and the dead?[33]

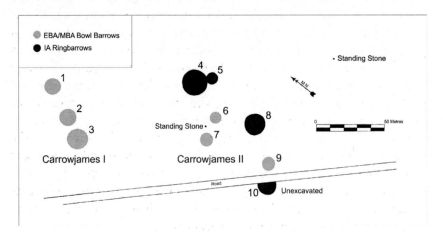

Fig. 1.4 The barrow cemetery at Carrowjames, County Mayo (after Joseph Raftery[34])

In tracing the development of the barrow cemetery on the Hill of Tara, Newman has established that there were recurring practices and principles involved. Tara had been a focus of Neolithic activity including the construction of the passage tomb known as the Mound of the Hostages. The Mound of the Hostages and the area to the north of it appear to have been the focus of activity in the later Neolithic and into the Bronze Age. Against this background of activity at Tara it is perhaps not surprising that of the two small groups of the earliest barrows (bowl barrows with outer bank and embanked ring-ditches), one is found to the south of the Mound of the Hostages. The second group occurs north of the east end of the Banqueting Hall and is separated from it by a small dry valley. Over the next millennium, these two clusters, which we can call for ease of reference the Mound of the Hostages cluster and the Rath Grainne cluster, became larger, more diverse in form, and developed in a strong linear fashion. Barrows were frequently placed beside or cut into earlier ones. In the first century BC, the construction of the large enclosure of Raith na Rig emphasized the central monuments in the Mound of the Hostages cluster. If we think in historical and social terms, it looks like the deliberate concentration of sites into clusters was predicated on the importance of placing monuments, but more importantly the individuals in the graves within them, close to and in relation to earlier, older sites.[35]

In trying to understand what was going on as this and other barrow cemeteries were sustained and enlarged through mortuary activities, including the construction of barrows, it is useful to refer back to the patterning in some of the earlier Bronze Age flat cemeteries. There, the main axis of burial, which focused on the graves of significant individuals, was linear. With the move during the centuries spanning the end of the Early Bronze Age and the Middle Bronze Age to reducing the focus on the grave in favour of greater visibility by being enclosed by a ditch and/or covered by a mound, the same principle of relationship and lineage was now expressed in the relative location of barrows. This constituted a further elaboration of the idea of the individual ancestor, with a lineage or lineages more specifically linked to that remembered individual in a more defined and close system of descent as cemeteries develop. Just as people deliberately opened graves to place later burials or placed later burials close to existing foci, so barrows were built to incorporate earlier ones.

In the developed Bronze Age, metalwork deposition and the recognition of different kinds of settlements are seen as reflecting a trajectory of social change. However, it is the barrow cemeteries that indicate these changes and their historical context most clearly. The settlement evidence suggests that the concepts of group identity and the size of groups extended in the centuries before 1000 BC. For a period of over a thousand years, from before 2000 BC, the focus seems to have been on local, small-scale networks of identity and interaction. It can be suggested that this was tied with a strong, local sense of bounded individuals. But matching the growing diversity of the settlement evidence and the use of metalwork there is a widespread presence of remains as well as echoes of the dead across the landscape. Both on hill and ridge tops and in low-lying, wet areas, barrow cemeteries were constructed against this cultural backdrop. The placement of graves and barrows within the cemeteries signified the relative importance of people and the lines of descent that could be recounted and remembered. The cemeteries provided lines of history that could be read as providing physical evidence to underpin social authority and legitimacy in the present. The extending social networks that we see, reflected both in the variety of occupation places for the living and locales for the dead, form a useful framework for understanding later prehistory.[36]

Memento Mori

This essay has focused on major 'turns' in the treatment of the dead by the living to illustrate both the richness of the archaeological record for mortuary practice in prehistoric Ireland and its critical value for our understanding of this period. With the exception of the Mesolithic period for which the evidence is limited, no attempt has been made to capture the full diversity of mortuary practice at any particular time in the prehistoric past. Rather, the emphasis has been on demonstrating that the post-mortem treatment by the living of the deceased, who were regarded as socially significant, as ancestors, was both complex and dynamic. The dead played a critical social role in prehistoric societies and they continue to be remembered in the present as key players in the narrative of Irish prehistory.

NOTES

1 See, for example, Thomas Bartlett, *Ireland: A History* (Cambridge: Cambridge University Press, 2010), p.1.

2 Patrick Vinton Kirch, *On the Road of the Winds: An Archaeological History of the Pacific Islands Before European Contact* (Berkeley: University of California Press, 2000), p.3.

3 See, for example, Mike Parker Pearson, *The Archaeology of Death and Burial* (Stroud: Sutton Publishing, 1999).

4 See Gabriel Cooney and Eoin Grogan, *Irish Prehistory: A Social Perspective* (Bray: Wordwell,

1994); John Waddell, *The Prehistoric Archaeology of Ireland* (Dublin: Wordwell, 1998) for general background and discussion.

5 Eileen Murphy, Barra Ó Donnabháin, Harry Welsh, Maria Tesorieri and Cormac McSparron, 'INSTAR: The People of Prehistoric Ireland Progress Report on Phase 2 – Synthesis of Osteological, Contextual and Chronological Data Relating to Irish Prehistoric Human Remains' (Report prepared for the Heritage Council, 2010). Another major project covering prehistoric burials is Mary Cahill and Maeve Sikora (eds), *Breaking Ground, Finding Graves – Reports on the Excavations of Burials by the National Museum of Ireland, 1927–2006* (Dublin: Wordwell/National Museum of Ireland, 2011).

6 See Parker Pearson, *The Archaeology of Death and Burial*, pp.72–123; Rosemary A. Joyce, *Ancient Bodies, Ancient Lives: Sex, Gender and Archaeology* (London: Thames and Hudson, 2009), pp.67–85; Joanna R. Sofaer, *The Body as Material Culture: A Theoretical Osteoarchaeology* (Cambridge: Cambridge University Press, 2006), pp.89–143. Each of these also discuss the relationship of sex and gender.

7 Tim Ingold, *The Perception of the Environment: Essays in Livelihood, Dwelling and Skill* (London: Routledge, 2000), pp.132–51.

8 Mary W. Helms, *Access to Origins: Affines, Ancestors and Aristocrats* (Austin: University of Texas, 1998), pp.34–54.

9 Tracy Collins and Frank Coyne, 'Fire and Water ... Early Mesolithic Cremations at Castleconnell, Co. Limerick', *Archaeology Ireland*, 17:2 (Summer 2003), pp. 24–7; Tracy Collins and Frank Coyne, 'As old as we felt...', *Archaeology Ireland*, 20:4 (Winter 2006), p.21.

10 Collins and Coyne, 'Fire and Water', pp.24–7.

11 For wider discussion see Chantal Conneller, 'Death', in eadem and Graeme Warren (eds), *Mesolithic Britain and Ireland: New Approaches* (Stroud: Tempus, 2006), pp.139–64.

12 For Killuragh, see Peter C. Woodman, 'Killuragh, Co. Limerick', in Isobel Bennett (ed.), *Excavations 1996* (Bray: Wordwell, 1997), p.67–8; for discussion of the use of caves in the Mesolithic and Neolithic in Ireland, see Marion Dowd, 'The Use of Caves for Funerary and Ritual Practices in Neolithic Ireland', *Antiquity*, 82 (2007), pp.305–17; and for Britain, see Conneller, 'Death', pp. 154–7.

13 For Rockmarshall, see G.F. Mitchell, 'Further Early Kitchen Middens in Co. Louth', *Journal of the County Louth Archaeological and Historical Society*, 12 (1949), pp.14–20; Peter C. Woodman, Elizabeth Anderson and Nyree Finlay, *Excavations at Ferriter's Cove, 1983–1995: Last Foragers, First Farmers in the Dingle Peninsula* (Bray: Wordwell, 1999), pp.102–3.

14 Jorgen Skaarup, 'Stone age-burials in boats', in Ole Crumlin-Pedersen and Birgitte Munch Thye (eds), *The Ship as Symbol in Prehistoric And Medieval Scandinavia* (Copenhagen: Danish National Museum), pp.51–8; Rick Schulting, 'Creativity's Coffin: Innovation in the Burial Record of Mesolithic Europe', in Steven Mithen (ed.), *Creativity in Human Evolution and Prehistory* (London: Routledge, 1998), pp.201–26.

15 A.E.P. Collins and D.M. Waterman, *Millin Bay, a Later Neolithic Cairn in Co. Down* (Belfast: HMSO, 1955); Gabriel Cooney, *Landscapes of Neolithic Ireland* (London: Routledge, 2000), p.124.

16 Richard Bradley, *The Prehistory of Britain and Ireland* (Cambridge: Cambridge University Press, 2007), pp.59–62.

17 Muiris O'Sullivan, *Duma na nGiall: The Mound of the Hostages, Tara* (Bray: Wordwell, 2005), pp.75–7, 225–6; Martin Smith and Megan Brickley, *People of the Long Barrows: Life, Death and Burial in the Earlier Neolithic* (Stroud: The History Press, 2009), pp.57–60, 82.

18 See Helms, *Access to Origins*, pp.28, 35.

19 Rick Schulting, Eileen Murphy, Carleton Jones and Graeme Warren, 'New Dates from the North and a Proposed Chronology for Irish Court Tombs', *RIA proc.*, 112C (2011), pp. 1–60; Gabriel Cooney et al., in Alasdair Whittle, Frances Healy and Alex Bayliss (eds), *Gathering Time: Dating the Early Neolithic Enclosures of Southern Britain and Ireland* (Oxford: Oxbow Books, 2011), pp.605–13, 637–57. For general discussion of megalithic tombs, see Carleton Jones, *Temples of Stone: Exploring the Megalithic Tombs of Ireland* (Cork: Collins Press, 2007).

20 Claire Foley, 'Prehistoric Settlement in Tyrone', in Charles Dillon and Henry A. Jeffries (eds), *Tyrone: History and Society* (Dublin: Geography Publications, 2000), pp.1–38; Jessica F. Beckett, 'Interactions with the Dead: A Taphonomic Analysis of Burial Practices in Three

Megalithic Tombs in County Clare, Ireland', *European Journal of Archaeology*, 14:3 (2011), pp.394–418; Andrew Powell, 'The Language of Lineage: Irish Court Tomb Design', *European Journal of Archaeology*, 8 (2005), pp.9–28.

21 For Tara, see O'Sullivan, *Duma na nGiall*, pp.119–21; for Knowth, see George Eogan, *Knowth and the Passage Tombs of Ireland* (London: Thames and Hudson, 1986), pp.135–9.

22 Patrick J. Hartnett, 'Excavation of a Passage Grave at Fourknocks, Co. Meath', *RIA proc.*, 58C (1957), pp.197–277; idem, 'The Excavation of Two Tumuli at Fourknocks (sites II and III), Co. Meath', *RIA proc.*, 71C (1971), pp.35–89.

23 See Cooney, *Landscapes of Neolithic Ireland*, pp.103–12; Hartnett, 'Excavation of a Passage Grave', pp.197–277; idem, 'The Excavation of Two Tumuli at Fourknocks (sites II and III), Co. Meath', pp.35–89.

24 Jones, *Temples of Stone*, pp.219–44; Neil Carlin, 'A Proper Place for Everything: the Character and Context of Beaker Depositional Practice in Ireland' (unpublished PhD thesis, UCD, 2011); William O'Brien, *Sacred Ground: Megalithic Tombs in Coastal South-West Ireland* (Galway: Department of Archaeology, NUIG, 1999).

25 For Early Bronze Age cemeteries, see Cahill and Sikora, *Breaking Ground*, pp.51–670; Waddell, *The Prehistoric Archaeology of Ireland*, pp.140–62; for an example of a recently excavated barrow, see Ian W. Doyle 'Excavation of a Prehistoric Ring-Barrow at Kilmahuddrick, Clondalkin, Dublin 22', *Journal of Irish Archaeology*, 14 (2005), pp.43–75.

26 Anna Brindley, *The Dating of Food Vessels and Urns in Ireland* (Galway: Department of Archaeology, NUIG, 2007) provides an important overview of the relationship and chronology of these different ceramic Styles.

27 Howard E. Kilbride-Jones, 'The Excavation of an Unrecorded Megalithic Tomb on Kilmashogue Mountain, Co. Dublin', *RIA proc.*, 56C (1954), pp.461–79.

28 Kilbride-Jones, 'The Excavation of an Unrecorded Megalithic Tomb', pp.461–79; James Eogan, 'Excavations at a Cairn at Coolnatullagh Townland, County Clare', *North Munster Antiquarian Journal*, 42 (2002), pp.113–50.

29 Cooney, *Landscapes of Neolithic Ireland*, pp.143–52 discusses the siting of wedge tombs in the context of other tombs. See also Bradley, *The Prehistory of Britain and Ireland*, pp.162–4 for the relationships between burials in cemeteries.

30 Eoin Grogan, 'Middle Bronze Age Burial Traditions in Ireland', in Helen Roche et al. (eds), *From Megaliths to Metals: Essays in Honour of George Eogan* (Oxford: Oxbow, 2004), pp.61–71.

31 Two important recent discussions are Jonny Geber, 'The Human Remains', in Melanie McQuade, Bernice Molloy and Colm Moriarty, *In the Shadow of the Galtees: Archaeological Excavations along the N8 Cashel to Mitchelstown Road Scheme* (Dublin: NRA, 2009), pp.209–40; Linda G. Lynch and Lorna O'Donnell, 'Cremation in the Bronze Age: Practice, Process and Belief', in Eoin Grogan, Linda O'Donnell and Penny Johnston (eds), *The Bronze Age Landscapes of the Pipeline to the West* (Dublin: Wordwell, 2007), pp.105–24.

32 Gabriel Cooney, 'Tracing Lines across Landscapes: Corporality and History in Later Prehistoric Ireland', and Tiernan McGarry, 'Irish Late Prehistoric Ring-Ditches', in idem, Katharina Becker, John Coles, Michael Ryan and Susanne Sievers (eds), *Relics of Old Decency: Archaeological Studies in Later Prehistory – A Festschrift for Barry Raftery* (Dublin: Wordwell, 2009), pp.375–88 and pp.413–23.

33 See Cooney, 'Tracing Lines across Landscapes', pp.378–82; Bradley, *The Prehistory of Britain and Ireland*, pp.164–8.

34 Joseph Raftery, 'The Tumulus Cemetery of Carrowjames, Co. Mayo', *Journal of the Galway Archaeological and Historical Society*, 19 (1940-1), pp.16–88.

35 Conor Newman, *Tara: An Archaeological Survey* (Dublin: Royal Irish Academy, 1997), pp.153–70.

36 See Cooney, 'Tracing Lines across Landscapes', pp.382–6.

2

BURIAL IN EARLY MEDIEVAL
IRELAND: POLITICS AND RELIGION

Elizabeth O'Brien and Edel Bhreathnach

Introduction

This essay is based on ongoing research being conducted by the 'Mapping Death' project based in the University College Dublin Mícheál Ó Cléirigh Institute for the Study of Irish History and Civilization and the Discovery Programme, and funded by the Irish Heritage Council's INSTAR programme. It is an inter-disciplinary project, which has as its focus the study of burials in Ireland from the first to the eighth centuries AD, combining archaeological evidence and primary documentary sources from Ireland, Britain and continental Europe. The aim of the project is to interpret burial practices in Ireland as indicators of social practices, social hierarchies, cultural intrusions, territorial boundary markers, the taking of territory, the establishment of dynasties, religious conversion and external relationships. A key object of the project is the compilation of a detailed and fully searchable online database of burial sites and graves, which will provide a guideline for the definitive interpretation of burial practices in Ireland from the late Iron Age to the early medieval period. This database is now available online and the input of information is ongoing.[1]

I

Burial rites and associated phenomena can provide a unique insight into a community's attitudes towards religion and other beliefs at any given moment in time. It is often assumed that burial rites and cemeteries were governed or overseen by the church in Ireland from the fifth century onwards given that Christianity had been introduced probably from as early as the end of the fourth century. However, literary sources suggest that the church did not seek to gain control over burial practices until the end of the seventh and into the eighth century and the archaeological evidence supports this conclusion.[2] It is useful, at the outset, briefly to sketch the background to burial rites in Ireland in the immediate pre-Christian and subsequent early medieval periods, before identifying archaeological examples of burial that were based on politics and family in which the Christian religion was not an issue.

During the later centuries BC and early centuries AD, the predominant burial rite in Ireland was that of cremation either deposited directly onto the ground surface or placed into small pits, sometimes covered by a low mound; alternatively, the cremation was placed in the central area and/or into the encircling fosse of a ring barrow, or into a burial monument of an earlier period. A majority of these cremations are not accompanied by grave goods, but a small number are, and those cremations with grave-goods dateable to the first century BC/AD provide evidence for possible outside contacts, influences, or intrusions (probably from Britain) during this period.[3] A very good example is that found at Stoneyford, County Kilkenny. This is a Roman type cremation burial contained in a glass urn, dateable to the first/second century AD, buried by people familiar with the burial rite that would not have been out of place in Roman Britain at that time.[4]

The short-lived phenomenon of crouched inhumation burial[5] was introduced into Ireland during the final centuries BC/first centuries AD, probably also due to influences spreading from Britain where this was the common native tradition at that time. In Ireland, this type of burial remained a minority rite, confined to a small area along the eastern coastline roughly from the Liffey to the Boyne; it was not absorbed into, nor adopted by, the native population.[6] Grave goods with crouched inhumations often match the small number of grave goods found with some cremations.

The rite of extended supine inhumation burial,[7] which by the later third century AD had almost completely replaced cremation throughout the Roman Empire, gradually spread into Britain, especially in areas near centres of Roman influence. At this early stage, orientation of the body varied; it could be laid out in either a north-south or west-east direction. However, during the fourth century, west-east orientation (with the head to the west) was fast becoming the norm. West-east extended supine inhumation was the burial rite adopted by Christians, but as its use was universal it cannot be seen as necessarily a sign of Christian burial especially in the early part of this period. As a result of contacts with the western and possibly the north/eastern fringes of Romanized Britain, extended inhumation was gradually introduced into Ireland from the later fourth or early fifth century onwards.[8]

In Ireland, burials during this early period tend not to be grouped in formal cemeteries: they can occur as single burials or in small groups in isolated places, and are often to be found inserted into or around prehistoric burial monuments.

The strong cultural and physical contacts that existed between Ireland and western Britain during this period are well documented.[9] We know, for instance, that in the fourth century the Irish (known to the Romans as the Scotti) had a trading agreement with the Roman authorities in Britain. According to the Roman historian Ammianus Marcellinus, this agreement was broken by the Irish in 360 AD when they raided the coast of Britain. We also know that the Déise of Waterford settled in south Wales at this time and that the Laigin (Leinstermen) had connections with the Llyn peninsula in North Wales. When the Roman army finally withdrew from Britain in 410 AD, the way became wide open for raids from Ireland and elsewhere: Patrick was only one of very many slaves taken around this time. There was contact between the Irish and Romano-Britons on many levels; culture and ideas were exchanged, and undoubtedly settlers moved in both directions bringing with them their own local customs. One of the new customs introduced into Ireland at that time was the Romano-British burial practice of west-east extended supine inhumation. As mentioned above, this was the burial rite adopted by Christians, but as its use was universal in the Romanized west, it cannot be interpreted as an indication solely of Christian burial. However, while some Irish burials of this period may well have been of Christians, it is now possible to demonstrate that by using burial as a means of creating links with the ancestors among whom they were being buried and ultimately with their land, the Irish were making as much a political as a religious statement. The Christian Church in Ireland had yet to legislate regarding burial. There are instances, however, of undeniably Christian burial in the fifth/sixth centuries. One example is the very interesting cemetery at a small Christian ecclesiastical site at Caherlehillan, County Kerry located in the Irish heartland of ogham inscriptions, an indicator of literacy that may have come with Christianity and of possible contacts with Irish settlements in Wales.[10]

By the seventh century, the standard burial rite in Ireland was extended supine inhumation, orientated west-east (head west) interred in organized cemeteries. Skeletons from this period onwards usually show indications that bodies were wrapped in a winding sheet or shroud with the legs and feet very close together and the arms remaining close to the body. Such burials normally do not have grave-goods, but a small minority were accompanied by a knife or a belt buckle. The use of coffins was unknown in Ireland at this time, although very occasionally a grave might be lined with wooden planks before the body was inserted.

The wrapping of a body in a winding sheet is a Christian custom, based on the description of Christ's burial as provided, for instance, in Luke 23:53, where it is indicated that the body was *involuit sindone* (wrapped in fine linen) before being laid in the tomb. The lower panel on the west face shaft of the early tenth-century Cross of the Scriptures at Clonmacnoise (amongst others) shows the Irish interpretation of this feature of Christ's burial.[11] At the end of the seventh century, Adomnán, describing the burial of Columba (who had died in the late sixth century), states that his body was wrapped in linen cloths and laid in the appointed burial place.[12] This was therefore regarded as the appropriate mode of burial for Christians in both Ireland and Britain by the eighth century.

Burials As Indicators Of The Politics Of Family And Territorial Claims, Not Religion

In 1976, Thomas Charles-Edwards published his paper 'Boundaries in Irish law' drawing on evidence contained in early Irish law tracts.[13] In the paper he describes how the boundary to a territory was marked by a *fert* (a grave-mound) or *ferta* (a collection of grave-mounds or a collection of burials in one mound). According to the legal procedure *tellach* (legal entry), which is described in the early law tract *Din Techtugad*,[14] a specific process was pursued in order to make a claim to land.[15] The ancestral boundary *fert* was an essential part of this process, the perception being that the ancestors who were buried in the *fert* acted as guardians of the land or territory. It was necessary to obtain the 'permission' of these guardians in order to legitimize the claim and to gain possession legally of the said land.

What was a *fert*? It was an ancestral burial place that often, but not always, involved the reuse of an existing prehistoric burial monument. When Bishop Tírechán referred to the burial of the two daughters of the king of Tara in his *Collectanea* written in the seventh century, he stated that they were buried in a *fossam rotundam* (circular ditch) after the manner of a *ferta* 'because this is what the heathen Irish used to do, but we call it *relic*'. Tírechán therefore regarded a *fert* as a non-Christian grave.[16]

Recent archaeological investigation at several *ferta* sites has provided evidence that from time to time during the later Iron Age (that is the first century BC/AD) and in the period 400–700AD burials were often inserted into ancestral *ferta*. Such burials were probably inserted either by the legitimate occupants of a territory in order to reinforce their valid title to their land when others sought to make a claim, or by intrusive groups who sought, by introducing their own 'guardians' into the *ferta*, to create a contrived form of continuity as a means of legitimizing a claim to territory. In either case, this is the deliberate incorporation of important individuals into the ancestral landscape, somewhat akin to the later literary tradition of inserting new ancestral names into a family genealogy. A further item of interest is the fact that many of the burials inserted during the fifth and sixth centuries AD were female.[17]

Map 2.1 Ancestral boundary *ferta* (mentioned in text)

When acting as territorial boundary markers, *ferta* (or ancestral burial mounds) are usually located in prominent positions overlooking or close to natural boundaries such as by a river, the coastline, a bog, or a ravine. While many *ferta* are reused prehistoric (or ancestral) burial mounds, others are natural hillocks which were probably perceived as ancient burial places; still others are primary mounds constructed in the early medieval period as imitations of ancient burial places.

For the purpose of this essay we have chosen to describe three examples from different parts of the country (see Map 2.1), which form part of an increasing list of such *ferta* sites:

Knowth, County Meath

Knowth could be regarded as the ultimate ancestral boundary *ferta*. It is the site of a famous Neolithic passage grave complex dateable to the fourth/third millennium BC.[18] This Neolithic necropolis, on the northern bank of the major political/territorial boundary formed by the River Boyne (see Map 2.1), was clearly regarded as an important ancestral burial place.

After the primary use of the site ceased, it lay undisturbed for millennia, but it was reused for burial starting in the Iron Age, around the first century BC/AD, with the insertion of crouched inhumations, which was, as described above, a burial rite hitherto unknown in Ireland.[19] Strontium and oxygen isotope analysis[20] on teeth from burials No. 8/9 (crouched males) have produced measurements which establish that the persons from which they derive were born outside of the Meath area, possibly in the northern regions of Ireland but more likely in the northern part of Britain.[21] The bodies were decapitated and were accompanied by gaming pieces and other small grave goods. Burial 10 (crouched female) was born either in the northern region of Ireland, or possibly eastern Britain.[22] These burials represent examples of newcomers being buried among the perceived indigenous ancestors. In other words, they were inserted and absorbed into the collective memory of the community.

There then occurred a further time-lapse of several hundred years during which the monument was not reused for burial until the insertion of extended inhumation burials in the seventh and eighth centuries AD.[23] It is noticeable that these particular burials were placed inside the smaller prehistoric ancestral tombs, as opposed to being placed in the open area around the tombs. In this way, an emphatic and symbolic statement of continuity with the ancestors was made by whichever dynasty or dynasties occupied Knowth during this time.

An extended double burial (No. 11/12), possibly a male and female, both aged over 20 years, which had been placed in the chamber of destroyed cruciform Passage Tomb 6 has produced a radiocarbon determination indicating a date of deposition in the seventh century.[24]

Burial 27 (who was born either in the northern region of Ireland or possibly in Britain) was placed together with a double burial No. 28/29 (male and female) in the chamber of Passage Tomb 15; and burial 30 was also placed into another passage tomb. All of these burials conform to the standard formal extended burial rite of the seventh/eighth centuries AD, and the general indications are that they were all more than likely Christians. Even though some were incomers, they were buried among the local ancestors.

There is one anomalous burial in the group. Burial No.14 – a tall, mature male dated to the seventh/eighth century[25] – was placed in the base of the outer ditch of the double-ditched enclosure dug around the main mound in the early medieval period when the site had become a royal complex. Even though some effort had been made to conform to normal practice by laying the body in a west-east direction in an extended position, the placing of the burial in the ditch suggests that the body had been disposed of in a furtive manner. There is also the fact that this person was apparently decapitated. It therefore cannot be regarded as a formal burial and one can only speculate on the reasons for this. One possible reason is provided by strontium and oxygen isotope analysis of the teeth, which suggests an origin for this person in eastern Scotland.[26] He may have had Pictish affinities, and it may be more than coincidence that a graffiti-type inscription on orthostat No. 56 in the main passage tomb commemorates a Pictish name 'Tolarg', indicating a possible Pictish presence at Knowth, during the eighth/ninth century AD.[27]

At the same time, four burials in west-east orientated slab-lined cists, laid in a row parallel to each other (Nos 32, 33, 34, 35), were inserted into flat ground on the western side of the main mound. Burial 32 was that of an extended, supine inhumation, possibly male, aged about 17 years. Radiocarbon dating of this burial places it in the eighth/ninth century AD (710–891 cal. AD) and strontium and oxygen isotope analysis of his teeth suggest that he was born outside of the Meath region, either in the northern part of Ireland or of Britain.[28] Burial 33 was an extended, supine inhumation, a female aged in her mid-twenties; strontium and oxygen isotope analysis of her teeth suggest that she was a local and was born in the Meath area. Perhaps she was a local girl married to an outsider whose ancestry was being integrated into the local genealogy.

Burial at the Knowth necropolis ceased after the eighth/ninth century. While the majority of the people who lived in and around Knowth in the seventh to ninth centuries were undoubtedly Christian and would normally have been buried at ecclesiastical sites such as Slane, which was the chief church of northern Brega, it is apparent that during this period a small number of individuals were still being selected for burial among the (pagan) ancestors.[29] The archaeological and scientific evidence indicates that many of these people in the Iron Age, and again in the early medieval period, were newcomers to the region. This raises many questions, the answers to which may lie in the turbulent historical background to the various dynasties that occupied Knowth during this period.[30]

Ballymacaward, County Donegal

Ballymacaward, Ballyshannon, County Donegal is located on the northern shore at the mouth of the River Erne at Ballyshannon Harbour (see Map 2.1). The River Erne has long been regarded as an important political and territorial boundary.[31] Excavation revealed a prehistoric Bronze Age cairn that contained two short cists (both empty) of a type datable to the first half of the second millennium BC (c.2000–1500 BC).[32] Like Knowth, the burial cairn then remained undisturbed for over a millennium, but continued to be recognized as an ancestral burial place because in the Iron Age two cremations, in small pits, were inserted into its surface. One of these cremations (an adult, probably female) produced a c14 date placing it in the second to first century BC.[33] After a further interval of more than a century, an extension was added to one side of the cairn into which deposits of charcoal and cremated bone were spread. This material has been c14 dated to between the first and third centuries AD.[34] We have no way of knowing who these people were, but it is interesting to note that one of the inlets recorded on the map attributed to Ptolemy, dating to approximately 150 AD, equates to the mouth of the River Erne, so that the area was known to mariners at that time. As at Knowth, there was a further time-lapse of several hundred years, after which four extended female supine inhumations in slab-lined long cists, oriented west-east, without grave goods, were inserted into the surface of the mound. One of these, a very elderly female, who suffered from post-menopausal osteoporosis of the spine, has been dated to the fifth to sixth century AD.[35] Once again, we have no way of knowing whether these particular burials were of pagans or of Christians.

44

The final period during which this monument was used involved the insertion in the sixth/seventh century of a minimum of several extended inhumations, all female, laid west-east, in unprotected dug graves. Some of these, at least, were probably Christian, as one of these female burials, dated to the sixth/seventh century AD, showed evidence of having been wrapped in a winding sheet.[36] After this, burial at this monument ceased. However, even after the cessation of burial in the seventh century this *ferta* probably continued to act as a boundary feature in the landscape well into the medieval period.

Eelweir Hill, Lehinch, County Offaly

The third *ferta* site, at Eelweir Hill, Lehinch, near Clara, County Offaly is located on a natural sand and gravel hillock on the northern bank of the political/territorial boundary formed by the River Brosna (see Map 2.1).[37] Excavation by Raghnall Ó Floinn in 1978/9 revealed that this hillock had originally been utilized for the deposit of Bronze Age cremations.[38] In the early medieval period the small hillock was still regarded as an ancestral burial *ferta* because after a lapse of perhaps two millennia, six extended supine inhumations were inserted into the mound. Burial III, a female (?), dated to the fourth to sixth centuries AD was accompanied by antler tine and some horse bones.[39] This is of particular interest because several other burials (predominantly female burials) from this same period in other parts of the country were also accompanied by antler and/or horse bones. Burial V, a male burial dated to the fifth/sixth centuries AD (somewhat later than the female burial), had been decapitated.[40] The head was missing when he was buried. In such cases, the head had either been deliberately buried elsewhere, which can happen for various reasons, or it had been taken as a trophy at the time of decapitation.[41] It is worth noting that this particular ancestral burial mound was not used for the insertion of any further burials after the sixth century AD. But here again it is likely to have continued to act as a territorial boundary marker.

This small sample suggests that ancestral burial mounds or *ferta*, when located on boundaries, had a crucial role to play in early Irish law, especially when a claim to territory was being made. These burials therefore have more to do with the politics of territorial claims than with pagan or Christian religious practices. It is of interest that of the 163 sites entered in the 'Mapping Death' database to date, thirty-five can be identified as probable *ferta* sites. Not all are located on recognizable boundaries, but the majority are likely to have been thus located.

Introduction of Ecclesiastical Legislation Regarding the Burial of Christians

Until the eighth century, burial in Irish church cemeteries was reserved for kings, bishops, abbots, clerics and patrons. The laity in general was probably buried in ancestral *ferta* and in familial cemeteries which could contain both believers and non-believers – a practice tolerated by the church because of the importance attached by the Irish to burial among their ancestors. This resulted in the proliferation of familial cemeteries, often with obvious ecclesiastical associations, located in or close to early medieval habitation sites.[42] It is impossible to differentiate between Christian and pagan burials for this period in Ireland because all graves look alike. This difficulty is brought sharply into focus by the seventh-century writers Muirchú and Tírechán[43] who relate a similar incident. Patrick, while travelling along a road, reputedly stopped at two new graves, one of which was marked by a cross. When questioned by Patrick, a voice from the grave marked by the cross admitted that he was a pagan and that the cross had been placed in error on his grave instead of that of his Christian neighbour. This incident was supposed to have taken place during the fifth century when Patrick was alive, but the fact that both Tírechán and Muirchú mention it indicates that they were still familiar with such a possibility in the late seventh century.

By the seventh/eighth century, the people who were still being buried in ancestral *ferta* and familial cemeteries were undoubtedly Christian, but the all-important statement being made was political. They were buried among their ancestors in their own territory and religious practice was not the primary consideration. It was only from the early eighth century onwards that the church started to define acceptable burial practices for Christians, probably in order to gain control over churches and their associated cemeteries. We see the beginnings of this trend in the late seventh century in the incident already mentioned regarding Patrick, which pointed out to the faithful the danger that graves of Christians risked not being recognized if they were located *inter malos* ('among pagans'), namely their ancestors. The *Collectio Canonum Hibernensis* (Collection of Irish Canons),[44] written in the early eighth century, includes the earliest canons that we are aware of urging the faithful to abandon burial among their ancestors in favour of church cemeteries.[45] The church was, however, conscious of the importance of ancestral graves and had to find ways to accommodate the change. Thus the canons refer specifically to traditional burial practices. Ancestral cemeteries were not to be totally abandoned. Christians were still held responsible for the upkeep of ancestral burial places. One canon emphasizes this point by including a reminder '... that it is a matter for blame if it (a burial) is neglected (by those) in the religious state ...'.[46] In other words, Christians were still responsible for the upkeep of their ancestors' graves. A further canon illustrates the point that although Christians were still being buried in ancestral cemeteries, they were now earnestly encouraged to consider burial in 'desert' places, which in this context meant church cemeteries, rather than *inter malos*, because they would then be more likely to be visited by angels.[47]

The church was obviously successful in dealing with the problem because by the eighth/ninth century, secondary burial in prehistoric ancestral burial mounds or *ferta* had ceased. Radiocarbon determinations currently being obtained suggest that many familial cemeteries also virtually ceased being used during the eighth/ninth century period. However, some cemeteries continued to function until the church reforms of the eleventh/twelfth centuries, and very occasionally even later than that. A possible explanation could be that some families were strong enough to reach a compromise with the church authorities, whereby certain family members were buried in the local ecclesiastical cemetery, while the remainder continued to be buried in the familial cemetery. Ultimately, however, the increasing power of the church, from the late seventh century onwards, influenced the abandonment of Christian burial among the pagan ancestors for political or familial purposes, and burial close to the saints gradually became an acceptable substitute for burial among the ancestors. In these circumstances, *ferta* did not cease to be used as boundary markers. Their inclusion in the early law tracts indicates that they were still recognized, but it was no longer politically correct to insert burials into them.

The archaeological and scientific evidence indicates that these changes did not happen until about three centuries after the introduction of Christianity into Ireland. In other words, the period of conversion was a long, drawn-out process. Eventually religion in the form of Christianity took precedence over, and dictated the future direction of, politics and family.

II

From an anthropological and historical perspective, the 'Mapping Death' project's exploration of late Iron Age, late antique and early medieval Irish society is beginning to provide us with a new image of that society. It is now possible to track the relationship between burial rites, cemeteries and Christian practices from the early stages of conversion to the gradual, but not total, move towards burial in and around large ecclesiastical cemeteries. Archaeology also provides a first-hand view of the political and social hierarchy of Irish society, and confirms the picture of a highly stratified society revolving around kin-groups manifest in early Irish law tracts.[48] Equally, the assembly of a corpus of knowledge on burial practices during the conversion period allows us to assess the survival of customs and practices associated with burial rites that were regarded disapprovingly by the stricter adherents of the church, such as the compilers of the *Collectio Canonum Hibernensis*.[49]

The Development of Churches and Cemeteries

Sanguis martyrum consecrat locum, non locus sanguine ('The blood of martyrs makes holy a place, not the place the blood').[50] This dictum occurs in the *Collectio Canonum Hibernensis* in the section on consecrated burials and is one of many references in early Irish ecclesiastical literature to places sanctified by the presence of the martyrs' remains. We know from such early sources as the *Liber Angeli*, the seventh-century founding charter of the church of Armagh, and the early Patrician dossier in the Book of Armagh that the relics of important martyrs of the church made their way to Ireland as they did throughout western Christendom.[51] For example, the *Liber Angeli* declares in relation to the city (*urbs*) of Armagh that:

> ... it ought to be venerated in honour of the principal martyrs Peter and Paul, Stephen, Lawrence and others. How much more should it be venerated and diligently honoured by all because of the holy admiration for a gift to us, beyond praise above other things, (namely) that in it, by a secret dispensation, is preserved the blood of Jesus Christ the redeemer of the human race in a sacred linen cloth, together with relics of saints in the southern church.[52]

This statement implies that by the seventh century, if not earlier, Armagh had a church that housed relics of saints, and the blood of Christ, and we encounter frequent reference to this consecrated space in Armagh through the early medieval records.[53] We have argued elsewhere that Armagh was deliberately called an *urbs* not just to emulate Rome as the seat of an apostle and a primatial seat, but also to demonstrate that the layout of the 'city' copied the house of martyrs on the Coelian Hill in Rome, which was developed by Pope Gregory the Great around the same time (*Altus Mache ... urbs*).[54] Tírechán mentions that Patrick established a *domus martirum* ('house of martyrs') in Druim Urchaille (near Donadea, County Meath) and in Mag Roigne, the plain surrounding modern Kilkenny city and the River Nore.[55] He associates one foundation of the 'Franks of Patrick', presumably a metaphor for early missionaries, with a *basilica sanctorum* ('basilica of the saints') identified as Baslick, County Roscommon.[56] Whether the Irish had their own native martyrs or not has yet to be established. Despite Patrick's intimations that his life was often in danger, the early sources do not admit to the martyrdom of missionaries during the period of conversion.[57] This did not preclude the early church in Ireland from using the bodies of native holy men and women as foundation graves of churches, and the Patrician dossier is replete with examples of such activity. A particularly curious example is related by Tírechán:[58]

> And he [Patrick] came to Mag Réin [plain in south Leitrim] and ordained Bruscus a priest and founded a church for him; Bruscus said something extraordinary after his death to another holy man, who was in the monastery of the family of Cothirbe (*in insola generis Cotirbi*): 'All is well with you because you have a son: I loathe my death because I am alone in a solitary church (*in aeclessia in diserto*), a church deserted and empty (*in aeclessia relicta ac uacua*), and no priests offer beside me'. For three nights (the holy man) had this dream; on the third day he got up, took an *anulum* and an iron shovel and dug up the grave mound (*fossa*) and took the bones of holy Bruscus with him to the monastery where they now are, and Bruscus spoke no more.

Can the phenomena of the translation of the saints' bodies or the circulation of reliquaries be detected in the archaeological record and if so, how early and in what form? Evidence is beginning to emerge that suggests that the idea of a *domus martirum* or *basilica sanctorum* may indeed be genuine. The complex site of Colp West, barony of Duleek Lower, County Meath, which was partly excavated in 1988 and has since undergone some recent geophysical surveying, overlooks the Boyne River estuary and is well-known in earlier Irish literature as Inber Colpdai.[59] One hundred and twenty burials (thirty males, thirty-five females, eighteen children and thirty-seven unidentified) were discovered buried within and outside a penannular circular enclosure measuring 15m in diameter. This enclosure, in turn, was surrounded by a very large triple-banked enclosure. To date, there is no evidence for a church or other structure on the site, although it is always difficult to identify early churches in Ireland due to the insubstantial nature of their architecture.[60] However, sherds of imported pottery (B and E ware) from continental and east Mediterranean containers along with imported glass were found in the large outer enclosure. It is highly likely that Colp was an emporium (trading post) and along with other sites such as Dalkey Island and Lambay Island was an important entry point to the east coast of Ireland.[61] Whoever controlled the entrance to the Boyne was economically – and consequently politically – powerful. Clearly such a place was also open to outside cultural influences including the reception of Christianity from Britain, Gaul and the Mediterranean. Two burials at Colp (B102F and B65M) have been c14 dated to between the sixth and seventh centuries AD.[62] A third burial (B161M) was particularly intriguing. It was inserted in a pit, which was dug into the outer edge of the penannular enclosure. The disarticulated bones of a male skeleton were placed in a wooden chest or box (70cm x 30cm) that was furnished with iron corner brackets. A bone sample from the skeleton has been dated to the fifth or sixth century (433–596 AD). The burial appears to be that of a man whose bones were collected and placed in the wooden box. Could this be regarded as evidence for a *translatio*, the removal of an individual's bones from their original grave and reburial elsewhere in a reliquary? Box burials are unknown in Ireland and are relatively rare in late antique Britain.[63] Of further interest is the fact that these remains could date to at least a generation earlier than the other known burials from the cemetery at Colp. The deepest burial (B65M) within the penannular enclosure has been dated to 558–644 AD. One might consider the possibility that the wooden box contained the *reliquiae* of a martyr or holy person from outside Ireland or a local person who was venerated in some way in a late antique manner. Isotopic analysis may enable us to identify his origin in the future. What can be said about this find so far is that it, along with imported pottery and glass, definitely links Colp with a wider economic and 'religious' culture that ranged from the east Mediterranean to late antique Britain and on to the east coast of Ireland.

Another possible example of a foundation burial may come from Dromiskin, County Louth. Two slab-lined stone cists (one male, one female) were discovered in 1862 near the church of Dromiskin, the site of Druim Inesclainn, a foundation closely associated with Armagh. There may have been a mound over the burials. One of the slab-lined cists contained a small stone box, and within it a smaller box made from yew wood (see Fig. 2.1).[64] The yew box, which had a sliding lid,

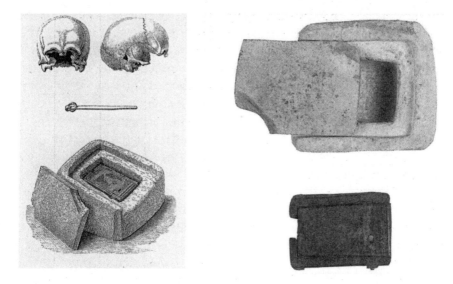

Fig. 2.1 Stone reliquary box with wooden box found at Dromiskin, County Louth

contained a small bronze pin of native manufacture and some charcoal. Were the stone and yew boxes to be placed in the cavity of an altar in the manner of Byzantine reliquary boxes? Or were they deliberately buried with a founder? The absence of human bone from the yew box should not prevent us from regarding this as a reliquary deposition. Non-corporeal relics became the norm in Ireland in the Middle Ages. A plausible version of the yew box occurs in Adomnán's seventh-century Life of Columba.[65] He relates how Columba became aware miraculously that the noble virgin Mogain, daughter of Daiméne of Clogher, County Tyrone (Clochar Macc nDaiméni) had broken her hip and was crying out for help by invoking Columba's name. Columba sent his monk Lugaid over to Clogher with a little pinewood box 'with a blessing inside it' (*sanctus pineam tradit cum benedictio capsellam*), and commended him to place the 'blessing' in water and to sprinkle the water on Mogain's hip. Lugaid did as he was told and the holy woman's hip was fully healed. While Adomnán does not specify the object put in the pinewood box, a bronze pin, similar to that discovered in the Dromiskin yew box, would not have been out of place, especially if owned by Columba.

The morphology of the cemetery at Caherlehillan, barony of Iveragh, County Kerry, opens up another horizon regarding churches and related cemeteries.[66] This site consisted of eighteen graves (unidentified as no bone survived) and is located on a terrace overlooking a river valley with a view towards Valentia Harbour. The graves were surrounded by an enclosure which also contained a small rectangular wooden structure defined by wooden corner posts, three decorated cross slabs and a possible stone shrine. The structure may be an early timber church and probably provides the best evidence to date for such a building. The timbers yielded c14 dates of the late fifth or sixth century. A post-hole in a central position close to the east end has been interpreted as evidence for a single-post altar of the type illustrated on a cross-shaft from Kilnaruane, County Kerry representing the meeting of SS Paul and Anthony in the desert.[67] The three fragmentary slabs are decorated with a cross of arcs surmounted by a bird – a peacock or a dove – which often appear on continental grave slabs until the seventh century. The Caherlehillan slabs are very similar in design, which might suggest that they were copied from imported representations. One of the graves shows features that marked it out as a special grave: it was one of the earliest, and the stones were more carefully cut than for other graves, and one stone at the head was in the form of a cross. This grave was later covered by a slab-lined shrine creating a raised platform or bed. This edifice may represent the tomb of the founder, the *érlam*. The concept of the *érlam* ('patron') is essential to understanding the founding of a church and its develop-ment in early Ireland. Pádraig Ó Riain has considered the role of the *érlam* in detail on the basis of a survey of genealogies, hagiography and laws.[68] The *érlam* was the heavenly patron of a church and was normally the saint who founded the church. He or she prescribed the rule of life for any community serving the church, and their kin-group often held on to its headship. The *érlam* was buried in the cemetery and was expected to be the protector at the Last Day of those who lay buried in the same cemetery. As handing over land to the church was included in the laws as part of the inheritance of kin-land, this land was not normally alienated from the kindred and was usually agreed within a kin-group. We should, therefore, regard cemeteries, be they clearly ecclesiastical (in that they exist close to or around a church) or otherwise, as part of the landscape of kindreds. Hence in this period, the use of the term 'secular settlement cemeteries' does not apply. All cemeteries were familial.

Familial Cemeteries: A Reflection of Local Polity at a Given Date
Familial cemeteries uncovered in excavations over the past two decades are sometimes characterized by a large number of burials amounting

to hundreds of graves. Industrial activity occurred on part of the site including milling, corn-drying, butchery and metalworking. The cemetery can be located close to a habitation site and has often developed around a primary burial. While the site may possess prehistoric origins, the main date range for use of the cemetery normally lies between the fifth and the eighth centuries and occasionally stretches into the late medieval period. For example, Raystown, barony of Ratoath, County Meath was in use between the fifth and ninth centuries and consisted of an extensive cemetery of which 133 burials were excavated.[69] As well as being a cemetery, this site was an early medieval farming complex with kilns and water-mills. To a certain extent, the dead were placed somewhat apart from the living as the cemetery was surrounded by enclosures but they were still within sight of the working community. The cemeteries of Holdenstown 1 and 2, barony Gowran, County Kilkenny, were located on a raised plateau overlooking the River Nore.[70] Holdenstown 1 consisted of two groups of burials within ring-ditches surrounded by a large enclosure and numbering eight graves (four male, two female, two unidentified), which were dated to between the fifth and seventh centuries. Isotopic analysis has identified one of the males as local, while a female originated from elsewhere in Ireland or from northern or western Britain.[71] Antler picks were found in the ring ditches. This cemetery has been classified as a *ferta*, an ancestral cemetery fittingly located on a strategic ridge overlooking the River Nore.[72] Holdenstown 2 consisted of ninety-four burials, roughly aligned in five rows containing a mixture of adult male and female burials. Though not as obviously neatly arranged as a modern graveyard, there is a plan to this cemetery and if it belonged to a certain kin-group, it is likely that responsibility for its upkeep lay with designated members of the kin. Burial 59, of fifth or sixth-century date, stands out as it was a male burial accompanied by an antler pick, similar to those recovered from Holdenstown 1. There is an overlap between the two cemeteries but clearly the concept of how to lay-out a cemetery changed between one and the other. An intriguing result from isotopic analysis of Burial 59 suggests that this man was not local. He may have come from elsewhere in Ireland, possibly from the south-east, or even from Britain.[73] Was he an *érlam* of a kin-group, either a holy man from elsewhere whose cult flourished among a community he converted, or was he the founder of a new dynasty, which claimed the earlier *ferta* to legitimize their new-found authority in the area? Various possibilities tentatively suggest themselves from the sources. This may be St Colmán, son of Ultán of Belach Buaidge (Holdenstown), who along with his brothers or companions Guaire and Máel Dub, are commemorated in the medieval saints' pedigrees.[74] An alternative explanation may be present in the inscription on an ogam stone from the nearby settlement of Dunbell Big.[75] It reads NAVALLO AVVI GENITACC '[Navallo] descendant of Gentech'. The Uí Gentig are mentioned among the genealogies of the Osraige, the early over-kingdom in which Holdenstown is located, and a saint Tecán of Tír Ua nGentich is listed in the saints' pedigrees.[76] This saint may be commemorated in the medieval dedication of Tempall Tegáin or 'Kiltakan' in the townland of Grenan near Thomastown.[77] Although associated with the Osraige, the Uí Gentig were not necessarily locals but may have come from an area around Clogher, County Tyrone.[78] One can only speculate but this is how archaeology and history overlap, and more often than not reflect the complexities of any society. In political terms, it is possible that the Holdenstown cemeteries were at the core of either a *túath* (minor kingdom) or even of the over-kingdom of Osraige. This region is in a very strategic location, and it acted as a buffer zone between the provinces of Leinster and Munster during the early medieval period. The Iron Age cult site of Freestone Hill[79] and the strategic corridor of Belach Gabráin (Gowran) are to the north-east of Holdenstown and the *ferta* (Holdenstown 1) overlooks the River Nore. Close by is Dunbell Big, a complex of enclosures and ringforts, where two ogam stones and objects dating to the fifth or sixth century and later, including a zoomorphic penannular brooch, were discovered during excavations.[80] Adjacent to Holdenstown 2, but not necessarily part of it, is a medieval church and graveyard. Is this the real landscape of late Iron Age and early medieval Ireland: the *ferta*, the familial cemetery, the medieval church and graveyard, ringforts and an assembly site?

Survival of Customs

Grave goods are not commonly present in Irish burials of this period, and if they occur they are normally unspectacular. The simple nature of objects implies that these were buried with individuals either as intimate possessions or related to popular customs. Why, for example, did twenty per cent of the graves at Holdenstown 2 contain quartz pebbles scattered over the body, some intentionally on the chest or in the pelvic area? A burial in the extensive cemetery found at Cabinteely, County Dublin had a stone box or cist constructed around its head and a pillow stone. A quartz pebble was deposited with the pillow stone. A burial of a woman, aged 25–35 years, dating to the fourth to sixth century from Cross, barony of Kilconnell, County Galway had a quartz pebble deposited in her grave. A sixth/seventh-century grave from the island 'monastic' site of Inishkea North, County Mayo had a quartz pebble on the individual's chest while an infant burial dating to sometime between 680–890 AD from the large cemetery at Parknahown, Clarmallagh, County Laois was found with an antler bead, a perforated horse tooth and a quartz pebble.[81] Although grave goods are uncommon, the repeated occurrence of a particular object suggests some form of practice, and one that can withstand conversion to a new religion and the strictures of canon law. Usually such customs relate to healing or fertility and, as in the case of the Parknahown infant burial, probably amulets. With regard to special stones, and apparently quartz in particular, Adomnán's Life of Columba illustrates the power of a simple white pebble for both 'pagan' and Christian ritualists.[82] Columba was competing with a druid Broichan in the court of the Pictish King Bridei. Broichan refused to release an Irish slave girl and the saint threatened that he would not have long to live. Coming to the River Ness, Columba picked up a white pebble and said 'Mark this white stone through which the Lord will bring about the healing of many sick people among this heathen race.' Meanwhile Broichan was struck by an angel and his glass cup broke in his hand just as he was drinking from it – resulting in a near-fatal seizure. Columba was called back to the king's fortress. He handed over the white pebble and ordered that it be dipped in water. Broichan was to drink the water and if he was willing to relent about the slave girl he would live. He relented and Adomnán continues:

> The stone was dipped in some water, where, in defiance of nature, it floated miraculously on the surface of the water like an apple or a nut, for that which the saint had blessed could not be made sink. When Broichan drank from it, though he had been near to death, he recovered completely his bodily health … The stone itself was kept in the royal treasury.

It healed many but not those whose time had come and that included King Bridei: when dying the stone was sought 'but it could not be found in the place where till then it had been kept'.

It is of little wonder that quartz pebbles remained popular and that Adomnán had to find a way in which his great érlam approved of them. Such insights, based on inter-disciplinary methods, abound in the burial record and the early sources. The 'Mapping Death' project – to which this essay provides an introduction – has the potential to open up completely new avenues in the exploration of early Irish society.

NOTES

1 See www.mappingdeathdb.ie.
2 For further information see Elizabeth O'Brien, 'Pagan or Christian? Burial in Ireland during the Fifth to Eighth Centuries AD', in Nancy Edwards (ed.), *The Archaeology of the Early Medieval Celtic Churches*, Society for Medieval Archaeology Monograph 29/Society for Church Archaeology Monograph 1 (London: Maney Publishing, 2009), pp.134–54.
3 O'Brien, 'Pagan or Christian', p.136.
4 E. Clibborn, 'Relating to Articles exhibited to him by a Mr Perry of Stoneyford, Co. Kilkenny' (RIA MS 24/E/34); Elizabeth O'Brien, 'Iron Age Burial Practices in Leinster: Continuity and Change', *Emania* 7 (1990), pp.37–4; Edward Bourke, 'Stoneyford: A First Century Roman Burial in Ireland', *Archaeology Ireland*, 3:2 (Summer 1989), pp.56–7; Edward Bourke, 'Glass Vessels of the First Nine Centuries AD in Ireland', *RSAI Jnl.*, 124 (1994), pp.163–209.
5 Where the body was placed on its side with the knees drawn up towards the abdomen.
6 O'Brien, 'Pagan or Christian', pp.136–8.
7 Where the body was placed on its back in an extended position.
8 O'Brien, 'Pagan or Christian', pp.143–5.
9 For list of documented sources, see O'Brien, 'Pagan or Christian', pp.143–4.
10 John Sheehan, 'A Peacock's Tale: Excavations at Caherlehillan, Iveragh, Ireland' in Edwards (ed.), *The Archaeology of the Early Medieval Celtic Churches*, pp.191–206.
11 For an illustration, see Peter Harbison, *The High Crosses of Ireland: An Iconographical and Photographic Survey* (3 Volumes, Bonn: Habelt, 1992), iii, fig. 909.
12 A.O. Anderson and M.O. Anderson (eds), *Adomnán's life of Columba* (2nd ed., Oxford: Oxford University Press), pp.230–31, lll.23.
13 T.M. Charles-Edwards, 'Boundaries in Irish law' in P.H. Sawyer (ed.), *Medieval Settlement: Continuity and Change* (London, 1976), pp.83–7.
14 *Din Techtugad* 'on legal entry': see *Corpus Iuris Hibernici* ed. D.A. Binchy (6 Volumes, Dublin: The Dublin Institute for Advanced Studies, 1978), i, 205.22-213.37.
15 This process is detailed in Charles-Edwards, 'Boundaries' and in Elizabeth O'Brien and Edel Bhreathnach, 'Irish Boundary *Ferta*, Their Physical Manifestation and Historical Context' in Fiona Edmonds and Paul Russell (eds), *TOME: Studies in Medieval Celtic History and Law in Honour of Thomas Charles-Edwards* (Woodbridge: Boydell and Brewer, 2011), pp.53–64.
16 Ludwig Bieler (ed. and trans.), *The Patrician Texts in the Book of Armagh* Scriptores Latini Hiberniae X (Dublin: The Dublin Institute for Advanced Studies, 1979) pp.144–5 §26.
17 O'Brien, 'Pagan or Christian', p.145.
18 George Eogan, 'Excavations at Knowth, Co. Meath', *RIA proc.*, 66C (1968), pp.299–400; idem, 'Report on the Excavations of some Passage Graves, Unprotected Inhumation Burials and a Settlement Site at Knowth, Co. Meath', *RIA proc.*, 74C (1974), pp.11–112; George Eogan et al. (eds), *Excavations at Knowth 5: the Archaeology of Knowth in the First and Second Millennia AD* (Dublin: Royal Irish Academy, 2012).
19 For table of dates for these burials, see O'Brien, 'Pagan or Christian', p.138, fig. 7.2.
20 Jacqueline Cahill-Wilson et al., 'Strontium and Oxygen Isotope Analysis on Iron Age and Early Historic Burials around the Great Mound at Knowth', in Eogan et al. (eds), *Excavations at Knowth 5: The Archaeology of Knowth in the First and Second Millennia AD*, Appendix 5.
21 The origin of these burials is more likely to be in Britain where this was the usual burial rite at that time.
22 See note 18.
23 See O'Brien, 'Pagan or Christian'.
24 GrN-15384: uncalib.1355±20 BP: calibrated at 2 sigma = cal. AD645–685.
25 GrN-1471. uncalib. 1270±25BP, calibrated at 2 sigma = cal. AD668–810.
26 Cahill-Wilson et al., *Excavations at Knowth 5*, Appendix 5.
27 F.J. Byrne, 'The Inscriptions in the Main Passage Tomb at Knowth', in idem et al. (eds), *Historical Knowth and its Hinterland* (Dublin: Royal Irish Academy, 2008), pp.115, 118.
28 Cahill-Wilson et al., *Excavations at Knowth 5*, Appendix 5.
29 F.J. Byrne and Pádraig Francis, 'Two Lives of Saint Patrick', *RSAI Jnl.*, 124 (1994), p.14.
30 F.J. Byrne, 'Historical Notes on Cnogba (Knowth)', in George Eogan, 'Excavations at Knowth, Co. Meath, 1962–5', *RIA proc.*, 66C (1968), pp.383–400; Cathy Swift, 'The Early History of Knowth', in Byrne et al. (eds), *Historical Knowth and its Hinterland*, pp.5–53.

31 For details of the political and historical background to the area, see O'Brien and Bhreathnach, 'Irish Boundary *Ferta*', pp.59–60.
32 Elizabeth O'Brien, 'Excavation of a Multi-Period Burial Site at Ballymacaward, Ballyshannon, Co. Donegal', *Journal of the Co. Donegal Historical Society*, 51 (1999), pp.56–61.
33 UB-4196, uncalib 2091±56BP, calibrated at 2 sigma = cal. 230BC–AD30.
34 UB-4425, uncalib 1804±51BP, calibrated at 2 sigma = cal. AD80–350.
35 UB-4171, uncalib 1592±20BP, calibrated at 2 sigma = cal. AD420–540.
36 UB-4172, uncalib 1448±21BP, calibrated at 2 sigma = cal. AD570–650.
37 For details of the political and historical background to the area, see O'Brien and Bhreathnach, 'Irish Boundary *Ferta*', pp.61–3.
38 Mary Cahill and Maeve Sikora, *Breaking Ground, Finding Graves – Reports on the Excavations of Burials by the National Museum of Ireland, 1927–2006* (Dublin: National Museum of Ireland, 2012).
39 GrA-24336, uncalib 1625±40BP, calibrated at 2 sigma = AD339–541.
40 GrA-24350, uncalib. 1550±40BP, calibrated at 2 sigma = cal. AD422–596.
41 See Elizabeth O'Brien, 'Literary Insights into the Basis of Some Burial Practices in Ireland and Anglo-Saxon England in the Seventh and Eighth Centuries', in C.E. Karkov and Helen Damico (eds), *Aedificia Nova: Studies in Honor of Rosemary Cramp* (Kalamazoo: Medieval Institute Publications, 2008), pp.283–99.
42 O'Brien, 'Pagan or Christian', pp.148–9.
43 Bieler (ed.), *Patrician Texts*, Muirchú, pp.114–5, §II. 2; Tírechán, pp.154–7, §41.
44 Herrmann Wasserschleben (ed.), *Die Irische Kanonensammlung* (hereafter referenced as *CCH*) (Leipzig: Tauchnitz, 1885). This collection of canons was compiled by Rubin of Dair-Inis (a monastery near Youghal), who died 725 AD, and Cú Chuimne of Iona, who died 747 AD.
45 For further details about these particular canons see O'Brien, 'Literary Insights'.
46 *CCH* LIBER LI Cap. 2, p.209.
47 *CCH* LIBER L Cap. 1, p.208.
48 Thomas Charles-Edwards, *Early Irish and Welsh Kinship* (Oxford: Clarendon Press, 1993).
49 Wasserschleben (ed.), *Die Irische Kanonensammlung*, passim.
50 Ibid., Liber XLIV, pp.178–9 Cap. 19.
51 Charles Doherty, 'The Cult of St Patrick and the Politics of Armagh in the Seventh Century', in J-M. Picard (ed.), *Ireland and Northern France AD 600–850* (Dublin: Four Courts Press, 1991), pp.53–94.
52 Bieler (ed.), *The Patrician Texts*, pp.186–7 §14 (19).
53 See, for example, the Middle Irish life of Patrick (*Betha Phátraic*) which relates that Patrick was granted the site of his church at Armagh by Dáire mac Findchada and adds the topographical aside *bale h-ita in Ferta indíu* 'where the ferta is today': Kathleen Mulchrone (ed.), *Bethu Pátraic* (Dublin: Royal Irish Academy, 1939), p.136 (line 2704).
54 Edel Bhreathnach, 'From *Fert(Ae)* to *Relic*: Mapping Death in Early Sources', in Chris Corlett and Michael Potterton (eds), *Death and Burial in Early Medieval Ireland* (Dublin: Wordwell, 2010), pp.23–9.
55 Bieler (ed.), *Patrician Texts*, pp.162–3 §51 (2), (4).
56 Bieler (ed.), *Patrician Texts*, pp.146–7 §29 (1)-(3).
57 *Confessio* §55 (for text see www.confessio.ie).
58 Bieler (ed.), *Patrician Texts*, pp.136–7 §16 (8)-(10).
59 Margaret Gowen, 'Colp West: Early Christian Enclosure, Cemetery', in Isabel Bennett (ed.), *Excavations 1988: Summary Accounts of Archaeological Excavations in Ireland* (Bray: Wordwell, 1989), p.32 (no. 51). Full list of publications at www.mappingdeathdb.ie under 'Colp West 1'. We wish to thank Margaret Gowen for providing us with details and a copy of recent geophysical survey of this site.
60 Tomás Ó Carragáin, *Churches in Early Medieval Ireland* (Yale: Yale University Press, 2010), pp.15–47.
61 I.W. Doyle, 'Mediterranean and Frankish Pottery Imports in Early Medieval Ireland', *The Journal of Irish Archaeology*, 18 (2009), pp.17–62.
62 For a detailed description of Colp West 1, see www.mappingdeathdb.ie.
63 Raghnall Ó Floinn, 'Early Christianity in Ireland Based on the Most Current Archaeological Research', in O. Heinrich-Tamásska, N. Krohn and S. Ristow (eds), *Christianisierung Europas* (Regensburg: Verlag Schnell-Steiner 2012), pp.11–35.

64 Full details including NMI reference in www.mappingdeathdb.ie.
65 Anderson and Anderson (eds), *Adomnán's Life of Columba*, ii, 5.
66 Sheehan, 'A Peacock's tale', pp.191–206.
67 Sheehan, 'A Peacock's tale', p.197; Ó Floinn, 'Early Christianity in Ireland', pp.28–9.
68 Pádraig Ó Riain, 'Irish Saints' Cults and Ecclesiastical Families', in Alan Thacker and Richard Sharpe (eds), *Local Saints and Local Churches in the Early Medieval West* (Oxford: Oxford University Press, 2002), pp.291–302.
69 Matthew Seaver, 'Against the Grain: Early Medieval Settlement and Burial on the Blackhill: Excavations at Raystown, Co. Meath', in Corlett and Potterton (eds), *Death and Burial in Early Medieval Ireland*, pp.261–79.
70 Excavated by IAC Ltd., Bray, Co. Wicklow – to whom we are grateful for providing information.
71 See Holdenstown www.mappingdeathdb.ie for details.
72 O'Brien and Bhreathnach, 'Irish Boundary *Ferta*', pp.53–64.
73 See Holdenstown www.mappingdeathdb.ie for details.
74 Pádraig Ó Riain, *Corpus Genealogiarum Sanctorum Hiberniae* (Dublin: Dublin Institute for Advanced Studies, 1985), §366; idem, *Dictionary of Irish Saints* (Dublin: Four Courts Press, 2011), pp.189–90.
75 *CIIC* I no. 30; Damien McManus, *A Guide to Ogam Maynooth monographs* 4 (Maynooth: An Sagart, 1991), p.108 §6.13.
76 Ó Riain, *Corpus Genealogiarum Sanctorum Hiberniae*, p.12.
77 Ó Riain, *Dictionary of Irish Saints*, p.569.
78 M.A. O'Brien (ed.), *Corpus Genealogiarum Hiberniae* I (Dublin: Dublin Institute for Advanced Studies, 1976), 129a9 and 130a30.
79 Raghnall Ó Floinn, 'Freestone Hill, Co. Kilkenny: a Reassessment', in A.P. Smyth (ed.), *Seanchas: Studies in Early and Medieval Irish Archaeology, History and Literature in Honour of Francis J. Byrne* (Dublin: Four Courts Press, 2000), pp.12–29.
80 Dunbell excavations: www.excavations.ie (Dunbell 1972: 0020; S561528 and 1990:07; S557521).
81 Tim O'Neill, 'The Changing Character of Early Medieval Burial at Parknahown 5, Co. Laois, AD400-1200', in Corlett and Potterton (eds), *Death and Burial in Early Medieval Ireland*, pp.251–60, at p.257.
82 Anderson and Anderson (eds), *Adomnán's Life of Columba*, II 33.

3

CROMWELL AND PLUNKETT: TWO EARLY MODERN HEADS CALLED OLIVER[1]

SARAH TARLOW

Bodies – and parts of bodies – have multiple and mutable meanings during life. This essay explores the actual and figurative journeys of the bodies, and particularly the heads, of two celebrated seventeenth-century men. In the process, what makes a body criminal or sacred, a person or a thing, a curiosity or a holy relic, an instrument of the state or a memorial of an individual are all called into question. In both cases, the criminality of the living person was mirrored through non-standard treatment of the dead body. In both cases, the material body, especially the head, was a synecdoche for a whole body and indeed a social identity. In both cases too, political, social and religious context is necessary for us to understand which of many multiple possible meanings should be attributed to a particular material treatment of the body: the display of Cromwell's head on a pike above Westminster Hall is very different to the display of Plunkett's in a glass case in St Peter's church, Drogheda, County Louth.

Oliver Cromwell after Death

Oliver Cromwell was a man of undistinguished origins who rose late in life through the parliamentary forces of the English Civil War to become a leader of the English Commonwealth in the period following the fall of King Charles I. He refused to accept the crown, but assumed the role of 'Lord Protector' from 1653 until his death five years later. During his lifetime, and continuing to the present day, Cromwell has been a controversial figure. Regarded by some as a tyrannical despot and a regicide, Cromwell has equally been painted as a champion of ordinary people against a corrupt monarchy, and a defender of liberty. His foreign policy – especially in Scotland and Ireland – was brutal, and his regime totalitarian, but his effective stance against many of the excesses and abuses of the previous regime was admired by many across the political spectrum.

Oliver Cromwell died a natural death on 3 September 1658. An account by the doctor who attended him in his final illness and carried out an autopsy immediately after his death (it was important to establish securely that his death was the result of natural causes) made much of the fact that even after removing his bowels and embalming the body, decay proceeded unusually rapidly and produced particularly putrid smells. Dr Bates claimed that even after enclosing the corpse in 'ceratis sextuplicibus' (six layers of wax-impregnated 'cerecloth' which normally provided an airtight shroud), a lead coffin and an outer wooden coffin, the bad smell was still detectable.[2] This, notes Ivan Root, proved to the Royalists the Protector's 'moral rottenness'.[3] While some authors have taken Bates at his word, he was not an impartial witness.[4] Indeed, he was a man of royalist sympathies and became surgeon to Charles II at the Restoration of the monarchy: thus he had an interest in representing Cromwell negatively. Some accounts of the time avow that Cromwell's untreated body was buried privately very soon after his death. Others maintain that his embalmed body was carried to burial at the time of his state funeral two months later.[5] There is additional folklore around the burial of Cromwell's remains. For instance, depending on the source, it was said that his body was sunk in the Thames, buried on the family estate in Huntingdonshire, taken to the battlefield at Naseby, the scene of his great victory against Royalist forces or, following the completion of the post-mortem, that he was taken to Northborough Priory in Yorkshire and remains hidden there.[6]

What is not disputed is that after his body was put into a coffin, an elaborate wax and wooden effigy was made and this effigy was then displayed in a series of sumptuously decorated rooms at Somerset House in London. Officials and members of the public were able to visit the lying-in-state and there was considerable comment on the monarchical trappings of the effigy – dressed in purple velvet trimmed with gold and ermine, with a crown upon his head and holding a sceptre and orb.[7] The treatment of the effigy was replete with exactly the kind of pomp that Cromwell himself avoided in life; Cromwell had always chosen to wear plain black clothes and refused a crown.

The state funeral took place on 23 November at an alleged cost of £60,000. The executed Charles I had not had a State funeral, obviously, but Cromwell's funeral was modelled on that of King James. There was really nothing to distinguish it from the funeral of a monarch of the blood. A lengthy procession of officials, foreign ambassadors and delegates, military and religious groups and important people made its way from Somerset House to Westminster Abbey. When the Quaker Edward Burroughs came across the funeral procession he was dismayed to see how Cromwell, formerly known for his low church, puritanical sympathies, and for tearing down idols, was at the centre of such pomp. Moreover, it was not even his body at the centre, but 'a dead invented Image of Wood or Wax'. Burroughs was disturbed by 'all this stir, and cost, and preparation ... all but to accompany an Image from one place to another ... as if it had bin some Poppit play'. He was prompted to muse: 'and is this the end and final farewell of once noble Oliver? What, only the sight of an image carried and set up?', he wondered.[8] But it was not Cromwell's final farewell; this was not to occur for several centuries.

At the point of Cromwell's funeral there were already multiple bodies – the real body, and at least one effigial body, which had represented Cromwell through the process of transition. These two material bodies were supplemented by a new political body – the new Cromwell, Oliver's son Richard who was his appointed successor. Kantorowicz's famous observations on the multiple royal bodies – material and spiritual that mediate the liminal moments of succession – are as true of Cromwell's death as of the crises of royal succession.[9]

Two years later, following the swift collapse of Richard Cromwell's government and the triumphant return of Charles's son to take the throne as Charles II, the House of Commons journals records a resolution on 4 December 1660 that the body of Cromwell, along with those of Henry Ireton, John Bradshaw and Thomas Pride, should be posthumously punished for their parts in the regicide of Charles I. All living signatories to the order of his execution who could be traced and arrested had been tried for treason earlier in the year, and mostly hanged, but some of the principal actors had, it was felt, escaped justice by dying a natural death before the Restoration. On 30 January 1661, the anniversary of the old king's execution, the disinterred bodies of Cromwell, Bradshaw and Ireton (still in their coffins) were dragged on hurdles to Tyburn where they were removed from their coffins, hanged until sunset and then cut down and taken away. Although he was named in the December resolution, Thomas Pride's body was not taken to Tyburn on that occasion; it might have been too decayed to exhume and hang or simply buried too far from London. Although the parliamentary Act stipulated that the bodies should be hanged in their coffins, numerous eyewitness accounts of the event tell us that the bodies were taken out of their coffins and then hanged: as one witness put it:

> The odious carcasses of O[liver] C[romwell], Major General
> Ireton, and Bradshaw were drawn in sledges to Tyburn, where
> they were hanged by the neck from morning till four in the
> afternoon. C[romwell] in a green-seare cloth, very fresh
> embalmed; Ireton having been buried long, hung like a dried rat,
> yet corrupted about the fundament. Bradshaw in his winding
> sheet, the finger of his right hand and nose perished having wet
> the sheet through; the rest very perfect, in so much that I knew
> his face, when the hangman, after cutting it [his head] off, held
> it up; of his toes I had five or six in my hand which the prentices
> had cut off. Their bodies were thrown into an hole under the
> gallows, in their seare cloth and sheet ... and their heads were
> set up on the south end of Westminster Hall.[10]

This account is confirmed by *Mercurius Publicus*, which reported that
their heads were then cut off their 'loathsome trunks' and their bodies
buried beneath the gallows. The heads were mounted on pikes and set
on the roof of Westminster Hall.

During the nineteenth and twentieth century, questions about
whether it was really Cromwell's body that was disinterred, or whether
it had been replaced by another, and where the authentic remains of
Cromwell's head and body were located dominated the historiography
of Cromwell's 'after-life'. William White Cooper, writing in the mid-
nineteenth century, did not believe that any body that had been coffined
for more than two years, especially one in the state of rapid decay
described by Dr Bates at the time, would be hangable at all.[11]

The head of Cromwell, however, had been treated immediately after
death – certainly a craniotomy had been performed because the account
of his post-mortem gives the weight of his brain; the removal of brains
and bowels, and the embalming of the corpse would have impeded
decay. It is also likely that the head was treated further before being
displayed. Pearson and Morant mention the possibility of 'tar' being
used.[12] If this is the case, we should not think of heavy caulking
bitumen, but of some lighter substance more like creosote.[13a] The heads
were certainly mounted by the time that Pepys visited Westminster Hall
on 5 February, and they seem to have remained there, on poles, above
the south end of the hall for many years.[13] The rest of the body was
thrown into a hole beneath the gallows with the bodies of the other
two, and at that point they depart the story. There are enough accounts
of this happening to conclude that the stories of its transportation to
Yorkshire, Naseby or Huntingdon are fanciful.

Cromwell's head remained on a spike for maybe as many as twenty to twenty-five years. We do not know exactly when the head came down, or how. The account of a French traveller records it as still on show in 1671; there is an ambiguous reference to it dating from 1681, which may suggest it had already fallen, though another account, albeit one which contains known inaccuracies, has it still in place in 1684.[14] By the early eighteenth century it was certainly no longer on Westminster Hall, although there is little clarity about where it actually was. Most sources agree that the head was blown down in a storm and picked up by a watchman. It was then either secretly kept by the watchman or passed to a Cromwellian sympathizer. In any case, its location was kept quiet at a time when possession of the head would probably be considered treasonable behaviour.[15]

The Body as Curio

The next mention of the head dates from 1710, when a German account records that the head was part of the collection of Claudius DuPuy, a Swiss calico-printer, residing in London, who owned four rooms of 'curiosities', which he displayed for private view rather than as a money-making venture.[16] Within fifty years of Cromwell's exhumation, the meaning associated with his head had thus changed entirely. At the time of its fall from the roof it was a political object whose possession was so dangerous it had to be kept secret. But by 1710, if the German account is reliable, it was part of a gentleman's cabinet of curiosities, the ownership of which afforded cultural capital to its possessor. From the eighteenth to the early twentieth century, Cromwell's head was an object of curiosity and exchange. This phase of the story blurs the distinction between body and artefact, as the body part was collected, exhibited, bought and sold.

DuPuy died intestate in 1738.[17] Either upon his death, or at some point previously, the head came into the possession of the Russells, a theatrical family. An account by a medallist called John Kirk mentions having seen the head in 1775 when it was in the possession of the Russells, although it is not clear whether it was commercially exhibited, or whether the writer was granted private access. In any event, the head was offered for sale *c.* 1770 to the master of Sidney Sussex College, Cambridge by Samuel Russell the elder, who was pejoratively dismissed as 'a strolling actor of drunken habits'.[18] Presumably Russell thought that Sidney Sussex College might have an interest in owning a part of their famous alumnus.

In 1780 James Cox, a jeweller of the City of London, saw the head exhibited near Claremarket in London when it was still owned by

Samuel Russell. The latter's version of the history, recounted through a third party, is that Cox tried many times to buy the head but Russell refused to part with it until he was in such debt to Cox that he was forced to sell it to him for £118 in 1787.[19] Cox thereafter sold the head on at a considerable profit to three men, perhaps called Hughes, who wanted to exhibit it in Mead Court, Old Bond Street. An advert and a 'narrative' was prepared for this exhibition by John Cranch in 1799.

Cranch's narrative is one of the main sources for the history of the head, but it also contains interesting explanations for the physical form of the relic. He notes, for example, that the ear is missing:

> This is accounted for by another of the (Russell) family traditions which is that when the Protector's relations and admirers were occasionally admitted to see the head, they took those opportunities to pilfer such small parts as could best be come at, or were least likely to be missed. The ear is said to have been taken away by one of the Russells of Fordham.[20]

The collection of minor body parts as souvenirs is not new, but it is interesting. The removal of Cromwell's ear by a visiting descendant compares with Sainthill's having five or six of Bradshaw's toes after his hanging. Again the body part is synechdocal of the person as a whole.

In 1814 the head was obtained by Josiah Henry Wilkinson, in whose family's possession it remained until the middle of the twentieth century. The novelist Maria Edgeworth describes being shown the head by Wilkinson at a private house on 9 March 1822. After breakfast, the whole group, of whom Maria Edgeworth was one, were told the story, while Wilkinson's sister and brother-in-law took turns to hold the head up for the hour that it took to tell the story. She observed, in an unpublished letter seen by Pearson and Morant, that 'Mr Wilkinson its present possessor doats upon it – a frightful skull it is …'.[21]

In 1935, when the study undertaken by Pearson and Morant was completed, the head was still in the possession of the Wilkinson family. Having been in the family for over a century, it was at that time owned by Canon Horace Wilkinson. Canon Wilkinson refused to allow the BBC to film the head in 1954, although he did permit personal visitors, friends and family to see it: there is a photograph dating from c. 1950 of Angela Thirkell holding the head in the archive of the writer's papers at Leeds University. Other twentieth-century photographs also exist: one of Canon Wilkinson with the head was on the Fitzwilliam Museum website at the time of writing this essay.[22]

In 1849 Carlyle, Cromwell's earliest authoritative biographer, dismissed as 'fraudulent moonshine' all claims that the body parts were authentic, but in the twentieth century, the debate over the authenticity of the head intensified. Numerous letters in periodicals during the early decades of the century traded anecdotes and folklore about the fate of Cromwell's body as well as his head, which seemingly cast doubt upon the status of the Wilkinson head. In order to allay doubt, 'scientists' were allowed to examine the head itself with the aim of making an objective assessment of its provenance and determining whether it was really Cromwell's head. Although he permitted members of the Royal Archaeological Institute to examine the head in 1911, Wilkinson did not allow them to publish their observations. However, in the early 1930s he granted Karl Pearson and G.M. Morant access to the head to make a thorough scientific study, taking many photographs and 'skiagrams', which were a form of early x-ray images. Their results were published by *Biometrika* in 1935 as *The Portraiture of Oliver Cromwell with Special Reference to the Wilkinson Head*. It was dedicated to, and acknowledged the assistance of Ramsay MacDonald, the Prime Minister at the time the research was carried out, and it is a serious product of respectable science. Although the dedication to Ramsay MacDonald describes the work as 'a slight token of gratitude', there is nothing slight about the volume, which is an extremely thorough and lengthy account of more than one hundred pages, plus numerous plates. The goal of the study was to demonstrate the authenticity of what had become known as the Wilkinson head. By scientific examination, Pearson and Morant moved from standard bio-anthropological determinations, like the age and pathologies of the man, to attempts to fit the head to all known portraits, busts and masks of the Protector. Their work was extremely thorough, and their conclusion 'that it is a "moral certainty" drawn from the circumstantial evidence that the Wilkinson Head is the genuine head of Oliver Cromwell', was widely regarded as persuasive.[23]

At the time Pearson and Morant carried out their study, they expressed no ethical qualms at all about examining and photographing the head. In 1952, however, William Kent, author of *London: Mystery and Mythology*, quizzed Canon Wilkinson about whether it was appropriate to keep the head on a mantelpiece, but only on the grounds that the remains of an important national figure surely ought to be on public view. Wilkinson's response was guarded, but negative:

> Canon Wilkinson demurs to this view on the grounds that they are Christian remains and there are descendants of Cromwell still

living. Perhaps he feels it would be dishonouring for the skull to be in a museum, but some will think it would be no more so than having it on a mantelpiece.[24]

This response – that Cromwell was a Christian, that his descendants are still alive, and that it would therefore not be appropriate to exhibit the head to the general public – manifests ethical concerns, albeit not strong enough for him to actually rebury the head. However, this was seen increasingly as the appropriate response during the later part of the twentieth century, when this is what happened.

If one wishes to see Cromwell's head today, it is not possible. In 1960, a few years after Wilkinson's death, the head was reburied (or re-immured) at an undisclosed location in or adjacent to Sidney Sussex college chapel. It intersects at this point with a set of cultural values relating to the dead body, which will be familiar to many archaeologists and museum professionals – that the display of dead bodies has become ethically troubling to our society. A new sensitivity to the way that the dead are treated had emerged by the mid-twentieth century; at first limited to the remains of Christians and concerns for living descendants, it expanded later, as a result of civil and indigenous rights movements' campaigns in the cultural realm, to include the bodies of other past people.

Oliver Plunkett's Head – A Post-Mortem History

Twenty-three years after Cromwell's 'execution', another symbolically powerful beheading occurred at Tyburn. The story of Oliver Plunkett's post-mortem journey is also remarkable, although far less extensively documented and discussed than Cromwell's, which has resulted in some asymmetry in my treatment of the two men. Oliver Plunkett was born into a wealthy and influential family of Anglo-Irish Catholics in County Meath in 1629, and he made a distinguished career for himself in the Church. He travelled around Europe and spent time in Rome until eventually he became the Bishop of Armagh. His involvement in both Irish and European Catholic politics made him enemies as well as friends. His execution in 1681 was the result of the machinations of his political and sectarian enemies who exploited English paranoia about Catholics seizing power. His fate was directly related to the anti-Catholic hysteria of the early 1680s, which culminated in the so-called 'Popish plot', a cooked-up story that the Pope was planning an invasion of England with help from Catholic France and elsewhere. Shortly after Plunkett's execution, it emerged that the whole story had been a fabrication, but in the paranoid and sectarian environment of Restoration England, the story was readily believed. Many Catholics were executed for treason. A number of disgruntled Franciscans, angered by Plunkett's decision in favour of the Dominicans in a land dispute, used the hysteria of the Popish plot to accuse Plunkett of planning to aid a French invasion of England. The story was ludicrous, as Plunkett pointed out during his trial, but this did not save him.[25] He was convicted of treason and sentenced to a traitor's execution – hanging, drawing and quartering. On 1 July 1681, sixteen days after his conviction, Plunkett was carried on a hurdle to Tyburn and there executed.[26]

Although the sentence specified in its conventional wording that the condemned should be still alive when he was taken down from the scaffold and disembowelled, it is likely that Plunkett was already dead. He had asked, in a final note written on the morning of his execution, that his body and clothes be placed at the disposal of Fr Maurus Corker, a priest he had befriended in prison.[27] A witnessed statement describes the dismemberment of the body that took place immediately after death:

> The under written John Ridley, chirurgen, and Elizabeth Sheldon, doe hereby certify and declare: that in the chist are included two tinne boxes, whereof the one being round containeth the Head; and the other being long containeth the two hands and armes from the Fingers End to the Elbow, of the Blessed Martyr Oliver Plunkett, Archbishop of Armagh, who was hanged, drane and quartered at Tyburn on the first day of July, A.D. 1681, for the holy Catholic religion; under pretence of a plott wrongfully imposed upon him and others of the same Religion. The said Head was cutt off from the Body at the tyme and place of execution. And on the same day the two hands, armes aforesaid were disjointed and separated from the rest of the said Body by one John Ridley, in the presence of Elizabeth Sheldon, immediately before the Quarters of the said Blessed Body were putt in to the coffin, in order to their interment, which Head, Hands, and armes were reserved by us out of the Coffin and placed in the said two Boxes of Tinne included in this, as is specifyed in witnesse whereof wee have hearunto sett our hands and seals this 29th day of May, An. Dmi 1682.
> John Ridley   Elizabeth Sheldon
> [endorsed on the back]
> Signed and sealed in the presence of
> Edward Sheldon   Ralph Sheldon

The other 'scattered remains' of Plunkett's body were gathered together and interred at St Giles in the Fields church close to the remains of a number of other Catholic victims of the 'Popish plot' scare.

Following Maurus Corker's release from prison a couple of years after the execution, Plunkett's body was disinterred and taken to Lambspring in Germany, one of the continental monasteries which specialized during the later seventeenth century in the education of novices and students from Britain and Ireland.[28] Corker erected a monument to Plunkett in the crypt at Lambspring and the body remained there until it was removed to Downside Abbey in England in 1882.[29] An anonymous scribe whose account survives at Downside Abbey notes that Plunkett's exhumation took place 'about two years after its burial, though a green woman had been buried upon it (Note: the woman had lain on it a year)'.[30] Plunkett's body must presumably have been embalmed and preserved in some way following his execution. Alice Curtayne commented in the early 1950s that the incision across the back of the head, where the scalp has been re-sewn with wire, is visible. This is likely to have been caused by the craniotomy carried out immediately after death, probably by John Ridley, to remove the brain. Packing the resulting cranial cavity with bran, sawdust, and aromatics was normal embalming practice.[31]

It was at this time that the dispersal of Plunkett's body parts began. One arm was sent to the Benedictine nuns in Paris; another was given to Archbishop John Brennan and thence through a succession of clerical keepers came into the hands of Cardinal Moran, Plunkett's biographer in the nineteenth century, who in turn gave it to the Dominican convent in Cabra, Dublin. Confusingly, yet another arm (or it might have been the one that went to Paris) was sent to the Franciscan convent at Goodings, Newbury, and then to Arundel, both in England.[32] One of Plunkett's legs was kept by Fr Bernard Lowick, who had helped Corker with the removal of Plunkett's body to Germany. Cardinal Moran described a number of cures and conversions associated with those body parts and other relics.[33]

The head, meanwhile, was given to Cardinal Howard in Rome in 1683/4, but was brought back to Ireland when Hugh McMahon became Archbishop of Armagh in 1715. According to one story, the head was smuggled into Dublin inside a grandfather clock,[34] and was given to the new Dominican convent of St Catherine of Sienna in Drogheda sometime between 1722 and 1737, where Catherine Plunkett, a close relative of Oliver, was prioress.[35]

In 1920, the same year that Oliver Plunkett was beatified, Cardinal Michael Logue petitioned the Sacred Congregation of Rites to have the head brought to St Peter's church in Drogheda, so that it might be more accessible to the growing numbers of visitors to the church, and his request was granted. The nuns at St Catherine's were unwilling to part with the relic, and mounted an appeal, but eventually bowed to the inevitable and released the head. They were allowed to keep the decorative ebony box which had been made for it during its time in Rome, and were sent a rib of Blessed Oliver, as he then was, from Hildesheim in Germany where his remains had been transferred after the closure of the Lambspring monastery.

Oliver Plunkett's head remains in St Peter's, Drogheda in open view. He was finally canonized in 1975. It is notable, however, that Plunkett's life up until his trial was by no means remarkable for a cleric of his period. Claims to his sainthood revolve upon his trial, imprisonment and execution, throughout which his dignity and faith were certainly impressive, and were 'consolidated through the reverence paid to his relics after death'.[36] The tradition and history of reverence in relation to the display of Catholic relics, including human body parts, has largely insulated Plunkett's head from the ethical anxiety surrounding the display of human remains in other contexts. Although there is an extensive literature on the ethics of displaying human remains in museums, the ethics of displaying Catholic relics have not been questioned.[37] In fact, while the twentieth-century response to the display of Cromwell's head ensured it was not brought into the public arena, and culminated in the decision in 1960 to remove the head from view, Plunkett's head was moved to a location where it would be *more* accessible.

Points of Convergence

Drogheda

While the post-mortem journeys of the two Olivers are in many ways opposites, there are actually numerous points of convergence. One could even argue that each story is textured and illuminated by the other. Certainly there are ghosts that haunt them both. The first, and most striking point of convergence, especially in Ireland, is Drogheda. St Peter's Church, which has housed Plunkett's head since 1920, was the location of Cromwell's notorious and brutal massacre of Irish and Royalist forces following the parliamentarian victory there in 1649. It was at St Peter's that the defenders of the city celebrated mass the Sunday before the attack.[38] Cromwell casts a long and black shadow over Drogheda, and his actions there have blighted Anglo-Irish relations to the present day. While in English historiography it has been possible to construe Cromwell as a people's hero and a champion of the ordinary folk,[39] in Ireland the brutality of his Irish campaign, exemplified by the Drogheda massacre, makes it hard to treat him other than as a monster, especially at a popular level.[40] Although there is little consensus among academics about the actual details of the massacre, and the extent of Cromwell's culpability, there is not much grey in the popular Irish view of Cromwell.

The translation of Plunkett's head from the private keeping of the convent to public display in St Peter's church in 1920 was primarily occasioned by the practical need to make his relics more accessible following his beatification. But the timing is also significant in the history of the Anglo-Irish relationship, since the head functioned as a potent reminder of English injustice towards the Irish. There is some irony in the fact that Cromwell's head became the object of detestation and then of vulgar curiosity, while at the scene of his atrocious massacre the head of a Catholic and a victim of the English secured a place of veneration and sanctity. In any case, the display of Plunkett's head in Drogheda facilitated its becoming a 'nationalist emblem', as Kilfeather has observed.[41] Throughout its history, then, Plunkett's head was co-opted for the purposes of nationalist or sectional political interest. One early example is the contrition of Hugh Duffy, one of the 'perfidious' Franciscans who perjuriously testified against Plunkett. Duffy came later to regret his role in Plunkett's death, and in 1721 visited Hugh McMahon, the Archbishop of Armagh responsible for returning Plunkett's head to Ireland. On hearing of Duffy's regrets, McMahon silently opened the door to a little shrine in his study, in which was Plunkett's head. Seeing this, Duffy fainted from emotion and remorse and subsequently became a 'true penitent'.[42]

The modern Catholic Church is keen to distance itself from accusations of relic idolatry, and presents the head more as a mnemonic and an aid to pious reflection than a miraculous object. One of the leaflets available at St Peter's numbers among Plunkett's significant achievements the opening of Ireland's first 'integrated school'.[43] While it is true that Plunkett did establish a school which was attended by a few sons of Protestant gentry as well as Catholic boys from good families, this was never a matter of religious politics, and his contemporary co-option by the integrated schools movement is merely one episode in a long history of appropriation, through which Plunkett's head has been used to buttress a socio-political framework or fulfil an ideological purpose – whether that be to admonish Franciscans, shame the English, embody the virtues of Catholic Ireland or champion integrated schooling.[44]

The Old King

Both heads are haunted by another seventeenth-century head – the one removed from Charles I. The relationship between Charles I and Oliver Cromwell is obvious and well known. Cromwell was one of those who tried and condemned the king, and his own post-mortem punishment was a twisted and grotesque parody of Charles' execution. Even the date chosen for hanging and beheading the bodies of the dead regicides – 30 January – was the anniversary of Charles' execution. A bizarre and, certainly, untrue rumour circulating around the time of Oliver Cromwell's punishment alleged that either deliberately or fortuitously, Oliver Cromwell arranged for the bodies of the old kings to be moved and swapped round with his own corpse, and that consequently the body on the scaffold was actually not Cromwell's but that of the king interred in his place – Charles I. It is inconceivable, however, that Charles I – who had already been decapitated – could be mistaken for Oliver Cromwell. In any case, the body of Charles I was exhumed in 1813 and found to be whole and in its proper place.[45] But the irony of the king's body being substituted for that of his killer was an irresistible elaboration of a parallel which was never very deeply hidden. Charles I's trial and beheading was symbolically matched by that of Cromwell.

Oliver Plunkett's association with Charles I was not so direct. Kilfeather notes that Charles' death was interpreted at the time as a religious martyrdom as well as a secular sacrifice.[46] Charles I's death became the model and referent for dignified martyrdom. Irish Catholics had fought alongside Royalist forces during the Civil War, not least at Drogheda, and it was not difficult to cast the death of Charles, with his Catholic sympathies and French wife, as a sacred sacrifice.

The Real Body and the Effigial Body

The damage done to Cromwell and Plunkett's actual bodies was, in both cases, presaged by destruction of their effigial bodies: a statue of Oliver Plunkett erected in the library of St Isidore's, a Franciscan foundation in Rome, was decapitated in about 1673 and several effigies of Oliver Cromwell, possibly including those constructed for his funeral, were destroyed by returning royalists in 1660. The attack on Plunkett's statue was carried out by disaffected Franciscans, whom Chaloner describes as 'parricides', and was the event to which Plunkett alluded in a letter sent shortly before his death when he wryly observed that 'those who beheaded me in effigy have now attained their intent of beheading the prototype'.[47] In Cromwell's case, several effigies were hanged or burned following the return of Charles II, possibly including at least one of those constructed for his funeral.[48]

71

Authenticity

The authenticity of Plunkett's head is essential to its spiritual power. Although the modern Catholic Church has distanced itself from any suggestion that the relic has supernatural powers, and requests that it should function instead as a focus for pious reflection and prayer, its popular appeal depends very heavily on its being the *real substance* of Plunkett's body. In the case of Cromwell, it was not the authenticity of the head that really mattered but its semblance. Indeed, in the case of the effigy that did duty for Cromwell at his funerary rituals, we know, as did everybody at the time, that it was not the actual body at all. By the twentieth century, however, mere verisimilitude would not suffice: an object purporting to be Cromwell's head had to really *be* Cromwell's head. The debate about its authenticity was not directed at any particular end – in other words, it did not really matter for any greater purpose whether the Wilkinson head was actually Cromwell's, but it was considered important to know (so important, in fact, that the Prime Minister of the day took an interest and made available to the investigators the art collections held at Chequers, his official country home).

One important set of questions, though, revolves around the extent to which the character and nature of the person inhere in the body, or body part. Does virtue, evil or criminality inhere in the body? In the case of Cromwell and Plunkett, their historiography is full of attempts to find in the surviving body evidence of the moral condition of the man. Bates' account of Cromwell's last illness, autopsy and embalming emphasizes the corruption of his flesh, and the Royalists made much of the rottenness of his body 'symbolising his moral rottenness'.[49] By contrast, Plunkett's head and body remained uncorrupted. The sweet fragrance of the head, alluded to by Archbishop McMahon in the early eighteenth century, was still evident to Cardinal Moran in the late nineteenth.[50] Curtayne, in her hagiographic treatment of Plunkett, sees his character in the features of his face that, in the mid-twentieth century, was 'still most human, in fact lovely'. She goes on to observe that his face evidences both gentility and resolution, and that 'generations of civilized living and culture went to the moulding of the temples and the fine chiselling of nose and lips'.[51]

What is a Criminal Corpse? A Different Kind of 'Top-Down' History
The actual material treatment of the dead body is part of what makes it criminal. We can see this most clearly by looking at what happened to those bodies whose categorization changed or was contested at and

after their deaths. The deaths of Oliver Cromwell and Oliver Plunkett occurred more than twenty years apart, but their post-mortem journeys look like they passed through much the same landscape, only moving in opposite directions. One body died the worst death of a criminal but, escaping bodily annihilation, eventually became an object of veneration, even a sacred thing. The other was buried with honour and accorded a State funeral of the most elaborate and prestigious kind, but was subsequently disinterred, dismembered and degraded as an object of vilification or curiosity. The journey from criminal to saint, in the case of Plunkett, is the reverse of the journey from social pre-eminence to criminal, in the case of Cromwell. But there are also curious parallels between the two.

The cases of Cromwell and Plunkett destabilize the notion of a criminal corpse. Plunkett was executed as the worst kind of criminal – a traitor – for whom the most brutal of punishments was prescribed. But from very shortly afterwards, his body began to transform from a most despised and abused object to a holy relic. A similar proximity of the criminal and the sacred is evident in the treatment of Sicillian *decollati*. These were originally beheaded criminals for whose souls some Catholics began to pray, as an act of mercy. Eventually, and in line with Sicilian Catholic practice, those who prayed came to expect some kind of reciprocity from the *decollati* and a cult developed wherein devotions to the *decollati* were undertaken in the expectation of receiving favours, pretty much indistinguishable from other Catholic saintly cults of the island.[52] Thus, criminal bodies come to possess powers similar to those of saints, and saints and sinners are both distinct from those who die a normal death. In Christian traditions, especially perhaps in times and places that are saturated with contentious Christianity, such as seventeenth-century England and Ireland, the archetypal criminal corpse is, of course, Jesus Christ himself. Executed as a criminal, the body of Christ was subject to physical pain and humiliation of execution. Yet the body of Christ was reinterpreted and thoroughly reclaimed as a locus of holiness by subsequent Christian traditions. Plunkett's martyrdom gains symbolic and religious force because his body underwent a similar journey of reinterpretation.

The post-mortem journey of Plunkett's body was reversed in Cromwell's case. At his death, Cromwell's body was subject to the treatment normally given to a royal body: autopsied, embalmed, buried in the most prestigious location, celebrated in effigy and given an enormous state funeral. But within a few years, his had become a criminal corpse and was subjected to the ignominy of public dismemberment and display.

The dead body or body part was not just a blank sheet on which society could inscribe its categorization of the worth of the deceased; it was actively involved in the creation of character, memory and historical legacy. In the case of these two emotive and symbolic seventeenth-century men, it seems probable that their bodies will continue to structure their historical meanings now and in the future.

NOTES

1 This chapter was prepared as part of the research programme 'Harnessing the Power of the Criminal Corpse' which is supported by the Wellcome Trust. Many thanks to Floris Tomasini for commenting on a version of this essay.

2 Dr Bates' account is given in William Cooper White, 'Historical Notes Concerning the Disease, Death and Disinterment of Oliver Cromwell', *Dublin Quarterly Journal of Medical Science*, 5:2 (May 1848), pp.339–70.

3 Ivan Roots, '*Cromwell's Head*', *Cromwelliana: The Journal of the Cromwell Association*, 1987, pp.27–30.

4 Cooper White's 'Historical Notes', p.22 discusses possible medical explanations. The anonymous author of *Flagellum: or the life and death, birth and Burial of O. Cromwell, the late usurper* (London, 1665), gleefully recounts that 'his milt was found full of corruption and filth ... strong and stinking' (p.196). The work is attributed to James Heath. Peter Gaunt *Oliver Cromwell* (Oxford: Oxford University Press, 1996) attributes it to an 'unsuccessful embalming'.

5 See, for example, Jonathan Fitzgibbons, *Cromwell's Head* (Kew: The National Archives, 2008).

6 Theories and stories about the ultimate fate of Cromwell's body, many of which appeared in *Notes and Queries* during the nineteenth century, are reviewed by Peter Gaunt, 'To Tyburn and Beyond: The Mortal Remains of Oliver Cromwell', *Cromwelliana*, 1987, pp.18–26.

7 There might have been a second effigy also involved in the display at Somerset House.

8 Edward Burroughs, *The Memorable Works of a Son of Thunder, and Consolation* (London, 1672), pp.457–60.

9 Ernst Kantorowicz, *The King's Two Bodies: A Study in Mediaeval Political Theology* (Princeton: Princeton University Press, 1957).

10 Edward or Samuel Sainthill (there is some inconsistency between sources) in a manuscript of Rev. T.R. Nash, cited by Karl Pearson and G.M. Morant, *The Portraiture of Oliver Cromwell, with Special Reference to the Wilkinson Head* (Cambridge: Cambridge University Press, 1935), p.45.

11 Cooper White, 'Historical Notes', p.33.

12 Pearson and Morant, *The Portraiture of Oliver Cromwell*, p.31.

13a There is now a considerable historiography on the subject of Cromwell's head, including Pearson and Morant's pioneering work, *The Portraiture of Oliver Cromwell*; Fitzgibbons, *Cromwell's Head*; Roots, 'Cromwell's Head'; Christopher Parish, 'The Posthumous History of Oliver Cromwell's Head', in D.E.D. Beales and H.B. Nisbet (eds), *Sidney Sussex College Cambridge: Historical Essays in Commemoration of the Quatercentenary* (Woodbridge: Boydell and Brewer, 1996); Sarah Tarlow, 'The Extraordinary Story of Oliver Cromwell's Head', in John Robb and Dušan Borić (eds), *Past Bodies: Body-Centred Research in Archaeology* (Oxford: Oxbow Books, 2008), pp.69–78. The history that follows is largely woven together from these sources.

13 Pearson and Morant, *The Portraiture of Oliver Cromwell*, p.58.

14 Ibid., p.22.

15 Ibid.

16 Ibid.
17 Ibid., p.13.
18 Ibid. p.14.
19 Ibid., p.15.
20 Ibid., pp.25–6.
21 www.fitzmuseum.cam.ac.uk/pharos/images/collection_pages/northern_pages/M2_1912/
TXT_SE-M2_1912.html [accessed 1 November 2012].
22 Pearson and Morant, *The Portraiture of Oliver Cromwell*, p.109.
23 William Kent, *London, Mystery and Mythology* (London: Staples Press, 1952).
24 Contemporary accounts of Plunkett's trial include a series of anonymous pamphlets published in 1681: *The condemnation of Oliver Plunket, titular primate and Arch Bp. of Dublin in Ireland and likewise of Edw. Fitz Harris, for high treason, at the Kings-Bench in Westminster-Hall, June 15, 1681* (London, [1681]); *An Account of some particulars in the tryal of Mr. Ed. Fitz Harris in Westminster-Hall, June 9, 1681, where he was found guilty of high-treason together with a brief relation of the tryal of Oliver Plunket, the popish primate of Ireland, at the same place the day before, who was likewise found guilty of high-treason* (London, 1681); *The traytors rewarded, or, the execution and confession of Edward Fitz Harris and Oliver Plunket, two notorious traytors, who were drawn to Tyburn on sledges, and there executed on the first of this instant July, 1681 for contriving, and trayterously carrying on the late hellish plot, by not only devising to destroy the life of his majesty, but to deliver up these kingdoms to a forreign power, &c.* (London, 1681); *The execution of Ed. Fitz-Harris and Oliver Plunket who was conveyed, one from the Tower and the other from Newgate, on the 1st of July to Tyburn upon a sledg, and there hang'd and quartered for high-treason in conspiring the death of his most sacred majesty, to subvert the government by endeavouring to raise rebellion, and to introduce an army to establish popery and arbitrary power and destroy the Protestants: with the manner of his behaviour in the Tower and at the place of execution* (London, [1681]); *The relation of the tryal and condemnation of Edvvard FitzHarris and Oliver Plunket who were tryed at the Kings-Bench on the 8th and 9th of this instant June, 1681, and there found guilty and condemned for high treason, for conspiring the death of the king, and to subvert the Protestant religion and government, by raising rebellion and leavying warr: with their last speeches and confessions at the place of execution* (London, 1681); *The tryal and condemnation of Dr. Oliver Plunket, titular primate of Ireland, for high-treason at the barr of the Court of King's Bench at Westminster, in Trinity term, 1681* (Dublin 1681); *The last speech and confession of Oliver Plunket titular primate of Ireland; with an account of his behavior in Newgate, since his condemnation, and also of Edw. Fitz Harris: at their execution at Tyburn upon Fryday July 1 1681, for high-treason, in conspiring the death of the King, &c* (London, [1681]); *The tryal of Edward Fitz-Harris, who was convicted at the Kings Bench-bar in Westminster-Hall, on the ninth of this instant June, 1681, for high treason, in conspiring the death of the King, and by several treasonable practices to subvert the government, with the several sercumstances that attended his trial, as also the tryal of Oliver Plunket titular Arch Bishop of Dubling, who was tryed at the Kings bench-bar, and there found guilty of high treason the eighth instant* (London, [1681]).
25 Plunkett's post-mortem adventures have received less historical attention than those of Cromwell. Most histories are of a hagiographical or devotional nature. They include Ethelbert Horne, 'The Body of Oliver Plunkett', *Dublin Review*, 167 (July-Sept. 1920), pp.19–24; Francis Patrick Moran, *Memoir of the Ven. Oliver Plunket, Archbishop of Armagh* (Dublin: Browne and Nolan, 1895); Alice Curtayne, *The Trial of Oliver Plunkett* (London: Sheed and Ward, 1953); Tomás Ó Fiaich and Desmond Forristal, *Oliver Plunkett: His Life and Letters* (Huntingdon, Indiana: Our Sunday Visitor, 1975); Tomás Ó Fiaich, *Saint Oliver of Armagh: The Life of St Oliver Plunkett* (Dublin: Veritas, 1981); Frank Donnelly, *Until the Storm Passes: St Oliver Plunkett, the Archbishop of Armagh who Refused to go Away* (2nd edn., Drogheda: St Peter's Church, 2000); Siobhán Kilfeather's 'Oliver Plunkett's Head', *Textual Practice* 16:2 (2002), pp.229–48 provides a thoughtful discussion of the cultural and political history of the head.
26 Curtayne, *The Trial of Oliver Plunkett*, p.198. Curtayne also claims that London Catholics had collected 200 crowns (an enormous sum) for Plunkett's funeral expenses.
27 See Derek Beales, *Prosperity and Plunder: European Catholic Monasteries in the Age of Revolution, 1650–1815* (Cambridge: Cambridge University Press, 2003).

28 Donnelly, *Until the Storm Passes*, p.22.
29 Ibid., p.15. The 'greenness' of the woman emphasizes the contrast between the uncorrupted body of the Archbishop and the decay of a more recently interred corpse. It is likely that even shortly after his death the possibility of Plunkett's future canonization was considered. The care taken in the preservation and disposition of his relics suggests something similar.
30 Seventeenth-century embalming procedures are described in P. Guibert, *The Charitable Physitian with the Charitable Apothecary* (London, 1639) and A. Read, *Chirugarum Comes; or the Whole Practice of Chirugery* (London, 1696).
31 These movements of body parts are described by the Downside scribe (Ethelbert Horne) and are considered in Moran, *Memoir of Oliver Plunket*, pp.430–51.
32 Moran, *Memoir of Oliver Plunket*, pp.446–7.
33 Donnelly, *Until the Storm Passes*, p.17.
34 Moran, *Memoir of Oliver Plunket*, pp.443–5.
35 Kilfeather, 'Oliver Plunkett's Head', p.233.
36 See Tiffany Jenkins, *Contesting Human Remains in Museum Collections: The Crisis of Cultural Authority* (London: Routledge, 2010) for a recent overview.
37 Micheál Ó Siochrú, *God's Executioner: Oliver Cromwell and the Conquest of Ireland* (London: Faber and Faber, 2008), p.84.
38 For a review of Cromwell's historiography, see Gaunt, *Oliver Cromwell*.
39 See, for example, some of the comments that appear after the online version of Dominic Sandbrook's appraisal of Cromwell's historiographical legacy in 'The man who wouldn't be king' in *New Statesman* [Online], 29 December 2010. Available from: www.newstatesman.com/society/2010/12/cromwell-god-essay-history [accessed 1 November 2012].
40 Kilfeather, 'Oliver Plunkett's Head', p.243.
41 Curtayne, *The Trial of Oliver Plunkett*, p.235.
42 Donnelly, *Until the Storm Passes*, pp.4–5.
43 This point is made most eloquently in Kilfeather, 'Oliver Plunkett's Head', p.244.
44 Robert B. Partridge, *'O Horrable Murder!': Trial, Execution and Burial of King Charles I* (London: Rubicon Press, 1998), pp.127–35.
45 Kilfeather, 'Oliver Plunkett's Head', p.234.
46 Cited in Curtayne, *The Trial of Oliver Plunkett*, pp.196–7.
47 Laura Knoppers, *Constructing Cromwell: Ceremony, Portrait and Print, 1645–1661* (Cambridge: Cambridge University Press, 2000), p.173.
48 Roots, 'Cromwell's Head', pp.27–30.
49 McMahon records in *Jus Primatiale*, section 22, pages 8–9, that the head and members of Oliver Plunkett were '*integra et incorrupta*' with a fragrant scent. This fragrance was still evident to McMahon in September 1893 when he described the condition of the head.
50 Curtayne, *The Trial of Oliver Plunkett*, p.236.
51 See, for example, E. Sidney Hartland, 'The Cult of Executed Criminals at Palermo', *Folklore*, 21:2 (1910), pp.168–79.

4

THE LAST GASP: DEATH AND THE FAMILY IN EARLY MODERN LONDON

VANESSA HARDING

D eath constituted one of the greatest of the many challenges faced by early modern urban societies. With the normal death rate some three to four times higher than at present, and periodic epidemics that raised it still further, the community of early modern London was confronted by the problem of how to survive the practical and psychic impact of enormously high mortality; how to dispose safely of thousands of bodies a year; and how to preserve social bonds and social harmony when death was constantly undermining relations and cutting short continuities. The struggle to resolve these issues was in some ways constructive, helping to constitute social relations within the city and within its communities. Dealing with the dead required local authorities, individuals, and wider but more marginal social groups to interact, and engaged them in a process that had to include negotiation, accommodation, and acknowledgement of a range of divergent interests. In the case of burial, the success of local leaders in balancing respect for traditions and sensibilities against practical considerations of space and hygiene, and in accommodating demands for privileged treatment without alienating the unprivileged, was crucial to the wellbeing of the local community.[1]

Responding to death took up a good deal of the citizens' spiritual and economic resources, and played a fundamental part in shaping their sense of themselves as a moral community. Death impinged on the everyday life of inhabitants, visibly and audibly, in terms of the spaces they could use and how they could use them. For a number of individuals, the death of others was necessary to their economic survival: as one London minister commented in 1638, à propos of his income from burial services, 'I may say, if people do not die, I cannot live.'[2] Searchers of the dead, gravediggers, sextons, clerks, clergy and lawyers all derived much of their income from death and dying. Funerals provided a substantial source of business for heralds, drapers, coffin-makers and, eventually, undertakers. The poor were supported by funeral doles and post-mortem distributions, and by employment in funeral ceremonies, while funeral feasts contributed to the network of sociable and charitable occasions that helped to sustain social relations.[3]

This essay engages with the central element in all of this, which is dying. Dealing with the dead in the early modern city was, among other things, about civic space and social order; dying brought together a small group in a smaller space, and foregrounded the dynamic of family and household. Death shaped the family in demographic terms, altered its size, composition, options, and prospect of survival. In addition, it shaped the family emotionally and psychologically as individuals were lost and roles and relationships changed. Dying assumed a large place in the life experience of early modern families and the majority of deaths were domestic.

There is, or was, a real tension between the idealized death, prescribed in the literature of the *ars moriendi* or held up as an example by sermonizing divines, and the majority of deaths, which took varied forms and were often somewhat disorderly. The idealized death was one in which the dying individual displayed fortitude, resignation, charity, religious awareness, sometimes to a heroic degree; in character, it was timely and orderly.[4] In reality, some achieved at least a respectable death, supported by family, friends, neighbours, medical attendants, or pastors. The disorderly death was recognized by moralists as the alternative from which they wished their audience to preserve themselves, and sometimes narrated as a warning. Many adults died accidentally, unprepared, away from home, or as vagrants or lodgers in a strange city; some died in hospitals, prisons or asylums. In addition, not all those who died in their own beds were necessarily spiritually or practically prepared for the event, or able to participate fully in the exchanges expected of them. If we want to understand the experience of dying and people's perceptions of death in early modern London, we need to take account of all of these deaths.

There are several ways to approach the subject of dying in early modern London. In this essay, I will begin by establishing, as far as possible, an overview of who died, at what age, and of what illness. I will then examine the evidence for spiritual preparation and psychological preparedness, for which will-making is a major guide; and finally, I will seek to piece together fragments – from wills and testamentary cases, and from personal writings – that tell us more about the circumstances of a particular death and contribute to more general conclusions.

The life histories of three individuals offer useful insights into death and dying in early modern London. Nehemiah Wallington (1598–1658), a Londoner born, a citizen and craftsman and a devout Puritan, wrote extensively about his spiritual and practical journey through life, and his world has been recreated in a masterly study by Paul Seaver; more recently, a selection of his writings have been edited and published by David Booy.[5] Richard Smyth (c.1590–1675) was born in Berkshire but migrated to London, trained as a lawyer, and held office in the Poultry Compter, one of the City's minor judicial institutions; he is best known now as a book-collector.[6] Samuel Pepys (1633–1703) is the most famous of the three and probably the seventeenth-century Londoner best known to present-day audiences. He held a government post in the Navy Office and lived in the city for much of his life, for which his personal diary for the 1660s, kept in cipher, is an extraordinarily full and candid record.[7] Each of these men experienced the deaths of many others, known and unknown to them, over the course of their long lives in London, and all survived at least one plague epidemic. Wallington thought and wrote a great deal about death, in the abstract as well as in relation to his own person; Smyth made a collection of expositions on the subject of baptism of the dead, and kept a remarkable record of the deaths of nearly 2,000 family members, friends and acquaintances, sometimes giving the cause or other details.[8] Pepys recorded in his diary his reactions to the deaths of others and his fears – usually quickly forgotten – for himself.[9] Since they were literate men of the broad middling class, these three do not fully represent the attitudes of the diverse and cosmopolitan London population – and the absence of a female perspective is important – but their responses to the phenomenon of death in the metropolis are instructive. Frequent contact with death and the dying was a shared urban experience, and all three display an interest in circumstantial detail fostered by the wide dissemination of information in the urban milieu.

How Death Was Encountered: Who Died, When And Why?

Early modern London experienced very high mortality. Over the sixteenth and seventeenth centuries, the city's population grew from around 50,000 to over 500,000, largely through migration from England and beyond. As a city of incomers it was particularly susceptible to epidemic disease, but even in ordinary years, mortality rates in the city were significantly higher than in rural areas, and probably averaged some 33 per thousand per annum.[10] Perhaps a million and a half people died in London between the early sixteenth and the late seventeenth centuries. The annual death toll was at least

4–5,000 a year in the late sixteenth century, reaching nearly 20,000 deaths a year in the 1670s. London probably lost between 10 and 20 per cent of its population in each of the five major plagues of the period; in 1665 alone, some 70,000 individuals fell victim.[11] Most of those who died were not what contemporaries – let alone what we – would call old. The largest contributor to this 'urban penalty' was very high infant and child mortality. Overall, however, London had a youthful population with large numbers in the 15–25 age group, the result of its migration pattern; inevitably, young migrants made up a significant number of the dead.

Some parish registers record the age at death, and these have been used in several studies. The caveat that there were significant local variations in the living population, and therefore the dead, must be borne in mind; the accuracy of age reporting has also been queried. The records also tend to cover relatively short intervals, up to a couple of decades, rather than extending consistently across the whole period. For the populous and rapidly growing suburban St Botolph Aldgate, the age at death is given for 98 per cent of the total buried from 1583 to 1599. Nearly half of all deaths (46 per cent) occurred below the age of ten. Eight per cent of deaths were of teenagers, 9 per cent of people in their twenties, 10 per cent in their thirties, 7 per cent in their forties, 6 per cent in their fifties, 6 per cent in their sixties, and 3 per cent in their seventies. Another 3.6 per cent of the dead were attributed ages from 80 years to over 100.[12] A similar picture emerges from a study of the neighbouring parish of St Botolph Bishopsgate. The age groups were defined differently, but the spread was similar.[13]

Why did people die? For causes of death, we depend largely on the annual Bills of Mortality, with their categories of 'diseases and casualties', not all of which represent real explanations to modern eyes, together with some more anecdotal evidence.[14] As already noted, a significant proportion of those who died were babies and small children. For these, several of the main 'causes' given in the Bills are simply statements of age or development: abortives and stillborn; chrisoms and infants; teeth.[15] The death of an infant often called for no further explanation. Richard Smyth lost two or three of his eight children in infancy or early childhood, and at least six grandchildren. He very rarely attributed a cause of death in the case of a small child, though in one case he noted 'convulsion fits'; interestingly, we also encounter 'fitts' and 'convoltion' in Nehemiah Wallington's account of his children's illnesses and deaths.[16] 'Convulsions' is the other major 'cause' applied predominantly to infants in the annual Bills of Mortality, accounting for 4.6 per cent of all deaths.[17]

Adults faced premature death in several guises.[18] Adult deaths fall into four main categories: accidental and very sudden deaths; gastric and intestinal complaints; infectious disease, including plague; and longer-term chronic illness including consumption and respiratory diseases.

Accidental and sudden death played a large part in the providential world-view of men like Wallington, and a smaller but still significant part in that of Smyth. Wallington looked for meaning in sudden deaths, and had a tendency to record the striking and especially the judgmental, but the more impassive Smyth also noted several alarming and fatal accidents: a man and his whole family were burned in bed; a woman was killed by a chimney falling on her; a young man was killed falling from a horse; an old man died after being hit on the head with a pot or jug at a local coffee-house.[19] Perhaps more worrying for the individual – who might feel that accidents would never happen to him – was the number of those who died unexpectedly but of natural causes. Richard Smyth noted that John de Gret, brewer in Red Cross Street, died suddenly in his bed at night in 1653, 'having been at church that day'; the baker Mr French in Moor Lane died about midnight in 1670, 'being well the day before'; Dr Robert Britten, Minister of Ludgate and Deptford, a good scholar and preacher, 'died ... at Deptford within two hours after he fell ill' on 16 February 1672.[20]

These deaths were remarkable because they were fairly rare: only a very small proportion of adults and adolescents, just over 3 per cent of the total, died suddenly and unexpectedly. A much larger number died from identifiable illness or complaint. Epidemic infections such as ague, fever, and smallpox, together with internal and gastric disorders, for instance colic or surfeit, caused just over 42 per cent of adult deaths.[21] Such afflictions could have killed quickly, leaving the individual little time to contemplate, or to prepare spiritually for, his or her own death.[22] But more would have had some days at least to prepare, and time to make a will if they had not already done so.

Deaths from more long-term causes made up about half the adult total – plague years excepted. Consumption may have been increased by the urban environment, and, along with other respiratory afflictions, was a major killer, but dropsy, gout, palsy, 'long sick', and similar chronic complaints also featured prominently in the Bills. Their impact varied according to age group. Where cause of and age at death can be correlated, the overall picture appears to be, perhaps not surprisingly, that the deaths of older people were more likely to be due to a long-term disease or complaint, such as consumption or dropsy, while those of younger adults were more often ascribed to an unpredictable and perhaps rapidly fatal complaint such as ague.[23] This might suggest –

especially since 'aged' was listed as a cause of death in the Bills of Mortality – that older people would have given more thought to death and to preparation for it, and that they were more likely either to have made, or to be ready to make a will; sudden or incapacitating illness may have prevented many of the younger dying from doing so.

Spiritual Preparation and Psychological Preparedness

A second way of thinking about the practice of dying and the circumstances of decease is by considering how well Londoners were prepared for death.

Prescriptions for Death

In their internal spiritual lives, citizens were constantly exhorted to remember death, and to consider the afterlife. Preaching and sermons contributed to this, but so too did the flourishing genre of advice literature in the form of versions of *ars moriendi*, the medieval book of the craft of dying, which was updated for a Protestant audience.[24] The late medieval genre of *ars moriendi* was widespread and popular, as is evidenced by the survival of some 200 Latin manuscripts from across Europe and at least fifteen English vernacular manuscripts. William Caxton (1415/24–*c*.1492) printed two related texts, as did Wynkyn de Worde (d. 1534/5). Protestant *ars moriendi* texts appear from the 1530s under various titles. Thomas Becon's *The sick man's salve*, which was written in the later 1540s, first appeared in print in 1561, and went through twenty-nine editions between *c*.1560 and 1632. Similar works, though none so popular, included William Perkins' *A salve for a sick man*, first published in 1595, and Jeremy Taylor's *The rule and exercises of Holy Dying*, first published in 1651. Use or even ownership of *ars moriendi* texts is hard to prove; few books are identified in wills, and Danae Tankard found none of this genre, but *The sick man's salve* was a small (if thick) book, intended for close reading, rather than for retention as a trophy or for presentation.[25] Some authors give a clue as to their expected readership: Samuel Ward, a preacher of Ipswich, published *The life of faith in death, exemplified in the liuing speeches of dying Christians* in London in 1622 (itself heavily plagiarized from Foxe), dedicating it to his mother and commending its contents 'chiefly ... to old sick persons, such especially, as die of lingring diseases, affoording them leisure to peruse such themes'.[26]

However, as Danae Tankard found, the gap between the deathbed envisaged in *The sick man's salve*, for example, and those depicted in contemporary accounts, was quite wide.[27] In practice, as we have seen, by no means all deaths took place under such favourable circumstances.

Nevertheless the literature of prescription offered a set of customs for model circumstances; perhaps these could not always be observed, but they helped both to establish norms and expectations and to shape practice more widely.

The Evidence of Will-Making

Christians were warned that death could occur at any moment, and some of them appear to have taken this to heart, as least as far as worldly arrangements went. Making a will was encouraged by the church as a form of spiritual exercise in itself, especially when distributions and bequests were seen as making a material contribution to the individual's chances of salvation. It was also an exercise undertaken by serious Protestants, for both spiritual and worldly reasons.

Sometimes will-making is portrayed in binary terms as a choice between precautionary or prudential will-making, when death was not imminent, and last-minute or even deathbed testimony. In fact, there seem to be at least three scenarios for will-making, though they are not always distinguishable in the surviving evidence. Apart from those who died intestate, there were those who made their first and only will on their sickbed or deathbed, either with time to sign and formalize a written will, or simply by a declaration before witnesses; those who made a will well in advance of death, but never revised or updated it, perhaps because sudden death overtook them; and those who made a will some time in advance, but revoked or replaced it shortly before dying. These distinctions are important when considering preparedness for death, and also the business of the deathbed. A man who had not hitherto made a will was likely to come under pressure to do so; while a man who had made one some time before might be prompted or encouraged to make a new one to reflect changed circumstances.

Prudential wills often include an explicit statement of motivation. Deryk Leke, about to travel overseas, made his will in 1536, 'seing that the liffe of man is shorte and the deathe sure and the howre of deathe unsure'.[28] Sir Thomas Gresham prefaced his will of 1575 with the words 'calling to minde howe certeynne it is that all mankinde shall leue and departe oughte of this transsitorye lieffe and how vncerteyne the tyme and mannor thereof is', before making the arrangements for his endowment of Gresham College.[29] In both cases, though, they failed to revise or update their wills. Deryk Leke returned from his trip abroad and lived for another ten years; Gresham lived for four years after making his will, but died quite suddenly in 1579, having spent the afternoon at the Royal Exchange.[30] Isaac Kendal, a young stationer to whose deathbed we will return later, made his will in his early twenties, 'being of good whole and perfect health and memory', with no reason to expect death any time soon (though it is possible he was moved to make a will by a falling-out with his family).[31] Among older men, Sir Stephen Soame was 'in perfect health' when he made his will; Robert Toft was 'well in body'; Sir Thomas Bennet was 'in good health of body'.[32]

Prudential will-making could have spiritual as well as secular motives. Alderman Richard Pyott made his will in September 1619 when he was 'weak in body' so that he should not be troubled at a later time when he ought to forget the world and concentrate on his salvation.[33] Nehemiah Wallington, as we shall see, made a spiritual exercise of will-making. John de Gret or Great, brewer, whose sudden death in 1653 was noted by Richard Smyth, made his will some three years before, 'in health of body', and in the language of redemption.[34] There is some evidence for an increase in 'prudential' will-making in the later seventeenth century, but it is difficult to attribute this to an increased fear of death, or to a greater responsiveness to the church's teachings on spiritual preparation: most wills are increasingly secular in preoccupation. It could also be that making a will in advance in fact allowed the individual to relax and to contemplate his or her own death. Richard Smyth made his will in 1670, five years before his death, when he was already 75 years old; as a man with legal training he was probably sensitive to the importance of settling his worldly affairs. He makes no reference to fear of death, and indeed seems confidently to have hoped to enjoy 'eternal happiness'.[35]

Nehemiah Wallington shows to a remarkable degree the intense preoccupation with sin, death and salvation that a serious religious upbringing could instil. Despite being strongly drawn towards suicide more than once, he did not believe himself ready to die; once he wrote '... I am sometimes afraid of sudden death, not only because things are out of order, but [because] I would not die in the act of sin nor in discontented condition'.[36] One of his notebooks contains many pages of meditations and reflections on the subject of death, supported with numerous quotations from Scripture. He believed we ought to remember death, and prepare for it, but he was aware that individuals often forgot to do so because remembering death is uncomfortable. In an attempt to counter this tendency, he suggested many comforts against the fear of death, principally that it translates us to a better state, and we are assured of life; whatever we think we may lose by it, we will in fact gain. A man with a clear conscience need not greatly fear death.[37] Despite this, he was for a long time not confident of his own salvation. Once he dreamed he was dead, and facing judgment; still not knowing if he would be saved or damned, he longed for a further chance to live well on earth.[38] Only late in life did he achieve a reassuring sense of certainty. He drafted a will in his notebook, when he was only 34, long before his own death at age 60, but clearly as part of a review of his life and of life itself.[39] It is not clear whether he drew up a legal will at the same time and we do not have his last will.

In Samuel Pepys we have a more secular approach to will-making and the settlement of affairs. Even as a young man he had made a will, which he subsequently amended in June 1664 following his brother Tom's death.[40] His response to the deaths and dangers around him during the plague of 1665 is interesting. He noted 'great fears of the sickness here in the city' at the end of April, but for many weeks he continued his normal life. Even when the disease invaded his neighbourhood, after raging elsewhere in the metropolis for some weeks, he only conceded that 'I beg[a]n to think of setting things in order', and it took him another two weeks to sort out his papers and make a new will. Once he had done so, it gave him considerable relief: 'so that I shall be in much better state of soul, I hope, if it should please the Lord to call me away this sickly time'.[41] He survived the plague, however, and lived for many years more; this will, like that which preceded it, must have been superseded. Pepys made his last will in August 1701, when he was aged 68 and in poor health, and he radically revised it by means of two long codicils on 12 and 13 May 1703, not long before his death on 26 May 1703.[42]

Despite his dilatoriness in 1665, Pepys was clearly a prudential will-maker, updating or rewriting his will to accord with changing circumstances. The evidence is less clear-cut in most other cases, but when the phrase 'I revoke all earlier wills' is used in sixteenth and seventeenth-century wills, it is reasonable to assume that an earlier will had been made, whether formally or informally. When Thomas Typlady wrote in 1540 that 'I utterly revoke and renounce all former legacies and bequests by me heretofore given to any person or persons ... and this to stand and be my very true will and last testament and none other', he presumably meant just that.[43] Others seem to have a specific document – 'my will in the keeping of so-and-so' – in mind that they wished to revoke. Adding a codicil was another way to update provision without having to make an entirely fresh will.[44]

However, many wills were made when the individual was within days of death, and even when there is no explicit reference to its imminence, they must have been shaped by that knowledge. Some of these wills contained phrases about the certainty of death but the uncertainty of the hour of its coming. More mentioned sickness as a reason for making their wills ('beynge seyke in my body', 'by the vesytation off my Lord God syckely and weke off my body', 'beyng syckly, fearing dethe', 'by age wearyed and weakned in bodey ... knowing the frayltie of this liefe').[45] Lord Mayor Sir Cuthbert Buckle made his will on 28 June 1594, 'being diseased in body'; he died on 1 or 2 July. The will is long and elaborate, naming 46 individuals to whom mourning was to be given; it seems likely that he had already drafted a will, but that planning his own exequies was part of his preparation for imminent death.[46]

Deathbeds and Dying

Deathbed wills lead us into and contribute to the third section of this essay, which will engage with when and how death occurred, and in whose presence.

Urban Characteristics

Were there any features unique to or characteristic of urban deathbeds, aside from the greater prevalence of epidemic disease and infant mortality? Apart from accidents and very sudden deaths, most deaths took place in a domestic setting. Early modern London was rather poorly provided with hospital beds, certainly compared with Paris, where nearly a quarter of all deaths took place in hospitals – the Hotel Dieu, particularly. London was also slow to establish pesthouses for plague victims.[47] There were a number of almshouses, where inmates commonly lived until death, but these reproduced, to some extent, the domestic environment, and drew on the same resources for care and attention as ordinary households.

The most significant feature of early modern London was the fragmented and diverse character of the household group. Although we do not have censal-quality records of family and household composition before the late seventeenth century, the evidence available indicates that households usually consisted of small conjugal family groups augmented by servants, apprentices, and lodgers or subsidiary family groups. Single adults, young and old, and single-parent family groups, were quite common. Poorer households might have fewer peripheral members, but wealthier ones could be complex and extensive. Migratory patterns meant that networks of kin in the immediate neighbourhood were often lacking, though many Londoners had relations scattered across the metropolis. Many individuals, therefore, lived with people to whom they were not related by blood. Even though ties of apprenticeship, service and affection might be present, Londoners often depended on non-kin to support and care for them in sickness and, eventually, in death. Particularly important in relation to deathbeds was the role of women as servants or landladies, and as carers, whether paid or voluntary nurse-keepers.

In crowded urban dwellings, a private and peaceful death might have been hard to achieve. While the wealthiest Londoners lived in large houses with numerous rooms for different uses, including well-furnished bedchambers, their servants occupied more makeshift quarters in the same houses, perhaps sharing beds or rooms dedicated to other uses. The middling and poorer sorts had still more cramped accommodation. In the poorest parts of London, whole families, or even unrelated adults, shared a single room, which must have encouraged prompt burial.

If these were not ideal circumstances in which to die, there was no shortage of neighbours to assist, admonish, and afterwards bear witness. Family, friends, and neighbours gathered to visit the dying or attend the deathbed; their presence is attested in witness lists and probate hearings. Knowledge of an imminent death in the immediate community is also important: news spread among neighbours, and the wider community was alerted by the tolling of a bell. The density of mutual knowledge and information in the city meant that citizens heard of many more deaths, through friends or general gossip, than in smaller or more dispersed communities.

There ought at least to have been no delay in obtaining professional attendance, whether of notaries, attorneys, clerks, or clergy in the metropolis. This was obviously important, since, as we have seen, many wills were written on the deathbed; other deathbed wills were made verbally, and subsequently proved with the assistance of those who had been present. The small size of most parishes in London, and the concentrations of clergy, should have meant that no city-dweller dying at home was without the services of a priest. Failure to obtain the sacrament, if desired, was more likely to be attributable to clerical negligence than the distance or difficulty of accessing it. Conscientious ministers took their duty in this respect seriously; Lancelot Andrewes, Vicar of St Giles Cripplegate, published a *Manual of directions for the sick* to help pastors manage their parishioners' journey towards death.[48] Many wills indicate a clerical or clergy presence (not always distinguishable) writing or witnessing the will, though this does not necessarily mean they attended to the point of death.

This is not the place for an extensive exploration of the medical assistance that was available for those who were dying, but Londoners had access, if they could afford it, to an array of professional and irregular medical practitioners, in addition to a plethora of books on self-help and self-medication, and a variety of therapies including patent medicines.[49] The intervention of medical practitioners in fatal illnesses is not well recorded, since our best source for this kind of activity is suits brought by disappointed, but living, clients. In the records of suits in which the patient had died, it is not always clear whether this was in spite or because of the practitioner's intervention, though the latter may quite frequently have been the case, given the violent purges, vomits, and fumigations so often prescribed.[50] Nor were doctors likely to advertise their association with deceased patients, and medical practitioners very rarely appear as witnesses to wills, at least in their professional capacity. But Wallington, a modest turner, consulted doctors over his children's illnesses, when his pregnant wife was seriously ill, and when he himself was sick and expected to die. He also brought in a woman who cured his son by applying plasters, and certainly employed women to look after his sick children.[51] Samuel Pepys' brother Tom was seen by two doctors, whose diagnoses (and, presumably, treatments) differed.[52] Nursing and nurse-keeping were widespread, if fairly casual, occupations for women; sometimes they were paid by the patient or the patient's family (or indeed out of the estate); sometimes the parish paid one poor woman to nurse other poor people; sometimes they may have acted out of neighbourly kindness.[53] But dying Londoners were probably at least as likely to be nursed by a comparative stranger as by a family member.

Concerns about inheritance dogged deathbeds at many social levels, but perhaps the disposable wealth of some city-dwellers, and their freedom of testamentary disposition, made their deathbeds a more charged and contested scene. A male citizen knew that even if he died intestate his goods would be divided according to the custom of London, that his widow was safe in her occupation of the home, and that the city would step in, if necessary, to safeguard his children's inheritance by appointing reliable guardians. If he wished to exercise any control, for example, by favouring some children over others, or by leaving legacies outside the conjugal family, he needed to say so; and of course many London testators were not citizens. Many early modern Londoners held a large proportion of their wealth in chattels and movables, and often in cash or bonds; wills suggest an attachment to clothing, jewellery, plate and household goods, which made disposing of them as much an emotional as a financial project. Widows in particular were often very specific about the distribution of such goods, effectively bequeathing the material nucleus of a new household to daughters, grand-daughters, or servants.[54]

Deathbeds

This essay concludes with a brief account of three deaths, each taken from a different kind of source. The evidence is essentially anecdotal, with limitations specific to each source, but they underline the importance of deathbed attendance and the largely secular nature of the concerns arising there.

The first source is the simplest: the narrative of verbal testimony that could stand for a written will. Such wills, sometimes known as nuncupative wills, comprised as much as 5 per cent of wills in the church courts, but no statistical survey has yet been undertaken. The value of these probate records is in the context they offer. Usually they are the only record we have, though in some cases the will can be linked to a burial record that may give further detail.

On the day before her death, 11 April 1593, Rian Freman, widow, of the parish of St Botolph Bishopsgate:

> being very sick in body and mistrusting that she should long live in this world, [but] being in perfect mind and memory lying on her death bed on the day last before her death ... uttered these words or like in effect with intent to make her last will and testament as follows, viz., my will and mind is that William Allot of this parish shall have all my goods and my child to bring up with the same goods, and I will my body shall be coffined and buried in the New Church Yard.

At least three individuals were present and heard these words; Thomas Jackson, Michael Pye, and Magdalen Jenkinson. Their relationship to Freman is not given, but all were of modest status: when they testified before the probate court on 12 April, Michael Pye could only write his initials, and Thomas Jackson made a mark. Magdalen Jenkinson, who was not asked to sign, could have been a neighbour or perhaps a nurse. It may be that Freman's failure to name an executor, thereby potentially undermining the legal status of this testament, is bound up with the humble rank of those present. In any event, the court sensibly granted administration to William Allott, the legatee and guardian of Freman's child.[55]

The role of neighbours as witnesses is emphasized in probate litigation, the second source for deathbed scenes. Litigation usually occurred when a will was contested, and in order to test its validity – the testator's competence and freedom of action being key points – the circumstances in which it was made are recounted by a series of witnesses under interrogation. Compared with nuncupative wills, these cases are often rich in detail, even though they do not necessarily record either the nature of the challenge or all the questions asked.[56]

In this particular case, the will had been made well in advance. The dispute seems to have arisen because the testator left almost everything to his master and employer, and not to his brother and sister, who presumably brought the case; but in the process we get a clear picture of his deathbed.[57] Isaac Kendall was a young man recently out of his apprenticeship, probably therefore in his mid-20s, living with and working for Cornelius Nealman, a stationer, when he fell sick in early 1585. He had made his will a year earlier, using a London scrivener, who was among those called to testify. We do not hear the nature of his last illness, though it is clear that it was not plague nor one that caused him to be shunned, but that it was understood or expected to prove fatal. He lay in an upper chamber in his master's house for several days before he died, and for at least some of the time he was fully *compos mentis*. He was attended by two older women – Mrs Thomson and Goodwife Arret – who were neighbours. Both implied that they undertook nurse-keeping out of neighbourliness; Goodwife Arret said she made her living from lace-making. Kendall was visited three days before his death by the parish priest, who said prayers with him and checked whether he had made a will, but he seems to have taken no further interest. On the afternoon of Monday 11 March, the day he died, he was visited by his sister and a female friend of hers, who tried to get him to change his will, a ploy he rejected vigorously. When he was told 'it is your sister Mary is come to see how you do and to know how you will bestow your goods', Isaac replied 'Why my sister came not for me for she is richer than I, and past my calling and my will is made already and I make none other' and turned his face from them. Later it appears that his brother also came for the same purpose and met with the same response.

That evening, the Nealmans and a couple of neighbours who had dropped in, hearing of Kendall's illness, were sitting by the fire downstairs after supper; one or more children were also present. Four witnesses testified to the following scene. Kendall sent down to the Nealmans by the woman who was sitting with him, asking them to go up to see him. They did, together with the neighbours, and Mrs Nealman urged Kendall to make a new will, if he wished, or to see his brother. But he refused, saying 'No, No, … for then there will be a Willing and a Willing and I will make no other will than I have done already for I give all to you and my master whom I have made executor'. He was then, one witness testified, 'in better memory and remembrance … than at any time in three days before'. Soon after, however, he apparently asked for the bell to be tolled for him. He died about two or three hours later; the neighbours heard of his death the next day.

Probate litigation often gives details of the scene, but for emotional interactions and interior feelings we are dependent on the third source – personal writings and diaries. Nehemiah Wallington's self-castigation for the excessive grief he experienced on the death of his children, and his failure to pray on the occasion of his sister-in-law's death is a good example,[58] but probably the fullest and most emotionally candid account of a death is that of Tom Pepys by his brother Samuel.[59] Tom was evidently a dissolute and improvident young man, a disappointment to his upwardly mobile older brother, who in 1664 was rising in the Navy Office. Samuel lived in Mark Lane near the Tower of London; Tom was a tailor, like their father, and lived in lodgings in St Bride's parish.

Samuel heard on 8 March 1664 that Tom, then aged about 30, was very ill, apparently of consumption, and went to see him. At first the situation did not seem too serious but five days later Samuel was informed that Tom was so ill it was thought he would not live, and alerted to the alarming rumour that Tom was suffering from the pox. Tom recognized Samuel when the latter visited a second time, but talked idly, 'and his face like a dying man'. A neighbour and family friend had arranged a nurse to be in attendance, as Tom had no wife, though he had an efficient and trustworthy maidservant. The next day, 14 March, Samuel visited Tom again, but found him delirious, and Samuel's anxieties about the shameful nature of Tom's illness were compounded by fears that his affairs were in a very poor state, and that he was possibly seriously in debt. He visited again, later the same day, and found him the same or worse. The next day, they heard he was somewhat better and that rumours of his having the pox were probably false, which relieved Samuel considerably; but his visit that night proved to be his last. Samuel attempted to bring his brother to face his condition but without great success: Tom seemed indifferent whether he would go 'the bad way' or 'the other way'. Even though death was clearly imminent, Samuel 'had no mind to see him die', and left the house; when he came back a quarter of an hour later, 'my brother was dead … lying with his chops fallen, a most sad sight'. As with Isaac Kendall, it was a hired nurse who sat with the patient as he died and closed his eyes, and reported the death to the family. Others involved and present at some point over the seven or eight days Tom was dying included the maid, two neighbours (Mrs Holden and Mrs Croxton), Tom's medical doctor (Dr Powell), another practitioner (Dr Wiverley, who declared him free of pox), two cousins (Mrs Turner and William Joyce), and Samuel's wife. Samuel was also in touch with other relations present in London, including his father and his maternal uncle, who were also therefore kept abreast of the situation.

Conclusion

What these three cases, and others like them, underline is the fairly public business of dying in early modern London, the likely presence of neighbours, and the spread of information about and interest in an imminent death. Information was spread from person to person (the neighbours who visited the Nealmans to ask after Isaac Kendall were the daughter and son-in-law of Mrs Thomson, one of his nurses) but could also be communicated by the passing bell. These cases are also revealing of the urban family and household, and the prominent presence of non-kin even at such critical moments as death. Family were clearly expected to play a part, though in Kendall's case his family of adoption mattered more than his actual siblings. In Pepys' case, though ties of family were acknowledged, Samuel baulked at playing an active role in caring for his brother. They also highlight the importance of women, including nursing attendants, whether professional or voluntary, at the deathbed, a point that others have made and examined in more detail.[60] Although spiritual and medical assistance might be called on as death approached, neither clergy nor doctors were necessarily present at the moment of death, and the conversation and concerns around the dying person were largely secular. No doubt there were ideal and highly morally edifying deaths among the more religious, but it seems likely that these deathbeds, low-key affairs with family and/or neighbours, not untouched by human failings such as greed and self-interest, were more typical of the generality of adult deaths in early modern London.

NOTES

1 The wider context for this paper is explored in Vanessa Harding, *The Dead and the Living in Paris and London, 1500–1670* (Cambridge: Cambridge University Press, 2002). Some points are also covered in eadem, 'Memento Mori: la Peur de l'Agonie, de la Mort et des Morts à Londres au XVIIe Siècle', *Histoire Urbaine*, 2 (Dec. 2000), pp.39–57.
2 T.C. Dale (ed.), *The Inhabitants of London in 1638* [Online] (London: Society of Genealogists, 1931), pp.210–24. Available from: www.british-history.ac.uk/report.aspx?compid=32076 [accessed 20 August 2012].
3 Harding, *The Dead and the Living*, Chapters 7–9.
4 R.A. Houlbrooke, *Death, Religion and the Family in England, 1480–1750* (Oxford: Clarendon Press, 1998), pp.57–80; L.M. Beier, 'The Good Death in 17th-Century England', in R.A. Houlbrooke (ed.), *Death, Ritual and Bereavement* (London: Routledge, 1989), pp.43–61.
5 P.S. Seaver, 'Wallington, Nehemiah (1598–1658)', in *Oxford Dictionary of National Biography* [Online] (Oxford: Oxford University Press, 2004 (hereafter *ODNB*). Available from: www.oxforddnb.com/view/article/28567 [accessed 10 September 2012]; Paul Seaver, *Wallington's World: A Puritan Artisan in Seventeenth-Century London* (London: Methuen, 1985); D. Booy (ed.), *The notebooks of Nehemiah Wallington, 1618–1654: a Selection* (Aldershot: Ashgate, 2007).

6   Vanessa Harding, 'Smyth, Richard (*bap.* 1590, *d.* 1675)' in *ODNB* [Online]. Available from: www.oxforddnb.com/view/article/25887 [accessed 10 September 2012]; Henry Ellis (ed.), *The Obituary of Richard Smyth, Secondary of the Poultry Compter* (London: Camden Society, no. 44, 1849) (hereafter, Smyth, *Obituary*).

7   C.S. Knighton, 'Pepys, Samuel (1633–1703)' in *ODNB* [Online]. Available from: www.oxforddnb.com/view/article/21906 [accessed 10 September 2012]; *The Diary of Samuel Pepys*, R. Latham and W. Matthews (eds) (12 Volumes, London: Bell and Hyman, 1970–83) (hereafter Pepys, *Diary*).

8   Seaver, *Wallington's World*, pp.199–205; LMA, MS CLC/521/MS00204 (formerly Guildhall Library MS 204), pp.357–68; BL, Sloane MS 1457; Smyth, *Obituary*, pp.ix, xx.

9   Pepys, *Diary*, v (1664), pp.87, 90; vi (1665), pp.93–342; xii (Companion), pp.350–4.

10 For London population figures and mortality rates, see Vanessa Harding, 'The Population of Early Modern London: A Review of the Published Evidence', *London Journal*, 15 (1990), pp.111–28.

11 Harding, *The Dead and the Living*, pp.14–26.

12 T.R. Forbes, *Chronicle from Aldgate: Life and Death in Shakespeare's London* (New Haven: Yale University Press, 1971), p.74.

13 T.H. and M.F. Hollingsworth, 'Plague Mortality Rates by Age and Sex in the Parish of St Botolph's Without Bishopsgate, London, 1603', *Population Studies*, 25 (1971), pp.131–46.

14 John Graunt, *Natural and political observations, mentioned in a following index, and made upon the bills of mortality ... with reference to the government, religion, trade, growth, ayr, diseases, and the several changes of the said city* [Online] (London, 1662). Available from: http://gateway.proquest.com/openurl?ctx_ver=Z39.88-2003&res_id=xri:eebo&rft_id=xri:eebo:citation:11824835 [accessed 10 September 2012]. See also Forbes, *Chronicle from Aldgate*, pp.100–02.

15 Graunt, *Observations*, pp.14–15.

16 Smyth, *Obituary*, p.30; Booy (ed.), *Notebooks of Nehemiah Wallington*, pp.68–9.

17 Graunt, *Observations*, p.15, and 'Table of Casualties' following p.74.

18 The following discussion is based on an analysis of the data in Graunt, *Observations*, pp.15–18, and 'Table of Casualties' following p.74, excluding plague deaths. See also Forbes, *Chronicle from Aldgate*, pp.86–118.

19 Seaver, *Wallington's World*, pp.54–8; LMA, MS CLC/521/MS00204, pp.512–14; BL, MS Sloane 1457; Smyth, *Obituary*, pp.57, 62, 74, 95; Vanessa Harding, 'Mortality and the Mental Map of London: Richard Smyth's *Obituary*', in Robin Myers and Michael Harris (eds), *Medicine, Mortality and the Book Trade* (Cheam: St Paul's Bibliographies, 1998), pp.49–71.

20 Smyth, *Obituary*, pp.34, 85, 94.

21 Graunt, *Observations*, 'Table of Casualties' following p.74.

22 See, for example, Smyth, *Obituary*, pp.87, 91, 97.

23 Forbes, *Chronicle from Aldgate*, tables 4 and 7, pp.74 and 103.

24 The source for the following discussion is Danae Tankard, 'Attitudes to Death in England, c.1480–1560' (unpublished Ph.D. Thesis, University of London, 2002), pp.23–40. See also Danae Tankard, 'The Reformation of the Deathbed on Mid-Sixteenth-Century England', *Mortality*, 8:3 (2003), pp.251–67.

25 Tankard, 'Attitudes to Death', p.38. The second edition (1561) of *The sick man's salve* is c.14 cm x 9.6 cm and contains 560 pages [Online]. Available from: http://gateway.proquest.com/openurl?ctx_ver=Z39.88-2003&res_id=xri:eebo&rft_id=xri:eebo:citation:99849879 [accessed 10 September 2012].

26 *THE LIFE OF FAITH IN DEATH, exemplified in the liuing speeches of dying Christians. By SAMVEL WARD preacher of Ipswich* [Online] (London, 1622), p.45. Available from: http://gateway.proquest.com/openurl?ctx_ver=Z39.88-2003&res_id=xri:eebo&rft_id=xri:eebo:citation:99846923 [accessed 10 September 2012].

27 Tankard, 'Attitudes to Death', pp.100–69.

28 Ida Darlington (ed.), *London Consistory Court Wills, 1492–1547* (London: London Record Society 3, 1967), no. 242.

29 J.G. Nichols and J. Bruce (eds), *Wills from Doctors' Commons: a Selection from the Wills of Eminent Persons Proved in the Prerogative Court of Canterbury, 1495–1695* (London: Camden Society, 1863), p.80.

30 Darlington (ed.), *Consistory Court wills*, no. 242; G.W.G.L. Gower, *Genealogy of the Family of Gresham* (London, privately printed, 1883), p.80.

31 LMA, DL/C/B/006/MS09272/012B, f. 115.

32 TNA, PROB 11/135, ff. 3, 26v, 36, 44; 11/151, ff. 170v-75.
33 TNA, PROB 1/135, f. 41.
34 TNA, PROB 11/227, f. 379.
35 TNA, PROB 11/347, ff. 289v-91.
36 Seaver, *Wallington's World*, p.56, quoting Folger Shakespeare Library, Washington, MS V.a. 436, pp.312–15.
37 LMA, MS CLC/521/MS00204, pp.352–68
38 Seaver, *Wallington's World*, pp.186, 195.
39 LMA, MS CLC/521/MS00204, pp.505–10; Seaver, *Wallington's World*, pp.195, 204.
40 Pepys, *Diary*, v (1664), p.192.
41 Pepys, *Diary*, vi (1665), pp.171, 173, 178, 187–9, 192, 208, 225.
42 TNA, PROB 1/9; Claire Tomalin, *Samuel Pepys: The Unequalled Self* (London: Penguin Books, 2002), pp.371–7.
43 TNA, PROB 11/28, f. 133.
44 E.g. TNA, PROB 11/ 43, ff. 327v-328; PROB 1/9.
45 Darlington (ed.), *Consistory Court Wills*, nos. 212, 228, 241; LMA, DL/C/B/004/MS09171/018 f. 16v.
46 TNA, PROB 11/84, f. 87v; Bodleian Library, Oxford, MS Ashmole 818, f. 45.
47 Harding, *The Dead and the Living*, pp.113–17; eadem, 'Burial of the Plague Dead in Early Modern London', in J.A.I. Champion (ed.), *Epidemic Disease in London Centre for Metropolitan History*, Working Papers 1 (London: Centre for Metropolitan History, Institute of Historical Research, University of London, 1993), pp.53–64.
48 Lancelot Andrewes, *A manual of directions for the sick with many sweet meditations and devotions of the R[ight] Reverend Father in God, Lancelot Andrews, l[a]te L[ord] Bishop of Winchester, to which are added praiers for the morning, evening, and H. communion. Translated out of a Greeke ms. of his private devotions. By R.D.B.D.* [Online] (London, 1655). Available from: http://gateway.proquest.com/openurl?ctx_ver=Z39.88-2003&res_id=xri: eebo&rft_id=xri:eebo:citation:99896184 [accessed 10 September 2012].
49 See Ian Mortimer, 'The Triumph of the Doctors: Medical Assistance to the Dying, 1570– 1720', *Transactions of the Royal Historical Society*, 6th ser., 15 (2005), pp.97–116.
50 Margaret Pelling and Frances White, Database of Physicians and Irregular Medical Practitioners in London, 1550–1640 [Online]. Available from: http://www.british-history.ac.uk/source.aspx?pubid=107 [accessed 10 September 2012]. For examples from the above cited database of patients dying apparently as a result of medical intervention, see George Butler, Robert Swaine, John Buggs, Leonard Poe, Samuel Lemm, Humfrye Beven, Edward Owen, and others.
51 Booy (ed.), *Notebooks of Nehemiah Wallington*, pp.56, 59–61, 68, 335.
52 Pepys, *Diary*, v (1664), pp.81, 84–6.
53 Peter Earle, 'The Female Labour Market in Early Modern London', *Economic History Review*, 2nd ser., 42 (1989), pp.328–53; Darlington (ed.), *Consistory Court Wills*, nos 37, 118, Appendix 4; Andrew Wear, 'Caring for the Sick Poor in St Bartholomew's Exchange, 1580–1676', in W.F. Bynum and Roy Porter (eds), *Living and Dying in London* (Medical History Supplement, 11) (London: Wellcome Institute, 1991), pp.41–60.
54 For examples, see TNA, PROB 11/42A ff. 264r-v; 11/43 ff. 402 r-v; 11/44 ff. 158v-159v, 201r-203r.
55 LMA, DL/C/B/004/MS09171/018 f. 23v. 'Reanna Freman' was buried on 12 April: A.W.C. Hallen, *The Registers of St Botolph, Bishopsgate, London* (London: privately printed, 1889), p.305. As the surname is quite common in this large parish, it has not been possible to trace her family.
56 For a variety of London testamentary cases see Tankard, 'The Reformation of the Deathbed in Mid-Sixteenth-Century England', pp.251–67.
57 The sources for this section are: LMA, DL/C/B/046/MS09585 (Diocese of London, Deposition Books, Testamentary Causes), ff. 67v-74; DL/C/B/001/MS09168/14 (Act book), f. 85; DL/C/B/006/MS09172/12B (Original wills), f. 115. No burial register, accounts or vestry minutes for the parish, St Mildred Bread Street, survive for this period.
58 Booy (ed.), *Notebooks of Nehemiah Wallington*, pp.59, 61, 64, 68, 309.
59 Pepys, *Diary*, v (1664), pp.79–87.
60 Elizabeth A. Hallam, 'Turning the Hourglass: Gender Relations at the Deathbed in Early Modern Canterbury', *Mortality*, 1:1 (1996), pp.61–82.

5

SUICIDE IN EIGHTEENTH-CENTURY IRELAND

JAMES KELLY

Introduction

S uicide was not perceived to be a serious social problem in Ireland as the seventeenth century drew to a close. Indicatively, officials made no attempt to conceal the fact that individuals took their own lives. Self-inflicted death (by hanging, poisoning and drowning) was afforded a separate category on the summary bill of mortality prepared for Dublin Corporation, but since the four cases included in the bill for the year 1683–4 constituted less than 0.2 per cent of the total number of people that had died in the metropolitan area, and since suicide was statistically eclipsed by fever, which accounted for 26 per cent of fatalities, consumption (nearly 16 per cent), smallpox (7 per cent), and measles (6 per cent), even capital punishment which accounted for ten deaths, the impression sustained was that suicide was not just uncommon, it was alien to Irish society.[1] Certainly, this was the image that opinion formers sought to promote. Explicitly denominated a 'British custom' in an account of the attempts by two old soldiers, 'both English', to kill themselves in Dublin in 1733, the anglophone Irish public was as disposed as its French equivalent to appeal to the stereotype of English people as suicide prone[2] to sustain the illusion that suicide did 'not prevail here', and to affirm the conviction that it was in the public interest that this should continue to be the case.[3]

Stern legal, religious, and social sanctions were, it was widely avowed, required to discourage the practice of self-murder, as suicide was emblematically denominated. As in England, the legal justification for the penalization of suicide derived from the common law. According to the law, as it was distilled and presented to Irish audiences by Edward Bullingbrooke, it was necessary in order to be deemed 'a *felo de se*, or felon of himself' to be 'of sound mind, and of the age of discretion', and to have killed oneself 'voluntarily'.[4] If this was the judgement of a jury 'of twelve men' in a coroner's court, then the 'goods and chattels, real and personal' of the suicide were forfeit, and, based on a handful of identifiable instances from the late sixteenth and early seventeenth centuries, it would appear that this sanction was enforced but that forfeited goods were acquired, not by or on behalf of the Crown, but by family members or local landowners.[5] Significantly, 'lands' owned by a *felo de se* were not subject to forfeiture for the simple reason that 'no man can forfeit his land, without an attainder by course of law'. This was sufficient to ease sensitivities with respect to the retention by families of heritable property, which encouraged juries in England and Scotland in the late seventeenth century to return verdicts of *non compos mentis* rather than *felo de se*, on the grounds that it was 'impossible that a man in his senses should' kill himself because it was 'so contrary to nature, and all sense and reason'.[6] It was also warmly contested.[7] The influential legal writer, William Hawkins (1681/2–1750) observed *à propos* in his popular textbook on English criminal law, first printed in 1716, that if this doctrine was allowed, it could be 'applied in excuse of many other crimes' on the grounds that they too were 'against nature and reason'.[8] Hawkins and, following him, Edward Bullingbrooke echoed the reservations of the great seventeenth-century jurist Sir Matthew Hale (1609–76), who had previously adverted to the dangers inherent in juries returning *non compos* verdicts in cases of 'melancholy or hypochondrical distemper' when he contended that such judgements ought to be restricted to those who were incapacitated by 'such an alienation of mind, as renders a person to be a madman, or frantick, or destitute of the use of reason'.[9]

While Bullingbrooke's necessarily brief commentary suggest that Irish officials shared Hale's and Hawkins' concerns at the preparedness of coroners' juries in the eighteenth century to return verdicts that secured suicides against legal sanction, there is no evidence to suggest that *non compos* verdicts were delivered with any frequency in seventeenth-century Ireland with this intention. Indeed, the slim corpus of recoverable evidence suggests that Irish authorities continued to authorize the seizure of the 'goods and chattels' of those adjudged to have committed suicide, but were disposed to restore such goods to the next of kin in cases of demonstrable poverty or financial distress. This is the import of the decision arrived at in 1682 by Dublin Corporation in one such instance:

That Mary Fromery, the widdow and relict of James Fromery, a *felo de se*, in respect of her great poverty, shall have the goods and chattels of her said deceased husband, now seized by the sheriffs of this cittie, for the use of the cittie, and that the said sheriffs be and are hereby desired to deliver the same into the hands of Alderman Mottley, whoe is to dispose of them to the use of the said Mary and her children, as the lord mayor and sheriffs of the cittie from time to time shall think fitt.[10]

It is not coincidental that the disposition (manifested by this case) not to penalize the families of individuals who took their own lives was in keeping with the comparable pattern, identified by Houston and others, in England and Scotland in the second half of the seventeenth century.[11] Yet, one cannot conclude on this basis that Ireland had also embarked on the transition, identified in several jurisdictions across Europe, from an era of draconian sanctions, such as were commonly introduced during the late Middle Ages, *en route* to the medical model of suicide that achieved ascendancy in the twentieth century.[12] There are a number of reasons. In the first instance, we are insufficiently informed as to how suicides were dealt with in Ireland between the late Middle Ages and the eighteenth century to draw any firm conclusions as to the implications of the manner in which suicides were treated. Second, and perhaps more indicatively, subsequent to the ratification by the Irish parliament in 1666 of the Act of Uniformity, the Church of Ireland adopted the Book of Common Prayer which explicitly ordained that 'the order for the burial of the dead' contained therein was 'not to be used for any that ... have laid violent hands upon themselves'.[13] Thirdly, the public at large was not neutral in its response to suicide. The public countenanced, indeed enforced sanctions (albeit in a minority of cases) through the eighteenth and into the nineteenth century that were palpably more severe than those provided for by the Church of Ireland and the other Christian churches.

Yet in Ireland, as in other jurisdictions, attitudes to self-murder were not unchanging. The pace of change was slow, uneven, and emphatically non-linear, as perceptions ebbed and flowed, mutated, went into eclipse and, on occasion, re-emerged after long absences. Certain trends, redolent of longer-term changes in disposition, attitude, and outlook, can be inferred from the response of the legal system, the sermons of churchmen, the reporting practices of newspapers, and the interventions of the public, but indicative as they may be, they ought not to be pursued at the expense of the challenge of establishing a social profile of those who sought to take their own lives, the means they utilized, and the factors that caused them to take this potentially irrevocable action. This is not easily accomplished. Richard Cobb famously claimed that it was all but impossible to explain what he denominated 'the most private and impenetrable of human acts'.[14] Jack Douglas' contention that Émile Durkheim's seminal effort to construct a sociology of suicide was destined to founder on the rocks of statistical and interpretative imprecision unless pursued on a case-by-case basis, might suggest that it is ill-advised even to try.[15] The challenge presented in the instance of early modern Ireland is compounded by the tantalizing character of the evidential record; there are virtually no court documents, detailed individual testimonies, or official statistics prior to the mid-nineteenth century. As a consequence, the reconstruction of the history of suicide presented here is built upon scattered evidential shards drawn primarily from typically skeletal reports in newspapers, amplified, as circumstances permit, by memoirs and private correspondence. These sources are less than forthcoming when one seeks to divine public attitudes, but religious literature and improving tracts help to fill this void until the emergence, in the second half of the eighteenth century, of the newspaper as a source of opinion as well as of news provides a more useful and usable evidential seam.

The picture these sources permit one to draw is sketchy in many aspects, but it does suggest that the phenomenon of suicide in Ireland during the late seventeenth, eighteenth and early nineteenth centuries cannot be embraced within a single explanatory theory. The most influential such interpretation is the 'secularization' model posited in the 1980s by Michael MacDonald and Terence Murphy; it claimed (based on the English experience) that the early modern period witnessed the eclipse and displacement of a religiously informed attitude that criminalized suicide with a secular view that believed that punishment was inappropriate and that conceived of suicide in essentially medical terms.[16] Critics of this interpretation maintained from the outset that it was overly schematic and did not take contrary or complicating evidence into account; some of this criticism has been robustly refuted, but the number of doubters has grown and the import of their criticism has acquired added authority in the interval.[17] The outcome, paradoxically, is that while it is now acknowledged that there is 'strong evidence for the growth of leniency', which diminished the disposition to penalize those who committed suicide, it is also accepted that the transition was 'more complex', more gradual, and less complete than MacDonald and Murphy perceived, since as well as new attitudes, older views and traditions persisted. In other words, instead of the 'displacement' of an intrinsically religiously informed hostility to suicide with an essentially secular perspective that paved the way for the adoption of a medical understanding, Europe embraced 'hybridization', where different viewpoints – some inherited, some adopted, some religious, some secular, some traditional, some modern – combined to determine public attitude.[18] The concept of 'hybridization' was coined by Susan Morrissey in her study of attitudes in nineteenth-century Russia to the *opoitsa* (the person who died from drink), but it has broader applicability, because it encompasses the complex reality of the situation in many contexts, seventeenth and eighteenth-century Ireland included.[19] Moreover, its articulation is in keeping with the greater receptivity to the multi-factorial explanation of suicide favoured today, to the recognition that the much-criticized sociological approach of Durkheim is still useful, and the acknowledgement that the medical model also does not provide a complete explanation. Guided by these insights and perceptions, and by a sample of cases that supports a multi-factorial explanation, this essay seeks in the first instance to delineate the main features of suicide as it was practiced in eighteenth-century Ireland; secondly, to outline the evolving nature of the public response; and, finally, to locate the phenomenon historically in its Irish and broader temporal, cultural and geographical context.

Profiling Suicide in Eighteenth-Century Ireland

The history of suicide in eighteenth-century Ireland is necessarily bound up with the history of the press, since the emergence of the newspaper as a conduit of domestic news was crucial over time to the normalization of self-murder in the public realm. This did not on its own prompt the adoption of a viewpoint that favoured understanding rather than condemnation, but it did favour an alternative perspective, which was less disposed to conclude that suicide was inspired by the Devil and to perceive it as a conscious affront to God.[20] The 1720s was an important moment in this respect, for though earlier examples have been identified, it was only then, as part of a paradigm shift in the public's consumption of news, goods and information, that the Irish press commenced carrying reports of self-inflicted death in numbers sufficient to permit an analysis of the practice.[21] Initially, and in contrast to the situation in Scotland where suicide among the social elite was largely kept out of the newspapers,[22] a substantial proportion of the cases brought into the public sphere were of individuals who had achieved notoriety or were socially well connected; thus Cavan Toole, who poisoned himself in Newgate Jail in the summer of 1712, did so while awaiting a date with the gallows for murder, while the son of Alderman Godly, who killed himself following his incarceration for debt, did likewise six years later.[23] Examples of 'gentlewomen', 'young gentlemen', 'eminent farmers', army officers and the 'sons' of good families who had taken their own life continued to attract disproportionate attention during the 1720s and 1730s.[24] The most celebrated was Ensign William Dixey, the son of Alderman Dixey of Drogheda, on Oxmantown Green on Christmas Day 1732. Dixey was discovered with his throat cut and a bullet in his temple, which caused some to conjecture that he had been murdered, but as it became clear that he had taken his own life, the level of public curiosity was such that, in addition to extensive reportage in the press, an enterprising printer produced a broadside account for those eager for more detail.[25]

As the coverage accorded the demise of William Dixey illustrates, and the expanding number of actual and attempted instances of self-murder reported in the press in the mid-eighteenth century suggest (see Table 5.1; Fig. 5.1), suicide was of compelling interest to the newspaper-reading public. On the reasonable assumption the news-paper proprietors knew their readership, it may be significant that a majority of the reports of suicide and attempted suicide published at this time were non-judgemental of the persons concerned since the legal and religious authorities continued to penalize suicides and their next of kin. Dublin Corporation, for example, resolved in January 1737 that the widow of a man guilty of 'self murder' could not receive an annuity even where a 'subscription' was made.[26] The main Christian churches were equally unaccommodating of the tendency, already well-established in England but not visible in Ireland before the late 1730s,[27] of coroners' juries returning *non compos mentis* verdicts in such cases. In keeping with the comprehensive statement constructed by Jeremy Taylor (1613–67), Bishop of Down, in his sprawling *Ductor Dubitantium* (1660), religious commentators condemned suicide as (in Taylor's words) an act of 'rebellion against God, and a violation of the proprieties and peculiar rights of God, who only hath power over our lives'.[28] It was, as John Sym (1581–1637), the author of the first book in English on suicide, makes clear, an 'evil', and references to suicide continued during the seventeenth century to denominate it 'barbarous' and 'inhuman', and to conclude that those who did so succumbed to 'the temptation of the Devil'.[29] The fact that it was also 'against the law and the very prime inclination of nature' – 'unnatural' – stiffened

Year	Male	Female	Total
1712-20	3	1	4
1721-30	14	3	17
1731-40	39	32	71
1741-50	25	15	40
1751-60	53	60	113
1761-70	44	29	73
1771-80	65	34	99
1781-90	66	73	139
1791-1800	43	29	72
1801-10	20	7	27
1811-20	19	1	20
Total	391	284	675

Table 5.1 Suicide: number and gender of sample, 1712–1820

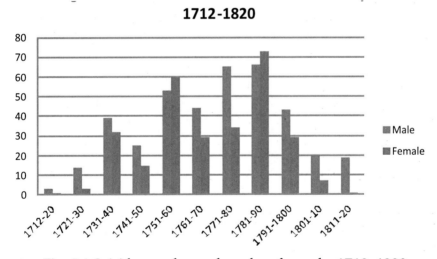

Fig. 5.1 Suicide: number and gender of sample, 1712–1820

opposition further. As a result, by the 1720s, when it was clear that 'the charity of modern juries', in 'attributing to temporary insanity what might often be more correctly traced to mortified pride and disappointed ambition', enabled offenders to escape unpunished, religious commentators unreservedly affirmed the traditional basis of their opposition. Isaac Watts (1674–1748), the prolific independent minister, who published a lengthy tract on the subject in 1726, acknowledged that there were many reasons why people chose to 'destroy themselves'. He identified 'the sceptical humour and growing atheism of the age', the growing disposition to indulge the 'lusts and passions of mankind', the 'horror of poverty and contempt and shame', and the lack of resourcefulness in the face of melancholy, jealousy and other debilitating emotions. He was unyielding, however, in his conviction that suicide was not an option open to any individual because, he pronounced, 'we dare not cut the thread of our own lives, nor fly from our present state of trial till our creator appoint the day of our deliverance'.[30]

Absolute belief in an omnipotent God, and in a last judgement was (as Taylor, Watts and others contended it should be) a powerful dissuasive for many potential suicides. The response of a young man named Neal, who 'languish'd' in 'a very distracted condition, as to the care of his soul' for eight days after taking poison in Dublin in 1730 offers some insight into the pangs of conscience it could generate.[31] Yet there were others, like the young woman from Youghal, County Cork, who lived for five hours after she shot herself in 1736, who 'would not hear of a clergyman coming to her, for she said she did not care where her body was laid, and she knew very well whither her soul would go'.[32] Indeed, as this case demonstrates, a majority of those who contrived to take their own lives were impelled to do so by difficult personal circumstances, which overwhelmed the complex of religious, natural and legal reasons critics of suicide fully believed invalidated this as a legitimate course of action.

Based on the temporal distribution of a sample of 675 cases of suicide and parasuicide reported in Ireland between 1712 and 1820 (see Table 5.1), there are sustainable evidential grounds for concluding, first, that the level of suicide increased in the course of the eighteenth century, and, second, that the rate of increase was not constant. One might reasonably have anticipated, given the substantial number of recorded instances dating from the 1750s, that this might have prompted a lively debate, but little commentary has been located prior to the late 1770s when the country experienced an increase in the reported suicide rate, which peaked in the 1780s, and extended into the 1790s.[33] Based on a contemporary estimation that fifty-five people took their own lives in the calendar year 1787, and a further forty-one in the first six and a half months of 1788, it can be concluded that the graph of the identified sample (see Fig.5.1) underestimates the number of instances of suicides, but it is equally clear that it captures the temporal trend.[34] If this is the case, then there are grounds also for accepting, based on the fact that the number of recorded cases involving women exceeded that involving men in the 1750s and 1780s, that the so-called 'gender gap', whereby in the modern era the number of male suicides exceeds that of women, was not an intrinsic feature of the suicide phenomenon in eighteenth-century Ireland.[35] It is notable also that the age profile of those who took their own lives ranged from ten to seventy, though it has not proved possible statistically to establish the preponderant ages of those who did so as adults because no attempt was made at the time to record that information.[36] Age was noted only when the deceased did not fit the adult standard. It is striking that a majority of those who took their own lives at an 'advanced' or 'old' age were female, and that a majority of those who took their own lives in their teens were male.[37] Teenage suicide was not an exclusively male preserve; at least two girls aged 13 or 14 killed themselves when suicide was at its peak in the late 1780s,[38] and they were considerably older that the youngest reported suicides – an 8-year-old girl who drowned herself in 1743 'to avoid being beat by a cruel uncle', and a 10-year-old boy who hanged himself in a cellar in George's Lane, Dublin in 1746, for no stated reason. The ages and circumstances of other teenage suicides varied; a 13-year-old boy from Tullamore, County Offaly, shot himself with his father's gun because he apprehended being 'chastised' for neglecting his school work, although a number of others, aged, 15, 16, and 17, took the more usual option of boys *and* girls, and ended their lives by hanging.[39]

While a positive correlation can be drawn between apprenticeship and attempts by teenage males to take their own lives, the profile of those who sought to commit suicide was not socially exclusive. Based on an analysis of that proportion of the sample with usable information (82 per cent of males and 64 per cent of females), it can be suggested that self-murder spanned the full social range from peers to the poor (see Tables 5.2. and 5.3; Figs 5.2 and 5.3). Interestingly, though those from the upper echelons accounted for some 14 per cent of the identifiable sample, they were outnumbered by those identified as respectable, which, if taken together with the small number of professional men who took their own lives, accounted for more than one fifth of the male sample (see Table 5.2). Yet it was some way shy of those in skilled employments, which in this instance also embraces apprentices, shopkeepers and dealers, who accounted for more than a

Year	Sample	Gentlemen	Respectable	Professions	Apprentices/Artisans	Soldiers	Prisoners	Servants	Lower level employees/Labourers	Poor
1712-20	3	1	0	0	0	0	2	0	0	0
1721-30	14	3	1	1	5	2	1	0	1	0
1731-40	35	2	6	1	11	8	2	0	4	1
1741-50	20	2	3	0	8	1	1	0	5	0
1751-60	42	1	6	0	12	3	3	7	7	3
1761-70	31	3	4	0	7	5	1	4	3	4
1771-80	48	7	8	0	16	7	2	1	5	2
1781-90	55	9	15	2	12	5	1	5	3	3
1791-1800	40	7	9	2	9	9	0	2	2	0
1801-10	15	1	4	1	4	2	1	1	0	1
1811-20	16	8	1	1	2	3	1	0	0	0
Total	319	44	57	8	86	45	15	20	30	14
%		14	18	2.5	27	14	5	6	9	4.5

Table 5.2 Suicide: social status, male, 1712–1820

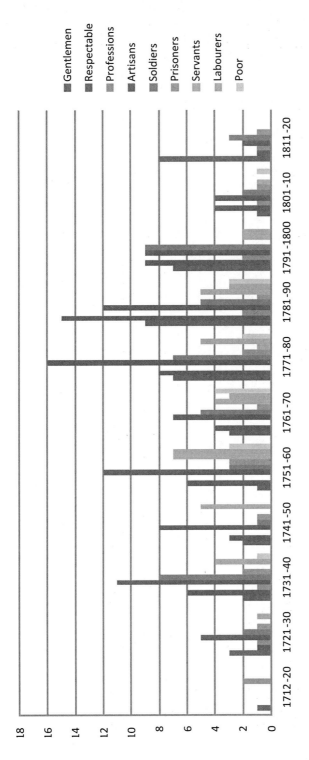

Fig. 5.2 Suicide: social status, male, 1712–1820

Year	Sample	Gentlewomen	Respectable	Artisan Level	Soldier's Wife	Prisoners	Servants	Lower Class employees	Poor
1712-20	1	1							
1721-30	1	1							
1731-40	21	2	3	5		4	3		4
1741-50	11	1	3	1		1	1		4
1751-60	33	2	6	5	1	1	9	5	4
1761-70	13		2	4			3	2	2
1771-80	21		4	2		1	7	4	3
1781-90	53	4	14	4	1	1	12	4	13
1791-1800	23	1	7	1			7	3	4
1801-10	5	1	2	1					1
1811-20									
Total	182	13	41	23	2	8	42	18	35
%		7	23	13	1	4	23	10	19

Table 5.3 Suicide: social status, female, 1712–1820

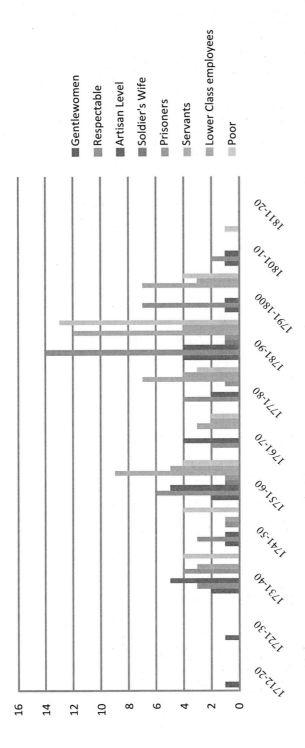

Fig. 5.3 Suicide: social status, female, 1712–1820

quarter (27 per cent). At the lower end of the social spectrum, the number of men described as poor who sought to take their own lives was a modest 4.5 per cent, but when this is combined with men in ill-paid and impermanent employments (9 per cent), and in service (6 per cent) the total is just short of twenty per cent. Significantly, the percentage of men in service who attempted suicide was not only of the same order as those consigned to prison for non-political offences (5 per cent), who attempted to do likewise in order to evade the humiliation of the gallows, but also less than half that of those in the military, who enjoyed preferential access to and knowledge of weaponry, and who were the most suicide-prone male social group (see Fig. 5.2).

Their female equivalents were servants, who account for nearly a quarter (23 per cent) of the approximately two-thirds of the female sample whose social profile can be identified (see Table 5.3; Fig. 5.3). Significantly, if combined with women described by contemporaries as poor (19 per cent), prisoners (4 per cent), and in lower socio-economic employments (10 per cent), together these account for more than half the total female reckonable sample and for nearly three times the male percentage in equivalent categories (19.5 per cent). By contrast, the proportion of gentle and respectable men and women that sought to end their own lives was comparable (32 per cent in the case of males and 30 per cent in the case of female), which meant that it was not only in the lower socio-economic ranks, graphically illustrated by the yawning 17 per cent differential between men and women in service, but also among those in the middling sort that the gender difference was evident. Indicatively, men employed as artisans and engaged in skilled manual labour (27 per cent) were twice as likely as women of this social station (13 per cent) to take their own life (see Tables 5.2 and 5.3).

The gender difference to which this attests is still more visible when one analyses the means by which men and women sought to end their own lives (see Tables 5.4 and 5.5; Figs 5.4 and 5.5). In keeping with latter day perceptions, men were more disposed than women to take the more violent option. This is most manifest in the recourse to firearms, which was the weapon of choice of seventy-four men (around 19 per cent of the available sample) but only three women (1 per cent). Given the efficiency of firearms (both the pistol and longer barrelled weapons) as a means of terminating existence, one might have anticipated a higher percentage, but other than soldiers, gentlemen and certain trusted servants,[40] access to firearms cannot be assumed, and it is notable that pistols were the weapons of preference of gentlemen

Year	Hanging	Gunshot	Cutting	Drowning	Jumping	Poison	Fire	Total
1712-20	1	0	0	0	0	2	0	3
1721-30	4	3	4	2	0	1	0	14
1731-40	11	11	8	7	1	2	0	40
1741-50	4	3	9	6	1	2	0	25
1751-60	16	5	16	13	2	2	0	54
1761-70	17	7	9	8	1	1	0	43
1771-80	17	4	18	17	6	4	1	67
1781-90	21	16	19	7	1	1	0	65
1791-1800	6	14	12	5	2	2	0	41
1801-10	2	3	4	6	0	1	0	16
1811-20	4	8	4	2	0	2	0	20
Total	103	74	103	73	14	20	1	388
%	26.5%	19%	26.5%	19%	4%	5%	0.258%	

Table 5.4 Suicide: means, male, 1712–1820

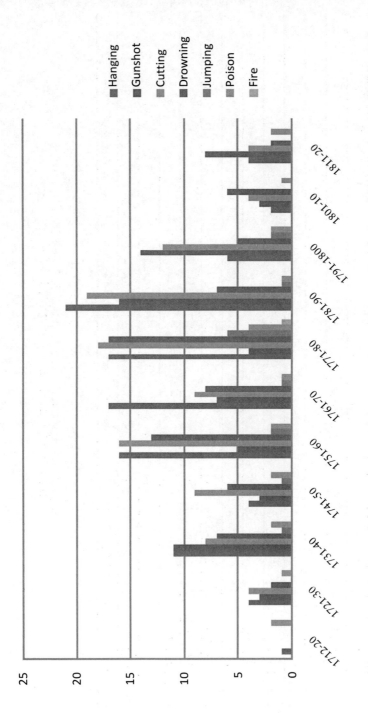

Fig. 5.4 Suicide: means, male, 1712–1820

Year	Hanging	Gunshot	Cutting	Drowning	Jumping	Poison	Total
1712-20	0	0	0	0	1	0	1
1721-30	0	0	0	2	0	1	3
1731-40	2	1	10	12	2	5	32
1741-50	2	0	1	9	0	4	16
1751-60	17	0	11	28	2	4	62
1761-70	9	1	6	10	2	1	29
1771-80	17	0	5	10	1	2	35
1781-90	28	0	4	34	2	6	74
1791-1800	10	1	0	13	2	2	28
1801-10	1	0	1	5	2	1	10
1811-20	0	0	0	1	0	0	1
Total	86	3	38	124	14	26	291
%	29.5%	1%	13%	42.5%	5%	9%	100%

Table 5.5 Suicide: means, female, 1712–1820

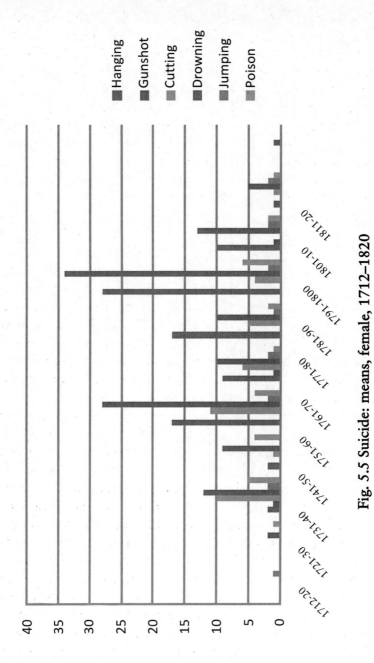

Fig. 5.5 Suicide: means, female, 1712–1820

and soldiers only.[41] Indeed, more men chose the options of death by hanging (26.5 per cent), by stabbing themselves in the abdomen or by cutting their throats (also 26.5 per cent) than by shooting. (Only one instance has been identified where an individual – a 'young gentlemen' in an inn at Kinnegad, County Westmeath – contrived to end it all 'by slitting his arm'.[42]) Recourse was also had to knives by 13 per cent of the women sampled, but this was significantly below drowning, which was the means of choice of 42.5 per cent of women who sought to take their own lives. This was substantially in excess of the respective figure for men (18.8 per cent), and of the percentage of women who sought death by hanging (29.5 per cent). Interestingly, the proportion of men and women who contrived to hang themselves was comparable; this was true also of death by jumping (3.6 per cent for men and 5 per cent for women); in obvious contrast, the percentage of women who had resort to poison (9 per cent) was almost double that of men (5.2 per cent).

Important differences are also manifest when we consider the reasons proffered as to why individuals sought to take their own lives (see Tables 5.6 and 5.7 and Figs 5.6 and 5.7). This is a particularly difficult area because phrases like 'disordered in his (or her) senses' or 'discontented of mind' were used in such a formulaic manner as to suggest that it assisted contemporaries to believe that those who perpetrated this 'detestable and inhuman action' were *non compos mentis*.[43] Yet contemporaries sought actively both to understand what prompted individuals to take their own lives, and did not hesitate to aver, when there was no other information available, or when (as often was the case) there were no identifiable reason, that 'there can be no cause assigned for this rash action'.[44] Insufficient information is available in 31 per cent of the total male sample and 40 per cent of the female sample to assign any cause but the fact that it is possible to ascribe some motive in a majority of reported instances permits certain conclusions in respect to both genders. The most salient is that in the judgement of contemporaries more than half of those who sought to take their own life did so because they were emotionally disturbed. This took different forms. The smallest, and at this remove arguably the most difficult to comprehend, are the 2 per cent of women and around 5 per cent of men who, it was reported, chose to end their lives 'having lost [their] senses in a fever', 'being delirious in a fever', 'in a paroxysm of raging fever', 'in a delirium', or simply 'in the height of a fever', but it may be, since some of these were 'ill for some time', that there were poorly understood underlying psychological issues.[45]

Year	Lunacy Deranged	Emotional despair Depression	Delerium Fever	Honour Reputation	Love Jealousy Domestic	Economic factors Poverty	Debt	Gallows Punishment	Total
1712-20	1	0	0	0	0	0	1	1	3
1721-30	3	0	0	0	4	0	1	1	9
1731-40	7	3	2	2	3	0	5	1	23
1741-50	5	2	0	1	2	1	1	0	12
1751-60	15	2	1	0	8	1	3	2	32
1761-70	17	3	1	0	3	1	0	4	29
1771-80	17	4	2	2	5	1	5	1	37
1781-90	12	16	5	1	10	1	10	0	55
1791-1800	15	6	2	2	4	0	10	4	43
1801-10	10	1	0	0	1	1	1	2	16
1811-20	4	2	0	1	0	0	5	0	12
Total	106	39	13	9	40	6	42	16	271
%	39%	14%	5%	3%	15%	2%	16%	6%	

Table 5.6 Suicide: motivation/cause, male, 1712–1820

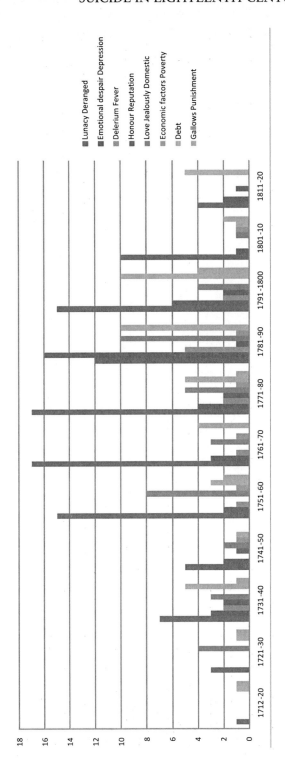

Fig. 5.6 Suicide: motivation/cause, male, 1712–1820

Year	Insanity	Depression	Delerium	Honour/Reputation		Love/Jealousy	Economic Factors			Punishment	Total
				Pregnant	Abandoned	Domestic	Finance	Poverty	Debt		
1712-20	0	0	0	0	0	0	0	0	0	0	0
1721-30	0	0	0	1	0	1	0	0	0	0	2
1731-40	5	4	1	1	0	0	0	1	0	4	16
1741-50	1	4	1	1	0	0	0	1	1	1	10
1751-60	19	6	0	2	3	6	1	0	0	2	39
1761-70	10	2	0	2	1	3	0	1	0	0	19
1771-80	5	1	0	1	0	6	0	0	1	1	15
1781-90	9	9	2	6	7	7	2	5	3	1	51
1791-1800	8	0	0	0	0	2	0	0	0	1	11
1801-10	3	0	0	0	0	0	0	0	0	0	3
1811-20	4	2	0	0	0	0	0	0	0	0	6
Total	64	28	4	14	11	25	3	8	5	10	172
%	37%	16%	2%	8%	6%	15%	2%	5%	3%	6%	

Table 5.7 Suicide: motivation/cause, female, 1712–1820

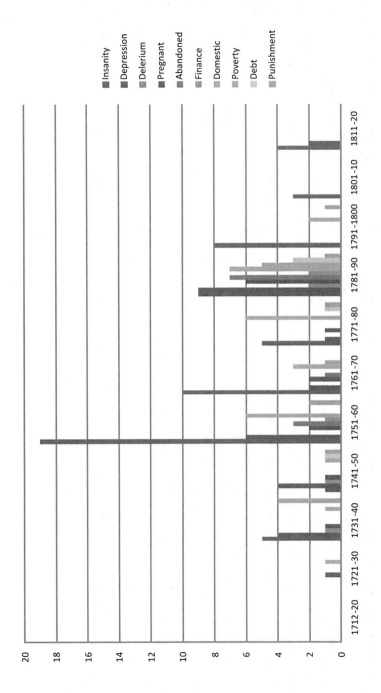

Fig. 5.7 Suicide: motivation/cause, female, 1712–1820

Mental instability was acknowledged as one of the primary causes of suicide in eighteenth-century Ireland from at least 1720, when William White, a young man of respectability, hanged himself 'out of some discomposure of mind'.[46] Significantly, the scepticism implicit in this report ceded thereafter to the more explicit acknowledgement that individuals who took their own lives were 'disordered', had manifested signs of 'odd behaviour', were 'somewhat discontented in his mind', 'melancholy', or 'out of his senses'.[47] The range of terms resorted to is illustrative of the lack of linguistic certitude that persisted until the mid-1730s, for though it is clear from the manner in which suicide was reported that the nature of the psychological distress experienced in such cases was barely comprehended, the adoption thereafter of the diagnostic explanation 'disordered in his [or her] senses' or 'disordered in his [or her] head' represented a step towards the development of a medical understanding of suicide.[48] These formulations were not used to the exclusion of all others,[49] but the frequency with which they were resorted to, and the proportion of self-murderers who were deemed to have killed themselves because they were 'disordered in their senses', 'under some discontent of mind' or acting 'from the distress of mind' by the 1750s attests to the linguistic, descriptive and interpretative ascendancy these inherently medical concepts had achieved by that date.[50] Moreover, this ascendancy was sustained through the 1760s and 1770s, and into the 1780s,[51] when they gave way incrementally to a still more medicalized concept of mental disorder, and, before the end of the century, to the utilization in popular discourse of the intrinsically legal terms 'lunatic' and 'insane'.

Suggestions that those who committed suicide did so because they were *non compos mentis* did not demand major attitudinal change by the Irish public in the 1780s. The 'lunacy' verdicts handed down by the coroners' courts from the 1730s were reported with sufficient frequency in the press to introduce the public to the term as well as the concept.[52] They also served to reinforce the tendency, already apparent in the description of those who committed self-murder as 'disordered', 'disturbed' and 'discontented', to conceive of suicide in medical terms, and this predilection was accentuated beginning in the 1760s and 1770s by the articulation of the view that many of those who chose to terminate their own lives were prompted to do so 'under a melancholy disposition' or by 'some disorder of mind'.[53] 'Despondency', 'melancholy', 'depression of spirits', 'dejection', and 'despair' were invoked to account for the actions of various individuals during the 1780s,[54] with the result that it did not require a great leap in imagination or interpretation to conclude that many of those who took their own lives did so either because they had been 'for some time previous disordered in ... understanding' or had 'lost [their] reason'.[55] This was a conclusion that some at least were well disposed to reach. Over half a century earlier, in January 1733, an 'old hospital man' who attempted to hang himself was 'sent to the madhouse' in the belief that this was the best place for him,[56] and while few outside of the coroner's court were willing then to make the link between suicide and insanity,[57] they had less difficulty from August 1774 when 'an opulent farmer' named Dornan killed himself in Cork jail, where he was detained for killing his three daughters, aged 9, 6 and nine months in a fit of jealousy.[58] Unable to account for Dornan's action other than by reference to the fact that his 'behaviour showed nothing but insanity', it was permissible thereafter to draw the same causal link, and before the 1770s were over, individuals with a history of mental instability who took their own lives were commonly described as having acted in a 'fit of' or 'in a state of insanity'.[59]

With the connection between suicide and insanity established, it was only a matter of time before other terms were brought into the public domain to describe those with psychological problems who took their own lives. 'Lunacy' was an obvious choice because it was the favoured term of coroner's juries until it was superseded by 'insanity' in the early nineteenth century.[60] The former was used with increasing frequency from the early 1780s, and it was joined before the decade was out by still more colloquial terms such as 'raving mad', and a 'fit of phrenzy'.[61] Since the use of such terminology could encourage stereotyping to the detriment both of those who were mentally unstable and those who killed themselves, it might be reasonable to contend that this was retrogressive, whereas there are good grounds for suggesting that both the terminology that was employed and the terms in which suicide was reported represented a hermeneutical advance. Thus the *Dublin Chronicle* newspaper observed sympathetically of a Miss Sullivan of Waterford who drowned herself in 1792 that her mental faculties had long been weakened, while it was said of another 'young lady' who took poison that 'her mental faculties were weak from ... infancy'.[62] These explanations did not entirely displace cruder, more stereotypical references to insanity, derangement and madness to which recourse was also made in cases of suicide, but the latter had to compete by the beginning of the nineteenth century with a language that accepted the reality that there were many for whom life was a burden, and that for those who could not cope because of mental impairment, suicide constituted a regrettable but explicable way out.[63]

A similar disposition to understand the action of the suicide is observable in the reports of those who were prompted to take their own lives by emotional upset. This could take many forms. In a significant 16 per cent of the reckonable sample of female cases, and 14 per cent of men, the publicly identified reason why they chose to attempt to end their lives was emotional distress. This can be ascribed in some instances to recognizable medical conditions such as *post partum* depression; others were prompted by bereavement. In a majority of cases, other than reporting that the person concerned was obviously in low spirits, no specific information is available.[64] It is certainly difficult to distinguish such cases from instances of emotional distress brought on by the breakdown of familial or sexual relationships, which account for an estimated 15 per cent of the usable sample in both genders (see Tables 5.6 and 5.7). Little can be ventured with certitude in a majority of such cases, but the frequency with which domestic disputes between married couples and personal rejection both within and without marriage caused individuals of both genders to take their own lives is illustrative of the strength of real and assumed emotional bonds. Based on the frequency to which it was appealed to explain the suicide of young men and women, it is apparent that the reading public of eighteenth-century Ireland not only had little difficulty with the suggestion that 'a disappointment in love' might precipitate an individual to self-destruction, but also that it was sufficiently firmly rooted for the phrase 'disappointed in love' to suffice as an explanation.[65] Moreover, this was the case long in advance of the publication in 1780 of the first of the five Irish editions of Goethe's *The Sorrows of Werther: A German Story*, which, it was widely maintained, legitimated if it did not glamorize the introspective self-pity that caused those disappointed in love to take their own lives.[66] Some, like the peripatetic Church of Ireland Bishop of Derry, Frederick Augustus Hervey (1739–1803), were certainly of this opinion. He did not hesitate to let Goethe know in person that 'Werther is a book altogether immoral and abominable' because it 'seduced people to commit suicide', but the Irish evidence does not sustain this conclusion.[67] It is a fact that interest in Ireland in *The Sorrows of Werther* coincided with a high in suicide numbers, and that the 1780s also witnessed a spike in the number of single people, male and female, that contrived to kill themselves for personal reasons, but introspective 'melancholy' of the kind encouraged by Werther was not cited as a precipitating factor in any of these instances. 'Melancholy' was invoked in more suicide reports in the 1780s than previously, but virtually all of these cases involved mature adults whose lives were blighted by depression.[68] It is more plausible for this reason to conclude that *The Sorrows of Werther* mirrored rather than generated a mood that encouraged an increased number of people both to contemplate and to attempt suicide.

By comparison with the modish emphasis on melancholy in accounts of suicide dating from the 1780s, 'jealousy' was one of the most consistently cited causes. However, because of the shortage of attendant detail, it can be difficult to divine accurately whether the jealousies referred to were sexual, reputational, financial or otherwise. One can conclude with confidence that the first two were at issue in those instances in which a woman ended her life because her husband had run 'off with a servant maid', or 'another woman', and in those cases in which a man did likewise because he was jealous of the relationship his wife had struck up with another man.[69] However, reports along the lines of that produced in 1795 that a soldier in a Highland regiment hanged himself 'in a fit of jealousy of his wife', which are more common, defy ready explanation.[70] They are probably best considered in the context of suicides prompted by domestic differences, intra-family animosities, and abusive relationships. These also resist easy generalization, but based on those instances that were reported, the primary precipitating factors were ill-considered 'words' or 'differences'; these were sufficient to cause certain men and women, and occasionally an unmarried son or daughter, to seek out an appropriate material with which to fabricate a hangman's noose or a river in which to drown. In other instances, women snapped because of the physical abuse they received from their partners, but since men also felt impelled to self-destruction by domestic pressures, it is evident that abuse was not unidirectional.[71]

Significantly, when women were prompted by domestic pressures to take their own lives, they generally did so because their reputations were at issue. The causes were many and the consequences varied. For example, in 1789 a young woman at Tralee, County Kerry, 'cut her throat in a most shocking manner' because she could not bear the humiliation of seeing her younger sister marry before her. Fifty years earlier, the daughter of a cutler on Ormond Quay in Dublin city threw herself into the River Liffey because 'her friends would not be reconciled to her' for marrying beneath her station. In another instance, a servant maid at Glasnevin, County Dublin, who was accused of 'having secreted a silver spoon', was only prevented from killing herself by hanging in 1755 by an unexpected interruption.[72] The women involved in each of these cases were clearly troubled individuals wrestling with reputational issues they were ill-equipped to handle. Sexual virtue was the primary index of female respectability in eighteenth-century Ireland; and, because the consequences of transgression were so acute, there was little that women caught in this maelstrom were not prepared to contemplate in order to escape the social sanction that followed the loss of reputation. Attention to date has focussed disproportionately on the phenomenon of infanticide, most of which was perpetrated by young women in a desperate attempt to rid themselves of the consequences of their venery, and the prospects of economic immiseration and social ostracism if they sought to live their lives as single parents.[73] Based on the number of cases brought to trial, it is clear that a large majority of women who committed infanticide evaded detection, but this possibility did not liberate them from the fear of apprehension, and, should they be tried, of being sentenced to death. Arising out of this, at least fourteen pregnant women chose to kill themselves not only 'to avoid shame' but also to evade the other implications of single parenthood.[74] This was not the only route chosen; a smaller number of women gave birth only to take their own lives and that of their child.[75] These are particularly arresting manifestations of the moral power of social convention; and this power was illustrated further by the eleven women who took their own lives when they were abandoned by the men to whose charm they had succumbed.[76] Suicide may be perceived of as an unjustifiably extreme response to the experience of seduction. But the reality was that, in common with the married woman from Arklow, County Wicklow, who was 'abused by some of her female neighbours, for want of that fidelity to her husband which is consistent with the character of an honest wife' when it was discovered that she had an affair, and the 14-year-old girl who was raped by a ploughman near Celbridge, County Kildare, these females chose to take their own lives because they perceived that this was preferable to living in a society that viewed them as tainted for having infringed the laws of female honour.[77]

Men too paid a high price when they were perceived to have behaved dishonourably. The most obvious evidence for this is the number of men who duelled to expiate insult, but every embarrassment did not lend itself to resolution by a preparedness to demonstrate personal bravery under fire.[78] Approximately 3 per cent of male suicides to whom a firm motive can be ascribed chose to take their own life rather than to be portrayed as dishonourable. Their plight can be illustrated by the decision of John Deseroy, whose father was an alderman in Kilkenny, to cut his throat rather than endure 'the slight he had received from some of his friends'; by the action of John S___n, who hanged himself to escape the shame arising out of his being discovered 'in a crime of a nature not to be spoken of', and, most famously, by the decision of Richard Power, the judge of the Court of Exchequer, who threw himself into Dublin Bay in 1794, rather than appear before the Lord Chancellor to answer charges of financial impropriety.[79]

While these incidents were readily accommodated within the male honour code, opinion was palpably more ambivalent as to whether a person was justified in taking one's life to escape the shame of imprisonment and to avoid the dishonour of capital punishment, yet this was a choice taken by as many as 6 per cent of male and female suicides (see Tables 5.6 and 5.7). Political radicals such as Rev. William Jackson (1795), Wolfe Tone (1798), Edward Roche (1798) and Denis Lambert Redmond (1803), who committed suicide 'to avoid the scandal and ignominy of being hang'd', were following a well-beaten path.[80] A considerable number of little-known figures sought in the course of the eighteenth century to cheat the gallows by taking poison, by opening their veins, or (less usually) by hanging themselves, while still others aspired to pre-empt sanction by taking their own lives in advance of the intervention of the judicial authorities. Ensign William Dixey whose suicide in 1732 created such a stir is an example of the latter; he took his own life in the wake of a quarrel in which he stabbed a man, to avoid the legal and disciplinary repercussions.[81] Examples of the former are more plentiful and they include a number of soldiers, sentenced to the lash for offences such as desertion and indiscipline, who sought to take their own lives to escape punishment.[82] Such actions may be accounted for by reference to the severity of the sentences that were pending, which in the case of the soldiers cited ranged from 200 to 1000 lashes, and in the case of a majority of civilians to death by hanging.[83] The main motivation in these cases may have been fear, but the wish to avoid the embarrassment of an 'ignominious death' was arguably still more important. This was a more vivid reality for women than for men because the standard capital sentence until 1790 was death by burning, and because women who were sentenced to public whipping for non-capital offences were stripped to the waist to facilitate the proper administration of the sentence. As a result, 'rather than suffer her descendents reputation to be sullied' and experience personal 'degradation', a woman was as likely as a man to seek to pre-empt the gallows and the stain of public censure.[84]

Financial embarrassment was another matter of compelling consequence for an individual's reputation, and, because the prevailing patriarchal order meant that males had disproportionate financial authority, it impacted men more acutely than women. Based on those cases to which a motive can be ascribed (see Tables 5.6 and 5.7), men were five times more likely to attempt to commit suicide for financial reasons than women. Moreover, as exemplified by Crosbie Morgell, the MP for Tralee, who killed himself in November 1794 because of the loss of an anticipated inheritance upon which he was reliant to restore his chaotic finances, a striking proportion of those men who took their own lives because they were experiencing financial problems were in the public eye.[85] This did not always mean they were major public personalities, but rather that they occupied a place of trust (be it in government, administration, or the community), which was grounded upon the perception that they were men of fiscal as well as personal probity. As a result, when this was shown to be misplaced, and the individuals concerned were faced with the ominous prospect of personal and financial ruin, some chose to take their own life rather than live with the loss of respect and reputation that must follow. This accounts for the suicide of respectable men consigned to debtors' prison; of gentlemen plunged into financial crisis by over-exposure to the South Sea Bubble; of officials who failed to acquit themselves of their responsibilities, such as the treasurer of the Workhouse (Charles Spranger), and Thomas Whitehouse, a former lottery office keeper; and of any number of merchants, traders, farmers and shopkeepers who encountered financial problems.[86] Significantly, their number appreciated in the course of the century, in keeping with the expansion of economic activity (see Table 5.6).

Commentators were not unsympathetic to those who were prompted to self-murder by financial distress. They were disposed to be sympathetic also to the still smaller number of people (5 per cent of reckonable females and 2.2 per cent of reckonable males) who were perceived to have killed themselves because they were impoverished.[87] By contrast, no compassion was extended to those who were deemed to have hastened their self-destruction because of gambling, inebriety or sexual licence, and where information to this effect was available it was made known.[88] This candour was in keeping with the enduring strength of the intrinsically religious conviction, delineated in 1726 by Isaac Watts, that suicide was part of 'a grand constellation of vice', and it is notable, the appreciating readiness to present the urge to self-destruct as a medical condition notwithstanding, that the religious perception of suicide as a sin continued to be strongly held. Thus suicide was openly linked in many minds with 'all the dissipations of the town' that those of a proper moral character and religious conviction consciously avoided.

Indicatively, the suicide of a 'poor washerwoman, named Flanagan, who hanged herself at her house in Hercules Lane' Belfast in 1785 was reported in the *Dublin Morning Post* as 'another melancholy proof of the fatal consequences attending the beastly custom of drunkenness'.[89] This was more than usually blunt; most reports established the connection without entering into such explicit judgement, because it was not necessary; once the link was made, the reader could be relied upon to arrive at the appropriate conclusion.

The implication that those who led irreligious or amoral lives were more likely than the God-fearing and personally disciplined to contemplate taking their own lives was reinforced by the suggestion, implicit in many suicide reports, that those who committed 'this rash act' did so on the spur of the moment and without forethought.[90] Many certainly did. There is a sufficiency of reports of individuals leaping into the River Liffey when the tide was out and of attempts at suicide that were ostensibly providentially interrupted to conclude that a distinct, but indefinable, proportion of those who sought to kill themselves gave the matter little prior thought.[91] However, there were also instances in which suicide was 'an act of agency rather than an act of hopefulness'.[92] Instances in which an individual succeeded, having failed previously, on one or more occasion, to end his or her life are an obvious case in point.[93] One may also include those who attached 'a considerable weight of stones' to their person in advance of jumping into a river.[94] But the intention is still more manifest in those cases in which an individual wrote a suicide note or put his (or her) affairs in order. In 1738 Colonel John Archer, who was agent to several military regiments, took the city of Dublin by surprise when he 'shot himself in the body and the head at his lodging in Dame Street, with three several pistols at different times, and had the fourth pistol lying on the chair ready at his hand'. Archer left a note in which he suggested, opaquely, that he was prompted to take this dramatic action by a desire 'to quit the malice of this world', but this elicited less attention than 'the deliberation and resolution' with which he had taken his own life. Having made his will one month previously, having had the pistols with which he took his life 'clean'd by a gunsmith' some ten days in advance, and having taken appropriate steps to ensure he was not interrupted, Archer drafted and sealed 'five or six letters' addressed to 'friends and creditors' explaining his actions before he shot himself in the head in the middle of the night.[95]

Though Archer's death contravened the prevailing idea that suicide was perpetrated by people who were emotionally unstable, or who overreacted to a reversal in fortune, he was not unique. Others left clear instructions as to what should happen to their possessions, and, a matter of particular concern to some, to their body. Thus the Rev. Daniel Keenan, who had ministered for a time in the Church of Ireland parish of St Brigid in Dublin, before he renounced it for Catholicism and embarked on a peripatetic existence which seems to have caused him to reconsider his conversion, left a letter in which he made clear his wish that his body be properly taken care of and he was properly buried in a coffin.[96] The contents of the notes or letters left behind were seldom so specific. But the fact that they were prepared and engaged on occasion with particular issues, or, as was the case with an elderly man from Ranelagh Road in Dublin, who justified his actions in 1785 on the grounds that 'when existence become a burden, death is the resting place of nature' illustrates that as far as certain individuals were concerned, suicide was a logical choice and a rational action.[97]

Responding to Suicide

Though no attempt was made in the accounts of self-murder presented to the public to deny that some people took their own lives having deliberated carefully upon the matter, suicide was a practice that society at large neither understood nor was disposed openly to tolerate. Like their equivalents in Scotland and England, the authorities in eighteenth-century Ireland did not believe it was appropriate any longer to punish the body of those who killed themselves, but neither the public, the legal system nor the churches were neutral on the subject, and each continued to impose sanctions in a proportion of cases. This was consistent with the dominant public attitude as expressed in the press, which routinely decried suicide as a 'horrid act', 'a horrid crime', a 'detestable and inhuman ... action', and, less commonly, 'an atrocious act'.[98]

Year	Number	Felo de se	Non compos mentis/Lunacy	Other	Unclear
1732-50	7		6	1	
1751-80	14	7	5	2	
1781-1800	15	4	10		1
1801-20	11	2	8		1
Total	47	13	29	3	2

Table 5.8 Suicide: Coroner's Court verdicts, 1732–1820

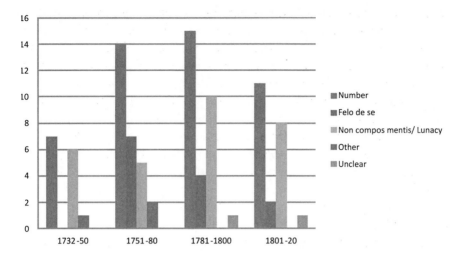

Fig. 5.8 Suicide: Coroner's Court verdicts, 1732–1820

If it appears, when these critical descriptions are set side by side with the non-judgmental tone of most press coverage, that Irish opinion was at best ambivalent in its attitude towards suicide, this impression is reinforced by the response of the law. In theory, every suicide should have been considered at a coroner's court before a jury of 12 men, who were required by law to view the body before presenting a verdict.[99] In practice, the logistics of convening a jury and of accessing bodies suggest that only a minority of cases were considered, but the absence of coroners' records means that this cannot be said for definite, and that we are obliged, once more, to rely disproportionately on what was carried in the newspapers for a perspective on what transpired. Based on a sample of forty-seven cases largely drawn from that source (see Table 5.8; Fig. 5.8), it can be suggested that Irish juries, like their English equivalents, were disposed to return verdicts of *non compos mentis*/lunacy in suicide cases by the 1730s. This was the verdict in six of seven cases heard in the 1730s and 1740s for which a record exists, and it is noteworthy in the one case in which another verdict was reached, that of Ensign William Dixey who took his own life on Christmas day in 1732, the coroner's inquest concluded prematurely that it was a case of 'wilful murder'.[100] However, this practice was not invariable, and certainly not sustained, since in the thirty years 1751–80, coroners' juries returned *felo de se* verdicts in 7 of 14 cases, a judgement of 'accessory to his own death' in one other, and lunacy in five cases.[101] It is not apparent, given the source of the sample, if these figures are representative of the cases heard by coroners' juries, but the fact that verdicts were returned in these proportions cautions against deducing that the legal system was disposed automatically to conclude, as one English medical practitioner observed in 1788, 'that every one who commits suicide is indubitably *non compos mentis*'.[102] Moreover, based on the example of Abraham Dondret, a suicide whose goods were forfeited to the Corporation of Cork in 1758, it is evident that the sanctions provided for by law were imposed, though it is not unlikely, as in this case, that the belief that it was inappropriate to penalize the next of kin ensured that the goods at issue were willingly 'given up' by the recipient and left in the possession of the family.[103] Since this had been the case for some time, it did not represent a reliable pointer to the future, but it can be suggested, based on the fact that *non compos mentis*/lunacy verdicts were returned in *c.*70 per cent of cases before coroners courts between 1781 and 1820, that coroners' juries echoed public opinion, which was increasingly accepting of the argument that those who killed themselves were *non compos mentis*. This outcome could not be assumed, however. At least 6 *felo de se* verdicts were returned by coroners' juries between 1781 and 1820, and while this constituted a reduced proportion of reported cases, it was indicative of the fact that suicide continued not only to excite divided opinions but also that there was significant legal support for the continuation of sanctions as a deterrent.

The societal ambivalence to which this attests was highlighted with particular vividness by the publication in a single issue of the *Dublin Daily Post* in 1739 of two ostensibly incompatible reports on the subject: the first, endorsed the coroner's inquest which returned the verdict of 'lunacy' in the case of Captain Maynard, 'a gentleman of a most excellent and pious character' who shot himself to escape chronic pain, on the grounds that 'nothing but absolute madness could reduce a person of his excellent understanding and exemplary life to such an act of desperation'; but the second, prompted by the case of a woman who attempted unsuccessfully to kill herself by drowning, elicited a call that 'attempts of this kind should be followed [by] some punishment' in order to 'prevent the many instances we have of this tremendous crime of self-murder'.[104] Guided by the latter instinct, the public intervened on occasion to express their disapproval of parasuicides by dispatching them to the 'mad house' or to the 'House of Correction'.[105] Yet it is surely significant that the number of socially responsible actions of this ilk was exceeded by those instances (indulgently reported in the press) in which individuals or groups assumed the entitlement to administer a public punishment. In 1754, for example, 'a gentlemen' who took it upon himself to 'discipline … with a horse whip' a young woman fished out of the ditch at Stephen's Green, Dublin, was warmly applauded for having administered a punishment that, it was piously pronounced, 'may perhaps be a means of preventing her from attempting to commit so rash an act in the future'.[106] Ducking was a popular punishment to which recourse was also had in such instances; in 1754 a woman who attempted to take her own life by jumping into the sea at Ringsend in Dublin in a state of intoxication was 'dragged several times through the water' on the assumption that it might 'give her an aversion to that element for the future'; while in 1789 another Dublin woman was given 'a severe ducking' with a similar intention.[107]

Public antipathy to parasuicides, of which these actions were a manifestation, possessed an obvious reformative intent; this cannot be said equally of the punishment visited on the bodies of suicides. Prompted by a well-established and enduring commitment 'to place suicides [permanently] outside the moral community, rather than to bring them back within it', the visceral antipathy that the body of a suicide could animate was highlighted in 1793 by the refusal of the fellow servants of an elderly woman who hanged herself in the house of a respectable family in King's Street, Dublin, 'to touch the body', with the result that the woman was not moved for twenty-four hours.[108] Communal disapproval was most commonly directed to ensuring that the final resting place of the deceased was not only set apart from the community at large but also that the manner in which suicides were conveyed into the ground was in keeping with the ignominious manner in which they died. This object was given official recognition by the prohibition provided for in the Book of Common Prayer on the use of the 'order for the burial of the dead' in cases of suicide, and by the proscription provided for in the code of Canon Law of the Catholic Church on the burial of suicides in consecrated ground. The enforcement of these religious exclusions in the eighteenth century depended largely on the status of the deceased, their social and personal standing in the community, and the skill with which family and friends were able to marshal support. But in those instances of contumacious suicide, separation was the least that the public expected, and they were not averse to taking the law into their own hands, particularly when responsibility for the deceased was not assumed by next of kin.[109] Moreover, families could not always be relied upon to ensure that suicides were afforded a proper burial; the body of a youth who took his own life because of 'a disappointment in love' was dumped in the Newry Canal, County Down, far from his place of abode, at the behest of his family in 1776.[110] In another instance, the relations of James Havern, a farmer from Dunmurry, County Down who hanged himself in his own barn in 1755, buried his body 'within the sea mark' privately late one Sunday night.[111] Strand burial, 'within the sea mark' or 'at low water mark', was the preferred option of those resident within reasonable distance of the sea in such cases. According to an observation dating from 1736, this was the fate of 'all suicides' at Youghal, County Cork, and since the same practice has been identified in counties Antrim and Down between 1733 and 1788, it may have been common practice.[112] It was not the only means by which the public expressed their disapproval, for though such practices may have declined in the course of eighteenth century, they were deeply rooted and were only slowly eradicated. They were, for example, strongly in evidence in Lisburn, County Down, in 1740 when a mob, affronted by the efforts of the family and friends of a local butcher, who had killed himself after several unsuccessful attempts, to afford him a decent burial, dug up the body, 'dragged it through the town on market day, and burned it to ash in the Market Square'.[113] This was an unusual, perhaps even unique surge of popular anger; in most instances in which the local community expressed objection to the burial of a person who took his own life, they were content once the body was not interred in consecrated ground. This is evidenced by a case at Waterford in 1787 when 'a tumultuous crowd' insisted on the removal from the parish graveyard of the body of a woman who had hanged herself, though this person had been interred 'privately and at night'. An acceptable alternative location was not always easily identified; the body of a carman who hanged himself in Dublin in July 1735 was dug up on a remarkable five occasions before an acceptable burial place was located 'under the gallows'. Others were buried at public crossroads. This was the Irish variation of the 'roadside burial' long commonplace in parts of England. Further inquiry may establish if this was common, but it is noteworthy that in one instance dating from 1818 in which a verdict of *felo de se* was returned, the suicide was interred with a stake, presumably through the heart. In other cases, bodies were interred in private spaces, usually in secret and not uncommonly by night.[114]

The persistence in such practices attests to the survival alongside an emerging proto-medical view of suicide into the nineteenth century of a more traditional viewpoint that perceived it as shameful as well as sinful. This was assisted by the failure of those who sought to break with the past and promulgate an alternative perspective that appealed to the public. As a consequence, self-murder retained its power both to embarrass and to shame, which meant, inevitably, that those who contemplated bringing about their own death not only did not discuss the matter with others, but also that families contrived where possible to conceal the fact. It may be, based on the more open reporting of self-murder among the middle and upper classes in Ireland than was the norm in Scotland, that suicide was not so hidden in the former, but reports of secretive midnight burials and the increasing tendency to conceal self-inflicted death suggests that the Irish were only slightly less sensitive than the Scots.[115] The public was certainly not assisted to embrace a more accepting attitude by a long-term disinclination to engage with the subject in the public realm. Indeed, other than Jeremy Taylor, whose authoritative statement of the traditional Christian position was prepared prior to his appointment to an Irish bishopric, nobody in a position of religious, political or moral responsibility in Ireland ventured forth with a considered statement on the subject during the seventeenth or early eighteenth centuries. Moreover, the issue was rarely discussed in the public prints during the same time period, though this did not matter greatly because Ireland and England were bound in a common sphere of print, and Irish anglophone opinion was content to follow English opinion on this issue. As a result, there was no shortage of authorities upon which those who were interested in the subject could draw, but their overwhelmingly conservative outlook ensured that the views and opinions expressed about suicide were not always at one with the coroner's court and the more tolerant echoes emerging from public sphere.

This remained the case, moreover, until the 1760s when the combined impact of the increase in the number of reported suicides (see Table 5.1), and of the inauguration in the 1750s of more news-oriented newspapers, paved the way for fuller engagement with the subject. At the outset, this was occasional and overwhelmingly anecdotal, and the press was largely content to reprint stories of the draconian treatment of suicides abroad on the grounds that 'certain circumstances attendant on death often carry more terror to the bulk of mankind than death itself'. Given the content of this material, its implicit message was that suicide might effectively be discouraged if the bodies of Irish suicides were hanged naked in a public place, as purportedly was the case in France, or 'delivered to the surgeons for dissection', but no such recommendations were made.[116] Instead, the press seemed content, as exemplified by the publication by the *Freeman's Journal* in 1765 of an extract from *A practical discourse concerning death* by William Sherlock (1639/40–1707), the Dean of St

Paul's, originally published in London in 1689, in which self-murder was deemed as sinful as murder, to echo the traditional religious condemnations of suicide.[117] Moreover, as evidenced by the republication in Dublin in 1776 of Caleb Fleming's *Dissertation upon the unnatural crime of self-murder*, which endorsed Isaac Watts' earlier contention that insanity was no 'excuse', and affirmed that suicide was against both nature and the law of God, it would appear this argument rang true with Irish readers.[118] They were evidently receptive also to the contention that suicide, like duelling, atheism, sexual excess, gambling, heavy alcohol consumption and the indulgence of other 'appetites' and 'lusts', was emblematical of 'the luxury and depravity of the age', and the tendency towards libertinism that was readily visible in the 1770s and 1780s.[119]

There was no more hard evidence for this than there was for the traditional argument that suicide was an English vice that was currently being imported into Ireland.[120] But as the number of reported suicides climbed during the 1780s towards its eighteenth-century peak, and attempts by the makers of proprietary medicine to suggest they had the remedies to 'drive away melancholy' failed to have the anticipated impact, religion alone was seen to provide the reservoir of moral, emotional and intellectual arguments that traditionalists invoked to sustain the case that suicide was unnatural as well as sinful.[121] They did this against a backdrop not only of bemusement at the rising number of people willing to take their life, particularly in Dublin, but also of a greater readiness in society at large at this time to consider other factors, most of which sat easily within an essentialist conservative world view that changes in behaviour and conduct were fundamental.[122] Thus as well as the enduring tendency to ascribe the greater propensity for self-harm to the 'contempt for religion, which had diffused itself among all ranks of people', and the corrupting effects of 'vices and follies' such as gambling and duelling, a variety of new and previously unacknowledged factors were invoked. These included the depressive impact of 'our climate'; the proliferation of debating societies and the emphasis placed on 'free will, free agency and predestination', which encouraged people to do as they pleased; the 'influence of those pernicious principles so successfully and fatally inculcated by the Voltaires and Humes, by the Rousseaus and Gibbons'; 'the unhappy effects of novel reading'; '*ennuie*', which sapped the will to live; and the permeation of 'cowardly despair and exasperated pride', which diminished the capacity to 'bear the slings and arrows of outrageous fortune'.[123]

The most problematic feature of this expanded, and revealing, menu of possible cases, was that the solutions proffered were over-whelmingly traditional in their thrust and purpose. The embrace of 'the religion of submission' rather than the 'pride of philosophy' was crucial according to one observer, who warned about the dangers of the 'passionate and impatient spirit' he detected in the expanding commitment to materialism: others just sought a return to the familiar or urged continued deference to the laws of God and nature.[124] Still others sought with varying degrees of success to reinforce the case against suicide by questioning the argument that it was ever 'judged a virtue' in 'antient Rome', but this had less obvious current purchase than the suggestion that the only way to reduce the suicide rate was to revive the tradition of punishing the body of the person who took his or her life.[125] With this end in mind, it was recommended that the bodies of those who took their own lives should be 'sent to the surgeon's theatre and there treated like all other murderers', and that their bones should be deposited in charnel houses to deter those who were 'jealous' of their 'personal honour' from taking such a fateful action. There was, to be sure, little or no prospect of this happening, as the moment when such punishments would be countenanced had passed.[126] Ireland may not have been ready at the end of the eighteenth century to embrace the implications of the analysis of William Rowley, a member of the London College of Physicians, that suicide was a medical issue that required a medical response, but the observation of another percipient commentator in 1812 that it was 'preposterous' to suggest that suicide could be prevented by 'act of parliament' summed up the prospects of the diverse portmanteau of legal sanctions to which appeal was occasionally made.[127]

Unsatisfactory as it was for those who genuinely believed that suicide was religiously sinful and socially detrimental, self-inflicted death was increasingly normalized within public discourse in the last quarter of the eighteenth century. This was both facilitated and encouraged by the increased coverage accorded the suicide of known public figures. An important moment was reached on 21 September 1788 when the MP for Banagher, and the Commissioner for Accounts, Edward Bellingham Swan, took his own life. Swan had been 'in a state of causeless discontent and gloominess for about a month' prior to his decision to 'put a pistol to his head', but this did little to mitigate the palpable 'shock' that a man 'possessing a clear property of £14,000' should take such a 'rash' action.[128] The suicide some five and half years later of Richard Power (c.1724–94), the second baron of the Court of

Exchequer, and onetime MP for Tuam, County Galway, did not generate quite the same stir in the print media, but it was the talk of the town, and the fact that Crosbie Morgell (c.1747–94), MP for Tralee, chose to kill himself at the same location in the same manner nine months later inevitably encouraged comment.[129] These were not the only MPs to take their own lives. Robert Downes (1708–54), MP for Kildare borough, killed himself in 1754; Edward Denny (c.1744–75), MP for Tralee, did likewise in 1775; in addition, Dudley, first Lord Cosby (c.1730–74), who represented Carrick-on-Shannon between 1763 and 1768, took a fatal dose of poison in 1774.[130] However, these fatalities were accorded few column inches by comparison with the deaths of Hervey Redmond Morres, second Viscount Mountmorres, who shot himself in London in 1797; of Theobald Wolfe Tone, whose celebrated intervention to save himself from the gallows in 1798 is still one of the most contested essays in Irish self-murder; of Wogan Brown, the liberal County Kildare landowner and member of the Whig Club, who died by his own hand in 1812; of Sir Thomas, second Baron French, who was prompted to take his own life in 1814 by bank failure; and of Robert, Lord Castlereagh, whose suicide in 1822 caused a sensation in both Britain and Ireland.[131] By this moment also, suicide had become sufficiently newsworthy, and Great Britain and Ireland sufficiently closely bound in the print sphere, for Irish newspapers routinely to carry stories of English suicides. Such coverage may have done little to promote a real understanding of suicide as a phenomenon, but by demonstrating that it was an everyday event, it accented the necessary process of normalization already well under way.[132]

Conclusion

Why did people kill themselves in eighteenth-century Ireland? It is tempting, because it would connect suicide to major historical and sociological trends, to echo those interpreters who have concluded that it was a consequence either of the emergence of a more secular world view or of the anonymizing impact of emerging social and economic forces associated with the industrial revolution. However, the reality suggested by Tables 5.6 and 5.7 is that there were identifiable social, economic, and moral forces at work, and that individuals were prompted to make the intensely personal decision to take their own lives by the interaction of these forces and their own personal and psychological circumstances. It is striking, for instance, that the largest definable category of suicides are those who experienced psychological problems. One cannot assume, of course, based on contemporary terminology, that everyone who committed suicide because of some perceived mental issue was clinically insane in the modern sense of the term, but the fact that an increasing number were so described, and that the more specific diagnoses of 'lunacy' and 'insanity' achieved greater favour in the course of the eighteenth and early nineteenth centuries, suggests not only that society at large was increasingly disposed to perceive insanity as legitimate grounds for self-murder, but also that it reflected the reality. There were, to state the obvious, disturbed, disordered and insane individuals in the eighteenth century who were prompted by derangement to seek to end their lives.

Suicide prompted by financial factors is more obviously amenable to sociological explanation in the tradition pioneered by Émile Durkheim, since there is good evidence that the pressure of debt, especially debt that was overwhelming or suddenly incurred, caused some individuals, stunned by the prospect of immiseration or enduring financial travail, to engage in self-destructive behaviour. However, suicide precipitated by financial problems can rarely be ascribed solely to impending fiscal difficulty; reputation was also a crucial consideration. Financial ruin, when experienced by an officeholder or member of parliament, was as likely as not to be interpreted as dishonourable, perhaps even shameful, and since honour and reputation were intrinsic both to the sense of self-worth of individuals and how they perceived they were viewed by others, it was deemed a legitimate reason to take one's own life. For those who took this course of action, suicide was an act of agency rather than an act of despair. Some may still have difficulty accepting that Wolfe Tone's decision to cut his own throat rather than face the gallows was an honourable action, but if it is set in the context, first, of the contemporary belief that it was singularly ignominious to die on the gallows, and, secondly, of the concept of a heroic suicide idealized in France in the 1790s, it was as logical as the decision of a man of honour to risk his life in a duel.[133]

Personal honour was certainly integral to the preparedness of women, who perceived that their virtue had been fatally compromised, to take their own lives. Moreover, it was not necessary for a woman to have been forsaken, pregnant, for this to occur; many women were plunged into such emotional despair by the experience of rejection by a man in whom they had vested their hopes, by a breach of promise or, even, by the apprehension of the prospect of being consigned to the less than entirely honourable space reserved for spinsters to take the fateful decision that life was no longer worthwhile.

It is difficult, of course, to separate such socially prompted acts of self-destruction from the intrinsically emotionally motivated suicide, perpetrated by men as well as by women, because of what was described as 'jealously'. Moreover, because this could be invoked to define situations that were socially constructed by the prevailing patriarchal order, which expected wives to yield to their husbands, which tolerated physical, emotional and sexual abuse, and viewed the deserted wife as more than faintly disreputable, it is also well nigh impossible to draw clear lines between what was a consequence of social structure and individual choice.

The most striking conclusion to emerge from an exploration of suicide in eighteenth-century Ireland is not 'the growth of leniency' but the enduring hostility toward 'self-murder' deriving from a complex of religiously inspired interdicts, legal proscriptions, and popular sanctions. These were not immutable, of course, but the fact that Irish society was only slightly less willing to condemn suicide in 1820 than it was in 1680 is a fair measure of how slowly entrenched attitudes changed, and of how far secular and medical perspectives had yet to permeate if suicide was not to continue to be penalized. As matters stood in the early nineteenth century, suicides were officially precluded a Christian burial by each of the three main religious denominations; the Presbyterian Church in Ulster deemed it legitimate to deprive the widows of ministers who took their own lives of access to the widow's fund, and it remained a criminal offence in law.[134] However, few now favoured burying suicides by the seashore, and still fewer sought to punish their bodies. The appreciation over a century of a medical understanding of suicide inherent in the realization that mental weakness was its primary cause did not herald the inevitable triumph of a medical explanation, but it greatly increased the likelihood, and with it the triumph, not of a secular view of suicide over a procrustean religious sensibility, but of the emergence of a more tolerable, but by no means tolerant attitude that was to achieve acceptance during the nineteenth century.

NOTES

1 'Dublin Bill of Mortality, 1683–4', in Sir John Gilbert (ed.), *Calendar of Ancient Records of Dublin* (19 Volumes, Dublin: Dollard, 1889–1944), v, pp.610-11.
2 See Roland Bartel, 'Suicide in Eighteenth-Century England: the Myth of a Reputation', *Huntington Library Quarterly*, 23 (1960), pp.145–58.
3 *Pue's Occurrences*, 20 Jan. 1733.
4 Edward Bullingbrooke, *The Duty and Authority of Justices of the Peace* (Dublin, 1788), p.426.
5 Ibid.; Clodagh Tait, *Death, Burial and Commemoration in Ireland, 1550–1650* (Basingstoke: Palgrave, 2002), p.22; *The Irish Fiants of the Tudor Sovereigns* (4 Volumes, Dublin: de Burca, 1994), iii, no. 6002.
6 Bullingbrooke, *The Duty and Authority*, p.426;
7 R.A. Houston, *Punishing the Dead? Suicide, Lordship and Community in Britain, 1500–1800* (Oxford: Oxford University Press, 2010), p.4.

8 William Hawkins, A treatise of the please of the crown: a system of the principal matters relating to that subject digested under the proper heads (2 Volumes, London, 1716–21).

9 H.J. Berman, Law and Revolution II: the Impact of the Protestant Reformations in the Western Legal Tradition (Harvard: Harvard University Press, 2006), p.296; Bullingbrooke, The Duty and Authority, p.426.

10 Gilbert (ed.), Calendar of Ancient Records of Dublin, vii, p.354.

11 Houston, Punishing the Dead?, pp.4, 238–9; Michael MacDonald and Terence Murphy, Sleepless Souls: Suicide in Early Modern England (Oxford: Clarendon Press, 1990); Michael MacDonald, 'The Secularisation of Suicide in England, 1660–1800', Past and Present, no. 111 (May 1986), pp.50–100.

12 Alexander Murray, Suicide in the Middle Ages, I: The Violent Against Themselves; II: The Curse of Self Murder (2 Volumes, Oxford: Oxford University Press, 1999–2000); Houston, Punishing the Dead?, passim; Jeffrey R. Watt (ed.), From Sin to Insanity: Suicide in Early Modern Europe (Ithaca: Cornell University Press, 2004), passim.

13 Bullingbrooke, The Duty and Authority, p.427; the Act of Uniformity: 17 and 18 Charles II, Chap. 6 (1666); A.J. Stephens (ed.), The Book of Common Prayer, 1666–7 (3 Volumes, London, 1849–50), iii, p.560.

14 Richard Cobb, Death in Paris, 1795–1801 (Oxford: Oxford University Press, 1978), p.101, cited in Houston, Punishing the Dead?, p.2.

15 Jack D. Douglas, The Social Meanings of Suicide (Princeton: Princeton University Press, 1967), passim.

16 MacDonald and Murphy, Sleepless Souls: Suicide in Early Modern England, passim; MacDonald, 'The Secularisation of Suicide in England, 1660–1800', passim; Michael MacDonald, 'The Medicalization of Suicide in England: Laymen, Physicians, and Cultural Change', The Milbank Quarterly, 67 Supplement 1 (1989), pp.69–91, also published in C.E. Rosenberg and Janet Golden (eds), Framing Disease: Studies in Cultural History (New Brunswick: Rutgers University Press, 1997), pp.85–103.

17 D.T. Andrew and Michael MacDonald, 'Debate: The Secularisation of Suicide in England, 1660–1800', Past and Present, no.119 (May 1988), pp.158–70.

18 For a review of recent writing on the subject of suicide, see Róisín Healy, 'Historiographical Review: Suicide in Early Modern and Modern Europe', Historical Journal, 49 (2006), pp.903–18.

19 S.K. Morrissey, 'Drinking to Death: Suicide, Vodka and Religious Burial in Russia', Past and Present, no. 186 (Feb. 2005), pp.119, 145; see also Healy, op cit., pp.903, 909, 918. Houston, Punishing the Dead?, passim but especially Chapter 6 which argues persuasively in support of 'hybrid understandings' (p.323).

20 Below, pp.113–25; Houston, Punishing the Dead?, p.315 ff.

21 See Robert Munter, History of the Irish Newspaper, 1685–1760 (Cambridge: Cambridge University Press, 1966); Andrew Hadfield and Raymond Gillespie (eds), The Irish Book in English, 1550–1800: The Oxford History of the Irish book, Volume 3 (Oxford: Oxford University Press, 2006), pp.222–4; James Kelly, 'Health for Sale: Mountebanks, Doctors, Printers and the Supply if Medication in Eighteenth-Century Ireland', RIA proc., 108C (2008), pp.1–38.

22 Houston, Punishing the Dead?, p.348 ff.

23 Dublin Intelligence, 21 June 1712; Pue's Occurrences, 9 Aug. 1718.

24 Dublin Intelligence, 11 Apr. 1719, 19 Feb. 1726, 10 Sept. 1728, 2 Aug. 1729; Harding's Dublin Impartial Newsletter, 30 Jan. 1720; Dublin Weekly Journal, 16 Nov. 1728, 20 Dec. 1729.

25 Dublin Gazette, 26 Dec. 1732; Pue's Occurrences, 26, 30 Dec. 1732; W. Cownley, A full and true account of the discovery of the terrible and bloody murder of William Dixey, esq (Dublin, 1732).

26 Gilbert (ed.), Calendar of Ancient Records of Dublin, viii, p.229.

27 See Gentlemen's Magazine, 1 (1731), p.397. The first Irish case that I have identified dates from 1737: see Dublin Daily Advertiser, 19 Jan. 1737, and below pp.127–8.

28 Jeremy Taylor, Ductor dubitantium, or the rule of conscience in all her general measures (London, 1660). Later editions were published in 1671, 1676, 1676 and abridged editions in 1701, 1710, 1725 and 1778. The passages quoted are from The whole works of Jeremy Taylor (3 Volumes, London, 1835), iii, p.423.

29 John Sym, *Life's preservative against self-killing* ... (London, 1637); *Sad and lamentable views from Brick Lane in the hamlet of Spittlefields, or a dreadful warning not to give way to the temptation of the Devil in the deplorable example of Mr John Child ... who ... committed a barbarous and unnatural murder upon his own person on 13 October 1684* (London, [1684]); *A full and true relation of the murther of Doctor Urthwait, archdeacon of the Isle of Man, who in an inhuman and barbarous manner cut his own throat ... on Wednesday the 20th of this instant December* [London, 1688].

30 Thomas Milner (ed.), *The life, times and correspondence of Rev. Isaac Watts* (London, 1834), pp.421–2; Isaac Watts, *A defense against the temptation to self-murther, wherein the criminal nature and guilt of it are display'd, the various pretences for it arte examin'd and answer'd; seasonable advice is proposed to those who have been deliver'd from this temptation* ... (London, 1726), pp.i–x.

31 *Faulkner's Dublin Journal*, 19 Dec. 1730.

32 *Dublin Daily Advertizer*, 14 Oct. 1736.

33 *Hibernian Journal*, 17 June 1776; *Freeman's Journal*, 21 Sept. 1784.

34 *Dublin Chronicle*, 22 July, 27 Sept. 1788.

35 This is not inconsistent with J.R. Watt's contention that the gender gap, absent in sixteenth and seventeenth-century Geneva, emerged in the course of the eighteenth century: J.R. Watt, 'Suicide, Gender and Religion: The Case of Geneva', in idem (ed.), *From Sin to Insanity*, pp.138–57.

36 An attempt to tabulate the age of those who sought to take their own lives was commenced, but it was not pursued because of the imprecision of a majority of age references.

37 *Pue's Occurrences*, 26 June 1731; *Hibernian Journal*, 15 June 1774; *Dublin Chronicle*, 4 Nov. 1790; *Freeman's Journal*, 15 July 1802.

38 *Dublin Courant*, 29 May 1788; *Dublin Weekly Journal*, 27 Nov. 1790.

39 *Pue's Occurrences*, 12 Oct. 1736, 21 June 1743, 10 Jan. 1744, 22 Feb. 1746; *Dublin Courant*, 4 Feb. 1746; *Hibernian Journal*, 27 May 1782; *Anthologia Hibernica*, 1 (1793), p.140.

40 See *Freeman's Journal*, 1 Feb. 1766, 21 Sept. 1784; Elizabeth Fitzgerald, *Lord Kildare's Grand Tour: the Letters of William Fitzgerald, 1766–69* (Cork: The Collins Press, 2000), p.93.

41 For a selection of gentlemen, respectable men and soldiers who killed themselves using a pistol, see *Dublin Weekly Journal*, 20 Dec. 1729; *Pue's Occurrences*, 10 Dec. 1734; *Universal Advertiser*, 9 Jan. 1753; *Dublin Chronicle*, 29 Dec. 1789 (soldier); *Pue's Occurrences*, 10 Aug. 1734, 3 Jan. 1767 (respectable); *Finn's Leinster Journal*, 24 Aug. 1775, 16 Jan. 1779 (gentlemen).

42 See *Dublin Mercury*, 15 July 1766. In another instance, Richard Dease, the Professor of Surgery at the College of Surgeons, may have killed himself by severing his femoral artery (Eoin O'Brien, 'A Day in Georgian Dublin', in idem (ed.), *Essays in Honour of J.D. Widdess* (Dublin: Cityview Press, 1978), p.178; *DIB*).

43 *Dublin Evening Post*, 29 Apr. 1735; see also below, p.127.

44 *Finn's Leinster Journal*, 3 Nov. 1774.

45 *Dublin Courant*, 23 Aug. 1748; *Public Gazetteer*, 7 Sept. 1762; *Finn's Leinster Journal*, 2 Sept. 1775; *Volunteer, Evening Post*, 1 Oct. 1785; *Freeman's Journal*, 4 Jan. 1791; *Hibernian Journal*, 10 Jan. 1791; *Clonmel Gazette*, 12 Jan. 1791; *Dublin Chronicle*, 29 Aug. 1789, 1 Jan. 1791, 20 Aug. 1793.

46 *Harding's Dublin Impartial Newsletter*, 30 Jan. 1720.

47 *Dublin Weekly Journal*, 8 Apr. 1727; *Dublin Intelligence*, 25 Mar. 1729, 31 Jan. 1730, 23 June 1731; 'Autobiography of Pole Cosby', *Journal of the Kildare Archaeological Society*, 5 (1906–08), p.269.

48 The first identified use of the term 'disordered in his senses' dates from 1725 (*Dublin Weekly Journal*, 19 June 1725); it achieved common currency in the 1730s and was used widely thereafter: see *Pue's Occurrences*, 15 July 1732, 16 Oct. 1736; 12 May 1733; *Dublin Evening Post*, 1 June 1734, 25 Oct., 14 Dec. 1735; *Dublin Gazette*, 21 Jan. 1738; *Dublin Courant*, 3 May 1746, 4 Apr. 1747, 15 Dec. 1753.

49 See, for examples, *Dublin Gazette*, 21 Feb. 1741, *Pue's Occurrences*, 22 May 1742, 11 Oct. 1755; *Freeman's Journal*, 3 Dec. 1765; *Dublin Mercury*, 21 Mar. 1767.

50 *Dublin Newsletter*, 13 June 1741; *Faulkner's Dublin Journal*, 24 Apr. 1744; *Dublin Courant*, 6 Jan. 1746; *Universal Advertiser*, 3 July 1753, 5, 12 Nov. 1754, 4 Jan. 1755, 10 Feb. 1756,

25 Jan. 1757, 24 July 1758, 19 June 1759, 18 Nov. 1760; *Pue's Occurrences*, 4 Aug. 1752, 18, 28 May, 4 June, 16 July 1754, 6 May, 3 June, 22 July, 7 Oct. 1755, 7 Feb., 3 Apr., 22 May, 9 Nov. 1756, 12 Apr., 21 June, 8 Nov. 1757, 13 May, 1 July, 7 Oct., 14 Nov. 1758; *Public Gazetteer*, 2 Dec. 1758, 18 Aug., 22 Sept. 1759; *Dublin Gazette*, 12 May 1759.

51 See, for example, *Public Gazetteer*, 20 Apr., 19 June 1762, 11 July 1763; *Freeman's Journal*, 22 Sept., 27 Oct. 1764, 25 Feb. 1766, 21 July 1770, 2 May 1775; *Dublin Gazette*, 29 June, 27 Aug. 1765; *Dublin Mercury*, 20 Jan., 7 Mar. 1767; *Hoey's Publick Journal*, 12 June, 31 July 1772; *Finn's Leinster Journal*, 11 Mar. 1767, 6 Aug., 7 Sept. 1774, 6 July, 11 Sept., 18 Dec. 1776, 3 Mar. 1779; *Pue's Occurrences*, 8 Apr., 24 June, 12, 19 Sept. 1769; *Hibernian Journal*, 23 June 1773, 22 May 1775, 26 Jan., 4, 10 July 1776, 8 Feb., 15 Apr. 1782; *Volunteer Evening Post*, 15 June, 23 Dec. 1784; *Dublin Morning Post*, 23 Dec. 1784; *Dublin Chronicle*, 4 Sept. 1788, 5 Nov. 1791; *Walker's Hibernian Magazine*, 1797, p.189.

52 See *Dublin Gazette*, 30 Jan. 1739, 6 Dec. 1740, 5 June 1742; *Dublin Daily Post*, 30 July 1739; *Freeman's Journal*, 18 Oct. 1766; *Finn's Leinster Journal*, 24 Jan. 1778; *Hibernian Journal*, 8 Aug. 1781.

53 See, for example, *Public Gazetteer*, 2 Feb. 1760; *Hoey's Publick Journal*, 31 July 1772.

54 *Freeman's Journal*, 5 June 1779; *Hibernian Journal*, 23 Apr. 1781, 5, 17 Aug. 1789; *Dublin Chronicle*, 11 Oct., 27 June, 30 May, 31 Dec. 1789; *Ennis Chronicle*, 4 June, 20 Aug., 9 Nov. 1789; *Clonmel Gazette*, 10 July 1790; *Dublin Weekly Journal*, 10 July 1790; Jean Agnew (ed.), *The Drennan-McTier letters* (3 Volumes, Dublin: Irish Manuscripts Commission, 1998–99), i, p.252; M.C. Lyons, *The Memoirs of Mrs Leeson* (Dublin: Lilliput Press, 1995), p.222.

55 *Dublin Chronicle*, 7 July 1789, 19 Apr. 1791.

56 *Pue's Occurrences*, 29 Jan. 1733.

57 See *Public Gazetteer*, 29 Sept. 1767, for an example.

58 *Finn's Leinster Journal*, 20, 24 Aug. 1774; *Freeman's Journal*, 25 Aug. 1774; *Hibernian Journal*, 17 Aug. 1774.

59 *Freeman's Journal*, 20 May 1775; *Hibernian Journal*, 23 June 1777, 12 June 1780; *Dublin Chronicle*, 20 Sept. 1788, 12 Sept. 1789; *Clonmel Gazette*, 2 Oct. 1788; *Ennis Chronicle*, 3 Feb. 1791.

60 For examples of the use of 'insanity' by coroner's courts in 1810, see *Freeman's Journal*, 12, 14 Jan., 17 Apr., 24 May, 17 Nov. 1810.

61 *Freeman's Journal*, 31 Oct. 1782, 12 Nov. 1785; *Dublin Morning Post*, 10 Jan. 1785; *Dublin Chronicle*, 30 Sept., 2 Oct. 1788, 8 July 1790, 3 Apr. 1792.

62 *Dublin Chronicle*, 7 Aug. 1792; *Cork Gazette*, 14 Aug. 1793.

63 *Freeman's Journal*, 28 May 1796, 16 May 1801, 2 Aug., 6 Nov. 1802, 12 Oct. 1809, 30 June 1810; *Walker's Hibernian Magazine*, Oct. 1798, p.284; *The Beauties of the Press* (London, 1800), p.383; Isaac Corry to [Thomas Pelham], 15 Jan. 1798 (NAI, Customs and Excise Establishment Papers, 1788–99 bundle, no 113); *Ennis Chronicle*, 8 Apr. 1818.

64 *Dublin Gazette*, 15 July 1732; *Corke Journal*, 6 Sept. 1756; *Universal Advertiser*, 9 Oct. 1753.

65 *Universal Advertiser*, 29 July 1755; *Pue's Occurrences*, 20 Jan. 1759; *Public Gazetteer*, 21 Aug. 1762; *Dublin Mercury*, 30 Sept. 1766; *Hoey's Publick Journal*, 2 Apr. 1773; *Freeman's Journal*, 24 Aug. 1771, 14 June 1785; *Hibernian Journal*, 29 Sept. 1773, 1 Mar. 1776, 1 Mar. 1780; *Finn's Leinster Journal*, 14 Aug. 1776; *Dublin Morning Post*, 14 June 1785.

66 Johann Wolfgang von Goethe, *The Sorrows of Werther: a German Story* (Dublin, 1780, 1785, 1790, 1791, 1794). This work was published in 1779.

67 John Hennig, 'Goethe and Lord Bristol, Bishop of Derry', *Ulster Journal of Archaeology*, 3rd ser. 10 (1947), p.102.

68 *Dublin Evening Post*, 12 Sept. 1786; *Dublin Chronicle*, 25 Sept. 1788; *Hibernian Journal*, 5 Aug. 1789, 7 July 1790; *Freeman's Journal*, 29 Nov. 1791, 27 May 1812; J. H. Gebbie (ed.), *An Introduction to the Abercorn letters, as Relating to Ireland, 1736–1816* (Omagh: Strule Press, 1972), p.355.

69 *Pue's Occurrences*, 18 Jan. 1755; *Universal Advertiser*, 18 Jan., 1 Mar. 1755; *The Corke Journal*, 15 July 1756; *Finn's Leinster Journal*, 16 Nov. 1776; *Freeman's Journal*, 2 Oct. 1802.

70 See, for examples, *Munster Journal*, 28 Jan. 1751; *Pue's Occurrences*, 10 July, 9 Oct. 1753; *Universal Advertiser*, 29 Oct. 1754, 21 Feb. 1756; *Freeman's Journal*, 10 Mar., 15 Sept. 1764, 27 Oct. 1769; *Volunteer Evening Post*, 21 Oct. 1784.

71 *Pue's Occurrences*, 4 Dec. 1733, 20 July 1742, 14 Nov. 1752, 17 Feb. 1767; *Universal Advertiser*, 22 July 1755; *Dublin Gazette*, 7 Sept. 1765; *Freeman's Journal*, 20 Mar. 1764; *Finn's Leinster Journal*, 30 Nov. 1774; *Hibernian Journal*, 5 Sept. 1780, 4 May 1781; *Volunteer Evening Post*, 6 Dec. 1783; *Dublin Chronicle*, 18 Sept. 1788.

72 *Ennis Chronicle*, 12 Feb. 1789; *Dublin Gazette*, 22 May 1739; *Universal Advertiser*, 7 Dec. 1754.

73 See James Kelly, 'Infanticide in Eighteenth-Century Ireland', *Irish Economic and Social History*, 19 (1992), pp.7–8; idem, 'Responding to infanticide in Ireland, 1680–1820', in Elaine Farrell (ed.), *'Tis Said she was in the Family Way': Pregnancy and Infancy in Modern Ireland* (London: Institute of Historical Research, 2012), pp.191–205.

74 *Dublin Mercury*, 15 July 1723; *Dublin Evening Post*, 13 July 1734; *Pue's Occurrences*, 13 July 1734; *Munster Journal*, 20 July 1749; *Dublin Courant*, 27 Apr. 1751; *Dublin Mercury*, 12 Aug. 1766; *Freeman's Journal*, 3 Sept. 1771, 25 Sept. 1787; *Hibernian Journal*, 11 July, 26 Dec. 1781; *Dublin Chronicle*, 19 Aug. 1788; *Dublin Weekly Journal*, 26 Mar. 1791.

75 For examples, see *Dublin Gazette*, 22 May 1739; *Pue's Occurrences*, 12 Dec. 1758, 15 Apr. 1769; *Dublin Mercury*, 4 Apr. 1767.

76 *Universal Advertiser*, 18 May 1754, 4 Jan. 1755; *Hibernian Journal*, 12 May 1777; *Dublin Chronicle*, 25 Sept. 1788, 14 Oct. 1790; *Freeman's Journal*, 25 Sept. 1788; *Dublin Weekly Journal*, 27 Nov. 1790.

77 *Dublin Courant*, 25 Jan. 1752; *Hibernian Journal*, 26 July 1782.

78 James Kelly, *'That Damn'd Thing Called Honour': Duelling in Ireland, 1570–1860* (Cork: Cork University Press, 1995).

79 O'Brien, 'A Day in Georgian Dublin', p.178; *Pue's Occurrences*, 23 May 1738; *Munster Journal*, 9 Aug. 1750; *Universal Advertiser*, 28 Jan. 1755; *Hibernian Journal*, 27 Mar. 1776; Ann Kavanaugh, *John FitzGibbon, Earl of Clare: Protestant Reaction and English Authority in Late Eighteenth-Century Ireland* (Dublin: Irish Academic Press, 1997), p.184.

80 *Dublin Gazette*, 15 Apr. 1740. For Jackson, see Stella Tillyard, *Citizen Lord: Edward Fitzgerald, 1763–1798* (London: Chatto and Windus, 1997), p.187; Daniel Gahan, *The People's Rising, Wexford, 1798* (Dublin: Gill and Macmillan, c.1995), p.298; Marianne Elliott, *Wolfe Tone: Prophet of Irish Independence* (London: Yale University Press, 1989), p.401; Patrick Geoghegan, *Robert Emmet* (Dublin, Gill and Macmillan, 2003), pp.211–12.

81 As per note 25 above. For the example of Dennis Connor, see Edward MacLysaght, 'Herbert Papers', *Analecta Hibernica*, 15 (1944), p.99.

82 *Public Gazetteer*, 3 Sept. 1763, 6 Sept. 1766; Waite to Wilmot, 2 Feb. 1768 (PRONI, Wilmot papers, T3019/5682); *Freeman's Journal*, 4 May 1771, 2 Apr. 1772; *Dublin Evening Post*, 23 June 1795.

83 *Dublin Intelligence*, 21 June 1712; *Dublin Gazette*, 15 Apr. 1740, 14 Sept. 1765; *Dublin Newsletter*, 21 Mar. 1741; *Universal Advertiser*, 3 Nov. 1753, 1 May 1759; *Finn's Leinster Journal*, 6 Dec. 1775, 16 May 1778; *Freeman's Journal*, 29 Sept. 1798.

84 *Dublin Evening Post*, 15 Nov. 1735; *Universal Advertizer*, 7 June 1755; *Dublin Mercury*, 30 Aug., 6 Sept. 1766; *Finn's Leinster Journal*, 9 May 1778; *Hibernian Journal*, 30 Dec. 1782; *Dublin Chronicle*, 17 June 1788; *Clonmel Gazette*, 1 Sept. 1790.

85 E. M. Johnston-Liik, *History of the Irish Parliament, 1692–1800* (6 Volumes, Belfast: Ulster Historical Foundation, 2002), v, pp.316–17; *Cork Gazette*, 15 Nov. 1794; *Hibernian Journal*, 12 Nov. 1794; *Dublin Evening Post*, 11 Nov. 1794.

86 *Pue's Occurrences*, 9 Aug. 1718, 10 Mar. 1733; *Dublin Evening Post*, 10 Aug. 1734; Rowena Dudley, *The Irish Lottery, 1780–1801* (Dublin: Four Courts Press, 2005), pp.100–02; *Dublin Gazette*, 18 Oct. 1740; *Faulkner's Dublin Journal*, 11 July 1741; *Hibernian Journal*, 21 Aug. 1775, 19 Aug. 1776; *Volunteer Evening Press*, 30 Oct. 1784; *Dublin Chronicle*, 21 June 1788, 6 Mar. 1790, 7 July, 1 Oct. 1791, 15 May 1792; *Freeman's Journal*, 22 Dec. 1789, 4 Oct. 1810; *Ennis Chronicle*, 31 Jan. 1818.

87 *Dublin Gazette*, 29 May, 5 June 1742, 14 May 1765; *Universal Advertiser*, 5 Feb. 1757; *Dublin Morning Post*, 30 Oct. 1784; *Dublin Morning Post*, 30 Oct. 1784; *Clonmel Gazette*, 2 June 1788; *Freeman's Journal*, 27 Oct. 1789; *Anthologia Hibernica*, 3 (1794), p.74.

88 See *Dublin Intelligence*, 8 Nov. 1726; *Dublin Daily Post*, 12 Feb. 1739; *Dublin Gazette*, 8 Dec. 1739; *Finn's Leinster Journal*, 14 Aug. 1776; *Dublin Chronicle*, 7, 26 Aug. 1788, 4 Aug. 1781 (for references to suicide and alcohol); *Finn's Leinster Journal*, 28 Sept. 1774;

Dublin Chronicle, 27 Mar. 1790; *Dublin Weekly Journal*, 11 Dec. 1790; *Clonmel Gazette*, 29 Dec. 1790; *Freeman's Journal*, 24 Nov. 1798 (for suicide and gambling); and *Dublin Chronicle*, 5 Feb. 1791 (for suicide and prostitution).

89 Watts, *A defense against the temptation to self-murther*, pp.37–9, 113–38; *Freeman's Journal*, 14 Apr. 1791; *Dublin Morning Post*, 6 Jan. 1785.

90 *Freeman's Journal*, 30 Sept. 1779; *Hibernian Journal*, 23 Sept. 1789.

91 For examples of unplanned suicide, see *Dublin Gazette*, 23 Oct. 1733; *Dublin Courant*, 25 Apr. 1747; *Dublin Mercury*, 17 Mar. 1767; *Pue's Occurrences*, 17 Mar. 1767; *Dublin Chronicle*, 26 Sept. 1789, 20 Mar. 1790.

92 The phrase, by Dalia A. Muller, features in her review of Louis A. Pérez, Jr, *To Die in Cuba: Suicide and Society* (Chapel Hill: University of North Carolina Press, 2005) in *Social History*, 3 (2006), p.376.

93 See, for example, *Dublin Intelligence*, 19 Feb. 1726; *Pue's Occurrences*, 14 Aug. 1736, 7 Aug. 1759; *Dublin Courant*, 8 Nov. 1746; *Universal Advertiser*, 28 Feb. 1756, 21 June 1760; *Freeman's Journal*, 23 Jan. 1768; *Finn's Leinster Journal*, 15 Apr. 1775; *Hibernian Journal*, 1 Mar. 1776, 13 Oct. 1780; *Dublin Chronicle*, 25 Oct. 1788; *Clonmel Gazette*, 20 Sept. 1794.

94 *Munster Journal*, 30 Nov. 1749; *Public Gazetteer*, 22 Apr. 1766; *Hibernian Journal*, 19 July 1773, 25 May 1795.

95 *Dublin Newsletter*, 14 Feb. 1738; *Dublin Gazette*, 14 Feb. 1738.

96 *Pue's Occurrences*, 6 Jan. 1747; *Dublin Courant*, 6, 10 Jan. 1747. Another case in point is that of Thomas Beach, the author of *Eugenio, or virtuous and happy life: a poem* (London, 1737), who cut his throat on 17 May 1737. Though the coroner's jury's verdict was 'lunacy', Beach left a note in which he observed that his suicide 'was not the effect of any discontent about his temporal affairs nor desperation; that he had a horrid gloom on his spirits by which his life was become a burthen to him'. He had, he went on, often asked God to take his life, but God not having obliged, he determined to do so himself to relieve him 'from insupportable misery': see Isaac Reed, 'Memoranda Relating to the Fashions, Manners and Customs of the Times' (Folger Shakespeare Library, Washington, M.b.37 pp.67–8).

97 *Pue's Occurrences*, 31 Dec. 1757; *Dublin Mercury*, 28 Feb. 1767; *Hibernian Journal*, 12 June 1780; *Volunteer Evening Post*, 15 Nov. 1785.

98 *Faulkner's Dublin Journal*, 19 Feb. 1726; *Dublin Evening Post*, 29 Apr. 1735; *Pue's Occurrences*, 16 July 1768; *Finn's Leinster Journal*, 24 July 1779; *Volunteer Evening Post*, 9 Sept. 1784, 16 June 1785; *Dublin Chronicle*, 24 June 1788; *Hibernian Journal*, 5 Nov. 1790; *Freeman's Journal*, 21 Sept. 1784, 18 Sept. 1788.

99 M. Dutton, *The office and authority of sheriffs ... and coroners* (Dublin: S. Powell, 1721), p.110; Houston, *Punishing the Dead?*, pp.16, 333.

100 *Faulkner's Dublin Journal*, 27 Dec. 1732.

101 John Butterly, a hawker of pamphlets and newspapers, who drowned himself in the river Liffey was adjudged 'accessory to his own death' (*Faulkner's Dublin Journal*, 13 Jan. 1759; *Public Gazetteer*, 13 Jan. 1759).

102 William Rowley, *A treatise on female, nervous, hysterical, hypochondrical, bilious, convulsive diseases; apoplexy and palsy. With thoughts on madness, suicide etc ...* (London, 1788), p.343.

103 Richard Caulfield, *Corporation Book of Cork* (Guilford: J. Billings and sons, 1876), p.705.

104 *Dublin Daily Post*, 27 Jan. 1739.

105 *Pue's Occurrences*, 20 Jan. 1733; *Universal Advertiser*, 19 Feb. 1754.

106 *Pue's Occurrences*, 16 July 1754.

107 *Universal Advertiser*, 30 July 1754; *Dublin Chronicle*, 27 Oct. 1789.

108 For an enlightening discussion of this, see Houston, *Punishing the Dead?*, pp.268–71; *Dublin Chronicle*, 31 Oct. 1793.

109 Above note 12; Code of Canon Law of the Roman Catholic Church (1917).

110 *Finns' Leinster Journal*, 15 Sept., 2 Oct. 1776.

111 *Pue's Occurrences*, 11 Oct. 1755.

112 *Dublin Gazette*, 26 June, 4 Dec. 1733; *Dublin Daily Advertizer*, 14 Oct. 1736; *Pue's Occurrences*, 11 Oct. 1755; *Dublin Chronicle*, 4 Oct. 1788.

113 *Dublin Daily Post*, 5 Mar. 1740.

114 *Dublin Gazette*, 5 Aug. 1735, 2 Apr. 1765; *Freeman's Journal*, 25 June 1774; Patrick Power, 'A Carrickman's Diary, 1787–1809', *Journal of the Waterford and South-East of Ireland Archaeological Society*, 14 (1911), pp.145–6; Robert Halliday, 'The Roadside Burial of Suicides: an East Anglian Study', *Folklore*, 121:1 (2010), pp.81–93; *Ennis Chronicle*, 26 Sept. 1818. Burial with a stake was outlawed in 1823.

115 Houston, *Punishing the Dead?*, p.335; *DIB sub nom* William Dease.

116 *Dublin Courant*, 14 Aug. 1750; *Munster Journal*, 16 Aug. 1750; *Universal Advertiser*, 28 Aug. 1753.

117 *Freeman's Journal*, 12 Mar. 1765.

118 Caleb Fleming, *A dissertation upon the unnatural crime of self-murder* (London, 1773), p.11 and passim.

119 Fleming, *A dissertation upon the unnatural crime of self-murder*, p.20; John Herries, *An address to the public, on the frequent and enormous crime of suicide* (2nd ed., London, 1781), p.3; *Hoey's Publick Journal*, 16 Aug. 1771.

120 *Hoey's Publick Journal*, 15 Jan. 1772; *Hibernian Journal*, 17 June 1776; *Dublin Chronicle*, 25 Sept. 1788; *Freeman's Journal*, 12 July 1788.

121 Between 1764 and 1771, a variety of proprietary medicines were offered for sale with the promise that they would combat 'hysterics and lowness of spirits', 'disorders of the nerves', 'melancholy' and 'irregular thoughts', and by 'strengthening the nerves' and 'enliven[ing] the spirits' prevent suicide. These included Redmond's Antimonial pills, and Dr Mead's Pills for hysterics and lowness of spirits: *Public Gazetteer*, 3 Jan. 1764; *Hoey's Publick Journal*, 29 Jan. 1760, 6, 13 June 1770, 14 Apr. 1771.

122 See above, p.113–25; Brian Henry, *Dublin Hanged: Crime, Law Enforcement and Punishment in Late Eighteenth-Century Dublin* (Dublin: Irish Academic Press, c.1994), pp.35–6, 211. The rise in suicide was commonly adverted to: see *Dublin Chronicle*, 22 July 1788, 10 Oct. 1789; *Freeman's Journal*, 19 June 1787, 10 Oct. 1789.

123 *Volunteer Evening Post*, 5 Feb. 1785, 29 May 1787; *Dublin Chronicle*, 27 Sept. 1788, 8 Sept. 1791; *Freeman's Journal*, 22 Dec. 1789; *Finn's Leinster Journal*, 23 Dec. 1789; *Dublin Weekly Journal*, 31 July 1790, 22 Jan. 1791.

124 *Dublin Chronicle*, 2 Oct. 1788, 8 Sept., 8 Nov. 1791; *Clonmel Gazette*, 2 Sept. 1788; *Volunteer Evening Post*, 23 June 1787; *Freeman's Journal*, 12 May 1792; *Cork Courier*, 24 Jan. 1795.

125 *Freeman's Journal*, 4 Oct. 1788; *Walker's Hibernian Magazine*, Dec. 1798, pp.530–1.

126 *Dublin Chronicle*, 11 Oct. 1788; *Freeman's Journal*, 10 May 1790; *Volunteer Evening Post*, 5 Feb. 1785. Interestingly, the decision of the authorities in revolutionary France to proscribe 'the barbarous custom of exposing the dead body of a suicide' was reported in Ireland (*Anthologia Hibernica*, 1 (1793), p.159).

127 Rowley, *A treatise on ... suicide*, p.344; *Freeman's Journal*, 24 July 1812.

128 Johnston-Liik, *History of the Irish Parliament*, vi, pp.370–1; *Freeman's Journal*, 25 Sept. 1788; *Clonmel Gazette*, 29 Sept. 1788; *Dublin Chronicle*, 23, 25 Sept. 1788.

129 Johnston-Liik, *History of the Irish Parliament*, v, pp.316–17, vi, p.110; Drennan to McTier, 3 Feb. 1794 in Agnew (ed.), *McTier-Drennan letters*, ii, p.13; above, p.123.

130 Johnston-Liik, *History of the Irish Parliament*, iii, p.519, iv, pp.50, 78; Daniel Beaumont, 'The Gentry of King's and Queen's County: Protestant Landed Society, 1690–1760' (unpublished Ph.D Thesis, TCD, 1999), pp.72–3.

131 *Freeman's Journal*, 26 Aug. 1797; *Walker's Hibernian Magazine*, Oct. 1797, pp.306–08; Lyons (ed.), *The Memoirs of Mrs Leeson*, pp.207–09; *DIB, sub nom* Wogan Browne, and Sir Thomas French; *Finn's Leinster Journal*, 24 Aug. 1822.

132 *Freeman's Journal*, 1 Feb. 1803, 5 Feb., 26 Apr. 1808, 1 Aug. 1810, 31 Aug. 1812, 12 June 1817, 9 Jan., 16 Mar. 1819; *Ennis Chronicle*, 23 Dec. 1818.

133 Dorinda Outram, *The Body and the French Revolution: Sex, Class and Political Culture* (New Haven: Yale University Press, 1989), pp.90–105.

134 Robert Black, *Substance of two Speeches, Delivered of the General Synod of Ulster at its Annual Meeting in 1812* (Belfast, 1812), pp.24, 31.

6

RETHINKING DEATH IN THE YEAR II: THE DECHRISTIANIZATION OF DEATH IN REVOLUTIONARY FRANCE[1]

Joseph Clarke

On 6 germinal year II, Mme Courbet, a 33-year-old widow, was arrested in Étrépagny in the Eure. At the height of the Terror, her offence was a song – something she had sung the day before:

> With bleeding hearts we watch
> Our altars destroyed ...
> Our dead are taken to their graves
> Without a prayer
> They are buried like Huguenots
> To rot in the earth ...

Doubting that a rustic, and a woman at that, could have come up with such verse, and sensing a clerical conspiracy to subvert Reason, the local *comité de surveillance* pressed her as to the real author, but to no avail. Mme Courbet insisted that she had composed the song in protest at the dechristianization that had taken place the previous winter.[2] That dechristianization was largely the work of the Parisian *armée révolutionnaire* as it swept through upper Normandy in late 1793. Even by the exacting standards of the year II, the *armée*'s passage through the Eure was exceptionally violent. Compelling clerics to abdicate or face arrest and converting churches into Temples of Reason, smashing roadside crosses and shrines, and hauling away church bells to be melted down for Republican cannon, the *révolutionnaires*' actions almost provoked 'a civil war' in some districts.[3] For our purposes, the

most immediate effect of the *armée*'s arrival was that it brought Joseph
Fouché's decree dechristianizing the cemetery in its baggage train. Word
of Fouché's dramatic decree, which directed that civic officials rather
than the clergy should conduct funerals, and that the slogan 'Death is
an Eternal Sleep' should replace all religious imagery in the cemeteries,
spread throughout France that winter.[4] With few priests on hand to
perform the last rites and still fewer churches functioning anywhere in
France by the spring of 1794, the business of dying was very rapidly
and very thoroughly stripped of all religious significance in the space
of about six months. Mme Courbet's bitter lament was one response
to what death had come to mean in a dechristianized republic.

Almost exactly a year later, Gaspard Delamelle published his
reflections on his mother's funeral in Paris during the Terror.[5] It is a
polished piece of work, more polished certainly than Mme Courbet's
song, but it describes an equally harrowing scene and conveys
equivalent revulsion for the Republic's apparent disregard for the dead.[6]
With its vivid account of drunken porters 'dragging' the dead woman's
body to 'a cesspit called a cemetery', its depiction of a mother's
uncoffined corpse left 'lying in the mire', and its searing sketch of a
civil servant's indifference to a son's loss, Delamelle's testimony was
just as scathing an indictment as Mme Courbet's of the 'scandal and
immorality' of contemporary funerals.[7] More importantly, it is also, for
all its manipulative eloquence, an essentially accurate account of how
the dead were disposed of in the year II, and a steady stream of authors
echoed Delamelle's indignation in the years that followed. Georges
Duval described similarly squalid scenes in the capital's cemeteries; Paul
Bontoux denounced 'the depravity, insensibility and omission of all
decency' seen there as a 'crime', and Jean-François Ducis deplored the
same disregard for the dead in verse:

A cadaver carried by hired hands
Without a cortège, without mourning, advancing alone
One would think he had no family, no friends ...[8]

Beyond the capital, François Etienne described the dead being 'dragged
shamefully through the streets' of Avignon without either priest or
procession to accompany them while in Évreux, again in the Eure, a
private society was formed in 1796 to attend funerals 'on account of
the indecency with which those charged with this mission have
acquitted it'.[9] Despite everything else that divided them, enlightened
Republicans and committed Catholics found common cause after the

Terror in condemning the 'scandal' of corpses carted to cemeteries like 'the carcasses of beasts of burden' and, with a single voice, denounced the 'indignity', and the 'brutality' with which the Republic dealt with its dead.[10] Both public life and private sentiment, it was frequently claimed, were diminished by 'the unseemly state of the cemetery' after the Terror.[11]

Mme Courbet was evidently not alone in her outrage and for that reason her song is as good an introduction as any to the French Revolution's impact on death. Short as it is, her song embodies both the immediacy and the intensity of the rupture that the Terror wrought as the familiar paraphernalia that enveloped death in eighteenth-century France – the funeral masses and processions, the tolling of church bells and crosses on tombstones – were swept aside by the arrival of a *représentant-en-mission* and the iconoclasm of the *armées révolutionnaires*. Indeed, the song's very existence, its articulation by an illiterate peasant woman in a remote Norman backwater, illustrates the extent to which this transformation in the everyday experience of death reached out beyond the cauldrons of Revolutionary political culture – the cities with their radical clubs and militant *sans-culottes* – to towns and villages across the entire country, and brought cultural conflict to cemeteries throughout France on a scale not seen since the wars of religion. Above all, it exemplifies the profound emotional response these changes inspired in communities across France, the sense of desolation and loss that emerge from Mme Courbet's despairing last line: 'to rot in the earth'.

From 1793 onwards, the French cemetery was a bitterly contested space. However, if we can identify parallels between the confessional conflicts of the sixteenth century when Catholics and Protestants frequently targeted one another's cemeteries, and the nineteenth century's culture wars when the 'war of the two Frances' was routinely played out at the graveyard's gates, the events of the 1790s are more than simply an echo of earlier conflicts or an anticipation of antagonisms to come.[12] Rather, death loomed large in Revolutionary politics from the very start. It furnished the Revolution with its most iconic images – David's martyr portraits of *Marat* and *Bara* – and its most resonant slogans. Moreover, the self-dramatizing 'Liberty or Death' was ever-present throughout the year II, and in Gillray's grotesque *sans-culottes* feasting on cadavers and *bonnet-rouge* bedecked skeletons, it fuelled the frenzied nightmares of conservative reaction. More immediately, the politics of death possessed immense political urgency throughout the 1790s. From the crusade to dechristianize death that began during the

Terror to the Napoleonic decree on cemeteries of 23 prairial year XII that finally closed a decade-long debate on the duties the new regime owed the dead, the attempt to redefine what death meant, and to reshape the rites that gave it meaning, was a recurring theme in Revolutionary discourse.[13] At times, the preoccupation with death can appear macabre, and the debates on the immortality of the soul that convulsed the Convention throughout the Terror could seem absurd if the political stakes had not been so high. Robespierre's insistence that the idea of an afterlife was an intrinsically Republican ideal, 'the immortality of the soul is a constant call to justice', like Saint-Just's suggestion that friends should 'dig each other's graves' might seem odd concerns in a wartime cabinet – but these questions went right to the heart of ideological debate and factional conflict in the Republic of Virtue.[14] Dismissing it simply as a fixation, a kind of collective 'necrophilia' as some scholars have done, not only fails to explain it; critically, it does not acknowledge its significance.[15]

Fortunately, other historians, Michel Vovelle, François Lebrun, Philippe Ariès and John McManners especially, have been more insightful in examining eighteenth-century attitudes towards death, and Vovelle's pioneering *Piété Baroque et Déchristianisation en Provence au XVIIIe Siècle*, in particular, has done much to define the terms of this discussion.[16] For Vovelle, and for many who have followed him, death was gradually dechristianized over the eighteenth century, and this long-term trend paved the way, at least in part, for the more explosive experience of the Revolutionary decade.[17] Even more promisingly, this secularization parallels the emergence of an increasingly scientific discourse of death and these two trends eventually culminated in the displacement of the dead, by royal decree in 1776, from medieval churchyards like the Saints-Innocents in central Paris to well-ventilated cemeteries on the outskirts of the city.[18] As the Enlightenment advanced, it seemed the educated public was no longer willing to invest either the time or the money once lavished on preparing for the good death of the *ars moriendi*, just as it was no longer inclined to tolerate the presence of the dead in its midst. In a 'total rupture with Christian tradition', death had become a subject of scientific study rather than religious reflection, and the dead had become something profoundly 'other', a source of contagion rather than a subject for contemplation, fit only, in the end, to be 'exiled' from view.[19]

This is still an influential body of literature.[20] And yet, for all the attention lavished on the evolution of elite attitudes towards death, this scholarship seems preoccupied with asserting the simple fact of change at the expense of exploring either its potential complexity or the continuities concealed beneath this apparent caesura. Studies of secularization seem too ready to downplay the resistance, up to and including rioting, that initiatives to relocate cemeteries provoked in some cities in the 1780s, and too ready to discount the immense sales that traditional devotional literature still commanded on the eve of the Revolution.[21] If these authors seem too keen to marginalize the 100,000 copies that preparations for death such as *L'Ange Conducteur* or *Pensez-y-bien* sold during the 1780s alone in favour of the century's racier 'forbidden bestsellers', they seem equally disinclined to consider the ritual world these works' readers occupied. Across much of France, the duties of the living towards the dead continued to define popular religious culture throughout the eighteenth century, and the ceremonies that expressed that sense of social and spiritual responsibility resisted the onset of secularization more tenaciously than any other religious practice.[22] Old habits died hard in rural France but they could be just as resilient in those crucibles of modernity, the bookshops of Paris, where John Quincy Adams was stunned to see 'everybody in the shop, but myself' falling to their knees as a priest bearing 'le bon dieu' to a dying parishioner passed by in March 1785.[23] There is very little indication of indifference here, and the evidence for sweeping secularization, as opposed to more mundane anticlericalism, seems just as slender in the scuffles that broke out in one Parisian parish in September 1789 when the *curé* refused to bury a local labourer.[24] Even as the Revolution began, events such as these, like the requiem masses held throughout the capital to honour those who died at the Bastille that summer, bear witness to the significance ordinary Parisians still attached to ensuring that the dead were given their customary due.[25] French Catholicism was certainly evolving but for all the changes in funerary culture that historians have identified under the *ancien régime*, and many of these involved the style as distinct from the substance of religious belief, continuity rather than change may well have been the chief characteristic of eighteenth-century attitudes towards death.

If studies of secularization in the eighteenth century have tended to stress cultural change more so than the stability that underlay it, this may be because the scholarship has been defined by two over-arching ideas. The first is the rather teleological assumption that Revolutionary dechristianization was not a contingency borne of specific political conflicts in the 1790s but possessed clearly defined, and quantifiable, cultural origins; the second is the premise that secularization is the logical corollary of the modernization process itself. Quite where this sub-Weberian process of disenchantment leaves Mme Courbet and her kind, the vast majority of French men and women who, as Le Bras argued, continued to 'believe and pray without a shadow of doubt or slackening' throughout the eighteenth century is unclear but this is not a problem that has ever unduly troubled studies of the 'secularization of the European mind'.[26] Margaret Anderson may be correct when she observed that this grand narrative of religious decline owed as much to 'the secularization of scholarship in the twentieth-century' as it did to the evolution of earlier societies but more recent scholarship is less in thrall to the sociological certainties, or ideological imperatives, of the 1960s and 1970s.[27] 'Religion', as Jonathan Sheehan recently declared, 'is back' on the historians' agenda and accordingly, a re-evaluation of the relationship between death and dechristianization in Revolutionary France seems somewhat overdue.[28]

At first, the Revolution's impact on the relationship between the living and the dead was limited. In principle, the National Assembly's decision to place all ecclesiastical property 'at the disposal of the nation' in November 1789 brought the nation's churchyards effectively under secular control but, in practice, the cemetery remained a predominantly parochial concern in 1790.[29] However, the measure did pave the way for the Assembly's decision to embark upon a far-reaching reform of the French Church and the rupture to which this gave rise brought conflict to cemeteries on a scale not seen since the Wars of Religion. The Civil Constitution of the Clergy, and more particularly the oath imposed upon all priests in November 1790, shattered the Revolutionary consensus. It split French Catholicism in two, and the schism rapidly spilled over into parish life as rival clergies wrestled for control of their congregations and command of their ceremonial spaces.[30] Where constitutional clerics were seen as interlopers or even worse, as heretics, parishes split, frequently spurning the 'intrus' and the sacraments they performed in favour of the refractory priests they had replaced.[31] The resulting scuffles over who should perform a baptism or administer absolution embittered parish politics to an unprecedented extent, but beyond these local skirmishes, this schism's consequences were immense. Increasingly weary of having to prop up constitutional clerics who commanded scant respect in the countryside and sparse congregations in the towns, the Revolutionary elites disengaged from their too troublesome clergy from 1791 onwards. Eager to disentangle themselves from the complexities of the religious question, and increasingly amenable to the shrill anticlericalism of the Parisian press, it was not long before the new regime assumed full control of the last preserve of the priest, the custody of the dead.

On 13 August 1792, just three days after the *journée* that ended France's brief experiment with constitutional monarchy, Paris' insurrectionary Commune embarked on the sweeping secularization of funerary practice in the capital. Ostensibly, these reforms aimed to extend 'the reign of equality' to every sphere of life, but the new rules governing funerals were explicitly anticlerical as well.[32] Insisting that 'every idea of superstition and fanaticism must be destroyed and replaced by the sentiments of a sound philosophy', the new code curbed the presence of priests in funeral cortèges and even banned mortuary drapes at requiem masses, and the Legislative Assembly soon followed suit, applying and extending the campaign nationwide.[33] By 20 September, when the Legislative Assembly disbanded, the parish councils that administered funerals were dissolved, the confraternities that attended them were suppressed, and the priests who presided over them were forbidden from appearing in public in clerical attire. Even more decisively, in one of its last acts, the Assembly transferred the registration of births, marriages and deaths from the parish to the municipality.[34] The laicization of *l'état civil* on 20 September 1792 radically redefined the legal framework, and the personnel, governing the nation's rites of passage. Dismissed from his place as the custodian of parish memory and indispensable officiant in public ceremony, the code reduced the priest to little more than an auxiliary, an optional and increasingly inconspicuous accessory in the ceremonial life of the community.

The Republican revolution of August 1792 inaugurated a sweeping secularization of civic life that would define Revolutionary politics for a decade to come. And yet, that barrage of legislation was simply the first salvo in a campaign that climaxed when dechristianization began in earnest a year later. That campaign's causes are complex, but the impact of religious schism, the links between refractory clerics and Counter-Revolution in the Vendée, and the association between the clergy and federalist revolt elsewhere all contributed to the growing conviction in 1793 that Revolutionary politics and the religion of the priests could no longer be reconciled. In June, a former Capuchin, François Chabot, elicited rapturous applause when he urged the Jacobins to 'cut the roots of superstition. Say openly that the priests are your enemies'.[35] In the months that followed, radicals seized on his counsel and set about the systematic 'eradication of Catholic religious practice, and Catholicism itself'.[36] Dechristianization has many possible starting points. The desecration of the royal tombs at Saint-Denis in August can be pointed to, but the movement only really took off following Fouché's decree replacing 'all religious signs' with the slogan

'Death is an Eternal Sleep' in the cemeteries of the Nièvre on 10 October.[37] Convinced, like all good Enlightened atheists, that the clergy owed its dominion to the uneducated's fear of damnation, Fouché's decree aimed to dispel that fear by abolishing the very idea of an afterlife and erasing all trace of the symbols and ceremonies that represented it. In declaring death the absolute end of all things, this decree made God, and the clergy who claimed to speak in His name, effectively redundant and this striking synthesis of materialist atheism and militant anticlericalism captured the radical imagination throughout the Republic in the months that followed.

The Convention never fully embraced dechristianization as its official policy. Many deputies were distinctly uneasy about its implications, and an increasingly anxious Robespierre thundered that 'atheism is aristocratic' from 21 November on.[38] Yet this did little to stop the movement spreading like wildfire, especially after Pierre Chaumette brought Fouché's decree back to Paris in late October.[39] The following month, plans were laid to raise statues of *Sleep* in the capital's cemeteries and an entirely secularized funeral ceremony was put in place, complete with tricolour-draped litters borne by porters in *bonnets rouges*.[40] Beyond Paris, it was more often than not the representatives-on-mission and *armées révolutionnaires* that carried Fouché's message into the regions. In early November, Dartigoeyte, one of the deputies charged with suppressing federalism in the southwest, boasted that Fouché's decree had been 'welcomed everywhere with enthusiasm' and promptly applied this 'sage and philosophical' policy across four Gascon departments.[41] Dartigoeyte was one of the Convention's most enthusiastic priest-baiters, and he went on to implement an identical policy in Toulouse in 1794, but even more moderate deputies followed Fouché's lead.[42] In late November, Couthon extended Fouché's decree into the Puy-de-Dôme and, in December, Jeanbon Saint-André did the same throughout the Manche.[43] Antoine Albitte applied Fouché's decree across the Ain in January, and his example was followed a fortnight later by Faure in the Moselle and the Meurthe.[44] In March, Etienne Maignet's plans for the cemeteries of the Bouches-du-Rhône and the Vaucluse were more ambitious still. Ordering the destruction of all crosses and statues still standing in the departments' churchyards, he stipulated that the slogan: 'Silence, they sleep' should take their place in these newly named 'Fields of Rest'.[45] Throughout the spring, identical decrees echoed across the Republic as wave after wave of Montagnard deputies, many of them (like Fouché) former priests, arrived in the provinces intent on exterminating all trace of 'the ecclesiastical vermin' from French soil.[46]

The representatives-on-mission led the charge against 'fanaticism and superstition', but sometimes the drive to dechristianize a district or even department came from within.[47] In October, the departmental authorities in Châlons imposed Fouché's formula across the Marne, and on 26 November, their colleagues in the Haut-Rhin followed suit, stripping the department's cemeteries of all religious symbols and ordering that all citizens, regardless of class or creed, should now be buried under a sign inscribed 'Equality'.[48] Elsewhere, individual communes, *commissaires civils* or *sociétés populaires* took the lead in secularizing their cemeteries and revolutionizing the rites that took place within them. In Montargis in the Loiret, Vierzon in the Cher, Verneuil in the Haute-Vienne, and Dieppe in Normandy, the initiative came from the local authorities as town councils, often spurred on by their *sociétés populaires*, ordered the removal of crosses and prohibited religious ceremonies in cemeteries in the name of 'universal morality'.[49] The communes and clubs all played some part in revolutionizing the last rites, but in the final analysis, as Richard Cobb remarked, 'dechristianization was an affair of the proconsuls'.[50] They provided its inspiration and they possessed the authority and the armed force, and Republican regeneration generally arrived well-armed, to see that the churches were closed, the crosses torn down and the cemeteries secularized.

It is, of course, difficult to measure how effective these edicts were. The representatives-on-mission were, by their nature, birds of passage, and despite their often-extravagant assessments of their achievements, they were also aware that their work could be easily undone after they moved on. As Roux-Fazillac observed in December 1793, it was much easier to pass decrees than to see them executed, and this was especially so when it came to establishing a new symbolic system for the French to live, and die, by.[51] For all the deputies' designs for edifying inscriptions and sombre sculptures, few of these were ever actually raised beyond the big cities and even there, Revolutionary statues tended to be impermanent affairs, wood and plaster expedients awaiting the war's end to assume a more durable form. In practical terms, the secularization of Republican space was much more successful in destroying the old symbolic order than in constructing a new one. But in the countryside, even this iconoclastic impact was sometimes in doubt. When François Mallarmé arrived in Toulouse two months after the Terror ended, he was shocked to see, despite Dartigoeyte's best efforts six months before, crosses still standing on graves throughout the Haute-Garonne, and he ordered their immediate destruction.[52] Jacques Pelletier encountered the same problem and ordered an identical solution in the Doubs in brumaire year III. The survival of these crosses is suggestive in two senses.[53] With so many other demands on their time, deputies could only devote so much attention to dechristianizing the countryside and, beyond their urban citadels, much of their work remained unfinished when the Terror ended in the summer of 1794. More significantly perhaps, the fact that crosses were spared on gravestones throughout the Haute-Garonne and the Doubs, and Heinrich Meister noted the same thing as he made his way from Nancy to Paris in 1795, suggests also some of the self-imposed constraints on Revolutionary iconoclasm.[54] While few militants entertained qualms about tearing crucifixes down from altars or roadside shrines, the reluctance to interfere with crosses in cemeteries implies, if not a residual respect for religion, then at least the wariness many *révolutionnaires* still felt when called upon to desecrate the place of their dead.

The Revolutionary crusade to reconfigure the cemetery as a Republican space was rarely realized in its fullest sense, and in many places, the campaign continued on well after every other aspect of the Terror came to an end. Dechristianization's impact on the nation's churchyards was more often destructive than constructive; but even so, its legacy endured long after the Terror, especially in terms of the ceremonial void it left behind. The crosses, statues and church bells the *représentants* succeeded in destroying were not easily restored, at least not until after the Concordat came into effect in 1802, and the priests they pressured into abdication or apostasy proved just as hard to replace across much of France. Where the legislation of autumn 1792 had driven the refractory clergy either underground or into exile, and between thirty and forty thousand priests fled France that winter, the dechristianization that followed devastated what remained of the French church.[55] Up to 20,000 clerics abdicated or abjured the priesthood, perhaps 6,000 married, and almost 3,000 were executed during the Terror.[56] Faced with arrest or worse, many more simply abandoned their parishes. Some clerics continued their ministry clandestinely, and nineteenth-century hagiographers revelled in reports of venerable pastors braving the wrath of the Republic to say mass in secret or covertly to bless the condemned on their way to the guillotine; but in practice, the majority did not. Estimates vary, but probably fewer than 200 of France's 40,000 churches openly celebrated Easter in 1794 and the effective cessation of religious practice had a very immediate effect on the way the dead were dealt with in the new Republic.[57]

On 1 March 1794, just as Jacques Frémanger launched a series of 'violent shocks against fanaticism' in the Calvados, the *curé* of Bellengreville, an inconsequential little commune about ten miles from Caen, was arrested as he buried one of his congregation in the churchyard.[58] Citizen Bacheley wore his vestments in public and he was to spend six months in prison as a result, only emerging when the jails started emptying after Thermidor. Bacheley's arrest, at gunpoint, before the open grave of one of his parishioners, might seem a slightly sensational example of how suddenly the everyday experience of death could come to a crashing halt during the Terror, but it is not. As the *déprêtrisation* campaign intensified that spring, similar scenes were played out in equally obscure settings across the Republic, and the consequences could be just as unsettling. Within a month of his arrival in the Lot, for example, Jean-Baptiste Bô boasted to his colleagues in Paris that there was scarcely one priest left in place in the department by mid-March.[59] For all its overstatement, and Bô was given to bluster, this claim rang true in the tiny village of Bégoux where the *curé*, under pressure from the authorities in Cahors, abruptly resigned his post after Sunday mass on 2 March and disappeared. A few days later, his church was stripped of its silverware and shut down and, when a local boy died shortly afterwards he became, according to the shocked entry in Michel Célarié's diary, 'the first to be buried in the cemetery without catholic ceremony'.[60] Célarié was a good revolutionary, but his diary's catalogue of children unbaptized and family and friends buried unblessed from March 1794 on, and this included his own wife in 1795, is evidence of dechristianization's intense and enduring impact, even in the remotest corners of the French countryside. In less than a year, a burial without benefit of clergy had become the norm throughout France.

In the clergy's absence, and this was undoubtedly dechristian-ization's most dramatic legacy, few Terrorists gave very much thought as to what should take the place of the religious rites, 'the pusillanimous practices' they had proscribed in the nation's cemeteries.[61] The thinking behind the slogan: 'Death is an Eternal Sleep' or the banner that preceded funeral processions in Paris: 'The just man never dies, he lives in the memory of his fellow citizens' was obvious, but elsewhere it was rarely this clear what idea of the afterlife, if any, underpinned the Republic's rites.[62] Having prohibited priests from participating in funerals in frimaire, Jeanbon Saint-André's decree never specified what 'the form of civil burial' he envisioned actually involved and many other decrees were equally ambiguous.[63] For all the energy the *révolutionnaires* devoted to dismantling the ceremonial conventions that encompassed death in eighteenth-century France – conventions last codified in Paul V's *Rituale Romanum* of 1614 – their ability to envisage any meaningful alternative, in the year II at least, rarely extended beyond instructing the officials charged with burying the dead to wear a *bonnet rouge* or tricolour sash.[64] Even in Marseille, where Maignet's decree was more detailed than most, the ritual to be followed in this newly secularized space remained uncertain. Aside from commanding that corpses be covered with a tricolour on their way to the cemetery, Maignet had little to say about what should take place in his 'Fields of Rest' once the dead arrived. Having 'expressly forbidden priests to be present', he simply stipulated that funerals 'should be the same for all, and entirely detached from any ceremony that might recall religious ideas'.[65] Whereas the Avignon edition of the *Rituale Romanum* devoted forty detailed pages to the liturgy of the dead in 1783, that single line constitutes the sum of the ceremonial set down for the Vaucluse a decade later.[66]

Most of these pronouncements were just as sketchy but some *révolutionnaires* were more inventive. In the Calvados, Honfleur's *société populaire* proposed a new kind of funeral rite in nivôse year II, a ritual designed to 'dismiss the memory of the ridiculous ceremonies which vanity and superstition once observed'.[67] These regulations deserve to be quoted at length:

> The commune will furnish six capes in black serge (large enough to suit all sizes) and six large mourning ribbons; the six closest relatives of the deceased will each wear one of these capes and attach the ribbons around the band of a three cornered hat; they will place this hat on their heads in such a manner that the ribbon, which will be at least a foot in width, covers their backs and falls a little below the belt. Their hair will be neither powdered nor tied up ... [B]efore the cortège leaves, the six closest relatives will don their capes and stand before the door of the deceased's house to receive the friends who arrive, who will abstain from offering all condolences. The six men in black capes will only respond to their salutations with a slight nod, without uncovering their heads; silence alone will express their grief. Every citizen who is to form the cortège having assembled, they will then march two by two in close order, in silence and at an orderly pace, preceded by the six men in black capes who will follow immediately after the corpse, to the burial ground, from whence they shall return to the deceased's house in the same

manner. There, they will stand before the deceased's house, facing the road, holding their hats with both hands on their stomachs ... and their heads bare. They will nod in recognition to those who have accompanied them from whom they will doubtless receive salutations.

The ceremony having ended, everyone will retire at once, without seeking either to enter the house of the deceased or to loiter in the road to exchange vain condolences ... For children up to the age of fourteen, two relatives and five or six mourners should suffice. This method, entailing no expense, can without difficulty be adopted by all citizens without distinction ...

In its ostentatious affordability and emotional asceticism, this careful choreography of ceremony, clothing and even bodily conduct served two immediate purposes. While explicitly intended to erase the social inequalities that centuries of flamboyant funeral services had expressed, this new rite aimed to instruct as well as to undo. In proposing the same 'honourable and decent' end for all, this Spartan ceremonial was intended to inculcate the egalitarian simplicity and sombre self-restraint expected of all good citizens in the Republic of Virtue. And yet, if this ceremony was conceived as a vehicle for political ideology, it aimed to achieve a more explicitly moral agenda as well. In completely recasting the ceremonial space and recalibrating every detail of the individual's actions and appearance before the prospect of death, this rite was intended to internalize a new experience and, by implication, a new understanding of what death meant in a dechristianized world. If, as John McManners argues, 'the Catholic liturgy of death was a blend of hope and menace' this ceremony's austere economy of emotion and expression is its very antithesis.[68] In its stoicism, its silence even, there can be neither faith in redemption nor fear of damnation, merely an unflinching acceptance of the absolute finality of death. Where other *révolutionnaires* struggled to find a ritual language to represent Fouché's 'Death is an Eternal Sleep', this ceremony seems, in every sense, its logical conclusion.

As the politics of regeneration progressively invaded every aspect of private life, the authorities aimed to redefine what death meant for both the citizen and for society as a whole. Yet, for all its ambition, the absences it entailed seem more significant than any of its innovations. At the height of the Terror, the clergy's expulsion was inevitable, but with them went the penitential confraternities and tradesmen's corporations that had accompanied so many funerals in the past. Both

155

organizations had displayed an almost 'obsessive concern with funerals for their members', and many confraternities existed for no other reason than to attend deathbeds and escort the corpses of the poor to the grave; but both had been abolished in 1792.[69] There was no place here for the conventional displays of collective identity and social solidarity that had defined a 'decent funeral' under the *ancien régime*. Women, too, seem equally absent from this unequivocally gendered cast of municipal officials and male mourners-in-chief. Where previously women had occupied centre-stage in caring for the dying and preparing the dead for their final journey, there was no obvious role for them here.[70] In the new regime, mourning was evidently men's business and perhaps in reflection of this, the most striking aspect of this idealized etiquette is its silence, not simply the strictly ordained silence of the mourners, but the silence of the space around them as well. There is no singing here, no *Libera* or *De Profundis* to accompany the funeral mass or march, no sobbing at the graveside and no chattering in the tavern afterwards. However much the Counter-Reformation clergy looked askance at the wakes that 'brought people together', and even the sternest cleric grudgingly accepted their inevitability, there is no compromise with customary codes of sociability here.[71] As Honfleur's regulations explicitly command, there will be no 'loitering' following the funeral, no 'vain condolences' in the cabaret afterwards.

Above all, there were no bells. From the handbell that preceded the priest as he carried the *viaticum* to the dying, and the knell that told that death had come, to the tolling that marked the time of the funeral, the sound of bells accompanied every aspect of death under the *ancien régime*. In both town and countryside, the death knell was an instantly comprehensible code, a clear means of distinguishing the sudden loss from the expected end and of determining the age and sex of the deceased. Perhaps most significantly, it did all of this in the subtle gradations of a rhythm that was unique to every parish. In this sense, *la sonnerie* did not just summon the congregation together but defined the community of the living and the dead in a uniquely resonant way.[72] By the summer of 1794, however, there were few bells left to toll; most had already been requisitioned for cannon or now lay buried, hidden from the Republic's rapacious view. In the Ain, for instance, Albitte claimed to have emptied every church-tower by February 1794; the Moselle alone sent some 800 bells to the foundries in *an II*, and, nationally, some 50,000 tons of church bells were melted down during the Terror.[73] This was enough to silence many parishes and even entire districts for decades to come. Of all the Republic's innovations, this was one of the most widely resented and the most frequently resisted. As one clergyman in Caen noted in 1795, his congregation longed 'to hear the sound of church bells again and they say that it is the Convention's will that no-one should tyrannise them any more'.[74] The implication was clear. In a world where a burial in silence had always been a stigma attached to suicides, heretics and unrepentant sinners, a prelude to damnation in effect, to deny the death knell could only be the work of a tyrant.

For this priest's parishioners, as for Mme Courbet, dechristianization demeaned their dead and a Republican funeral, however 'honourable and decent' it might seem, could only ever be a source of shame. It is small wonder then that the secularization of cemeteries and the descent of church bells encountered such widespread and varied resistance, even during the Terror when resisting the Republic was an especially foolhardy thing to do. The opposition dechristianization provoked in 1793–4 has never received the sustained study it deserves.[75] And yet, at its most intense, the defence of a graveyard cross or church bell often involved the resort to arms. The official correspondence of the year II is littered with reports of threatening mobs and armed assemblies mobilizing in defence of the symbols that shaped the contours of the community in customary culture: in the Yonne, the *armée révolutionnaire*'s 'excess of zeal' in tearing down crosses everywhere they found them provoked wholesale riots in several rural communes in November 1793; and the Cher, in close proximity to the epicentre of Fouché's campaign in Nevers, witnessed similar disturbances throughout December.[76] In the village of Argent, for example, two *commissaires*' attempts to eradicate all signs of religious worship provoked 'a real riot' on Christmas Eve and order was only restored after the unfortunate officials signed a document authorizing the villagers to keep their crosses, and 'the *curé* to convey the dead to the cemetery and the free exercise of their faith as in the past'.[77] Once that was conceded, the crowd dispersed but violence erupted that very week in nearby Villequieurs when an armed mob attacked the local authorities screaming: 'We want our religion and we will die to defend it'.[78]

Such disorders were not necessarily counter-revolutionary although they were sometimes confused. In January 1794, 'a large assembly' in Artonne broke up the municipality's attempts to celebrate 'Herod's law' in their former church with cries of 'we want the republic but we want our religion too'.[79] There was no contradiction between religious practice and Revolutionary patriotism here but, in general, it suited the authorities to represent these riots as 'liberticide uprisings' requiring immediate and exemplary repression.[80] In the Loire, for example, rioting broke out repeatedly as churches were closed and cemeteries secularized across the department in December. Feurs, Chazelles and Saint-Germain-Laval all experienced serious disturbances that month but in Belmont, the disorder degenerated into a stand-off when an angry mob of women occupied the cemetery in protest against the 'religion of goats' that was being foisted upon them.[81] Riots and armed assemblies like this erupted sporadically throughout the year II, but while these episodes were eye-catching, they were exceptional, chiefly because the consequences were almost always the same. Whatever compromise a beleaguered local official might concede in the short-term, violent resistance to authority inevitably provoked a stern response during the Terror and Belmont's experience is exemplary in this respect. After enduring the women's sit-in in the cemetery for several days, the Mayor finally called in the National Guards from nearby Thizy to deal with his cantankerous *concitoyennes*. Sticks and stones were no match for the Guards' rifles and after several volleys of gunfire, the assembly was dispersed and the ringleaders taken for trial.[82]

The open recourse to arms to reopen a chapel, restore a cross in a cemetery or ring a church bell would become a commonplace after the Terror.[83] Official complaints that 'everyone is fanaticised here ... they replant crosses and retake the temples' rang out across the Calvados from the year III onwards while 'the loutish, barbarous and fanatical' population of the Haute-Loire baffled, and frequently butchered, Republican officials in defence of their 'bloodthirsty priests' throughout the late 1790s.[84] The Directory was dogged by its inability to control the countryside, but during the Terror, when radical resolve was backed up by impressive force, this kind of open defiance was much less common. In place of outright opposition, and all the risks it entailed, rural communities resorted instead to what Scott describes as 'the weapons of the weak' when confronting what appeared to be authority's unreasonable demands.[85] Where armed resistance seemed doomed to fail in the year II, feigned ignorance, foot-dragging and false compliance were the order of the day instead. Some, it seems, simply tried to ignore the new order of things. In February 1794, for example, André Bernard was outraged to find priests still presiding over funerals in Franche-Comté 'with their crosses, candles and lugubrious croaking' and ordered their immediate arrest and the removal of the authorities that had permitted this offence against Reason.[86] Such complaints were common in early 1794 but as more *représentants* and *agents nationaux* fanned out across France that year, obstructionism became increasingly difficult, and alternative strategies had to be deployed.

Some tried to reach an accommodation with the authorities. In March 1794, for instance, the commune of Chapelles petitioned Paris seeking an exemption from Albitte's edict ordering the removal of all church bells on the grounds that a mountainous frontier community needed its bell to sound the alarm in case of *émigré* attack. The matter was referred back to Albitte who refused this 'fatal deal with fanaticism' because the community had already asked him to spare its bells as 'they wished to live and die in the faith of their fathers'.[87] Where an attempt at negotiation failed, and negotiations almost always failed with men like Albitte, an outward show of orthodoxy probably seemed a more sensible option. Well after Maignet had decreed the secularization of cemeteries in the Vaucluse, the Jacobins of Jonquières were still plaintively seeking an explanation as to what they were supposed to do with their churchyard.[88] The terms of Maignet's decree had been abundantly clear but Jonquières' churchyard still remained obstinately unreformed and the *sociétaires* sought clarification. However, given their embarrassingly recent enthusiasm for marking Republican solemnities with special masses, not to mention the *société*'s warm welcome for the restoration of religious freedom a year later, this apparent anxiety to conform seems suspect at best.[89] Pragmatism rather than principle probably dictated this kind of calculating conformity and it should certainly not be confused with any genuine conversion to the new orthodoxy. In an increasingly authoritarian order, these village Jacobins were just making sure that they were seen to toe the line, but they did it as slowly and as ineffectually as they dared, and this procrastination suggests that they had little real stomach for overseeing the secularization of their own churchyard.

Obfuscation, evasion and the appearance of orthodoxy might delay the inevitable but in practice there was very little anyone could do to hold the tide of Terror back. Once a priest was arrested or abdicated, the administration of the last rites and the celebration of the funeral mass effectively ceased, and the grim reality that Mme Courbet decried descended across much of France. Confronted by the prospect of seeing their own dead dispatched with the same humiliating lack of respect that French Protestants had been forced to endure for well over a century, one final form of resistance remained. As French Catholicism was driven steadily underground, the anxiety to maintain a respectable ritual minimum in the community's dealings with the dead sometimes saw the laity step into the void left by its priests. Accounts of lay-led masses and funeral services surface in a whole range of settings throughout the Terror and beyond, and women, as Olwen Hufton notes,

159

often led the way. In the Haute-Loire, for example, lay sisters, the *béates*, tried to ensure some continuity with the customary past by baptizing newborns and burying the dead with religious rites, often at night and with armed support – and this kind of surrogate ceremonial was common in the Doubs too.[90] Some kind of religious life survived in parts of the Yonne also where Canon Duplessis noted that 'couples were married and the dead buried according to Catholic rites although the *curé* was absent while incarcerated' in *an II*, and the practice continued in places long afterwards.[91] In 1796, 'dry masses' were still being said by proxy priests, school-teachers and sacristans in the Vaucluse, 'elderly celibates' in the Haute-Garonne, and even inn-keepers in the countryside around Compiègne, as communities struggled to fulfil their duties to the dead despite their clergy's absence.[92]

In one town after another, from the Ain to the Vaucluse, the Republican regeneration of the last rites was accomplished 'with weapons in hand'.[93] And yet, the popular reaction this unexpected rupture in the social and cultural order provoked is hard to reconcile with the steady advance of religious indifference, the gradual 'dechristianization of death' that Vovelle and others have described. On the contrary, the varied forms of resistance dechristianization aroused testify instead to the ongoing attachment vast swathes of the French public felt for their church bells and funeral processions and illustrate the resilience of popular religious culture rather than its decline. However, if the experience of the year II raises questions the conventional narrative of eighteenth-century secularization cannot easily answer, its long-term consequences are equally contentious. According to Richard Cobb, dechristianization left little lasting trace after the Terror. It was, in his view, 'more spectacular than effective' and for all its anarchic energy, 'even iconoclasm was an admission of impotence and failure'.[94] In many respects, Cobb's conclusions seem convincing and the religious revival that followed the Terror would appear to support this verdict. With the laws of 3 ventôse and 11 prairial year III, the Convention grudgingly conceded that the Republic's war against religion could not be won and restored the right to worship. By June 1795, many of the capital's churches had reopened and in the provinces, the public celebration of the mass had resumed in cities like Caen, Évreux and Toulouse by the end of the month.[95] Naturally, the timing of this revival varied according to the availability of a priest and the attitude of the authorities but it was nationwide.[96] By the end of June 1795, even tiny Bégoux had secured the services of a priest from Cahors to say Sunday mass, although its church still lacked a chalice and its steeple remained silent.[97] And yet, even as the churches reopened in 1795 and some semblance of normal service resumed, death remained dechristianized because to all intents and purposes, Fouché's edict remained in effect throughout France long after the Terror ended.

Religious liberty was restored in the year III, but crucially that liberty was never extended to the grave where the ban on 'les signes extérieures du culte' and the prohibition on priests appearing in public outlawed the conduct of anything even remotely resembling a Christian burial for the rest of the 1790s.[98] Admittedly, the reopening of the churches permitted the public celebration of the requiem for the first time in two years, but beyond this, the legislation of the year III made few concessions to the customary culture of death. From the procession of the *viaticum* to the bell-ringing and graveside prayers that traditionally defined a good death, even the most basic elements of a decent funeral remained proscribed by law, and fresh legislation in the year IV copper-fastened the constraints imposed in *an III*.[99] The decision to uphold, and even extend, these restrictions did not go unchallenged, even under the Directory. In July 1796, for example, Jacques-Michel Coupé proposed that the law let 'everyone honour the dead according to their own lights', while Michel Talot demanded the right to 'be buried as he pleased' but both were unceremoniously shouted down in the Councils.[100] The following year, Camille Jordan's call to extend freedom of worship to the cemetery and relax the restrictions on bell-ringing prompted more considered debate but it was ultimately shot down with emotive allusions to the 'fanaticism' of the Vendée and claims that church bells were either a 'useless' ostentation or the clarion call of *chouannerie*.[101] For all the Directory's anxiety to distance itself from the excesses of *an II*, the official conduct of funerals remained, as a result, remarkably consistent after the Terror.[102] Admittedly, the *mise en scène* of the Republican funeral did evolve a little over time. The statues of Sleep that Chaumette had placed in Paris' cemeteries were renamed Immortality, and after lengthy debate, the capital's civil servants acquired black plumes in their hats when attending funerals in the year IV, but neither of these modifications did much to dispel the dismal utilitarianism of the year II.[103] Otherwise, little really changed after the Terror, or as one priest put it bluntly in 1796, 'burials in my parish remain the same as under Robespierre's tyranny'.[104]

Paradoxically perhaps, given Robespierre's opposition to the policy from the very start, the state-sponsored dechristianization of death proved to be one of the Terror's most lasting legacies. As the *curé* of Cheniers in the Creuze lamented in January 1800, 'much remains to be done; the people would like to be let hear the sound of their bells and see the *viaticum* carried openly in the streets again ... and the cemeteries are still in the most terrible state.'[105] Indeed, in most urban centres, the laicization of the last rites remained in effect until well after the Concordat. In Le Puy, for example, where dechristianization had been especially intense in *an II*, Doctor Arnaud's diary made a special note of 9 December 1802 because this was 'the first time in a long time that a funeral has been performed publically by a priest'; and the same could be said of any large town where the Republic had a real official presence.[106] Across much of rural France, however, the situation was quite different and in the parishes around Le Puy, Arnaud noted that 'the sound of church bells, the Angelus, processions and funerals' were all back 'on the old footing' by late 1796.[107] Despite the occasional show of force, as in March 1796 when the authorities in Toulouse dispatched one hundred Guardsmen to deal with 'fanatical women' ringing church bells in St Nicholas-de-la-Grave, the Republic's writ did not run very far beyond the cities and garrison towns under the Directory.[108] On the contrary, in a countryside where Republican authority was met with 'sullen hostility' more often than respect, where armed 'assemblies' regularly escorted refractory priests at religious rites and where mayors were repeatedly chastised for turning a blind eye to the ringing of church bells and the reappearance of clerics and crucifixes at the head of funeral cortèges, it proved increasingly impossible to impose *la police des cultes* after *an II*.[109] As Jordan reminded his colleagues in 1797, the Directory's inability to enforce its own laws in the cemeteries did more to discredit the regime than dissuade the wrong-doer. But despite his advice, the campaign to keep the clergy out of the nation's cemeteries staggered grimly on until the regime itself collapsed in 1799.[110] With the passage of Napoleon's law on cemeteries in prairial year XII and the restoration of all 'ceremonies previously employed in funerals, according to the different religions', the campaign to dechristianize death finally came to a close over a decade after it had begun.[111]

Throughout the 1790s, the Revolutionary state, in all its guises, had resolved that 'nothing which can encourage the priesthood's pretentions' could be tolerated in the nation's cemeteries; but with the coming of Napoleon, resolution crumbled.[112] In ceremonial terms, the old order was slowly reasserted in cemeteries from the Channel to the Pyrenees from the Concordat on, but even then, the effects of the year II continued to be felt in parishes throughout France. In terms of both men and materiel, the Terror left the French church in tatters and those effects endured long after the Napoleonic *rapprochement* with Rome.

Whereas the First Estate had numbered 170,000 souls in 1789, of whom half were secular clergy, the Napoleonic church was reduced to some 36,000 practising priests, and as late as 1816, 15 per cent of a much reduced parish network remained unmanned.[113] In numerical terms at least, the French Catholic church never really recovered from this loss, but if the institutional wreckage dechristianization wrought can be measured readily enough, the social and psychological damage it did is harder to quantify. And yet, that damage is apparent in many ways and for this reason, Cobb's description of dechristianization as an explosive but ultimately ephemeral experience seems rather inadequate. To dismiss its impact in these terms, to discount it because so few towns retained their Revolutionary names and so few citizens observed the Republican calendar, is to overlook the deep social divisions and profound personal traumas the dechristianization of death gave rise to.

At its most basic, the experience of dechristianization left many communities bitterly divided and the violence that erupted in villages like Avignonet, when families like the Treys found the church locked when they came to bury a family member, was common throughout the late 1790s.[114] Confrontations like this could not be easily forgotten and mayors and municipal officials from Normandy to the Pyrenees paid for comparable displays of officious enthusiasm with their lives throughout the late 1790s. Incidents like this pitted family against family and poisoned village politics for years to come – but their legacy was more profoundly ideological as well. That legacy is apparent in the resentment felt towards a Republic that declared its commitment to the rights of the individual citizen but that still saw fit to interfere in the most intimate details of the individual conscience. As one embittered Catholic cried out in 1796:

> Is it up to you to teach me how to mourn? To console myself I need my religion, its spectacles and its chants. I have no need of Cato stabbing himself or Socrates drinking the hemlock. I need Christ suffering on the cross ... My sorrow, is it seditious?[115]

In a Republic where sorrow could seem seditious, the conflict over what could take place, and who should take precedence, in France's cemeteries had opened up an enduring ideological chasm. Between the Republic's determination to redefine what death meant and how it should be marked and the repeatedly expressed resolve of ordinary French men and women to live and more importantly 'to die in the rites of our religion', there could be no compromise.[116]

The Terror had profoundly politicized the living's relationship with the dead and this bitter contest to redefine the meaning of death resonated all the more because its effects were so intensely personal and so utterly irrevocable. Of all dechristianization's many effects, the psychological damage a decade of shabby civic funerals in fetid 'fields of rest' did was perhaps the most enduring. That damage is palpable in the despair that Mme Courbet and Michel Célarié, Gaspard Delamelle and Jean-François Pilat expressed as they endured the spectacle of loved ones 'taken to their graves without a prayer', 'deprived of the simplest honours … and delivered up to disdain' by an 'indifferent' *commissaire civil*.[117] These accounts express the revulsion a Republican funeral evoked but also the trauma it inflicted and this was an experience that left lasting emotional scars. Decades later, as he described his childhood in the 1790s, Florentin Fortin remembered the divisions the Revolution had given rise to but recalled that 'the most painful thing for any family was to see their dearest relatives deprived of a Christian burial'.[118] That pain was all the more intensely experienced because a Republican funeral was not simply a social humiliation; it was a spiritual transgression too. These testimonies speak of real torment, an anguish born of the fear that a family member or friend had been 'plunged into oblivion' by the absence of absolution and the denial of a decent burial.[119] Catholic theologians had long preached that a lifetime of piety was more efficacious than any deathbed ritual, but in a popular religious culture where 'a good death' still required a priest's presence to anoint the dying, the denial of the last rites was not just an indignity, it imperilled an immortal soul.[120]

Salvation was at stake on these occasions and unlike the other sacraments, the baptisms and marriages, that were performed when a suitable cleric became available again after the Terror, extreme unction could not be administered after the event.[121] In many places, indeed, absolution could never be assured again after the Terror and for that reason, dechristianization's catastrophic effect on the ecclesiastical demography of France also represented a seismic shift in the spiritual economy of entire communities. Where once the parishioners of villages like Bégoux could rely on their priest being present in the event of an accident or unexpected illness, they now saw a cleric only on Sundays, and under these circumstances, no parishioner could have any confidence of receiving absolution, and with it hope of salvation, if the end should come without warning.[122] The fear of sudden death loomed very large in the French countryside, and with the disappearance of their priests during the Terror or the demotion of their parish under the Empire, much of rural France had to live with this kind of spiritual uncertainty for years following the Revolution.[123] In all of these ways, dechristianization's impact on the relationship between the living and the dead was both profound and enduring. It cannot be easily quantified, but its most lasting legacy is probably best seen in the trauma of the men and women who experienced its most harrowing effects in a cemetery and in the spiritual insecurity it left in its wake. By 1799, many of these men and women had probably any number of reasons for turning their backs on the Republic but the crusade to dechristianize death, and the very real and very lasting damage it did, was certainly one of them.

NOTES

1 The author would like to acknowledge the Irish Research Council's support in facilitating research for this essay.
2 Cited in Richard Cobb, *Les Armées Révolutionnaires: Instrument de la Terreur dans les Départements, Avril 1793–Floréal an II* (2 Volumes, Paris: La La Haye, Mouton and Co., 1961–3), ii, p.647, n 25.
3 Ibid., pp.665–6.
4 Joseph Fouché, 'Arrêté du Représentant du People près les Départements du Centre et de l'Ouest sur l'Exercice des Différents Cultes et la Sépultures des Morts', in M.J. Guillaume, *Procès-verbal du Comité d'Instruction Publique* (7 Volumes, Paris, 1895), ii, pp.630–1.
5 G. Delamelle, *Réflexions sur l'enterrement de ma mère, ou sur les cérémonies des funérailles et la moralité* (Paris, an III).
6 *Réimpression de l'Ancien Moniteur, Depuis la Réunion des États-Généraux Jusqu'au Consulat, Mai 1789–Novembre 1799* (29 Volumes, Paris 1840–45) (henceforth AM), no. 206, 26 germinal an III, p.202.
7 Delamelle, *Réflexions*, pp.5, 6 and 11.
8 Georges Duval, *Souvenirs de la Terreur de 1788 à 1793* (4 Volumes, Paris, 1841), iv, pp.319–21; Paul-Benoit-Francois Bontoux, *Des Devoirs à rendre aux morts, question envisagée sous le rapport politique et moral* (Paris, an IV), p.4; *Journal de Paris*, 20 vendémiaire an V.
9 François Etienne to Henri Grégoire, 11 ventôse an IV (Bibliothèque de la Société de Port-Royal (henceforth BPR), Henri Grégoire corr. (Vaucluse) GR1895 ms); Nicolas Rogue, *Souvenirs et Journal d'un Bourgeois d'Évreux: 1740–1830* (Évreux, 1850), pp.109–10.
10 E. Pastoret, 'Rapport au nom de la commission de la classification et de la révision des lois', *AM*, no. 288, 18 messidor an IV, p.1150; J.-F. Pilat, 'Réflexions sur l'indécence et immoralité des inhumations aujourd'hui', *Annales de la Religion*, no. 25, 4 floréal an IV, pp.577–90 and 601–10, at p.577; L. M. de La Revellière-Lépeaux, *Réflexions sur le culte, sur les cérémonies civiles et sur les fêtes nationales*, in La Revellière-Lépeaux, *Mémoires* (3 Volumes, Paris, 1895), iii, pp.7–27, at p.20; Legouvé, 'Le sépulture', *Annales de la Religion*, 7 (May 1798), pp.360–7, at p.366.
11 F.-A. Daubermesnil, *Rapport fait au nom d'une commission spécial sur les inhumations, le 21 brumaire an V* (Paris, an V), p.1.
12 Natalie Zemon Davis, 'The Rites of Violence: Religious Riot in Sixteenth-Century France', *Past and Present*, no. 59 (1973) pp.51–91; Keith P. Luria, 'Separated by Death? Burials, Cemeteries, and Confessional Boundaries in Seventeenth-Century France', *French Historical Studies*, 24 (2001), pp.185–222; James McMillan, 'Priest Hits Girl': on the Front Line in the 'War of the Two Frances', in Christopher Clark and Wolfram Kaiser (eds), *Culture Wars: Secular-Catholic Conflict in Nineteenth-Century Europe* (Cambridge: Cambridge University Press, 2003), pp.77–101.
13 'Décret impérial sur les sépultures, le 23 prairial an XII', *Bulletin des Lois de l'Empire Français*, xxv, pp.75–80.

14 Maxmillien Robespierre, *Œuvres de Maxmillien Robespierre* (10 Volumes, Paris, 1957–67), x, pp.451–2; L.-A. Saint-Just, *Fragmens sur les institutions républicaines* (Paris, 1831 edn.), p.60.
15 Emmet Kennedy, *A Cultural History of the French Revolution* (New Haven: Yale University Press, 1989), p.287; Jean Starobinski, *1789: the Emblems of Reason* (Charlottesville: University Press of Virginia, 1982), p.117.
16 See, in particular, Philippe Ariès, *L'Homme Devant la Mort* (2 Volumes, Paris: Seuil, 1977); Pierre Chaunu, *La Mort à Paris, 16e, 17e et 18e Siècles* (Paris: Fayard, 1978); R.A. Etlin, *The Architecture of Death: The Transformation of the Cemetery in Eighteenth-Century Paris* (Cambridge, MA: MIT Press, 1984); François Lebrun, *Les Hommes et la Mort en Anjou aux XVIIe et XVIIIe Siècles: Essai de Démographie et de Psychologie Historique* (Paris: La Haye, Mouton and Co., 1971); John McManners, *Death and the Enlightenment: Changing Attitudes to Death in Eighteenth-Century France* (Oxford: Oxford University Press, 1985); Michel Vovelle, *Piété Baroque et Déchristianisation en Provence au XVIIIe Siècle: Les Attitudes Devant la Mort D'après Les Clauses Des Testaments* (Paris: Plon, 1973).
17 Vovelle, *Piété Baroque*; Chaunu, *La Mort à Paris*; see also Jean Quéniart, *Les Hommes, l'Église et Dieu dans la France du XVIIIe Siècle* (Paris: Hachette, 1978) pp.241–74.
18 Ariès, *L'Homme*, pp.200–5; Madeleine Foisil, 'Les Attitudes Devant la Mort au XVIIIe Siècle: Sépultures et Suppressions de Sépultures dans le Cimetière Parisien des Saints-Innocents', *Revue Historique*, 251 (1974), pp.303–30.
19 Michel Vovelle, *La Mort et l'Occident de 1300 à nos Jours* (Paris: Gallimard, 1983), p.461.
20 Timothy Tackett, '*Piété Baroque et Déchristianisation* Thirty Years Later', *French History*, 19 (2005), pp.145–51.
21 Alain Lottin, 'Les Morts Chassés de la Cité; «Lumières et Préjugés» Les Émeutes à Lille et à Cambrai Lors du Transfert des Cimetières', *Revue du Nord*, 60 (1978), pp.73–117; Julien Brancolini and Marie-Thérèse Bouyssy, 'La vie Provinciale du Livre Français', in Genevieve Bolleme et al., *Livre et Société dans la France du XVIIIe Siècle* (2 Volumes, Paris: Mouton, 1970), ii, pp.3–38 at p.14.
22 See, for example, Lebrun, *Les Hommes et la Mort*, p.358; P.M. Jones, *Politics and Rural Society: The Southern Massif Central, c.1750–1880* (Cambridge: Cambridge University Press, 1985), p.134; Gérard Bouchard, *Le Village Immoble: Sennely-en-Sologne au XVIIIe Siècle* (Paris: Plon, 1972), p.306.
23 J. Quincy Adams, *The Diary of John Quincy Adams*, David Grayson Allen et al. (eds) (Cambridge, MA: MIT Press, 1981), i, p.235.
24 *Révolutions de Paris*, no. 12, 3 Oct. 1789, p.28.
25 S.-P. Hardy, *Mes Loisirs, ou Journal d'Événements tels qu'ils Parviennent à ma Connoissance* (Bibliothèque Nationale, Ms. Fonds Français, no. 6687, Vol. viii, pp.395–6).
26 Gabriel Le Bras, *Études de Sociologie Religieuse* (2 Volumes, Paris: Presses Universitaires de France, 1955–56), i, p.244.
27 M.L. Anderson, 'The Limits of Secularisation: On the Problem of the Catholic Revival in Nineteenth-Century Germany', *Historical Journal*, 38 (1995), pp.647–70.
28 Jonathan Sheehan, 'Enlightenment, Religion and the Enigma of Secularisation: A Review Essay', *American Historical Review*, 108 (2003), pp.1061–80.
29 Nigel Aston, *Religion and Revolution in France, 1780–1804* (London: Macmillan, 2002), pp.133-7.
30 Timothy Tackett, *Religion, Revolution and Regional Culture in Eighteenth-Century France* (Princeton: Princeton University Press, 1986).
31 See, for example, J.-C. Meyer, *La vie Religieuse en Haute-Garonne sous la Révolution* (Toulouse: Toulouse Publications de Université de Toulouse-Le Mirail, 1982), pp.135–40; Olwen Hufton, *Bayeux in the Late Eighteenth Century* (Oxford: Oxford University Press, 1967), p.192; Timothy Tackett, 'Women and Men in Counter-Revolution: The Sommières Riot of 1791', *Journal of Modern History*, 59 (1987), pp.680–704.
32 Maurice Tourneux (ed.), *Procès-Verbaux de la Commune de Paris, 10 Août 1792-1er Juin 1793* (Paris, 1894), pp.55–7.
33 Ibid., p.55.
34 *Archives Parlementaires de 1787 à 1860: Recueil Complet des Débats Législatifs et Politiques des Chambres Françaises* (100 Volumes, Paris, 1867–2000) (henceforth *AP*), Vol. 50, pp.179–84.

35 *Journal de la Montagne*, no. 5, 6 June 1793, pp.37–8.
36 Frank Tallett, 'Dechristianizing France: the Year II and the Revolutionary Experience', in idem and N. Atkin (eds), *Religion, Society and Politics in France since 1789* (London: Hambledon Press, 1991), pp.1–28, at p.1.
37 Fouché, 'Arrêté … sur l'Exercice des Différents Cultes et la Sépultures des Morts'.
38 Robespierre, *Œuvres*, x, p.117.
39 *AM*, no. 27, 27 vendémiaire an II, p.137.
40 *AM*, no. 63, 3 frimaire an II, p.482, no. 114, 24 nivôse an II, p.195.
41 *AP*, vol. 79, pp.232–4. The four departments were the Gers, Landes, the Hautes and Basses-Pyrénées.
42 Dartigoeyte, 'Arrêté du 21 Floréal an II' (Archives Départementales de la Haute-Garonne (henceforth AD HG), 1L, 197).
43 Y.-G. Paillard, 'Fanatiques et Patriotes dans le Puy-de-Dôme', *Annales Historiques de la Révolution Française* (henceforth *A.h.R.f.*), 50 (1978), pp.372–404, at p.388. For Jeanbon Saint-André see Francois-Alphonse Aulard (ed.), *Recueil des Actes du Comité de Salut Public avec la Correspondance Officielle ses Représentants en Mission et le Registre du Conseil Exécutif Provisoire* (30 Volumes, Paris, 1889–1951) (henceforth Aulard, *CSP*), ix, p.360.
44 L. Meunier, 'Albitte, Conventionnel en Missions', *A.h.R.f.*, no. 103 (1946), pp.238–77, at p.264; Aulard, *CSP*, x, p.408.
45 E. Maignet, *Arrêté du représentant du peuple envoyé dans les departéments des Bouches-du-Rhône et du Vaucluse, 9 germinal an II* (Marseille, 1794).
46 Former clerics like Lakanal, Ysabeau, Monestier and Châles were among the most violent dechristianizers. For André Dumont's main priority on mission in Amiens, Aulard, *CSP*, ix, p.125.
47 Aulard, *CSP*, xi, p.491.
48 *AP*, Vol. 79, pp.174–75; Paul Leuilliot (ed.), *Les Jacobins de Colmar: Procès-Verbaux des Séances de la Société Populaire, 1791–1795* (Strasbourg: Istra, 1923), p.77.
49 *AP*, Vol. 80, p.85, Vol. 81, p.186, Vol. 82, pp.114–5. For Verneuil, see Louis Pérouas and Paul d'Hollander, *La Révolution Française: une Rupture dans le Christianisme? Le cas du Limousin (1775–1822)* (Paris: Editions des Monedieres, 1988), p.180.
50 Cobb, *Les Armées Révolutionnaires*, ii, p.683.
51 Aulard, *CSP*, ix, p.292.
52 F. Mallarmé, 'Proclamation et Arrêté du Représentant du Peuple Délégué dans les Départements du Gers et de la Haute-Garonne, fait à Toulouse le 14 Vendémiaire an III' (A.D. H-G, 1L 200).
53 Jules Sauzay, *Histoire de la Persécution Révolutionnaire dans le Département du Doubs, de 1789 à 1801* (10 Volumes, Besançon, 1867–73), vi, p.403.
54 Henri Meister, *Souvenirs de mon Dernier Voyage à Paris, 1795* (Paris: Picard, 1910 edn.), p.56.
55 Francois Lebrun (ed.), *Histoire des Catholiques en France* (Paris: Privat, 1981), p.281.
56 Pierre de la Gorce, *Histoire Religieuse de la Révolution Française* (5 Volumes, Paris: Plon-Nourrit et cie, 1912–23), iii, p.362; Michel Vovelle, *The Revolution against the Church* (Columbus: Ohio State University Press, 1991), pp.64 and 84.
57 André Latreille, *L'Église Catholique et la Révolution Française* (2 Volumes, Paris: Hachette, 1950), i, p.166.
58 Bacheley to Henri Grégoire, 22 thermidor an III (BPR, Grégoire corr. (Calvados) GR.2820 ms). For Frémanger's plans for the Calvados, see Aulard, *CSP*, x, p.739.
59 Aulard, *CSP*, xii, p.96.
60 Michel Célarié, *Journal d'un Bourgeois de Bégoux: 1771–1836*, C. Constant-Le Stum (ed.)(Cahors: Publisud, 1992), p.165.
61 'Arrêté des conseils généraux du district et de la commune de Dieppe réunis le 6 frimaire' (*AP*, Vol. 82, p.114).
62 *AM*, no. 63, 3 frimaire an II, p.482.
63 Aulard, *CSP*, ix, p.360.
64 Avril, 'Rapport sur l'inhumation des citoyens, le 21 nivôse', *AM*, no. 114, 24 nivôse an II, p.195.
65 Maignet, 'Arrêté du représentant du peuple…' le 9 germinal an II, articles xxii, xxvii and xxviii.

66 *Rituale Romanum, Pauli V. Pontificis Maximi Jussu Editum* (Avignon, 1783).
67 Michel Biard (ed.), *Procès-Verbaux de la Société Populaire de Honfleur (Calvados) (Janvier 1791–Février 1795)* (Paris: Cths editions, 2011), p.452.
68 McManners, *Death and the Enlightenment*, p.275.
69 W.H. Sewell, *Work and Revolution in France: The Language of Labour from the old Regime to 1848* (Cambridge: Cambridge University Press, 1980), p.36. See also Maurice Agulhon, *Pénitents et Francs-Maçons de l'Ancienne Provence* (Paris: Fayard, 1968).
70 M.-F. Gueusquin, 'Gardiennes et Portefaix: de la Prééminence de la Femme dans le Travail Funéraire d'une Commune Rurale de la Nièvre', *Ethnologie Française*, 13 (1983), pp.129–38.
71 Arnold Van Gennep, *Le Folklore Français* (4 Volumes, Paris: Robert Laffont, 1998 edn.), i, p.607.
72 On the death knell's place in customary culture, see McManners, *Death and the Enlightenment*, pp.270–80, Lebrun, *Les Hommes et la Mort*, pp.467–9; Alain Corbin, *Village Bells: Sound and Meaning in the Nineteenth-Century French Countryside* (New York: Columbia University Press, 1998), pp.165–9.
73 Aulard, *CSP*, xi, p.492; Corbin, *Village Bells*, p.21. On Albitte's long-term legacy, see Philippe Boutry, 'Les Mutations du Paysage Paroissial: Reconstructions d'Églises et Translations de Cimetières Dans les Campagnes de l'Ain au XIX Siècle', *Ethnologie Française*, 15 (1985), pp.7–34.
74 Gervais to Grégoire, 17 Juin 1795 (BPR, Grégoire ms. (Calvados) GR.2836 ms).
75 Vovelle's survey of dechristianization, for example, paints a quite inadequate picture of resistance nationwide: Michel Vovelle, *La Révolution Contre l'Église: de la Raison à l'être Suprême* (Paris: Editions Complexe, 1988).
76 Aulard, *CSP*, viii, p.237.
77 Aulard, *CSP*, ix, pp.665–6.
78 Ibid., and p.759.
79 Fernand Martin (ed.), *Les Jacobins au Village: Procès-Verbaux de la Société d'Artonne* (Clermont-Ferrand: P. Juliot, 1902), p.111.
80 Aulard, *CSP*, xii, p.356.
81 Etienne Brossard, *Histoire du Département de la Loire Pendant la Révolution Française* (2 Volumes, Paris: H. Champion, 1907), ii, pp.28–9; Edouard Herriot, *Lyon n'est Plus* (4 Volumes, Paris: Hachette, 1937–40), iii, p.229.
82 Ibid.
83 See, for example, 'Le commissaire du Directoire Exécutive près l'administration centrale du département de la Haute Garonne, 3 messidor an VI' (AN, F1cIII Haute-Garonne, 8).
84 'Compte-rendu de l'agent national près du district de Vire, germinal an III' (AN, F1cIII Calvados, 7); Portal, 'Situation politique du département de la Haute-Loire, ventôse an VI' (AN, F1cIII Haute-Loire 4).
85 J.C. Scott, *Weapons of the Weak: Everyday Forms of Peasant Resistance* (New Haven: Yale University Press, 1985).
86 Aulard, *CSP*, x, p.721.
87 Aulard, *CSP*, xii, pp.304, 449.
88 'Régistre de la société populaire de Jonquières, le 1 floréal an II' (Archives Départementales de Vaucluse, 6L 9).
89 Ibid., entries of 14 pluviôse an II and 30 ventôse an III.
90 Olwen Hufton, *Women and the Limits of Citizenship in the French Revolution* (Toronto: University of Toronto Press, 1999), pp.120–2; Frank Tallett, 'Religion and Revolution: The Rural Clergy and Parishioners of the Doubs, 1780–1797' (unpublished PhD Thesis, University of Reading, 1981) pp.355–60.
91 H. Forestier, 'Les Campagnes de l'Auxerrois et la Déchristianisation d'après la Correspondance d'Edme-Antoine Rathier Agent National du District d'Auxerre (Pluviôse an II – Germinal an III)', *Annales de Bourgogne*, 19 (1947), pp.185–206, at p.205.
92 BPR, Grégoire corr. (Vaucluse) GR1899 ms, 18 nivôse an IV; ADH-G, 1L, 1075, Cintegabelle, le 27 pluviôse an IV. For the 'cabaretier' saying mass near Compiègne, see J. Brenet, 'Les Limites de la Déchristianisation de l'an II Éclairées par le Retour au Culte de l'an III', *A.h.R.f.* (1998), pp.285–99, at p.291.

93 Aulard, *CSP*, viii, p.675.
94 Cobb, *Les Armées Révolutionnaires*, pp.667, 687.
95 *Annales Religieuses*, no. 19, 19 fructidor, an III, p.237; Rogue, *Souvenirs*, p.99; *L'Anti-Terroriste ou Journal des Principes*, no. 48, 7 thermidor an III, p.193; BPR, Grégoire corr. (Calvados) GR.2836 ms.
96 On this revival, see Olwen Hufton, 'The Reconstruction of a Church, 1796–1801', in Gwynne Lewis and Colin Lucas (eds), *Beyond the Terror: Essays in French Regional and Social History 1794–1815* (Oxford: Oxford University Press, 1983), pp.21–53; Suzanne Desan, *Reclaiming the Sacred: Lay Religion and Popular Politics in Revolutionary France* (Ithaca: Cornell University Press, 1990).
97 Célarie, *Journal*, p.167.
98 *AM*, no. 10, 11 vendémiaire an IV, pp.78–80.
99 This point was repeatedly reaffirmed by ministerial instructions. See, for example, 'Le Ministre de la Police Générale aux commissaires du pouvoir exécutif, le 26 pluviôse an IV' (ADH-G, 1L1075, no. 30); Antonin Debidour (ed.), *Recueil des Actes du Directoire Exécutif: Procès-Verbaux, Arrêtés, Instructions, Lettres et Actes Divers* (4 Volumes, Paris, 1910–17), ii, p.129.
100 J.-M. Coupé, *Des Sépultures en Politique et en Morale* (Paris, an IV), p.9; *AM*, no. 298, 28 Messidor an IV, p.1192.
101 C. Jordan, *Rapport sur la police des cultes* (Paris, an V); *Opinion de Jourdan de la Haute-Vienne sur les projets de résolutions présentés par la commission chargé de la révision des lois sur les cultes* (Paris, an V), p.6; *Opinion d'Eschasseriaux ainé sur le projet rélatif à la police des cultes* (Paris, an V), p.7; *Opinion de Trouille, depute du Finistère, sur l'usage des cloches ...* (Paris, an V), p.5.
102 F.-A. Daubermesnil, *Rapport fait au nom d'une commission spéciale sur les inhumations, le 21 brumaire an V* (Paris, an V).
103 Coupé, *Des Sépultures*, p.4; Pilat, *Réflexions sur l'indécence et immoralité des inhumations*, p.577.
104 François Etienne to Henri Grégoire, 11 ventôse an IV (BPR, Grégoire corr. (Vaucluse) GR1895 ms).
105 Mariston to Grégoire, 5 pluviôse an VIII (BPR, Grégoire corr. (Creuse) s.n.).
106 J.-A. Arnaud, *Recueil des événemens qui ont eu lieu au Puy et aux environs depuis l'an 1775 jusqu'en 1815 inclusivement ou journal de ce qui s'est passé de remarquable durant cette période* (Le Puy: Editions de la Société académique, 1931), p.272.
107 Ibid., p.173.
108 'Arrêté de l'administration centrale du département de la Haute-Garonne, le 11 ventôse an IV' (ADH-G, 1L 135).
109 AN, F1cIII, Calvados, 7, 20 brumaire an IV. For an example of such armed assemblies, see ADH-G, IL, 1064, and for similar complaints concerning the 'public officials in many communes [who] shamefully collaborate with fanaticism, tolerate bell-ringing and protect refractory priests': ADH-G, IL, 107. See also BPR, Grégoire corr. (Calvados) GR.2870 ms; AN, F1cIII, Haute-Garonne, 8, 3 messidor an VI.
110 Jordan, *Rapport sur la police des cultes*, p.24.
111 'Décret impérial sur les sépultures', article xviii, in *Bulletin des lois de l'Empire Français*, Vol. 25, p.77.
112 *AM*, no. 298, 28 messidor an IV, pp.1191–2.
113 Lebrun, *Histoire des Catholiques*, p.240; G. Cholvy and Y.-M. Hilaire, *Histoire religieuse de la France, 1800–1880* (Toulouse: Éditions Privât, 1990), p.16.
114 ADH-G, 1L, 1075, Avignonet, 19 messidor an IV.
115 Rebour, 'Sur les sépultures', *Annales de la Religion*, iii, no. 24, 24 vendémiaire an V, p.575.
116 'Pétition des Catholiques romains de Toulouse' (ADH-G, 1L, 1058).
117 Pilat, *Réflexions sur l'indécence et immoralité des inhumations*, p.603; Delamelle, *Réflexions*, pp.4 and 5.
118 F.-J. Fortin, *Souvenirs* (2 Volumes, Auxerre, 1865), i, p.6.
119 Pilat, *Réflexions sur l'indécence et immoralité des inhumations*, p.603.
120 On the popular belief that the last rites were essential for 'a good death': see Philippe Ariès, *The Hour of our Death* (New York: Alfred A. Knopf, 1982), p.303.

121 On the resumption of these sacraments see, for example, ADH-G, 1L 1075, Blagnac, 8 pluviôse an IV.
122 Célarié, *Journal*, p.167.
123 On the fear of sudden death in nineteenth-century France, see Ellen Badone, *The Appointed Hour: Death, Worldview and Social Change in Brittany* (Berkeley: University of California Press, 1989), pp.55–7.

7

FORGETTING TO REMEMBER ORR: DEATH AND AMBIGUOUS REMEMBRANCE IN MODERN IRELAND[1]

GUY BEINER

Modern Ireland is haunted by the memory of the dead. Although the topic of Irish social remembrance has been explored extensively in recent years, critical attention should also be paid to forgetting, as recent psychological studies have concluded that 'the study of forgetting cannot be separated from the study of memory'.[2] In his ruminations on the relationship of history, memory and forgetting, the philosopher Paul Ricoeur floated 'the paradoxical idea that forgetting can be so closely tied to memory that it can be considered one of the conditions for it', suggesting an 'imbrication of forgetting in memory'.[3] This essay argues similarly that forgetting was part and parcel of remembrance – even in the case of Ireland's most revered heroes – and that it reflected deeply embedded anxieties and internal conflicts.

It is instructive in this regard to reconsider the opening verses of John Kells Ingram's canonical poem 'The Memory of the Dead' – first published anonymously in *The Nation* (1 April 1843) and included as a song in *The Spirit of the Nation* (1845). It was recycled endlessly in broadsides and songbooks thereafter, and became an unofficial anthem of Irish nationalists when it was reverentially sung as a hymn in the centennial of the 1798 Rebellion:

Who fears to speak of Ninety-Eight?
Who blushes at the name?
When cowards mock the patriot's fate,
Who hangs his head for shame?[4]

171

While assertively trumpeting the memory of dead United Irishmen, the poem acknowledges disapprovingly the embarrassment (manifested in blushing, mocking and shame) they caused to some. Commenting on this 'remarkable combination of attitudes', Joep Leerssen attributes the poem's success to the fact that it epitomized a 'traumatic paradigm' typical of Irish engagement with the past, whereby, 'on the one hand, the 1798 rebellion (and Irish history and politics generally) became unmentionable almost, in a rictus of discreet "don't mention the war" avoidance, while on the other hand, there was much eloquent preoccupation with the painful topic'.[5] This tense ambivalence – embodied in the paradox of vocally proclaiming reticence – entwines remembering with an apprehension of disremembering, thus facilitating a complex mode of social memory that could be labelled 'social forgetting'.

Whereas conceptualization of social forgetting along these lines can call attention to the ambiguities implicit in Irish memory at large, it is more noticeable in certain historical contexts, and the legacy of the 1798 Rebellion in Ulster offers particularly fruitful ground for tracing its dynamics. These can be illustrated through a case study of the remembrance of William Orr, the proto-martyr of Irish republicanism. Although repeated evocation of the motto 'Remember Orr' appears to have secured his position in the Irish national pantheon, closer inspection reveals that constructions of his memory have been subject from the outset to pervasive considerations of forgetting.

I

On 17 July 1796, a warrant was issued for the arrest of William Orr, a formidable Presbyterian farmer from Farranshane, County Antrim, described by a contemporary historian as 'a man of good family and connexions'.[6] Orr, who had contributed articles to the United Irish organ, the *Northern Star*, was a known supporter of the republican cause who had previously been brought to the attention of the authorities by an informer.[7] It was alleged that in April he had sworn in to the secret society of the United Irishmen two soldiers (Hugh Wheatley and John Lindsay) of the Fifeshire Fencibles, a Scottish regiment stationed in Ulster as part of the government's counter-insurgency measures. He went into hiding to avoid arrest but was apprehended in September, charged with high treason under the recently enacted Insurrection Act, and held in prison without trial for a year. He was finally brought before the Antrim assizes in mid-September 1797, convicted, and sentenced to death. Orr's public execution at the 'Three Sister Gallows' outside Carrickfergus on 14 October 1797 was a highly contentious event, which proved to be a formative moment for United Irish mobilization towards rebellion. Moreover, in the words of the Victorian historian William Edward Hartpole Lecky, 'this memorable and most unhappy case' left a residue of 'bitter and enduring memories'.[8] From the perspective of the history of memory, contemporary representations of Orr's ordeals constitute a 'pre-memory' of 1798.

Modern traditions of political martyrdom have a long history in Ireland, extending back to early modern struggles of the Reformation and Counter-Reformation.[9] However, William Orr was to become Ireland's first *republican* martyr, preceding, even, the 'father of Irish republicanism', Theobald Wolfe Tone. The patterns of martyrdom established with his execution in 1797 were to mould the ways in which other United Irishmen were to be remembered following the suppression of the rebellion in 1798. In his pioneering study of remembering, the psychologist Frederic C. Bartlett claimed that memories of events are shaped by schemata that incorporate recollections of earlier events.[10] In other words, even as we experience history we construct its memory in accordance with already existing memories. It can therefore be argued that memory has a pre-memory. In this elementary sense, though seemingly counter-intuitive, the example of Orr clearly demonstrates how the construction of the memory of 1798 actually began before 1798.

But there is also a more immediate sense in which the case of William Orr exhibits the workings of pre-memory. During his lifetime, even as the affair was moving towards its tragic outcome, several interested parties – Orr included – embarked on competing attempts to shape the way he would be remembered. Concerns of forgetting would play a key role in these pre-memory contestations. Paradoxically, before Orr was executed he was already being discussed in terms of possible oblivion, expressing a discourse that could be termed 'pre-forgetting'. It would appear that before history occurs, it is not only being remembered but is perhaps even being forgotten!

The struggle over what would be forgotten and what would be remembered, and how it would be remembered, permeates historical knowledge of Orr. Even the accounts of his physical appearance were subject to partisan representations. Sensing that 'the Irish nation feels highly interested in whatever relates to the unfortunate William Orr', a sympathizer who had visited him in jail published in the United Irish newspaper *The Press* two months after the execution a detailed 'description of that ever to be venerated martyr'. Perfectly handsome – 'nothing can be conceived more completely formed than every part of his body' – and impeccably dressed, Orr was depicted as an ideal image of manliness: 'it is a question if a finer fellow could have been found'. In writing this flattering pen portrait, the anonymous author (who used the pseudonym Humanitas) observed: 'I am the more scrupulous and minute, as I understand some of the Irish artists are meditating an engraving of their countryman.'[11] This deliberate effort to formulate an iconic visual memory was successful insofar as it was later considered authentic.[12] Its lasting influence is apparent in artistic portraits of Orr, which over a century later would be modelled on this romanticized depiction.[13]

However, such valorizing was unacceptable to those loyal to the Crown, and was disputed by the man who apprehended Orr – Arthur Chichester Macartney (at the time a student in Trinity College Dublin), whose father George, the Church of Ireland vicar of Antrim, was the magistrate who had issued the arrest warrant. When interviewed by the historian of the United Irishmen Richard Robert Madden some three decades later, Macartney (then, vicar of Belfast) observed that Orr 'was a very ordinary man, a wild and dissipated young man of very loose morals'. He acknowledged that Orr was 'popular among his class', but ascribed his popularity to the fact that he was 'a frequenter of cockfights, drinking bouts in public houses, and a fair-going boisterous sporting young man', and insisted that, rather than 'a patriot of great and noble qualities', he was 'irregular in his habits and of very moderate abilities'.[14] Madden maintained that this was a trustworthy source, stating that 'this gentleman would have served the party to which he unfortunately belonged at the expense of his life, but, to the best of my opinion, not at the expense of truth',[15] and he even claimed that 'a clearer statement of facts and opinions in reference to this subject I never heard given by any person on either side'.[16] Nonetheless, Madden's partiality towards eyewitness testimonies was overruled by his unbridled sympathy for the United Irishmen and so he chose to sanitize this hostile account and omit the deprecatory comments from his published history.[17] His multi-volume *The United Irishmen: Their Lives and Times* practically defined the pantheon of early republican heroes (including Orr) and ensured that they would be remembered. But, as the case of Orr vividly manifests, Madden's valorization of the United Irishmen was permeated with subtle instances of erasure. Such canonization necessitates selective editing, which involves deliberate forgetting.

The widespread sympathy aroused by Orr's plight could be translated into non-verbal action. In October 1797, the *Belfast News-Letter* noted that, while in prison, Orr 'had his entire harvest cut down by some 600 of his neighbours, in a few hours'.[18] In Ulster, as the contemporary French traveller de Latocnaye observed, it was 'an old custom with the peasantry here to assemble at the end of the autumn and to dig up the potatoes of persons for whom they have any sort of affection'.[19] The United Irishmen utilized such acts of communal solidarity as a form of propaganda by deed, which in the case of Orr assisted with his elevation into a *cause célèbre* deemed worthy of remembrance.[20]

Recognizing that the case struck a chord with the local population, the United Irishmen appointed a talented legal team to mount Orr's defence. It included John Philpot Curran and William Sampson, who sought to exploit confusion over the expiry of the 1796 Insurrection Act.[21] Despite their efforts, a guilty verdict was delivered after a single day of court proceedings (18 September 1797). The visible concern of the many spectators who attended the trial left a strong impression; as reported by 'an eminent Stenographer' (probably William Sampson): 'during the whole of the trial the silence and anxiety of a crowded audience were singularly solemn and striking'.[22] This deafening silence did not mark acquiescence, or consent to forgive and forget.

The clear-cut verdict of treason was undermined by what can be described as an alternative unofficial trial, which took place in the public sphere. Martha McTier had previously written her brother, the noted United Irishman William Drennan, of fabricated evidence, 'which will soon be brought to light'.[23] Though the key incriminating fact that Orr had been present at a United Irish initiation remained unshaken, his culpability was challenged by the public's refusal to accept the legitimacy of the martial law under which he was captured and prosecuted. Radicals refused to accept Orr's guilt; they alleged that a flagrant miscarriage of justice had been perpetrated, citing revelations that members of the conspicuously packed jury had been drunk during the deliberations. In a letter which detailed allegations that a member of the jury was coerced into conferring the death sentence, Mary Ann McCracken wrote her brother Henry Joy McCracken, a key Belfast United Irishmen then imprisoned in Kilmainham jail: 'Orr's trial has clearly proved, that there is neither justice nor mercy to be expected.'[24]

Expressions of sympathy emanated from far beyond the core radical cliques. Maintaining that Orr had 'a character without reproach', the moderate liberal Dr Alexander Henry Haliday noted that pleas were made on his behalf 'by most respectable people, and on strong grounds'.[25]

Even Lady Londonderry, mother-in-law of the influential Lord Castle-reagh (who had played a key role in Orr's incarceration, deterring the possibility of release following his arrest), tried to intercede and prevent his execution. These appeals for clemency were brushed aside by senior figures in the Irish administration, who were determined to make an example of Orr in order to demonstrate the government's ability to crack down on the United Irish organization in Ulster. Both the lord lieutenant, Lord Camden, and the chief secretary, Lord Pelham, were adamant that the sentence should be carried out, and refused to avail of a temporary reprieve to issue a stay of execution. The ineffective efforts to spare Orr's life encouraged open contestation of his guilt, which would evolve into a struggle over memory. By rejecting his castigation as a traitor, his supporters were intentionally fashioning him as a martyr even before he was executed.

William Orr was an active agent in the attempt to predetermine his memory. He issued a 'Dying Declaration', dated 5 October 1797, in which he denied the 'false and ungenerous' confession, which his brother James had published in the *Belfast News-Letter* in the hope of securing a pardon.[26] This recalcitrant text, as Kevin Whelan has pointed out, effectively reinvented and politicized the popular eighteenth-century genre of gallows speeches. It inaugurated a new literary form of speeches by condemned republicans that would flourish in the nineteenth century and achieve canonical status in the numerous editions of the key text of nationalist hagiography, *Speeches from the Dock* (in which Orr's 'Dying Declaration' was placed after Wolfe Tone's courtroom speech).[27] Concerned about his reputation – 'which is dearer to me than life' – and the prospect that he might be remembered unfavourably, or even forgotten, Orr's final appeal included a plea 'that all my virtuous countrymen will bear me in kind Remembrance'.

A letter from Carrickfergus, written on the day of the execution, described a solemn demonstration of silent solidarity:

> The inhabitants of this town, man, woman, and child, quit the place this day, rather than be present at the execution of their hapless countryman, Mr. Orr. Some removed to the distance of many miles. Scarce a sentence was interchanged during the day, and every face presented a picture of the deepest melancholy, horror, and indignation.[28]

Once again, silence was employed as an expression of protest. Denied a public audience at the gallows, Orr was left to read the declaration to the military guard. Nevertheless, his appeal to be remembered was not forgotten, as popular print provided a readership.

Orr's rousing declaration was printed in advance on handbills in order that it would be available for distribution at the funeral. Striving to counteract its effects, the high sheriff of County Antrim and the sovereign (Mayor) of Belfast immediately issued a refutation (published in the *Belfast News-Letter* and *Freeman's Journal* on 15 October 1797), which alleged that Orr had confirmed the confession in their presence.[29] In addition, the military was charged with confiscating the printed sheets, but, as the soldiers could not prevent further prints, they were unable to suppress the declaration's circulation.[30] Three days after the execution, it was published in the *Press* (17 October 1797)[31] and it reappeared soon after in United Irish publications in Ireland and abroad.[32] From beyond the grave, Orr triumphantly continued to avow: 'I glory in my innocence.'

Straight after the execution, an attempt was made to resuscitate the corpse.[33] Among those involved was Samuel Kirk, 'a warm, Loyalist friend of the condemned man', as recounted later by his son.[34] Since such actions have been recognized as expressions of popular disproval of capital punishment, this would appear to offer an indication that the execution was considered unwarranted also by certain loyalists.[35] The Presbyterian minister Rev. Adam Hill was arrested after Orr's corpse was waked surreptitiously at his meeting-house in Ballynure, but he was then released, in the absence of witnesses willing to testify against him.[36] William shared a grave with a family member, Ally Orr (who had passed away in 1791), in Templepatrick.[37] Though his name was not added to the tombstone, this anonymity should not be mistaken as an act of forgetting, as identification of the unmarked grave would be tenaciously recalled in local tradition.

In stark contrast to the dearth of spectators at the execution, multitudes thronged to the funeral procession, where 'an amazing concourse of people crouded [*sic*] the road and the adjacent Hills'.[38] The ultra-loyalist historian Sir Richard Musgrave described the event as 'a most splendid funeral, which was attended by a numerous body of United Irishmen, who lamented in doleful accents the fate of this martyr to republican liberty, and bedewed his hearse with tears of sympathetick civism [*sic*]'.[39] The burial was reputedly undertaken by Orr's freemason brethren.[40] However, Musgrave omitted any reference to masonic rites at the funeral, as elements of their ritual had been adopted both by United Irish revolutionaries and loyalist Orangemen and were therefore deemed a delicate issue.[41] The authors of historical accounts, whether writing from a loyalist or republican perspective, had no qualms about editing out inconvenient information with the intention of predicating memory on selective forgetting.

Repudiation of the death sentence was manifest on the night of 27–28 February 1798, when Orr's executioner was dragged naked from his bed and violently assaulted by a party of men who 'feloniously cut the ears out of his head and left him for dead'.[42] There is evidence to suggest that members of the jury that convicted Orr were also subject to reprisal.[43] This outright conflict between enforcement of the King's law and its popular rejection was mirrored in public memory, which, as put by the American historian John Bodnar, is situated at 'the intersection of official and vernacular cultural expressions'.[44] If popular memory indeed emerges from 'the relation between dominant memory and oppositional forms', it follows that such conflict inevitably entails acts of 'popular forgetting'.[45] In the struggle over shaping popular remembrance, each side sought to invalidate, essentially consign to oblivion, the opponent's claim on truth and justice.

The *Press* – the main vehicle for expressing support of Orr – published on 27 October 1797 an open letter to the lord lieutenant, which claimed that the execution was regarded by 'the nation' as 'one of the most sanguinary and savage acts that had disgraced the laws'. Repeating allegations that Orr had been convicted through 'perjury, drunkenness, and reward', the pseudonymous author (signed Marcus) alleged that, in denying a pardon, Lord Camden had acted 'inhumanly, wickedly and unjustly'.[46] The authorities could not sit back idly as the United Irish mouthpiece, which enjoyed a print run of 6,000 copies and was marketed extensively, brazenly recast Orr as an innocent victim of government repression.[47] Moreover, the newspaper, which sensed that 'the public have felt much interested in every circumstance relating to the much lamented Mr. Orr',[48] was determined to continue publishing in this vein and declared that 'the death of Mr. Orr is a topic that should never be relinquished'.[49] This defiant editorial policy effectively provoked a clampdown.

The proprietor of the *Press*, Arthur O'Connor, was a senior United Irishman who distanced himself from the newspaper in public. In his stead, the nominal printer Peter Finnerty was sued for seditious libel. Though vigorously defended by the same counsellors – Curran and Sampson – that had represented Orr, Finnerty was convicted and sentenced to stand in the pillory for an hour, serve in prison for two years, pay a fine of twenty pounds, and to provide on his release hefty securities (in total of one thousand pounds), guaranteeing his 'good behaviour for seven years'.[50] The prosecution of Finnerty, which took place two months after the execution (22 December 1797), represented a government attempt to assert control over the public memory of Orr. The verdict of libel and its overly severe punishment was intended to silence criticism and to stem the growing popularity of an oppositional narrative. Yet the authorities were incapable of effacing this counter-memory. Two months later, in February, the Lord Chancellor, Lord Clare, was obliged to refute in the Irish House of Lords persistent accusations of misconduct at Orr's trial.[51]

The possibility of legal sanction encouraged prudence in those who chose to support Orr in print. One strategy adopted to circumvent the government and to sustain radical memory was to have recourse to 'literary mischief'. A fortnight after the execution, on 31 October 1797, the *Press* published an elegiac poem simply entitled 'William' and signed 'The Minstrel'. The author was William Drennan, who was aptly described by Madden as 'the penman of the United Irish Society'.[52] Drennan's purpose was to break the literary silence that followed Orr's death:

> Are your springs, oh ye Muses, run dry?
> Has horror suspended their source?
> That no tribute – no tear and no sigh,
> Oh William! has hallowed thy corpse.

Describing with pathos how the hopes that Orr's life would be spared were frustrated, the poem concluded with a resounding condemnation of the authorities:

> Oh wither the pitiless hand
> Could execute such a decree,
> And the heart that could give the command,
> A stranger to *peace* let it be.[53]

This composition was followed by Drennan's poetic masterpiece 'The Wake of William Orr', which called for restrained and muted remembrance:

> Here our brother worthy lies,
> Wake not him with women's cries;
> Mourn the way that mankind ought;
> Sit, in silent trance of thought.

This is a sophisticated use of silence, which had already been utilized to great effect in response to the trial and execution. It amounts to a 'conspiracy of silence' through which, as discussed by the sociologist Eviatar Zerubavel, the absence of speech actually creates a presence of significance, leaving an unavoidable 'elephant in the room'.[54]

Penned in 1797, and titled 'To the Memory of William Orr' when it first appeared anonymously in the *Press* (14 January 1798), the poem was published in 1815 in a collection of Drennan's poems under the unspecific title 'The Wake'.[55] It was described by Madden as 'a piece written with great power, and which, probably, had more effect on the public mind than any production of the day in prose or verse'.[56] Yet William Orr is not mentioned by name throughout the poem. For Drennan, he was to be commemorated guardedly, through feigned silence and discreet coded references, which were recognizable to the intended readership but, to discourage recrimination, were not made explicit. In this formulation, Drennan created a poetic genre of veiled mourning that was distinct from the flagrantly sentimental expressions of grief in contemporary English literature.[57] This style would be perfected by Thomas Moore in his celebrated poem 'Oh! Breathe Not His Name', which implicitly commemorated Robert Emmet – the executed hero of the United Irish attempted rebellion in 1803 – by depicting a hidden ritual of mourning:

And the tear that we shed, though in secret it rolls,
Shall long keep his memory green in our souls.[58]

The call for silence, not actual silence, embedded a discourse of omission into the initial stages of memory formation.

It must not be mistaken for submission to government censorship, however. Hushed remembrance was employed as a subversive tactic, intended to sustain resistance through clandestine vigilance in anticipation of future resurgence, as hinted in Drennan's poem:

Here we watch our brother's sleep;
Watch with us, but do not weep;
Watch with us through dead of night,
But expect the morning light.

In its many republications, the poem, which ends with a vision of resurrection cum insurrection ('The day is come – Arise, arise!'), functioned as an 'invisible bullet' (to borrow Stephen Greenblatt's term). It was endorsed by Young Ireland and appeared in the multiple editions of Charles Gavan Duffy's popular ballad anthology.[59] In the mid-twentieth century, a writer would refer to it as 'that heart-quickening work which we, as youngsters of the early-nineteen-hundreds, were ever ambitious to recite'.[60]

In contrast to the wary endorsement of silence by prudent radicals, hot-blooded revolutionaries threw caution to the wind. Eager United Irishmen sang 'Though perjury doomed thee, Oh Orr to the grave, Thy blood to our union, more energy gave'[61] and toasted 'The memory of ORR, who died a martyr to Irish Freedom'.[62] Their audacity may have been encouraged by declarations by English radicals. At a London birthday party for the Whig parliamentarian Charles James Fox, toasts purportedly included: 'The memory of William Orr, basely murdered' and 'May the Lord Lieutenant, and the Irish Cabinet, be seen in the situation of William Orr.'[63] The London *Courier* described Orr's execution as 'Murder most Foul'.[64]

In Ireland, revolutionary popular politicization explicitly appealed to memory through reiteration of the motto 'Remember Orr'. This motto came to symbolize defiance in the face of state terror, and was adopted as a rallying cry in the preparations for a rebellion in 1798. At the arrest of the brothers John and Henry Sheares – the first United Irish leaders to be tried and executed for high treason following the outbreak of the rebellion – the police magistrate William Alexander found a handwritten proclamation, which, in its inflammatory rhetoric, would secure their conviction:

Vengeance, Irishmen, Vengeance on your Oppressors – Remember what thousands of your dearest friends have perished by their [Murders, Cruel plots (scratched out)] Merciless Orders. Remember their burnings, their rackings, their torturings, their Military Massacres, and their legal Murders. Remember ORR.[65]

Henry Grattan Jnr. (son, and namesake, of the famous reformist politician) would later recall the prevalence of this seditious catchphrase: '"*Remember Orr! – Remember Orr!*" were words written everywhere – pronounced everywhere. I recollect, when a child, to have read them on the walls – to have heard them spoken by the people.'[66]

A range of commemorative artefacts dedicated to William Orr served as potent *aide-mémoires*. The production of these mementoes originated in a spontaneous act at the scaffold, when, following the execution, the cap placed over Orr's head was cut up and the pieces were distributed among his friends, who, according to a near contemporary account, 'cherished it as a most precious relick [*sic*]'.[67] Madden retained one of these pieces, which was given to him in the mid-nineteenth century by Robb McGee of Belfast,[68] and another piece was still in the possession of a member of the Orr family a century later.[69] Specially designed souvenirs were distributed within United Irish circles. 'Remember Orr' was inscribed on 'mourning rings', some of which had Orr's hair set in them (and others were wrought with silk). The Belfast antiquarian Francis Joseph Bigger described one such ring, which became his prized possession a century later:

> a little thin finger or scarf ring, hand-made, of gold. On one side is a round plate enclosing a green enamelled shamrock, with white enamel surrounding it. On the opposite side in an oval are the words, 'Remember Orr,' and on each side of the plate in gaelic letters *Erin go bragh*. Engraved inside are the letters 'presented by Robert Orr'.[70]

Henry Joy McCracken, the leader of the rebels in Antrim, wore a similar ring (presented to him by his friend Thomas Richardson). Prior to his execution, he was incarcerated in Carrickfergus jail, the same prison in which Orr had been held. In a pre-memory gesture, which signified his willingness to imitate Orr's martyrdom, McCracken bequeathed his 'Remember Orr' ring to his mother and, following her death, it was reverently kept by his sister.[71]

The slogan was also engraved on commemorative medals. One such medal, owned by an antiquarian in the late-nineteenth century, was described by the Newtownards journalist Wesley Greenhill Lyttle:

> It is made of copper; in size it is about that of a penny piece of the old coinage. The obverse has the words: 'May Orr's fate nerve the impartial arm to avenge the wrongs of Erin.' On the reverse there appears the Irish harp with the spear and cap of freedom, and the motto 'Liberty – remember William Orr.'[72]

A 'Remember Orr' silver medal was faithfully retained in private possession for half a century and then put on display at an exhibition of antiquities at the Belfast Museum in 1852.[73] In addition, memorial cards, silk rosettes and custom-made watch-paper featured commemorative texts with the dedication 'Sacred to the Memory of William Orr', and the entreaty 'Let us bear him in steadfast memory'.[74]

The exhortation to 'Remember Orr' was phrased as a hallowed commandment, which transcended the particular circumstances of the historical present and enshrined republican aspirations in an eternal timeframe of mythic redemption, similar to the rituals of remembrance discussed by Yosef Hayim Yerushalmi in his treatise on Jewish history and memory, *Zakhor*.[75] The popular inculcation of the phrase became apparent when, during the rebellion of June 1798, it was used as a battle cry by insurgents in Antrim and Down. Despite the crushing defeat they experienced, it would gain lasting currency as a marker of anti-establishment militancy. Thirty years later, in 1828, when the campaign for Catholic emancipation was at its peak, Daniel O'Connell observed: 'the young blood of Ireland is in a ferment. I detected a boy of 13 years of age a few days since, drilling a regiment of boys – they had a flag on which was emblazoned, "Remember Orr."'[76]

Rechristened in republican popular print 'The Martyred Orr',[77] his example was imitated by United Irishmen in 1798. For example, the United Irish Catholic priest Rev. James Coigly consciously fashioned himself after the 'Immortal Orr' when he issued an 'Address to the People of Ireland' prior to his execution.[78] Functioning as a pre-memory, the constructed martyrdom of Orr was ultimately adopted as the mnemonic template, a kind of master schema, for apotheoses of republican heroes. Its influence is particularly noticeable in the ornate remembrance of Robert Emmet, which became a centrepiece of Irish republican martyrdom.[79]

Nonetheless, in spite of its apparent sacrosanct endurance, overt remembrance suffered from an inherent insecurity. Folk traditions vividly recalled the dangers of being caught in possession of paraphernalia commemorating Orr. The nineteenth-century local historian Hugh McCall claimed that the United Irishman confidant Tom Armstrong was executed in Lisburn after a cockade marked with 'Remember Orr' was discovered in the lining of his hat.[80] Similarly, a man found in Hillsborough with a 'Remember Orr' token concealed in his shoe was also reported to have been hanged.[81] In consequence, treasured souvenirs had to be carefully hidden, even destroyed. Bigger noted that his commemorative ring (described above) was 'repaired in several places, the explanation being that it was smashed in pieces by Orr's daughter and then thrown away to hide it from the eyes of the soldiers who were on the look out for such "treasonable" articles'.[82]

Mnemonic references in other artefacts were purposely fashioned in a way that would render them less conspicuous to outsiders. For example, a set of corn-mill scales from Straid, near Gracehill, County

Antrim, that was inscribed with William Orr's name and dated 1803 (the year of Emmet's failed rising), may have had a secret commemorative function, as explained by a curator at the Ulster Folk and Transport Museum (which acquired the item in the mid-1980s): 'In 1803 the metaphorical symbolism of this inscription would have been evident to most men using the Straid Mill: the scales of "justice", with the inscription of a heart motif and the name of William Orr on a beam which would jerk with scaffold-like violence each time a sack of grain was thrown on.'[83] Commemoration could assume even more subtle forms, as in imitation of Orr's style of clothing, about which it was noted that 'the colour of his coat at the time he suffered became a kind of uniform dress'.[84]

Even when explicitly proclaiming the imperative to 'Remember Orr', commemorative texts reflected concerns that his memory would be forsaken. A memorial card with an evocative text, which was attributed to Wolfe Tone and believed to have originated as an epitaph intended for the tomb of William Orr, included a pre-emptive denunciation of forgetting: 'when YE *forget* HIM ... May you be debar'd THAT LIBERTY he sought, and *forgotten* in the Hist'ry of Nations; or, if rem'ember'd, remember'd with disgust and execration, or nam'd with scorn and horror.'[85] In a popular poem beginning 'Sad is the sleep of Erin', which appeared on rosettes, the ghostly 'spirit of Orr' fails to awaken Ireland in what appears to echo an anxiety that even determined remembrance cannot triumph over forgetful apathy.[86]

In a strictly cognitive sense, as first hypothesized by Hermann Ebbinghaus in 1885, memory retention exponentially declines over time in accordance with a 'forgetting curve', by which the most substantial loss occurs in the initial stage.[87] Surprisingly, it seems that expressions of pre-forgetting actually strengthen the durability of social memory. To sum up the arguments concerning pre-forgetting discussed above: from its germination, remembrance of the United Irishmen was dialectically tied in with dis-remembrance so that different types of memory were constructed through engagement, in some form or other, with forgetting. Popular disavowal of official memory generated an alternative radical memory, which confronted the government prohibitions that attempted to overwrite and efface this counter-memory. In certain cases, remembrance was muted, as wariness of suppression encouraged an underground subaltern memory, but even public expressions of defiant remembrance masked inhibitions. Overall, concerns of oblivion assisted in shaping and sustaining a memory, which was founded on anxieties. The context of remembrance and forgetting, however, would substantially change following the suppression of the rebellion in counties Antrim and Down in June 1798, allowing for the introduction of new anxieties.

II

Although Ulster-Scot Dissenters formed the backbone of the insurrection in the North, following its failure, many Presbyterians renounced their radicalism. In a mass trend known locally as 'mushroom loyalty', former rebels publicly declared their allegiance to the Crown, enlisted to the yeomanry and, even, joined ultra-loyalist Orange lodges.[88] A year after the rebellion, Lord Castlereagh, who by then was chief secretary in Dublin Castle, noted with satisfaction: 'The Protestant Dissenters in Ulster have in a great degree withdrawn themselves from the Union [i.e. the United Irishmen], and become Orangemen.'[89] Six years after William Orr's execution, the lack of enthusiasm in Ulster for Robert Emmet's rising, which culminated with the execution of Thomas Russell in Downpatrick (21 October 1803), seemed to demonstrate that the spirit of 'Remember Orr' was no longer around. Previously radical communities succumbed to disillusion. Four decades after the rebellion, an Ordnance Survey memoirist noted in William Orr's home parish of Templepatrick that 'since the lesson they got in 1798 they have meddled but little with party politics'.[90] Admittedly, pockets of republican resistance remained in the Presbyterian heartland for several years after 1798.[91] Amongst the disaffected in Antrim, William Orr was toasted, alongside other prominent dead United Irishmen.[92] Yet by and large, over the nineteenth century, areas in north-east Ulster formerly implicated in rebellion were to become bastions of staunch unionism. With the realignment of political allegiances, the republican heritage of 1798 became a discomforting skeleton in the closet for Ulster unionists and was subject to self-censorship.

At the same time, Ulster Protestants who were still willing to acknowledge their previous association with the radical politics of the 1790s were repulsed by what they considered as the brash co-option of the memory of the United Irishmen by Irish nationalism, which, following Daniel O'Connell, became inseparably associated with Catholics. Images on Home Rule banners displayed in the 1870s at nationalist rallies in Ulster featured William Orr alongside the pope and O'Connell.[93] The nationalist takeover of republican memory is also noticeable in songbooks, as exemplified in the ballad 'By Memory Inspired', with its recurring verse 'Here's a memory to the friends that are gone'. The song, which dates to the early part of the second half of the nineteenth century, opens with 'a tribute to O'Connell that is gone' and then devotes a stanza to reiterating the accusations of miscarriage of justice in Orr's case:

In October Ninety-Seven,
May his soul find rest in Heaven!
William Orr to execution was led on;
The jury, drunk, agreed
That Irish was his creed,
For perjury and threats drove them on, boys, on.[94]

This interpretation started off locally as a subaltern counter-memory, but by the mid-nineteenth century it had become the dominant narrative, confidently put forward by an increasingly assured nationalist memory. Its general acceptance can be attributed in no small part to the impact of Madden's writings. His detailed account of the 'case of William Orr' made use of documentary evidence to put forward a strong condemnation of the authorities ('Lord Camden's cause to "Remember Orr"'), which was of seminal influence on popular nineteenth-century nationalist historiography.[95] In his pioneering study on collective memory from 1925, the French sociologist Maurice Halbwachs emphasized the crucial role of social frameworks (*cadres sociaux*) in shaping memory.[96] The political conversion, at least in public, of Presbyterian communities and their apparent disavowal of the memory of 1798, in conjunction with its adoption by Catholics, fundamentally changed the social frameworks at the centre of local 1798 remembrance, facilitating classic conditions for collective amnesia among Ulster Protestants.

Nonetheless, despite the strong incentive to forget a past which was incongruous with the prevailing politics of the present, this was not a case of total oblivion. While acknowledging that 'Ulster Protestants have sometimes engaged in a process of remembering to forget', Ian McBride has perceptively identified 'the survival of a "hidden" history of the '98 in the Ulster countryside'.[97] Unusually, this vernacular folk history was documented on different occasions by collectors with diverse political views. These included not only unrepentant radicals, who bemoaned the defeat of the rebels, and liberals, who still harboured affections to the United Irish ideology while voicing objections to violence, but also conservatives, who opposed the rebellion and yet found themselves fascinated by it. For example, some three decades after the rebellion, the Carrickfergus shopkeeper Samuel McSkimin, a former yeoman who may have even informed on United Irishmen in his home area of Ballyclare, travelled around the Ulster countryside plying common people with drink at considerable personal expense, in order to cajole them into recounting recollections of 1798, which he then incorporated into his posthumously published history of the rebellion.[98]

The narrators of local traditions, whom the various collectors interviewed, included both supporters and opponents of the rebellion, and in some cases their relatives who had fought on both sides of what was clearly a civil war. Accordingly, the collected oral traditions reveal the ambiguous nature of 1798 remembrance in Ulster, as indicated in McSkimin's clarification of the name by which the rebellion was popularly referred to in local parlance: 'In speaking of this insurrection it is very rarely called a rebellion, but commonly the "turn out"; the call used at the time, to those who appeared tardy to come forth to the ranks.'[99] This was neither a case of wholesale forgetting nor of subaltern counter-memory persisting intact in face of defeat, but a complex combination of memory and forgetting marked by ambivalence.

Traces of continued remembrance of William Orr can be discerned within such works of alternative historiography, which sought to counter the domineering influence of the sectarian 'matrix of memory' established by Musgrave and elaborated in subsequent loyalist Protestant polemics.[100] In his tireless efforts to access all available sources for the biographies of United Irishmen, Madden made extensive use of oral history, tracking down surviving former rebels as well as interviewing friends and relations. His manuscript notes offer glimpses of apocryphal stories told about Orr locally, among them an anecdote, found by Mary Ann McCracken in the papers of the veteran rebel Jemmy Hope, which recounted how Orr declined a plan hatched by a Belfast spirit merchant (William McClean of North Street) to spring him out of prison.[101]

Folk remembrance could also assume non-narrative forms. One way of subtly remembering William Orr was to name children after him. This commemorative practice began with the christening of his daughter Wilmhelmina, who was born shortly after his execution, and it achieved wide popularity thereafter. For example, in 1798, Joseph McGaw and Laetitia Thoburn from the parish of Carnmoney in County Antrim expressed their indignation at the execution by calling their son William Orr.[102] Moreover, such customs crossed political divides. The historian of the Orange Order Robert Mackie Sibbett, who hailed from Portglenone, County Antrim (nearby Ballymena), observed in the early twentieth century: 'To this day the name is popular among those who are in sympathy with sedition, notwith-standing the fact that it also belongs to men conspicuous for loyalty.'[103] Even if the original reason for this trend in children's names was not always discussed openly, and for some may have become obscure over time, it appears that loyalists did not completely forsake all association with the memory of United Irishmen.

If republicanism went underground in Ireland in the immediate aftermath of the rebellion, it was allowed to thrive in the Irish diaspora. Kerby Miller's inspection of Ulster Presbyterian immigrant corre-spondence suggests that, in the first half of the nineteenth century, there was a mass exodus to the United States of radicals who were unwilling to conform to unionist politics.[104] Invited in 1831 to speak before a predominantly Irish audience at a dinner in Philadelphia's Congress Hall, William Sampson (who had been living in America since 1806) was toasted as 'the defender of William Orr'. In his 'affecting and effective' speech, the trial and execution were presented as 'the epitome of Ireland's history'. Sampson, like other former United Irishmen, was wary of being forgotten. Exhorting his audience to 'Remember Orr', he added 'may you remember me when you remember Orr. And whilst I live I shall be grateful to you.'[105] Republican memory was expressed freely in exile and transmitted to future generations of Irish-Americans, who could then export it back to Ireland. Speaking in Philadelphia in 1895 at an event dedicated to the commemoration of Robert Emmet, Rev. George Whitfield Pepper of Cleveland, Ohio, who was originally from Ballinagarrick in County Down (born to a loyalist father and a republican mother) and who became a Fenian supporter in the aftermath of the American Civil War, dwelt on the memory of Orr. He described his death as 'one of the noblest incidents in history' and considered the resolution to remember Orr an appropriate way of marking all forms of oppression in Ireland.[106]

In 1824, from the safety of Philadelphia and the pseudonym Solomon Secondsight, James McHenry, originally from Larne in County Antrim, wrote *O'Halloran; or The Insurgent Chief*, which was an early attempt to forge a cultural memory of 1798 in Ulster.[107] Though a work of historical fiction, he considered mention of William Orr unavoidable:

> To give a minute account of the sufferings of this greatly lamented favourite of the people, would interfere too much with the main design of this history; but his fate was too closely interwoven with, and had too important an influence on many

transactions, which it will be incumbent on us to relate, to permit us to pass it over in silence.

In addition to several references made in passing, a chapter is devoted to a detailed account of Orr's trial and execution. Towards the end of the novel, the author concludes that the persecution of Orr was the main cause of the rebellion:

> The blood of martyrs has been truly said to be like seed to the cause for which they suffered; and perhaps, in no portion of the history of nations, has this truth been more clearly illustrated than in that we have just recited. The unnecessary, unjust, impolite, and cruel execution of William Orr, almost instantaneously resulted in thousands of William Orrs, or rather of characters such as he was accused of being, starting into existence, and vowing revenge upon his persecutors.[108]

In 1843, writing an appendix 'containing biographical memoirs of the principle characters' for a new Belfast edition of his novel, McHenry noted with regard to Orr:

> The narrative given in the novel, of the sufferings of this victim of a cruel and ill-fated policy adheres closely, in all its parts, to the real facts. The story was of a character too solemn and melancholy, as well as of too much publicity, to warrant an interference of invention, and too impressive and affecting to require it.[109]

Unlike the other characters, which were loosely based on historical personages, Orr was considered inviolable.

Though the southern nationalist writer Charles Kickham doubted 'Whether our Northern friends "remember Orr"', references to Orr continuously reappeared in popular historical novels on 1798 in Ulster.[110] Most notably, Wesley Greenhill Lyttle's local bestseller *Betsy Gray or, Hearts of Down* (originally serialized in the *North Down Herald and Bangor Gazette* in 1885–6 and repeatedly republished thereafter) included chapters titled 'Remember Orr!' and 'The First Victim'. Referring to his use of the slogan 'Remember Orr' in his critically acclaimed *The Northern Iron* (1907), the Belfast-born author George A. Birmingham (pseudonym of the Church of Ireland clergyman James Owen Hannay) added: 'even now his name is not wholly forgotten'.[111] As indicated by their reissue in multiple editions, such literary writings appealed to readers in Protestant Ulster. They contributed to the popularity of the memory of Orr, despite the mainstream political shift towards unionism, and constituted what could be labelled works of 'cultural unforgetting'.

Towards the end of the nineteenth century, a group of concerned Belfast antiquarians, who were unwilling 'to allow records and investigations into the past history and antiquities of our Province to pass into oblivion', committed themselves to collecting 'the immense mass of information still existing in the possession of private persons, ere it be utterly lost'. In reviving the *Ulster Journal of Archaeology* as their main platform, they explicitly pronounced that 'space will be given to the Insurrection of '98'.[112] Robert Magill Young, who was disturbed that 'the social and local details of the struggle in Ulster are dying fast out with their narrators', gathered folklore of 1798 in Ulster, 'with the hope of preserving some material of this description, however scanty'.[113] Among the traditions Young collected from his relatives was information on 'the way that the spy who informed on William Orr and his friends got their names'. He also took down a story attributed to Samuel Skelton, the agent of Lord Massereene and a yeoman, which told of an unsuccessful attempt by a female acquaintance of Orr to secure by bribe the appointment of a supportive jury member.[114] In compiling *Memories of '98*, Rev. William Sunderland Smith noted that 'many of the events of a minor character, hitherto unrecorded, connected with the Insurrection of 1798, are fast becoming the merest traditions'.[115] He collected an account from a loyalist family acquainted with Orr's relatives which told how jail officials had buoyed their hopes 'with the belief that he would not really be put to death at the time appointed for his execution, but only partially so' in order to enable his resuscitation.[116]

Francis Joseph Bigger, the most prominent of these antiquarians, followed in the footsteps of Madden and devotedly compiled sources for biographies of 'The Northern Leaders of '98', professing that 'it has fallen to me to be a chronicler of their lives and actions'. In 1906, he published *Remember Orr* – a comprehensive presentation of all available information on William Orr, including documentary and folklore sources, written in hagiographical style.[117] Although he has been labelled 'a somewhat unreliable historian', Bigger has been credited for his 'unerring instinct for choosing popular-themes and a remarkable ability to inspire ordinary people'.[118] Regardless of the book's dismissal from a positivist perspective as 'quaint and rather lopsided', it stands out in cultural terms as a landmark of memory revival.[119] Details drawn from it would be repeated by the Belfast raconteur Cathal O'Byrne, an admirer of Bigger, whose writings would enjoy local popularity and reappear in several local editions.[120] Memory Studies have stressed the crucial role of memory agents or, to use a term coined by Brian Conway in relation to Northern Ireland, 'memory choreographers' in mediating and reshaping social remembrance.[121] Bigger's vigorous commemorative initiatives, alongside his encouragement of the work of other collectors, confronted the waning of folk memory in Ulster.

The revival of memory facilitated by the publication of these *fin de siècle* folklore collections fed into the centenary celebrations of the 1798 rebellion, which effectively commenced with the centennial of Orr's execution. In October 1897, Thomas Fitzpatrick, the leading cartoonist of the constitutional nationalist *Weekly Freeman*, sketched an image of conciliation whereby unionists, lead by Edward Sanderson, joined with moderate nationalists, lead by John Dillon, in combined commemoration of William Orr.[122] Contrary to this fanciful vision of unity, the centennial commemoration of the United Irishmen turned out to be highly contentious, pitting unionists against nationalists, as well as fermenting bitter competition between rival nationalist factions. After constitutional nationalists declared their intention, at the first public meeting of the Belfast United '98 Centenary Association (4 October 1897), to use the celebrations to reunite the Irish parliamentary party and promote Home Rule, separatist republicans were concerned that they would be side-stepped in the commemorative organizations. The Irish Republican Brotherhood appealed to the Dublin '98 Central Committee and received its support for the establishment of an all-inclusive Ulster '98 council, to be elected on the anniversary of Orr's execution. However, the commemorative demonstration that took place on 14 October 1897 at St Mary's Hall was organized by John Dillon's northern lieutenant, Joseph Devlin, as an exclusively Irish Party affair.[123] In this partisan spirit, Dillon, alongside other nationalist members of parliament, led a procession of mostly Catholics through the streets of Belfast city centre in which banners of 'Remember Orr' were waved alongside 'Ulster wants Home Rule'.[124]

Memory of Orr featured prominently throughout the centennial commemorations. The first of the national '98 Centenary Committee's publications was a penny pamphlet entitled *The Story of William Orr*, issued in January 1898, which was inscribed 'Remember Orr' and dedicated to 'the first martyr of the United Irishmen'.[125] Several local '98 clubs established in Ulster that year were named after him, and others made sure that he was commemorated in some form. For example, the Belfast centenary club on Stephen Street put on display a pike-staff attributed to William Orr, which was 'acquired through a descendent of the Martyr' and 'given a place of honour on the walls of the club'.[126] At a meeting of the Belfast William Orr '98 Club in St Mary's Hall on 6 May 1898, a great-grandson of William Orr ceremoniously unfurled a new 'Remember Orr' banner in which Orr's portrait was encircled by images of prominent United Irish heroes – Wolfe Tone, Thomas Russell, Henry Joy McCracken, and Lord Edward Fitzgerald. In a hostile report, the unionist *Belfast News-Letter* scoffed at how the participants were exhorted 'to "remember" various "martyrs" and *pathriots* [sic] of the '98 movement, and they were remembered accordingly more or less vociferously', while pointing out that the date coincided with the anniversary of the Phoenix Park murders (1882) – a more recent atrocity which loyalists were 'unable to forget'.[127]

In the polarized politics of the time, nationalist commemoration of rebellion was unacceptable to loyalists. The Grand Master of the Orange Order in Belfast, Rev. Richard Rutledge Kane, passionately argued that 1798 was 'a subject full of the most painful memories' and that it would be best to 'rather have that terrible year forgotten and forgiven'.[128] At the same time, he called upon loyalists to 'abstain from any interference whatever with the demonstrators'.[129] Nonetheless, the indignation of Protestant loyalists reached boiling point that summer. In reaction to a nationalist commemorative procession in the Belfast Catholic area of Hannastown, which celebrated the anniversary of the Battle of Antrim (6 June 1898), violent rioting broke out on the unionist Shankill Road. In return, the Orange commemorations on 12 July were perceived by nationalists as a loyalist attempt to eclipse the memory of 1798, and were met with rioting in Belfast's Catholic neighbourhoods. A month later, trains carrying the northern participants in the main national 1798 demonstration in Dublin (15 August) were attacked on their return to Belfast and rioting spread to the city centre.[130] These outbursts of sectarian rowdiness seem to signify the ultimate purging of the United Irishmen from Ulster Protestant memory and the completion of the appropriation of the memory of 1798 by predominantly Catholic nationalists.

De-commemorative vandalism rarely results in total amnesia, however. Critical studies of iconoclastic attempts to obliterate the memory of tyrants in ancient Rome – labelled by classicists *damnatio memoriae* – have revealed that this 'was not exactly about the destruction of memory, though ancient sources insist that it was' and 'what actually occurred was a highly symbolic, universal display of pantomime forgetfulness'.[131] Consequently, '*damnatio memoriae* did not negate historical traces, but created gestures which served to *dishonour* the record of the person and so, in an oblique way, to confirm memory'.[132] Similarly, by opting actively to oppose nationalist demonstrations, Protestants unwittingly engaged with commemoration of the United Irishmen. Their advocacy of contrived forgetting paradoxically encouraged the niggling persistence of memory.

Mainstream unionist histories attempted to airbrush the local 1798 experience out of Ulster history, as in Ernest Hamilton's *The Soul of Ulster* (1917), which included a chapter on the 1798 Rebellion but omitted any reference to the rebellion in the North, and to William Orr.[133] Checked by traditions of ambiguous remembrance, the popular reception of this historiographical omission was ultimately limited. Innovative studies of silence as a 'socially constructed space' have shown that avoidance of speech does not necessarily promote forgetting at the expense of remembering, but can function as a mediator between memory and oblivion.[134] In contrast to the official line of wilful amnesia, the Presbyterian historian Rev. James Barkley Woodburn answered the rhetorical question 'how far was the Ulster Scot concerned in this rebellion?' by arguing that 'it is certain he was embroiled more deeply than most of the historians allow'. His popular history of *The Ulster Scot* (1914) included extensive chapters on the United Irishmen and the 1798 rebellion in Ulster, with a section on William Orr (which drew heavily on Bigger).[135]

Conversely, nationalist resolve to 'Remember Orr' did not produce spectacular results. For all the commemorative assertiveness of the centennial, perhaps due in part to intra-nationalist squabbles, no monument was erected in William Orr's memory in 1898. In comparison with the centennial fervour, subsequent nationalist commemoration was low-key and easily forgotten. In 1913, one of the clubs of the republican youth movement Na Fianna Éireann, which attended a march from the Falls Road to Cave Hill in commemoration of the 150th anniversary of the birth of Wolfe Tone, was named after William Orr.[136] In 1924, a Gaelic football club in Antrim town was named after William Orr, reviving a tradition dating from the inception of the GAA in County Antrim, when several clubs (Carnally in 1887 and Belfast in 1888) were named after him, but this club ceased to function in the late 1930s.[137] In 1938, the London-based bookseller Joseph Fowler devoted to William Orr the first leaflet in the series

'Who Fears to Speak of '98?', issued for the 140th anniversary and 'launched at a price and in a form that would reach the humblest of people'.[138] In 1948, Orr appeared on a banner that was waved at a sesquicentennial commemorative march down the Falls Road.[139]

Republican activists tirelessly reiterated the call to 'Remember Orr' in various minor publications and at countless political gatherings. Apart from bringing the United Irish legacy in Ulster to the attention of nationalist-minded people, they were – in the words of Aodh de Blacam – determined constantly to remind 'Northerners who have forgotten it'.[140] This self-serving rhetoric was spurned by the majority of Presbyterians in Northern Ireland. The impact of nationalist memorialization for most of the twentieth century falls short of the earlier achievements of Madden or Bigger and its overall unimpressive record casts doubt on the sincerity of republican self-confidence, which may have been covering up anxieties about its incapability. The most noticeable shortcoming, when compared to the numerous memorials erected for other United Irishmen, was the consistent failure to mark the grave of William Orr. This glaring presence of absence, which would only be amended at the end of the century, embodies the ambiguous essence of social forgetting, which allows for private remembrance yet prevents its fulfilment in the public sphere.

III

Commemoration of the United Irishmen would once again peak in the 1798 bicentennial, which was launched on 14 October 1997 with an event at Templepatrick Old Presbyterian Church, organized by a purposely-designated Remember Orr Society. A packed hall heard the Presbyterian minister and local historian Rev. Dr John Nelson deliver a lecture on Orr, which was accompanied by harp and uileann pipes. That afternoon, Orr's grave was ceremoniously marked with a small plaque, though significantly not by a full-size monument. Over the following year, numerous events commemorated the 1798 rebellion in Ulster, and it was generally maintained that this allowed a 'reclaiming by many Presbyterians of an important part of their history, which had in large part been forgotten or banished from communal memory'.[141]

In the conciliatory spirit of the concurrently brokered Good Friday Agreement, 1798 bicentennial commemorations in Northern Ireland often brought together Catholic nationalists and Presbyterians unionists. With the financial support of the Cultural Diversities Programme of the Community Relations Council, the United Irishmen Commemoration Society launched at the Linen Hall Library in Belfast on 4 June 1998, a facsimile reprint of Bigger's *Remember Orr*, making this remarkable resource, which had long gone out of print and become a collector's item, once again readily available.[142] Newly introduced consociational policies of 'parity of esteem' fed into cultural revivalism, which rekindled in Presbyterian communities an interest in their United Irish lineage. In 2004, the Ulster-Scots Folk Orchestra added to its traditional repertoire an emotive tune composed by the Antrim musician Willie Drennan titled 'William Orr's Farewell'. According to accompanying notes, it attempted to redress local ignorance, whereby 'the story of William Orr of Faranshane is unfortunately not well known and the principles he stood for often misunderstood'.[143] Once again, a Drennan was remembering Orr in a non-verbal form.

The south Antrim Presbyterian writer Niall McGrath published in 1998 a poem entitled 'Remembering Orr' in which he mused on the marking of the grave:

For the first time in two hundred years
your burial place is acknowledged
with a plaque, your memory is permitted
openly, is no longer the whispered shame
farmers would mutter about in remote fields.

Reflecting on the proximity of the modest tombstone to the ostentatious mausoleum of the local landlord family – the Uptons – and relating this to the contemporary political context in which the commemoration occurred, he pondered:

Would you think it fitting your death is marked
at this fateful time, when successors strive
to come to terms with similar cohabitation?[144]

In 2003, the east Belfast Protestant poet John Stevenson also published a poem 'Remember Orr', which touched on the theme of unbroken memory and 'constant scribbling', offering a reminder that local preoccupation with Orr had never ceased and that he had never been entirely forgotten.[145] With certain similarities to contemporary arrangements of 'truth and reconciliation' elsewhere, the amnesty provided by the new politics of peace in Northern Ireland was not grounded in oblivion but in restorative retelling of memory or, to use a term introduced by Graham Dawson, 'reparative remembering'.[146] This new-found remembering of Orr addressed a long history of social forgetting, which had cultivated memories riddled with inhibitions and beset by contestations.

NOTES

1 The research for this essay was initially sponsored by the Irish Research Council for the Humanities and Social Sciences, followed by a grant by the Israel Science Foundation (grant no. 810/07). It has also benefited from a National Endowment for the Humanities fellowship at the Keough-Naughton Institute of Irish Studies in the University of Notre Dame.

2 Roberto Cubelli, 'A New Taxonomy of Memory and Forgetting', in Sergio Della Sala (ed.), *Forgetting* (Hove and New York: Psychology Press, 2010), p.42.

3 Paul Ricoeur, *Memory, History, Forgetting* (Chicago: University of Chicago Press, 2004), pp.418, 426.

4 G.D. Zimmerman, *Songs of Irish Rebellion: Irish Political Street Ballads and Rebel Songs, 1780–1900* (Dublin: Four Courts Press, 2002), pp.226–7.

5 Joep Leerssen, '1798: The Recurrence of Violence and two Conceptualizations of History', *Irish Review*, 22 (1998), pp.37–45, at p.39.

6 J. Gordon, *History of the Rebellion in Ireland, in the Year 1798, &c. containing an impartial account of the proceedings of the Irish revolutionists, from the year 1782, till the suppression of the rebellion* (London: T. Hurts, 1803; orig. edn. 1801), p.82 n.

7 The informer, who is mentioned anonymously by the Victorian historian James Anthony Froude, was identified by W.J. Fitzpatrick as Samuel Turner (alias Richardson) of Newry: see J.A. Froude, *The English in Ireland in the Eighteenth Century* (3 Volumes, New York: Scribner, Armstrong, and Co., 1873), iii, pp.179–80; W.J. Fitzpatrick, *Secret Service under Pitt* (London and New York: Longmans, Green, and Co., 1892), p.55.

8 W.E.H. Lecky, *A History of Ireland in the Eighteenth Century* (5 Volumes, London: Longmans, Green, and Co., 1913; orig. edn. 1892), iv, pp.103, 115.

9 See Alan Ford, 'Martyrdom, History and Memory in Early Modern Ireland', in Ian McBride (ed.), *History and Memory in Modern Ireland* (Cambridge: Cambridge University Press, 2001), pp.43–66; Clodagh Tait, 'Catholic Martyrdom in Early Modern Ireland', *History Compass*, 2, 1 (2004), unpaginated.

10 F.C. Bartlett, *Remembering: A Study in Experimental Social Psychology* (Cambridge: Cambridge University Press, 1932), pp.197–214.

11 *The Press*, 21 Dec. 1797. A similar adulatory description appeared in a contemporary sympathetic account of the trial, which added that 'above all, there was in his aspect a mixture of firmness and sensibility which seemed to shew [*sic*] him gifted by nature with a generous and elevated spirit': see *A Brief Account of the Trial of William Orr, of Farranshane, in the County of Antrim* (Dublin, 1797), p.35. For the idealization of Orr as 'a widely accessible model of manly behaviour' see N.J. Curtin, 'Reclaiming Gender: Transgressive Identities in Modern Ireland', in Marilyn Cohen and N.J. Curtin (eds), *A Nation of Abortive Men': Gendered Citizenship and Early Irish Republicanism* (New York: St Martin's Press, 1999), pp.40–2.

12 'Notes and Queries', *Ulster Journal of Archaeology*, 2nd. ser., 1, 1 (1894), p.78.

13 A painting and sketch by Edwin Arthur Morrow (1877–1952) and a drawing by Joseph William Carey (1859–1937) were reproduced in F.J. Bigger, *Remember Orr* (Dublin: Maunsel and Co., 1906), pp.10, 78 (Morrow), 41 (Carey).

14 TCD, R.R. Madden Papers, MS 873/267, reproduced in R.H. Foy, *Remembering all the Orrs: the Story of the Orr families of Antrim and their Involvement in the 1798 Rebellion* (Belfast: Ulster Historical Foundation, 1999), pp.25–6.

15 R.R. Madden, *The United Irishmen: their Lives and Times*, 2nd ser. (2nd edn., Dublin: James Duffy, 1858), ii, p.254 n.

16 TCD, MS 873/267.

17 The published account reads: 'he was a man of very moderate abilities; athletic in his frame, active, and somewhat of a sporting character among his class': see R.R. Madden, *The United Irishmen: their Lives and Times*, 2nd ser. (2 Volumes, London: J. Madden and Co., 1843), ii, p.461.

18 *Belfast News-Letter*, 14 Oct. 1797; reproduced in Henry Joy, *Historical Collections Relative to the Town of Belfast from the Earliest Period to the Union with Britain* (Belfast: G. Berwick, 1817), p.444.

19 Chevalier de Latocnaye [Jacques Louis de Bourgenet], *A Frenchman's Walk through Ireland, 1796–7*; John Stevenson (trans.) of *Promenade d'un Français dans l'Irlande* [1797] (Belfast: McCaw, Stevenson and Orr: Dublin: Hodges, Figgis and Co., 1917), p.209.

20 N.J. Curtin, *The United Irishmen: Popular Politics in Ulster and Dublin, 1791–98* (Oxford: Clarendon Press, 1998), pp.241–5.

21 W.N. Osborough, 'Legal Aspects of the 1798 Rising, its Suppression and the Aftermath', in Thomas Bartlett et al. (eds), *1798: A Bicentenary Perspective* (Dublin: Four Courts Press, 2003), p.438, n. 2.

22 'Exact statement of the trial of Mr. Orr, taken down by an eminent stenographer', *The Press*, 19 Oct. 1797.

23 Martha McTier to William Drennan, 9 Oct. 1797 in Jean Agnew (ed.), *Drennan-McTier letters* (3 Volumes, Dublin: Irish Manuscripts Commission, 1998), ii, p.341; cited in Catriona Kennedy, '"Womanish epistles?" Martha McTier, Female Epistolarity and Late Eighteenth-Century Irish Radicalism', *Women's History Review*, 13:4 (2004), p.658.

24 Mary Ann to Henry Joy McCracken, 27 Sept. 1797, in Madden, *The United Irishmen*, 3rd ser. (4 Volumes, Dublin: James Duffy, 1846), i, p.164; also 2nd ser. (2nd edn., 1858), ii, pp.254–5.

25 Alexander Haliday to Lord Charlemont, 6 Oct. 1797, in J.T. Gilbert (ed.), *The Manuscripts and Correspondence of James, First Earl of Charlemont* (2 Volumes, London: H.M.S.O., 1891), ii, pp.306–7.

26 *The Press* subsequently published an account by James Orr admitting that he had forged the confession (28 Oct. 1797), as well as a copy of letter by William Orr (dated 10 Oct. 1797) that was sent to Lord Camden after the trial and which stated that the confession 'was base and false' (21 Nov. 1797): see Madden, *United Irishmen*, 2nd ser. (2nd edn., 1858), ii, pp.256–7.

27 Kevin Whelan, 'Introduction to Section V', in Bartlett et al. (eds), *1798: A Bicentenary Perspective*, p.388; T.D. Sullivan, 'Remember Orr', in idem, A.M. Sullivan and D.B. Sullivan, *Speeches From the Dock: or, Protests of Irish Patriotism* (23rd Dublin edn., Providence, R.I.: H. McElroy, Murphy and McCarthy, 1878), pp.28–31; cf. James Kelly, *Gallows Speeches from Eighteenth-Century Ireland* (Dublin: Four Courts Press, 2001).

28 Extracts of the letter were published in the *Press* and later reproduced in T.J. Howell, *A Complete Collection of State Trials and Proceedings for High Treason and Other Crimes and Misdemeanors* (33 Volumes, London: T.C. Hansard, 1809–25), xxxiii, p.906.

29 *The Trial of William Orr, at Carrickfergus Assizes, for Being an United Irishman; with his Dying Declaration* (Philadelphia, 1798), pp.16–18.

30 *A Brief Account of the Trial of William Orr*, pp.41–2.

31 For a reproduction see W.A. Maguire, *Up in Arms: the Rebellion of 1798 in Ireland: a Bicentenary Exhibition* (Belfast: Ulster Museum, 1998), p.168.

32 Orr's declaration was included in partisan accounts of the trial; see *A Brief Account of the Trial of William Orr*, pp.38–40; *The trial of William Orr*, pp.15–16. See also *Billy Bluff and 'Squire Firebrand: or, a sample of the times, as it periodically appeared in the Northern Star* (Belfast, 1797), p.28.

33 Richard Musgrave, *Memoirs of the Different Rebellions in Ireland, From the Arrival of the English* (3rd edn., 2 Volumes, Dublin, 1802), ii, p.217.

34 Testimony of James Kirk of Whinpark: W.S. Smith, *Memories of '98* (Belfast: Marcus Ward and Co., 1895), pp.42–3.

35 See Kelly, *Gallows Speeches*, p.39.

36 David Hume, *'To Right Some Things That We Thought Wrong': The Spirit of 1798 and Presbyterian Radicalism in Ulster* (Lurgan: Ulster Society, 1998), pp.40–1. A century later, the incumbent minister at Ballynure – Rev. Andrew James Blair – took pride in his predecessor's involvement with the wake: see Ian McBride, 'Memory and Forgetting: Ulster Presbyterians and 1798', in Bartlett et al. (eds), *1798: A Bicentenary Perspective*, p.491.

37 Although commonly believed to be the grave of William's 'favourite sister', it has been suggested that it may actually be the grave of his mother; see Foy, *Remembering all the Orrs*, p.33 n. 14.

38 *A Brief Account of the Trial of William Orr*, p.41.

39 Musgrave, *Memoirs*, p.217.

40 Samuel McSkimin, *The History and Antiquities of the County of the Town of Carrickfergus, from the Earliest Records till 1839; also, a statistical survey of said county, new edition, with notes and appendix by E.J. M'Crum* (Belfast: Mullan and Son, 1909), p.97 n. William Orr's

name is not listed in any of the masonic lodges in his area (though part of the register of lodge 783 Antrim for the 1790s is lost); see Petri Mirala, *Freemasonry in Ulster, 1733–1813: A Social and Political History of the Masonic Brotherhood in the North of Ireland* (Dublin: Four Courts Press, 2007), p.193.

41 Jim Smyth, 'Anti-Catholicism, conservatism, and conspiracy: Sir Richard Musgrave's *Memoirs of the Different Rebellions in Ireland*', *Eighteenth-Century Life*, 22, 3 (1998), p.71.

42 Charles Dickson, *Revolt in the North: Antrim and Down in 1798* (Dublin and London: Clonmore and Reynolds, 1960), p.182.

43 Shortly after the trial, jury member George Casement was attacked near Larne: see Rob Davison, 'George Casement and the United Irishmen', *North Irish Roots*, 9, 2 (1998), p.12. According to oral traditions collected in the mid-nineteenth century by Rev. Classon Porter of Larne, Casement went into hiding after receiving advance warning: see R.M. Young, *Ulster in '98: Episodes and Anecdotes* (Belfast: Marcus Ward and Co., 1893), p.50.

44 J.E. Bodnar, *Remaking America: Public Memory, Commemoration, and Patriotism in the Twentieth Century* (Princeton: Princeton University Press, 1992), pp.13–5.

45 For conceptualization of popular memory see Popular Memory Group, 'Popular Memory: Theory, Politics, Method', in Richard Johnson et al. (eds), *Making Histories: Studies in History-Writing and Politics* (London: University of Birmingham Press, 1982), pp.205–52 at p.211.

46 Madden identified the author as Deane (Theophilus) Swift (1774–1858): Madden, *United Irishmen*, 2nd ser. (2nd edn., 1858), pp.259–62.

47 For the newspaper's circulation see Kevin Whelan, 'The United Irishmen, the Enlightenment and Popular Culture', in D. Dickson et al. (eds), *The United Irishmen: Republicanism, Radicalism and Rebellion* (Dublin: Lilliput Press, 1993), pp.278–9.

48 *The Press*, 21 Nov. 1797.

49 *The Press*, 5 Dec. 1797.

50 *Trial of Peter Finerty, late printer of* The Press, *for a libel against his excellency Earl Camden, lord lieutenant of Ireland, in a letter signed Marcus, in that paper* (Dublin, 1798).

51 *The Debate in the Irish House of Peers on a Motion made by the Earl of Moira, Monday, February 19, 1798* (Dublin: John Milliken, 1798), pp.61–9.

52 Madden, *United Irishmen*, 1st ser. (1842), ii, p.45; also 2nd ser. (2nd edn., 1858), ii, p.262.

53 Reproduced in R.R. Madden (ed.), *Literary Remains of the United Irishmen of 1798 and Selections from other Popular Lyrics of their Times* (Dublin: James Duffy, 1887), pp.43–4.

54 Eviatar Zerubavel, *The Elephant in the Room: Silence and Denial in Everyday Life* (Oxford and New York: Oxford University Press, 2006).

55 William Drennan, *Fugitive Pieces, in Verse and Prose* (Belfast: F.D. Finlay, 1815), pp.79–81.

56 Madden, *The United Irishmen*, 1st ser. (1842), ii, p.45; also 2nd ser. (2nd edn., 1858), ii, p.262 [dated mistakenly to 1791].

57 Cf. E.H. Schor, *Bearing the Dead: The British Culture of Mourning from the Enlightenment to Victoria* (Princeton: Princeton University Press, 1994), esp. pp.48–52.

58 Thomas Moore, *Irish melodies* (revised edn., London: J. Power, 1821), p.10.

59 C.G. Duffy, *The Ballad Poetry of Ireland* (40th edn., Dublin: James Duffy, 1869; orig. edn. 1845), pp.70–2.

60 F.P. Carey, 'The Shrines of the Patriot Dead', in Seamus McKearney (ed.), *Ninety-Eight* (Belfast: The 1798 Commemoration Committee, 1948), pp.59–61. Francis Patrick Carey, who was a recognized authority on sites of pilgrimage (having authored essays on Lough Derg and Knock, among other places) took the poem too literally, maintaining that: 'Drennan nobly kept that watch. He was grandly the pioneer-pilgrim to the grave-shrines of Ninety-Eight. Neither the infirmities of age, nor yet the effects of his own privations when arrested and tried for complicity in the Rebellion, discouraged him in that weekly visit of reverence to Templepatrick, where Orr is buried.'

61 This verse appeared in the United Irish song 'Oh Union for ever', which was included in the revolutionary songbook *Paddy's Resource*; see *The Irish Harp (Attun'd to Freedom): A Collection of Patriotic Songs, Selected for Paddy's Amusement* (Dublin, 1798), p.88; also Madden, *Literary Remains*, p.23.

62 See list of 'Toasts and Sentiments' appended to a 1798 volume of *Paddy's Resource*. The toast also appeared as incriminating evidence in extracts of another printed list produced at the trial of Wicklow United Irishman Michael-William Byrne on 5 July 1798: see William

Ridgeway, *A Report of the Trial of Michael-William Byrne, Upon an Indictment for High Treason* (Dublin: John Exshaw, 1798), p.128.

63 John Gifford, *A History of the Political Life of the Right Honourable William Pitt, including some Account of the Times in which he Lived* (6 Volumes, London: T. Cadell and W. Davies, 1809), vi, pp.434–5. These toasts entered the folklore of political circles and appear in several variations in subsequent histories. For example, Samuel McSkimin has the second toast as 'May the Irish cabinet soon take the place of William Orr'; in Henry Grattan's memoirs, as written by his son, it appears as 'May the execution of Orr provide places for the cabinet of St. James's at the Castle'; Lecky's rendition of the first toast is 'to the memory of the martyred Orr': see McSkimin, *History and Antiquities*, p.97; Henry Grattan, *Memoirs of the Life and Times of the Rt. Hon. Henry Grattan* (5 Volumes, London: Henry Colburn, 1839–46), iv, p.319; Lecky, *A History of Ireland*, iv, pp.103–4.

64 *Courier*, 25 Dec. 1797; quoted in W.J. Fitzpatrick, *The Life, Times and Cotemporaries* [sic] *of Lord Cloncurry* (Dublin: James Duffy, 1855), p.126 n.

65 *The Report from the Secret Committee of the House of Commons* (Dublin, 1798), Appendix 20, p.208.

66 Grattan, *Memoirs*, iv, p.319.

67 Musgrave, *Memoirs*, p.217; see also McSkimin, *History and Antiquities*, p.97.

68 TCD, MS 873/336.

69 Young, *Ulster in '98*, p.89.

70 Bigger, *Remember Orr*, p.56.

71 Madden, *United Irishmen*, 2nd ser. (1843), ii, p.485.

72 W.G. Lyttle, *Betsy Gray or, Hearts of Down: a Tale of '98* (Newcastle, County Down: *Mourne Observer*, 1968; orig. edn. 1888), p.134. In the early twentieth century, such a medal was in the possession of the London antiquarian coin dealers Messrs. Spink and Son; see R.D., 'A Memorial of 1798', *Journal of the Cork Historical and Archaeological Society*, 2nd ser., 12 (1906), pp.102–3.

73 *Descriptive catalogue of the collection of antiquities and other objects, illustrative of Irish history, exhibited in the museum, Belfast on the occasion of the twenty-second meeting of the British Association for the Advancement of Science, September, 1852* (Belfast, 1852), p.27.

74 See Young, *Ulster in '98*, pp.89–90; Bigger, *Remember Orr*, pp.55–8; Maguire, *Up in Arms*, pp.167–8.

75 Y.H. Yerushalmi, *Zakhor: Jewish History and Jewish Memory* (Seattle: University of Washington Press, 1982).

76 *The Annual Register, or a View of the History, Politics, and Literature, of the Year 1828*, 70 (1829), p.127.

77 *The Press*, 28 Oct. 1797.

78 James Coigly, *The life of the Rev James Coigly, an address to the people of Ireland, as written by himself during his confinement in Maidstone Gaol* (London, 1798), p.60; see also Dáire Keogh, *A Patriot Priest: A Life of Reverend James Coigly* (Cork: Cork University Press, 1998), p.1. Already during his trial, Coigly's defence counsel referred to 'the fate of the unfortunate Mr. Orr'; see *The trial of James O'Coigly, otherwise called James Quigley, otherwise called James John Fivey, Arthur O'Connor, esq., John Binns, John Allen, and Jeremiah Leary for high treason, under a special commission, at Maidstone, in Kent, on Monday the twenty-first and Tuesday the twenty-second days of May 1798, taken in short-hand by Joseph Gurney* (London: M. Gurney, 1798), pp.381–2.

79 For Emmet's memory, see Marianne Elliott, *Robert Emmet: The Making of a Legend* (London: Profile, 2003); Ruan O'Donnell, *Remember Emmet: Images of the Life And Legacy of Robert Emmet* (Bray: Irish Academic Press, 2003); Kevin Whelan, 'Robert Emmet: Between History and Memory', *History Ireland*, 11, no. 3 (2003), pp.50–54.

80 Young, *Ulster in '98*, p.80; see also *Some Recollections of Hugh McCall* (Lisburn: J.E. Reilly, 1899), p.16.

81 Bigger, *Remember Orr*, p.55.

82 Ibid., p.57.

83 P.S. Robinson, 'Hanging Ropes and Buried Secrets', *Ulster Folklife*, 32 (1986), pp.8–9. With reference to a contemporary esoteric code, Robinson proposes that the date may have been an encrypted religious reference to I.N.R.I., thus evoking Orr's martyrdom by drawing an analogy to Jesus.

84 Samuel McSkimin, *Annals of Ulster; or, Ireland Fifty Years Ago* (Belfast: John Henderson, 1849), p.91.
85 For facsimile reproductions, see Young, *Ulster in '98*, p.90; Bigger, *Remember Orr*, p.58. The italics in the quotation are carried from the original text. The provenance was first noted by Mary Ann McCracken, who identified for Madden the author as Wolfe Tone; TCD, MS 873/33. This claim was subsequently recognized in social memory; see '98 Centenary Committee, *The Story of William Orr* (Dublin: James Duffy, 1898), pp.13–14.
86 Bigger, *Remember Orr*, pp.55–6; Maguire, *Up in Arms*, p.167. An indication of the poem's popularity can be gathered from it migrating across the Atlantic and reappearing in United Irish republican circles in the United States: see D.A. Wilson, *United Irishmen, United States: Immigrant Radicals in the Early Republic* (Dublin: Four Courts Press, 1998), p.162.
87 See Hermann Ebbinghaus, *Memory: A Contribution to Experimental Psychology* (New York: Teachers College, Columbia University, 1913).
88 Allan Blackstock, *Loyalism in Ireland, 1789–1829* (Woodbridge: Boydell, 2007), pp.99–105.
89 Castlereagh to the duke of Portland, 3 June 1799, in C. Vane (ed.), *Memoirs and Correspondence of Viscount Castlereagh, Second Marquess of Londonderry* (4 Volumes, London: Henry Colburn, 1850), ii, p.326.
90 The village of Templepatrick was described as a 'hotbed of mischief' in 1798 and was consequently burned by the Crown forces; see memoir of James Boyle (dated Nov. 1838) in Angélique Day and Patrick McWilliams (eds), *Ordnance Survey Memoirs of Ireland*, 35 (Belfast: Institute of Irish Studies, Queen's University Belfast, 1996), pp.123–4.
91 J.G. Patterson, *In the Wake of the Great Rebellion: Republicanism, Agrarianism and Banditry in Ireland After 1798* (Manchester and New York: Manchester University Press, 2008), pp.13–79.
92 R.B. McDowell, *Public Opinion and Government Policy in Ireland, 1801–46* (London: Faber and Faber, 1952), p.50.
93 Neil Jarman, *Displaying Faith: Orange, Green and Trade Union Banners in Northern Ireland* (Belfast: Institute of Irish Studies, Queen's University Belfast, 1999), pp.34–5.
94 Despite its reference to 'the memory of John Mitchel that is gone!', the ballad antedates Mitchel's death in 1875 and was already hawked as a broadside in 1864; see Duncathail [R. Varian] (ed.), *Street Ballads, Popular Poetry and Household Songs of Ireland* (2nd edn., Dublin: McGlashan and Gill Co., 1865), p.88fn.
95 Madden, *The United Irishmen*, 2nd ser. (2nd edn., 1858), ii, pp.253–63. Evidence of the influence of Madden's account can be found in seminal popular histories, see for example: John Mitchel, *The History of Ireland, from the Treaty of Limerick to the Present Time* (New York: D.J. Sadlier & Co., 1868), p.277; M.F. Cusack, *The Illustrated History of Ireland from the Earliest Period* (London: Longmans, Green, and Co., 1868), pp.548–9.
96 Maurice Halbwachs, *On Collective Memory* (Chicago: University of Chicago Press, 1992).
97 McBride, 'Memory and Forgetting', pp.478–96.
98 McSkimin, *Annals of Ulster*; re-issued as *History of the Irish Rebellion in the Year 1798 Particularly in Antrim, Down and Derry* (Belfast: John Mullan, 1853). See also 'Samuel McSkimmin, Historian of Carrickfergus', *The Nation*, 4 Mar. 1843, p.329.
99 McSkimin, *Annals of Ulster*, p.112.
100 The term 'matrix of memory' is borrowed from Kevin Whelan, *The Tree of Liberty: Radicalism, Catholicism and the Construction of Irish Identity 1760–1830* (Cork: Cork University Press, 1996), pp.135–8. For Musgrave's interpretation of 1798 and its impact, see James Kelly, *Sir Richard Musgrave, 1746–1818: Ultra-Protestant Ideologue* (Dublin: Four Courts Press, 2009), pp.90–125 (esp. pp.115 and 119–20); see also Stuart Andrews, *Irish Rebellion: Protestant Polemic, 1798–1900* (Basingstoke and New York: Palgrave Macmillan, 2006).
101 M.A. McCracken to R.R. Madden, 2 July 1844 (TCD, MS 873/155).
102 W.O. McGaw, 'Notes on the Parish of Carnmoney, Co. Antrim', *Ulster Folklife*, 1 (1955), p.56.
103 R.M. Sibbett, *Orangeism in Ireland and Throughout the Empire* (2 Volumes, Belfast: Henderson, 1914), ii, p.28.
104 K.A. Miller, '"Heirs of Freedom" or "Slaves to England"? Protestant Society and Unionist Hegemony in Nineteenth-Century Ulster', *Radical History Review*, 104 (2009), pp.17–40.

105 *Hazard's Register of Pennsylvania*, 8, no. 19 (1831), pp.299–303.
106 G.W. Pepper, *Under Three Flags; or, The Story of my Life as Preacher, Captain in the Army, Chaplain, Consul, with Speeches and Interviews* (Cincinnati: Curts and Jennings, 1899), pp.524–5. Pepper was born in 1833; his Episcopalian father was master of the local Orange lodge and his mother's family had been United Irishmen; he emigrated to America in 1854 and was known there as an untypically Protestant advocate of Irish nationalism.
107 Charles Fanning, *The Irish Voice in America: 250 Years of Irish-American Fiction* (Lexington: University Press of Kentucky, 2000), pp.46–50.
108 Solomon Secondsight, *O'Halloran; or the Insurgent Chief: An Irish Historical Tale of 1798* (2 Volumes, Philadelphia: H.C. Carey and I. Lea, 1824).
109 James McHenry, *The Insurgent Chief; or, the Pikemen of '98: A Romance of the Irish Rebellion, to which is added an appendix, containing biographical memoirs of the principal characters and descriptive of the scenery of the work* (Belfast: John Henderson, 1844), p.461.
110 'Our Protestant Compatriots – the Wild Justice of Revenge' (12 July 1862), reproduced in C.J. Kickham, *Sally Cavanagh; or the Untenanted Graves: A Tale of Tipperary* (Dublin: W.B. Kelly, 1869), p.xx.
111 Lyttle, *Betsy Gray*, pp.26–30; G.A. Birmingham, *The Northern Iron* (Dublin: Maunsel and Co., 1907), p.113.
112 'Prospectus', *Ulster Journal of Archaeology*, 2nd ser., 1:1 (1894), p.1.
113 Young, *Ulster in '98*, preface.
114 Ibid., pp.70–1.
115 *Ulster Journal of Archaeology*, 2nd ser., 1:2 (Jan. 1895), p.133; republished in Smith, *Memories of '98*, p.7.
116 *Ulster Journal of Archaeology*, 2nd ser., 1:3 (Apr. 1895), p.216; republished in Smith, *Memories of '98*, pp.42–3.
117 Bigger, *Remember Orr*. It was sold for a shilling and distributed in Belfast by the Catholic Book Company; see *Ulster Herald*, 26 May 1906, p.3.
118 Roger Dixon, 'Heroes for a new Ireland: Francis Joseph Bigger and the Leaders of the '98', in T.M. Owen (ed.), *From Corrib to Cultra: Folklife Essays in Honour of Alan Gailey* (Belfast: Institute of Irish Studies, 2000), pp.29–37 (esp. pp.37–8).
119 P.K. McIvor, 'Regionalism in Ulster: an Historical Perspective', *Irish University Review*, 13:2 (1983), pp.184–5.
120 Cathal O'Byrne, *As I Roved Out* (facsimile of 3rd edn., Belfast: Blackstaff, 1982; orig. edn. 1946), pp.378–85.
121 Brian Conway, *Commemoration and Bloody Sunday: Pathways of Memory* (Basingstoke and New York: Palgrave Macmillan, 2010).
122 *Weekly Freeman*, 16 Oct. 1897; see L.W. McBride, 'Visualizing '98: Irish Nationalist Cartoons Commemorate the Revolution', *Eighteenth-Century Life*, 22:3 (1998), p.109.
123 Owen McGee, *The IRB: the Irish Republican Brotherhood from the Land League to Sinn Fein* (Dublin: Four Courts Press, 2005), p.253; see also Cathal O'Byrne, 'Maud Gonne in Belfast Long Ago', in McKearney (ed.), *Ninety-Eight*, pp.29–32.
124 A.C. Hepburn, *Catholic Belfast and Nationalist Ireland in the era of Joe Devlin, 1871–1934* (Oxford: Oxford University Press, 2008), p.55.
125 '98 Centenary Committee, *The Story of William Orr*.
126 *Shan Van Vocht*, 3, 2 (7 Feb. 1898), p.31.
127 *Belfast News-Letter*, 7 May 1898, p.7.
128 *Belfast News-Letter*, 21 May 1898.
129 *Belfast News-Letter*, 2 June 1898.
130 Peter Collins, *Who Fears to Speak of '98? Commemoration and the Continuing Impact of the United Irishmen* (Belfast: Ulster Historical Foundation, 2004), pp.38–43, 47.
131 Peter Stewart, 'The Destruction of Statues in Late Antiquity', in R. Miles (ed.), *Constructing Identities in Late Antiquity* (London and New York: Routledge, 1999), p.167.
132 C.W. Hedrick, *History and Silence: Purge and Rehabilitation of Memory in Late Antiquity* (Austin: University of Texas Press, 2000), p.93.
133 E.W. Hamilton, *The Soul of Ulster* (New York: E.P. Dutton & Co., 1917).
134 Efrat Ben-Ze'ev, Ruth Ginio and J.M. Winter (eds), *Shadows of War: A Social History of Silence in the Twentieth Century* (Cambridge and New York: Cambridge University Press, 2010).

135 J.B. Woodburn, *The Ulster Scot: His History and Religion* (London: H. R. Allenson, 1914), pp.274–279.
136 Brian Walker, *Past and Present: History, Identity and Politics in Ireland* (Belfast: Institute of Irish Studies, 2000), pp.55–6.
137 'Gaelic Games in Antrim Town' [Online]. Available from: http://stcomgallsgaa.com/history.htm [accessed 1 October 2011]. My thanks to Dr Dónal McAnallen for sharing with me his knowledge of the subject.
138 J.H. Fowler, *William Orr* (London: St Giles Bookshop, 1938).
139 Collins, *Who Fears to Speak*, p.72.
140 Aodh de Blácam, *The Black North; An Account of the Six Counties of Un-Recovered Ireland: Their People, Their Treasures, and Their History* (Dublin: M.H. Gill, 1950; orig. edn. 1938), p.xi; for reference to Orr, see pp.161–4.
141 Collins, *Who Fears to Speak*, p.81.
142 Ibid., p.95.
143 Ulster Scots Folk Orchestra, *Bringin it Thegither* (Fowk Gates, 2004). My thanks to Willie Drennan for providing me with the music track and album notes.
144 Niall McGrath, 'Remembering Orr', *Books Ireland*, 215 (1998), p.228.
145 John Stevenson, *The Cherry Tree* (Belfast: Lapwing, 2003), p.18.
146 Graham Dawson, *Making Peace with the Past? Memory, Trauma and the Irish Troubles* (Manchester: Manchester University Press, 2007), esp. pp.77–85 and 315–8; cf. Andrew Schaap, *Political Reconciliation* (London and New York: Routledge, 2005), pp.124–37.

8

VARIETIES OF IRISH FAMINE DEATH[1]

CORMAC Ó GRÁDA

Introduction

The demographic toll of famines is a controversial issue, and for two quite separate reasons. The first is that famines are nearly always blamed on somebody, and excess mortality is reckoned to be a measure of guilt. The second is that famines are more likely to occur in economically backward regions and countries, where demographic data are often poor or non-existent, and where non-crisis deaths are not easily separated from famine mortality. Today, it is excess mortality in China during the Great Leap famine and in Ukraine in 1931–33 that creates the most controversy, but not so long ago the death toll in Ireland during our own Great Famine was equally controversial. The most heated debates about excess mortality tend to be not between demographers, but between historians with contrasting views about the role of human agency and culpability.

The main focus of this essay is not on aggregate mortality, but on what people died of during famines. Our standard images of famine victims are images of starvation: pot-bellied children; gaunt, scarecrow-like adults; and the grass-stained mouths of the dead. Such grim images are all too real, yet throughout history the great majority of famine victims have succumbed to infectious diseases rather than outright starvation. Weakened immune systems and social disruption allowed diseases present in normal times to wreak havoc during famines. Some of these diseases were closely related to malnutrition, but some were not.

Most of what we know about the causes of death during the Great Irish Famine is based on William Wilde's contributions to the 1851 population census. The material available to Wilde was flawed since many deaths were unrecorded, but it is by no means useless. Mokyr

203

and Ó Gráda found that, after due adjustment for lacunae in the data, causes other than outright starvation were responsible for over nine famine deaths in ten.[2] Much more important as causes of death were diseases such as typhus, relapsing fever, dysentery, and diarrhoea. Most famines in the past would have followed a broadly similar pattern. The Soviet famine of 1932–33 seems to have marked a transition in this respect, with the public health advances made in the 1920s reducing the proportion succumbing to infectious diseases.[3] The main causes of death during several Second World War famines in Europe – in Greece in 1941–43, in the Warsaw ghetto before its final destruction in 1942, in the western Netherlands in 1944–45, and during the Leningrad blockade of 1941–43 – were dystrophy, oedema, pneumonia, and literal starvation.[4] However, this change did not extend to all Second World War famines; in Bengal in 1943–44, and, presumably, in Vietnam in 1945 the main causes of excess deaths were the age-old ones.

This suggests a distinction between traditional and 'modern' famines: the latter are purely the product of human agency in locations normally no longer famine-prone, and where a combination of public health and higher living standards prevent widespread mortality from infectious disease. In most famine-prone countries in the past, however, infectious disease was endemic in non-crisis conditions, and so it was the main cause of mortality during famines.

This is a somewhat disconnected essay. Part one is a discussion of the causes of death during Ireland's other 'great' famine, that of 1740–42. It sets out in some detail how one contemporary medical practitioner described the main causes of death. Part two focuses on the issue of famine cannibalism.

1. Ireland's Other Great Famine

The cold spell that struck Europe toward the end of 1739 and lasted until the summer of 1741 is the coldest on statistical record. In 'central England', where continuous monthly observations are available from 1659 onwards, 1740 was the coldest year, with a mean temperature of 6.8 degrees centigrade.[5] The weather in Ireland cannot have been that different. Figure 8.1 describes the average monthly temperature at the time in central England, the temperature between January 1740 and December 1741, and the gap between them. January 1740, when the mean temperature was seven degrees below the mean was worst of all, but the following month also stands out.

What caused the cold spell is still unclear. It is sometimes blamed on a volcanic eruption on Kamchatka peninsula in Russia, and this may

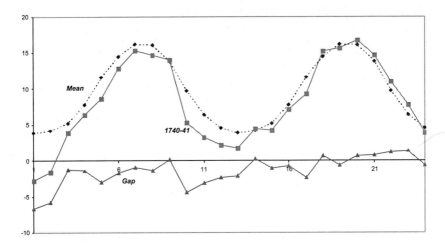

Fig. 8.1 Monthly temperature, 1740–41 *versus* the mean

well be so, since an eruption in the Tolbachik volcanic cluster in 1740 is noted in the long list of eruptions of the volcano published by Russian specialists.[6] The bad weather wreaked havoc in much of northern and eastern Europe.[7] Even in England, where it is claimed that the era of famines ended in the 1620s, parish register evidence implies a considerable rise in deaths and reduction in births in 1740–42.[8]

The famine is expertly described in David Dickson's *Arctic Ireland*; it is also analysed by Michael Drake and Louis Cullen.[9] Still, source material is scarce, particularly when compared to what there is for the 1840s – although the crisis prompted elegiac poems that have survived in Latin,[10] Irish,[11] and English.[12] For Gaelic poets, the crisis was '*an cogadh so an tseaca do fearadh ón Airdrí orainn* (this frost war that was waged by God on us)', '*fuacht, gorta 's anró* (cold, famine and woe)', and '*an cruatan géar so* (this severe hardship)'.[13] The weather lent the famine a peculiarly macabre quality:

> In yards of burial rows of coffins lie,
> Fill'd with their dead, implorers to the skie;
> Earth, grown unkind, refuses to receive
> Her clayey Children in her peaceful grave ...
>
> And Man, athirst, scarce lift the ax to cleave
> A moist subsistence from the harden'd wave,
> Or force with prongs of steel the marbled ground,
> In search of roots, and ev'n those roots unsound ...

The Sailor, beaten by th'inclement skie,
His rudder froze, lab'ring to port should plie;
The ropes within their pullies clog'd should stand,
Nor run in office to his gripeless land:
Yet, thro' kind Providence by pitying gales,
The Wind to port should set his stiffen'd sails,
Candied in frost, the ropes all glitt'ring bright:
At once a beauteous and a piteous sight!
Down from the yards the coral'd ice should grow,
The deck and sides a rock of crystal'd snow.
The pilot at the helm, congeal'd by cold,
Erect in death, should still the rudder hold.[14]

These are excerpts from a long 'poem founded upon facts' on the famine composed at the time by 19-year-old Thomas Hallie Delamayne.[15] Delamayne also describes how Richard Wellesley's stately castle at Dangan in County Meath was reduced to a ruin by fire because 'though nigh around, lakes, streams, and ponds commanded lie, those treach'rous servants to all help were froze'.[16]

The cold weather destroyed the potato, already an important item in the diet, particularly in the south of Ireland. Its role is well reflected in contemporary verse:[17]

Is iomdha maith fairis san aicme gan chuibheas,
Le braon na bó ba leor a milseacht;
Ba rómhaith iad le hiasc is le hím glan,
'S níor hitheadh riamh bia ba shaoire.[18]

Potáta plúrach dhúntaibh Éireann,
Crann an bheatha an meacan cléibh-so,
Ba gheal gáire i lár méise,
Só is rósta phóir Mhilésius.[19]

Famine conditions prevailed during much of 1740 and 1741, and excess mortality lasted until 1742. Delamayne notes that the rich were not immune:

Nor Sickness, only on the Poor to prey,
Should through their meaner habitations stray;
Contagion, like the screaming bird of Night,
Perch'd on the Palace dome's resplendent height,
Should thro' its column'd courts in order lead

The fable fun'rals of their stately Dead;
Th' attending tapers through the shade should gleam,
And real sorrows from the Mourners stream.
Here Crowds should seem a Wainwright to deplore,
Here mourn a Rogerson and there a Gore.[20]

John Wainwright, who died on 15 April 1741, was Baron of the Exchequer; Sir John Rogerson was Chief Justice of the Court of King's Bench; and Lady Elizabeth Gore was one of 'many others of great distinction, who all died of fevers in the common calamity'.[21]

Dickson, Ó Gráda, and Daultrey have attempted to infer excess mortality from the decline in the number of hearths between 1732 and 1744.[22] They reckon that between 310,000 and 480,000 out of a population of about 2.4 million perished. That is just an informed guess, and the implied proportionate mortality – up 15–20 per cent of the population – is certainly very high. John Rutty noted in his valuable *Chronological History of the Weather and Seasons and of Prevailing Diseases in Dublin* an estimate that one-fifth of the population perished – presumably referring to the loss of 'upwards of 400,000 souls' in the anonymous *The Groans of Ireland* (1741) – but he thought that fraction exaggerated.[23]

The Dublin Bills of Mortality imply significant mortality in the capital in 1740 and 1741 (when 3,304 and 2,792 deaths, respectively, were recorded) relative to the average of 1735–39 and 1742–45 (2,189 deaths). None of these figures captures all deaths in a city of 130,000 or so souls, however; the implied non-crisis death rate of sixteen per thousand is surely too low for that. But even assuming an under-count of one-third, this would still mean an excess mortality of no more than 2,600 [$1.5*(3,304 + 2,792 – 4,398)$] or 3 per cent or so in 1740 and 1741.[24] Of course, death rates outside the city were undoubtedly much higher. For the sake of comparison, in the 1840s the excess death rate in the capital was about 4 per cent, whereas aggregate excess mortality was about one in eight or nine.[25] In the early 1740s, the suffering was worst in the south, west, and midlands; Ulster, it would seem, escaped relatively lightly.[26]

Rutty's *Chronological History* is our best-known source on the causes of death in 1740–42. It mentions 'fever, dysentery, and famine' in that order. Also noteworthy are his remarks about male mortality in 1741: 'Another notable circumstance seems worthy of being recorded, in relation to the subjects which this fever generally attacked, both here and in England viz. that they were generally men and those of a middle age, and strong, but few women; also children were but more rarely attacked.'[27] This age-gender pattern recalls that of the great influenza epidemic of 1918–19.

The inseparability of fever and famine highlighted by Rutty are also clear in Delamayne's verses:

Hence naked Want and Famine lean should spring,
And pale Disease spread wide her putrid wing,
The Fever hence, attended by Despair,
Its blood-shot eyes should, fix'd on Pity, glare.
Here the sick Mother fall, and at her breast
The famish'd Infant cling, and drink the pest.[28]

The rest of this section is devoted to a little-known source on the causes of death in 1740–42, Mauritio O'Connell's *Morborum acutorum, et chronicorum quorundam, observationes medicinales experimentales, Sedulâ complurium annorum praxi, tum Corcagioe, tum in locis circumjacentibus, exantlatâ comprobatae*, which was published in Dublin in 1746.[29] The cumbersome title and the use of Latin are typical of medical treatises of the day. O'Connell's work was a late contribution to a genre dating from the Renaissance.[30] He dedicated his work to the celebrated London physician Richard Mead (1673–1754), and an acknowledgment from Mead is included as a foreword. Letters follow from Hieronymus David Gaubius (1705–80), a well-known medical practitioner and author based in Leiden, and one Doctor Michael Connell, who lived in London's Old Burlington Street at the time.[31]

Little is known about Maurice O'Connell. According to one account, he was born near Mallow.[32] *Observationes Medicales* is based on information gathered during twenty-five years of practicing medicine in Cork and its hinterland.[33] It is an unusual document, and its detailed description of the diseases prevalent in 1740–42 is particularly interesting. Although cited by Rutty, it hardly features in scholarship on *blianta an áir*. O'Connell devotes thirty-one pages (pp. 325–55) or about four thousand words in *Observationes Medicinales* to the famine period.[34] Here some of the most important elements are summarized.

The account of the famine is spread over two chapters in the third section of the book. The preceding chapter contains an account of dysentery ('the bloody flux'), which it links to the crisis of the late 1720s, but which, doubtless, was also very much present in 1740–42. His account of *blianta an áir* opens with a depiction of the extreme weather conditions, beginning with the severe winter of 1739–40, which persisted without respite into the spring months. The damage to livestock, crops, and plants was enormous. Birds and wild animals, sources of supplementary food in normal times, were decimated. But worst of all was the destruction of the tuberous plant, which the people called '*battata*', and which O'Connell dubbed 'the steady and exclusive staple of this country's poor and its small farmers'. Mortality among the poorer sections of the population was immense.

A murderous cocktail of diseases and epidemics ensued. In April 1740, when the frost came to an end, these included 'pleurisy, *angina, peripneumonia, ophthalmia*, and several other inflammatory diseases'. Smallpox also struck virulently during 1740. It peaked in mid-1740, decreasing in intensity from July onwards. By the middle of the autumn, there were few signs of it. Infants and children under ten were its main victims, and an incredible number succumbed to it. In August 1740, an epidemic of dysentery and diarrhoea spread, increasing in intensity in the autumn, and wreaking terrible havoc in the following winter. Late August witnessed the outbreak of a fever epidemic, which attacked people almost indiscriminately and overran dysentery and all other epidemics in its intensity, particularly affecting the common people. It persisted into 1741. In 1742, 'inflammatory sicknesses, pleurisies, *v.g.angina*, and *peripneumoniae*' were pervasive; and fever made a comeback. In retrospect, however, it attacked fewer people, and by the following summer it had disappeared.

The second chapter on the famine is entitled 'On the continuous epidemic fever of 1740–42'. It describes that fever's symptoms graphically and lists the 'cures' proscribed; its depiction of the symptoms of famine fever – typhus – has an immediacy that stems from O'Connell's own experience:

> Stiffness and hair standing on end attack the sick person more often, and recurs randomly, even several times, sometimes many, sometimes just a few days after the first onset. During this time, a mild and inconstant heat often recurs in intervals when the hair stands on end, an unaccustomed and universal cold [i.e. head cold], lack of appetite, dullness, unaccustomed languor of strength, often a dizzying, heavy, or sleep-inducing headache, nausea, and not infrequently rheumatism, or pains like lumbago, sometimes coughing, and bothersome headache between coughing, red or thick urine, a moist, pale, and clammy tongue torture the man.
>
> All these symptoms are rather mild in the first days of the illness, and are accompanied by somewhat difficult and necessarily quickened breathing; with the result that for a few days from the initial infection, if not feverish, the sick man does not think himself seriously ill.

The mild character of the fever lulled the patient and his family and friends into a false sense of security; they linked the symptoms to a chill or some other mild ailment. But thereafter the victim's condition took a turn for the worse.[35] The symptoms described above are exacerbated, and the victim's pulse quickens. The tongue dries up, the abdomen swells, sleeplessness persists, breathing becomes laboured; other symptoms include delirium and mental confusion, nosebleeds, comatose sleep, and in many cases red, purple, or black spots *(petechiae)* on different parts of the body. The symptoms described by O'Connell bear a close resemblance to those described by Sir William MacArthur in his medical history of the 1840s.[36] Interestingly, O'Connell does not distinguish between typhus and relapsing fever, as MacArthur did.[37] Indeed, he may have confused the two. Rutty, however, drew attention to 'a fever altogether without the malignity of [typhus], of six or seven days duration, terminating in a critical sweat, as did [typhus] also frequently, but in this the patients were subject to a relapse, even to a third or fourth time, and yet recovered'.[38] The symptoms of typhus in its early stages and relapsing fever differed: the latter was more intense, and associated with nausea and much vomiting.

Nor does O'Connell draw a link between the spread of the disease and lice: that link would not be scientifically established until the 1900s. Instead, he believed that it was due to the 'very cold and frozen winters' and the resultant 'putrid nourishment from bad moisture' which led through reduced perspiration and an increased rigidity of solids to 'inflammatory putrefaction' of the blood. Fever was 'the established mechanism' of this illness, and dictated how it should be treated.[39]

O'Connell's patients endured the standard Hippocratic 'cures', beginning with 'ten ounces of blood to be drawn at once', and soon followed by 'a softening enema' (a procedure for entering liquids into the body via the rectum as a bowel stimulant), with a washing of the feet and shins with hot water. If vomiting resulted, on the following day he prescribed 'a light emetic' (or vomit-inducing agent), after which sleep was to be encouraged, if necessary with the aid of 'a light opiate'. O'Connell would follow with 'somewhat sour liquids ... to duly dilute and moderate the blood'; he also administered 'amygdaline emulsions' (otherwise a cure for female frigidity) and reviving juleps (*julapii*). If diarrhoea was a problem, 'a white decoction, a tincture of roses, or almond emulsion' was to be substituted for the usual liquids. He also prescribed warm baths and steam vapours to the face, nose, and throat. In cases of delirium, acute headaches, or persistent sleeplessness, he listed footrests (*suppedanea*) or softening poultices (*cataplasmata*) for the feet and soles, and cutting of the jugular vein (*saphena*) was often 'observed to be useful and necessary'. Few of the remedies prescribed by O'Connell and his fellow practitioners can have been effective. Yet a significant proportion of those attacked by famine fever – and of those treated by medical practitioners – survived, lending some credibility to the cures described in *Observationes Medicales.*

As for food, 'The right diet in this fever, was a little broth of oatmeal, barley, bread boiled in water (*panatella*), acidic juice of bitter orange, and sweetened by very pale sweetener; to which is added, for the great languor of strength, especially when the disease is in place and in decline, some spoonfuls of wine from the Canaries.' The patient ought to recline in a dark place on as soft a couch as possible. Should none of the above treatments relieve the accompanying delirium or sleeplessness, O'Connell suggested 'nothing with more successful experience in this strait of affairs, than the right dose of an alleviator (a medicine that induces vomiting and nausea), in proportion to the exigency of the symptoms, brought out without delay'.

The pride of place given to typhus in O'Connell's *Observationes* is a reminder of the important part played during famines throughout history by illnesses that are not very nutrition-sensitive.[40] The spread of typhus and relapsing fever was due more to the social disruption caused by the shortage of food than to starvation *per se.* This accounts for the untimely deaths of Sir John Rogerson and Lady Gore and, more generally, helps to explain why elites throughout history have had some interest in preventing and mitigating outbreaks of famine.

O'Connell, as Rutty noted, provides an estimate of excess mortality.[41] He does not reveal how he arrived at his lower bound estimate of 80,000, but simply states that it was supported by the 'opinions of several perspicacious individuals who observed this murderous event'.[42] This figure, he surmised, matched or exceeded that from the plague that affected Ireland in an earlier age. O'Connell's depictions of the causes of death and the long-drawn character of the famine point to a crisis of apocalyptic proportions.

2. Famine Cannibalism

In 1866, a controversial paper presented to the Anthropological Society of London asked the question whether cannibalism had ever been practiced in Europe.[43] Admitting that the subject was unpalatable to Europeans and that 'few would believe it', the author doubted whether ritual cannibalism had ever been part of European culture in the past. But he then proceeded to provide several examples, some fanciful and some plausible, of 'cannibalism caused by sheer famine'. The discussion that followed the presentation of the paper was inconclusive, with one irate contributor protesting that 'it was absurd to rest an anthropological discussion on the illusions of poetical fancy and the tales of old women'.

Danish anthropologist Kirsten Hastrup has argued that when famine results in cannibalism, it has gone 'far beyond mensurational reach' to a level of 'hardship so extreme that humanity itself seems at stake'.[44] Of all the horrors of famine, cannibalism is probably the worst. While never widespread and never responsible for more than a miniscule fraction of famine deaths, examples of it recur throughout history.[45] Hastrup does not distinguish between what is termed 'survivor cannibalism' – survivors consuming the corpses of those who have already died – and, what is surely more horrific and depraved, the killing of people for the purpose of consuming them. The latter might be dubbed 'murder-cannibalism'. Yet one striking feature of accounts of famine cannibalism is the degree of understanding, if not outright empathy, sometimes displayed towards those engaging in the practice.

A recent best-selling history of the Chinese Great Leap Forward famine devotes a four-page chapter to cannibalism. Inconclusive about its extent, it concludes that 'in the midst of state-sponsored violence ... necrophagy was neither the most common nor the most widespread way of degrading a human being'.[46] Nor was famine cannibalism new in China: it was reported in Henan in 1942, in Sichuan in 1936, in Gansu in 1929, in Shan-Si in 1900 (where 'human flesh is offered for sale, and officials are unable to prevent it'), and in northern China during the 'incredible' famine of 1876–78.[47] Hastrup's distinction between survivor cannibalism and murder-cannibalism is implicit in three stock phrases regarding cannibalism that recur in gazetteers' accounts of the 1876–78 famine: 'people ate each other', 'exchanging children and eating them', and variants of 'people ate each other to the point that close kin destroyed each other'.[48]

In the Soviet Union in 1920–21, and again in 1932–33, cannibalism was also present, although its extent is impossible to gauge. In the latter case, the authorities punished cannibalism, though 'not nearly as severely as say the theft of a horse or a cow from a collective farm'.[49] Grim photographs,[50] and graphic oral testimonies of famine in the Soviet era survive:

> Every day there were cases of cannibalism. Mothers killed their children and ate them up. In such villages as Kordyshivka, Soshenske, [and] Pytiiv, cannibalism was very widespread. It was awfully dangerous for a person who looked good to go there. I don't know why people change so much. Ukrainians are very

generous and very kind people, but during that hunger they looked like wolves.[51]

Evidence for cannibalism during the blockade-famine of Leningrad during the Second World War is plentiful. At the height of the crisis, between December 1941 and mid-February 1942, nearly 900 people were arrested for unspecified crimes relating to cannibalism.[52] And during the Soviet Union's last famine in Moldova in 1946–47, 'the eating of corpses took place on a large scale'.[53]

Yet although cannibalism is a recurring feature of accounts of famine, by no means all famines led to it. There is no evidence for it during the Great Bengal Famine of 1943–44, for example, and nineteenth-century Indian famines also seem to have been free of it. One exceptional example refers to a woman belonging to an obscure flesh-eating caste who survived the famine of 1896–97 on corpses floating in a river. Recent famines in sub-Saharan Africa have yielded little evidence of cannibalism either. According to Tom Keneally's recent *Three Famines*, the official responsible for relief during the Ethiopian famine of 1984–85 witnessed cannibalism 'in an inadequate feeding centre in the Ethiopian highlands', for which (according to his informant) 'these people were not to blame'. But cannibalism does not feature in accounts of major famines in the Sahel, in Biafra, and elsewhere.[54]

What of Ireland? As Nicholas Canny noted almost four decades ago, dubbing the native Irish 'canyballs' was a feature of early English colonialist rhetoric, but the allegation has a much older history.[55] In *Foras Feasa ar Éirinn*, Seathrún Céitinn traced it back to the Roman writer Strabo. If by this is meant ritual cannibalism, there is no hard evidence for it in the historical record. But insofar as famine cannibalism is concerned, Céitinn's rejection of the claims '*gurab lucht feola daoine d'ithe na h-Éireannaigh* (that the Irish were cannibals)' on the basis that documentary evidence for it is lacking ('*óir ní léaghtar i san Seanchus go raibhe neach i n-Éirinn riamh ler' cleachtadh feoil daoine d'ithe ...*') is far from correct.[56]

According to the medieval *Annals of Tigernach*, in 698–700 AD '*fames et pestilentia iii annis in Hibernia facta est, ut homo hominem comederet* (famine and disease raged for three years in Ireland so that man ate man)'.[57] The *Chronicon Scotorum's* entry for 1116 AD notes that in the wake of an attack on Thomond by Toirdhealbhach Ó Conchubhair '*Gorta mor isin errach go recad an fer a mac & a ingin ar biadh & go n-ithdís na daoine cidh a chéle ann & na coin. Fasughadh Laigen uile {acht beg} & a sgaoiledh fo Eirinn ar gorta* (Great famine in the spring so that a man would sell his son and his daughter for food and men would even eat one another, and dogs. All Leinster was *almost* emptied, and scattered throughout Ireland on account of the famine).'[58] The sale of children is a common feature of famine, but the reference to cannibalism does not imply that they were sold to be consumed. Cannibalism was also recorded in 1316 AD during Robert the Bruce's Irish campaign.[59] Edmund Spenser's *View of the Present State of Ireland*, describing Munster in the 1580s, reported that 'they (the surrendering rebels) looked like anatomyes of death, they spake like ghostes crying out of theyr graves; they did eat of the dead carrions, happy where they yf could finde them, yea, and one another soone after ...'.[60] Less than two decades later, Fynes Morison wrote of war-induced famine in County Down:[61]

> Captain Trevor and many honest gentlemen lying in the Newry can witness, that some old women of those parts used to make a fire in the fields, and divers little children driving out the cattle in cold mornings, and coming thither to warm them, were by them surprised, killed and eaten, which at last was discovered by a great girl breaking from them by strength of her body, and Captain Trevor sending out soldiers to know the truth, they found the children's skulls and bones, and apprehended the old women, who were executed for the fact.

A later commentator, more sympathetic to the old women, added: 'The authors of the famine were the authors of cannibalism, not the unfortunate hags, who were driven by the extremity of hunger to that shocking sustenance.'[62]

Tarlach Ó Mealláin, a Franciscan friar, kept a *cín lae* (diary) while on the run during the early stages of the Confederate Wars in Ulster in 1643. This was a time of widespread famine.[63] Ó Mealláin's reference to cannibalism is probably to survivor cannibalism:

> There are people in the country, Ó Catháins, O'Devlins, O'Haras (*muintir Ára*), and the people of Iveagh, all of Clandeboy and the Route [reduced to] eating horses and steeds; the end of spring; stealing; carrying off cats; dogs; eating humans [corpses?]; rotten leather (*leathar carbaidhí*); and undressed leather (*leathar fo na aon*).[64]

Richard Lawrence, referring to the same period, wrote of seeing 'miserable creatures plucking stinking carrion out of a ditch, black and rotten' and of being 'credibly informed that they digged corpses out of the grave to eat'.[65] Note that all the above instances except (perhaps) the first occurred during periods of civil war or colonial conquest.

Evidence for cannibalism is also lacking during the famine of 1728–30, even though this crisis, which also led to excess mortality in parts of England, prompted Jonathan Swift's *A Modest Proposal for preventing the children of poor people in Ireland from being a burden to their parents or country, and for making them beneficial to the public*, which was published in 1729. Nor is there evidence for cannibalism during the much more serious famine in 1740–42, which has been discussed above. The next reference is to an incident in Wexford in 1798 as described by Sir Jonah Barrington. It is worth citing, although it does not refer to a context of famine:

> During the rebellion ... Mr. Waddy, a violent loyalist ... fled to a castle at a considerable distance from the town of Wexford ... He dreaded discovery so much that he would entrust his place of refuge to no person whatsoever and, as he conceived, took sufficient food to last until he might escape out of the country... Here Mr. Waddy concealed himself, and everybody was for a long time utterly ignorant as to his fate ... At length, it occurred to certain of his friends, to seek him through the country ... Their search was in vain, until approaching by chance the old castle, they became aware of a stench, which the seekers conjectured to proceed from the putrid corpse of murdered Waddy. On getting nearer this opinion was confirmed, for a dead body lay half within and half without the castle, which the descent of the portcullis had cut nearly into equal portions ... [T]o their infinite astonishment, they perceived it was *not* Waddy, but a neighbouring priest who had been so expertly cut in two; how the accident had happened nobody could surmise ... [T]the other half of the priest was discovered immediately within the entrance, but by no means in equally good condition with that outside; inasmuch as it appeared that numerous collops and rump-steaks had been cut off the reverend gentleman's hindquarters by Waddy who early one morning had found the priest thus divided; and being alike unable to raise the portcullis or get out to look for food, certain indeed, in the latter case, of being piked by any of the rebels who knew him, he thought it better to feed on the priest, and remain in the castle till fortune smiled, than run a risk of breaking all his bones by dropping from the battlements, his only alternative.[66]

What of the Great Famine of the 1840s? Metaphorical references to cannibalism, such as Thomas Carlyle's account of a gombeenman who had 'prospered … by workhouse grocery-and-meal trade, by secret pawnbroking – by eating the slain' or John Mitchel's gothic depiction of the workhouse in Glenties as 'a Temple erected to the Fates, or like the fortress of Giant Despair, whereinto he draws them one by one, and devours them there', capture the horrors of the famine but prove nothing about cannibalism.[67] However, William Carleton's reference to cannibalism in *Red Hall*, a novel written during the Great Famine, is in a different league:

> … fathers have been known to make a wolfish meal upon the dead bodies of their own offspring. We might, therefore, be carried on our own description up to the very highest point of imaginable horror, without going beyond the truth.[68]

Carleton may well have been thinking of one or two incidents that had attracted attention a few years earlier. In May 1849, Rev. James Anderson, rector of Ballinrobe in County Mayo, wrote a long open letter to Lord John Russell, the Prime Minister, in the course of which he described a starving man who had extracted the heart and liver from a ship-wrecked corpse 'and *that* was the maddening feast on which he regaled himself and his family'. Anderson's letter was widely reported in the press and raised in the House of Commons by Henry Arthur Herbert, MP for Kerry.[69] Russell felt compelled to reply in some detail to the charge of famine-induced cannibalism.[70]

In his statement to the House of Commons Russell revealed that the alleged incident had occurred the previous November in the Clifden union and claimed that the culprit was a well-fed labourer 'of singularly voracious appetite … not at all suffering from distress himself' (although two of his sisters were on relief). Initially, according to Russell, the culprit did not identify the corpse as human, but on being apprised of this by neighbours, 'it does not appear that he ate any portion of the flesh, whatever his original intention might have been'. Russell's disingenuous statement was widely reported, and was the focus of a long rebuttal in the *Freeman's Journal* a few days later.[71] The *Freeman's* protested that the only detail on which Anderson had erred was 'the eating of the putrid heart', and took particular exception to Russell's assertion that 'the Clifden cannibal', one Patrick Diamond[72], was well fed or, as claimed by the London *Times*, 'a fat man':[73]

Patrick Diamond, the fat labourer, must be as great a curiosity as the extinct *Dodo*. We believe he is the only man of his race on whom a pound of Indian meal per diem has raised the thick coat of fat, which gives the *Times* the power of triumphant refutation. Such miraculous obesity cut away the ground from the Rev. Mr. Anderson, and raises the presumption that all the Irish are shamming ... But, after all, it did appear that Diamond did cut out the heart – nay more, that this 'fat and well-fed labourer' did meditate the eating thereof until he was told, what his eyes must plainly have told him before, that the trunk was that of a human body! This could not well be got over, and how is it explained? Well, by another fact of equal singularity with the fabulous fatness – that Diamond had a most voracious appetite, and of such abnormal irregularity, that he would devour rank weeds or green grass to satisfy its enormous cravings! We leave this satisfactory explanation untouched. Is there a human being, Lord John and the *Times* inclusive, who believes it?

Which is the less plausible, Patrick Diamond's girth or his failure to distinguish the corpse as human? Was this cannibalism? What actually transpired is lost in the 'spin' of the different reports.

Thomas Keneally has recently drawn attention to a second instance of cannibalism during the Great Famine:

In 1851, the Irish census stated that a stipendiary magistrate in Galway City heard the case of a prisoner arrested for stealing food, who was discovered in his cabin with his family and a part-consumed corpse. With astounding tolerance, the magistrate found there were extenuating circumstances, since the man was subject to the mania that struck people in the late stages of starvation.[74]

Both cases refer to survivor cannibalism rather than to murder-cannibalism. So far, I have not found any further contemporary evidence for cannibalism in the 1840s. Folk memory, as represented by the archives of the Irish Folklore Commission, does not even hint at the possibility, although this may have been because it reflected twentieth-century sensitivities rather than nineteenth-century realities.[75]

Still, until further evidence is forthcoming, given the massive and horrific scale of the Great Famine in relative terms and the extent of excess mortality over such a long period, perhaps it is the paucity of evidence for cannibalism in the 1840s that is surprising. Yet acknowledging even the possibility of cannibalism can only add to our understanding the horrors of famines such as the Great Irish Famine.

217

NOTES

1 This is a revised version of the paper presented to the Conference of Irish Historians, Maynooth, June 2011. Many thanks to Andrew Carpenter, Perry Curtis, David Dickson, and to Breandán Mac Suibhne for several helpful suggestions and to Madeleine Jones for translating sections of Maurice O'Connell's *Observationes Medicales*.

2 Joel Mokyr and Cormac Ó Gráda, 'What do People Die of during Famines? The Great Irish Famine in Comparative Perspective', *European Review of Economic History*, 6:3 (2002), pp.339–64.

3 Sergei Adamets, 'Famines in Nineteenth- and Twentieth-Century Russia: Mortality by Age, Cause, and Gender', in Tim Dyson and Cormac Ó Gráda (eds), *Famine Demography: Perspectives from the Past and Present* (Oxford: Oxford University Press, 2002), pp.158–80.

4 Hionidou Violetta, 'Why do People die in Famines? Evidence from Three Island Populations', *Population Studies*, 56:1 (2002), pp.65–80; Cormac Ó Gráda, *Famine: A Short History* (Princeton: Princeton University Press, 2009).

5 The details are available at: http://hadobs.metoffice.com/hadcet/mly_cet_mean_sort.txt [accessed June 2011].

6 A.A. Gusev et al., 'Great explosive eruptions on Kamchatka during the last 10,000 years: self-similar irregularity of the output of volcanic products', *Journal of Geophysical Research* [Online], 108 (B2) (2003), pp.1–18, at p.9. Available from: http://geo.web.ru/Mirrors/ivs/bibl/sotrudn/stgusev/gusevetal2003vul%5B1%5D.pdf [accessed June 2011].

7 John D. Post, 'Climatic Variability and the European Mortality Wave of the Early 1740s', *Journal of Interdisciplinary History*, 15:1 (1984), pp.1–30; idem, *Food Shortage, Climatic Variability, and Epidemic Disease in Pre-Industrial Europe: the Mortality Peak in the Early 1740s* (Ithaca: Cornell University Press, 1985).

8 B.M.S. Campbell, 'Four famines and a pestilence: harvest, price, and wage variations in England, 13th to 19th centuries', in Britt Liljewall et al. (eds), *Agrarhistoriapåmångasätt; 28 Studier om Manniskan och Jorden. Festskrift till Janken Myrdal på hans 60-årsdag* (Stockholm: KSLAB, 2009), pp.23–56, at pp.19–26; M. Kelly and C. Ó Gráda, 'The Poor Law of Old England: Institutional Innovation and Economic Regimes', *Journal of Interdisciplinary History*, 41:3 (2010), pp.339–66.

9 David Dickson, *Arctic Ireland: The Extraordinary Story of the Great Frost and Forgotten Famine, 1740–41* (Belfast: White Row Press, 1997); idem, 'The Other Great Irish famine', in Cathal Póirtéir (ed.), *The Great Irish Famine* (Cork: Mercier, 1995), pp.50–59; idem, *New Foundations: Ireland, 1660–1800* (2nd edn., Dublin: Irish Academic Press, 2000), pp.90–1; Michael Drake, 'The Irish Demographic Crisis of 1740–41', in T.W. Moody (ed.), *Historical Studies* VI (London: Routledge and Kegan Paul, 1968), pp.101–24; L.M. Cullen, 'The Irish Food Crises of the 1740s: the Economic Conjuncture', *Irish Economic and Social History*, 37 (2010), pp.1–23.

10 William Dunkin, 'Hyemes Glaciales apud Hibernos', in idem, *Select Poetical Works of the Late William Dunkin DD in Two Volumes* (Dublin: W.G. Jones, 1769), pp.430–43.

11 Cormac Ó Gráda and Diarmaid Ó Muirithe, 'The Famine of 1740–41: Representations in Gaelic Poetry', *Éire-Ireland*, 45:3 and 4 (2010), pp.41–62.

12 T[homas] H[allie] D[elamayne], *To Francis Bindon, esq. on a picture of his grace Dr. Hugh Boulter, Lord Arch-Bishop of Armagh, set up in the Work-house, near Dublin, in commemoration of his charities in the years 1739–40 and 1740–41* (London: J. Williams. 1767); Andrew Carpenter (ed.), *Verse in English from Eighteenth-Century Ireland* (Cork: Cork University Press, 1998), pp.248–52.

13 Ó Gráda and Ó Muirithe, 'The Famine of 1740–41', pp.1–22.

14 Delamayne, *To Francis Bindon, esq. on a picture of his grace Dr. Hugh Boulter*, pp.10, 11, 17.

15 Delamayne graduated from Trinity College Dublin in 1738. Author of several satirical and dramatic poems and a barrister-at-law, he died in London in 1794: *Gentleman's Magazine*, June 1794, p.578.

16 Delamayne, *To Francis Bindon, esq. on a picture of his grace Dr. Hugh Boulter*, pp.15–16.

17 The author of the poem is not known. It is titled *Tuireamh na bhfataí bliain an tseaca mhóir. i. 1739* (Royal Irish Academy, MS 24 M 5 pp.93–4). For a consideration of the authorship of the poem, and a transcript of the text with translation see Ó Gráda and Ó Muirithe, 'The Famine of 1740-41', pp.46–9.

18 'It was also a boon to those without property / With a drop from the cow its sweetness was adequate; / They were great with fish and pure butter / And a cheaper food was never consumed.'

19 'The floury potato of the forts of Ireland / Tree of life, this darling root / It was the bright smile in the middle of a dish / Comfort and sustenance of the race of Milesius.'

20 Delamayne, *To Francis Bindon, esq. on a picture of his grace Dr. Hugh Boulter*, p.13.

21 John Wainwright (1689–1741) died of fever contracted while on assize at Limerick (F.E. Ball, *The Judges of Ireland* (2 Volumes, London, 1926), ii, pp.202–03); John Rogerson (1676–1741) was MP for Dublin city, 1714–27, prior to his elevation to the Court of King's Bench. He died on 24 Aug. 1741 at his Henry Street home (E.M. Johnston-Liik, *History of the Irish Parliament, 1692–1800* (6 Volumes, Belfast, 2002), iv, p.284); Lady Elizabeth Gore (d. 7 Dec.1741) was wife of Sir Ralph Gore (1674–1733), MP for County Donegal, 1713–27 (ibid., vi, pp.187–9).

22 David Dickson, Cormac Ó Gráda and Stuart Daultrey, 'Hearth-Tax, Household Size and Population Change 1672–1821', *RIA proc*, 82C (1982), pp.125–81, at pp.164–8; Dickson, *Arctic Ireland*, pp.69, 72.

23 John Rutty, *Chronological History of the Weather and Seasons and of Prevailing Diseases in Dublin* (Dublin, 1770), p.86.

24 Rutty, *Chronological History*, passim; Patrick Fagan, 'The Population of Dublin in the Eighteenth Century', *Eighteenth-Century Ireland: Iris an Dá Chultúir*, 6 (1991), pp.121–56, at p.148.

25 Cormac Ó Gráda, *Black '47 and Beyond: The Great Irish Famine in History, Economy, and Memory* (Princeton: Princeton University Press, 1999), Chapter 5.

26 Dickson, *Arctic Ireland*, pp.62–9.

27 Rutty, *Chronological History*, pp.86–97.

28 Delamayne, *To Francis Bindon, esq. on a picture of his grace Dr. Hugh Boulder*, p.10.

29 Mauritio O'Connell, *Morborum acutorum, et chronicorum quorundam, observationes medicinales experimentales, Sedulâ complurium annorum praxi, tum Corcagioe, tum in locis circumjacentibus, exantlatâ comprobatae* (Dublin: Faulkner & Kelly, 1746).

30 Maedhbhín Ní Urdail and Cormac Ó Gráda, 'Tadhg Ó Neachtain agus Muiris Ó Conaill ag Trácht ar Bhlianta an áir, 1739–42', forthcoming.

31 See www.british-history.ac.uk/report.aspx?compid=41494&strquery=Michael+connell [accessed June 2010].

32 William Kearns Tanner, 'A Retrospect: Surgery in Cork', *British Medical Journal*, 9 (Aug. 1879), pp.225–7.

33 O'Connell, *Morborum acutorum*, p.iii.

34 Ibid., pp.325–55.

35 Ibid., pp.333–4.

36 Sir William P. MacArthur, 'Medical History of the Famine', in R.D. Edwards and T.D. Williams (eds), *The Great Famine: Essays in Irish History* (Dublin: Browne & Nolan, 1956), pp.263–315, at pp.265–6.

37 MacArthur, 'Medical History of the Famine', pp.267–8.

38 Rutty, *Chronological History*, p.90.

39 O'Connell, *Morborum acutorum*, p.337.

40 Mokyr and Ó Gráda, 'What do People Die of during Famines?', passim.

41 Rutty, *Chronological History*, p.91; O'Connell, *Morborum acutorum*, p.327.

42 O'Connell, *Morborum acutorum*, p.327.

43 Richard Stephen Charnock, 'Cannibalism in Europe', *Journal of the Anthropological Society of London*, 4 (1866), pp.xxii–xxxi.

44 Kirsten Hastrup, 'Hunger and the Hardness of Facts', *Man*, n.s., 28:4 (1973), pp.727–39, at p.730.

45 Ó Gráda, *Famine: A Short History*, pp.63–8.

46 Frank Dikötter, *Mao's Great Famine: The History of China's Most Devastating Catastrophe, 1958–1962* (New York: Walker & Co., 2010), p.323.

47 *New York Times*, 30 Dec. 1900, 22 May 1929; Kathryn Edgerton-Tarpley, *Tears from Iron: Cultural Responses to Famine in Nineteenth-Century China* (Berkeley: University of California Press, 2008).

48 Edgerton-Tarpley, *Tears from Iron*, p.223.

49 Dana Dalrymple, 'The Soviet Famine of 1932–34', *Soviet Studies*, 15:1 (1964), pp.250–84.

50 See Bruce Patenaude, *The Big Show in Bololand: The American Relief Expedition to Soviet Russia in the Famine of 1921* (Stanford: Stanford University Press, 2002).

51 Harvard Project on the Soviet Social System, Case 333; see http://pds.lib.harvard.edu/pds/view/5608007?n=25; see too *New York Times*, 28 Feb. 1922 (report by Walter Duranty).

52 Boris Belozerov, 'Crime during the siege' in John Barber and Andrei Dzeniskevich, (eds), *Life and Death in Besieged Leningrad, 1941–44* (London: Palgrave Macmillan, 2005), pp.223–4.

53 Michael Ellman, 'The 1947 Soviet Famine and the Entitlement Approach to Famines', *Cambridge Journal of Economics*, 24:5 (2000), pp.603–30 at p.617 n 1.

54 Thomas Kenneally, *Three Famines* (Melbourne, 2010); Ó Gráda, *Famine: A Short History*, pp.67–8.

55 Nicholas P. Canny, 'The Ideology of English Colonization: From Ireland to America', *William and Mary Quarterly*, 3rd ser., 30:4 (1973), pp.575–98, at p.587.

56 www.ucc.ie/celt/online/G100054/, Chapter 2.

57 www.ucc.ie/celt/published/G100002.html.

58 www.ucc.ie/celt/published/G100016.html.

59 G.O. Sayles, 'The Siege of Carrickfergus Castle, 1315–16', *IHS*, 10 (1956), pp.94–100, at p.95.

60 Edmund Spenser, *View of the Present State of Ireland* (1596). The text, and the quotation, can be located at www.ucc.ie/celt/published/E500000-001/index.html.

61 This observation by Fynes Morison is widely cited: for example Dennis Taaffe, *An Impartial History of Ireland from the Period of the English Invasion to the Present Time* (2 Volumes, Dublin: Christie, 1810), ii, pp.100–01.

62 Taaffe, *An Impartial History of Ireland*, ii, p.101.

63 W.J. Smyth, *Map-Making, Landscapes and Memory: A Geography of Colonial and Early Modern Ireland, c.1530–1750* (Cork: Cork University Press, 2006), p.161.

64 Charles Dillon, 'Cín lae Uí Mhealláin: Friar Ó Meallan Journal', in idem and Henry A. Jeffries (eds), *Tyrone: History and Society* (Dublin: Geography Publications, 2000), pp.327–402, at p.350. For the original, see Tadhg Ó Donnchadha, 'Cín lae Ó Mealláin', *Analecta Hibernica*, 3 (1931), pp.1–61.

65 Richard Lawrence, *The Interest of Ireland in its Trade and Wealth Stated* (2 parts, Dublin, 1682), pt. 2, pp.86–7), cited without attribution by John Gamble, *Society and Manners in Early Nineteenth-Century Ireland*, Breandán Mac Suibhne (ed.) (Dublin: Field Day Publications, 2011), p.213. I am grateful to Dr Mac Suibhne for this reference.

66 Sir Jonah Barrington, *Personal Sketches of his own Times* (3 Volumes: London, 1827–32), Ch. XXII. I wish to thank Perry Curtis for this reference.

67 Thomas Carlyle, *Reminiscences of my Irish Journey in 1849* (New York: Harper, 1882), p.160; John Mitchel, *The Crusade of the Period: And the Last Conquest of Ireland (Perhaps)* (New York: Lynch, Cole, and Meehan, 1873), p.212.

68 William Carleton, *Red Hall, or, the Baronet's Daughter* (3 Volumes, London: Saunders and Otley, 1852), ii, pp.34–5.

69 *House of Commons Debates (Hansard)*, 25 May 1849, vol. 105, col. 978.

70 *House of Commons Debates (Hansard)*, 1 June 1849, vol. 105, cols 1033–4.

71 See, for example, *Trewman's Exeter Flying Post or Plymouth and Cornish Advertiser* (Exeter, England), 7 June 1849; *Scotsman*, 2 June 1849.

72 Could this be Patrick Diamond, born Rusheen, County Galway, 1814; died Fountainhill, County Galway, 1894?: see www.mcdade.bravepages.com/i77.html#i27617 [accessed 8 October 2012].

73 *Freeman's Journal*, 4 July 1849.

74 Keneally, *Three Famines*, p.59.

75 Compare Cormac Ó Gráda, *Ireland's Great Famine: Interdisciplinary Perspectives* (Dublin: UCD Press, 2006), pp.228–33.

9

SUICIDE STATISTICS AS MORAL STATISTICS: SUICIDE, SOCIOLOGY AND THE STATE

DAVID LEDERER

Suicide, History and a Theory of Practice

Statistics provide a veritable reservoir of actionable information for modern societies. Since the nineteenth century, government bureaucracies have instrumentalized statistics as objective and self-explanatory measures of the state and its empirical qualities. In the wake of the publication of Durkheim's classic study of suicide, *Le Suicide* (1897), many concluded that statistics had literally become social facts.[1] When cleverly presented as such, statistics can presume an authoritative and unassailable status as arbiters of state policies. Those familiar with British university life, for example, can attest to the rapid increase in quantitative exercises in recent years. Managerial culture has embraced bibliometrics to equate performance across disciplinary lines in order to enhance a corporate sense of discipline and deference to administrative structures. The attendant emphasis on outcomes encourages targeted and cyclical hiring practices through the Research Excellence Framework (REF), successor to the Research Assessment Exercise (RAE). Such best practice is predicated upon the presumption that numbers tell stories which, after all is said and done, count.[2]

Or do they really? As an omnipresent feature of quantitative sociology, suicide statistics have been telling stories since the birth of that discipline, coinciding with the rise of modern national states. This essay will consider the emergent quantitative methods of social measurement in an overview of suicidology during the nineteenth century. In doing so, something quickly becomes evident; the measurement of social phenomena remains a largely *qualitative* endeavour involving value judgments particular to specific places at specific times. The very phenomena we choose to count as the subjects of quantitative analyses says just as much about the values of the society or the particular social group undertaking the analysis, as it does about the phenomenon in question. By preferring certain subjects and certain units of analysis over others, researchers constantly engage in value-laden decision-making which consequently influences the inputs and outcomes of their research. As a result, our analytical choices gradually, but systematically erode distinctions between objective and subjective discrimination, revealing quantitative social analyses for what they truly are: the measurement of qualities.

This story, which begins in the nineteenth century, continues to this day. In order to demonstrate the implications of a theory of practice, please entertain the following useful digression from the present day before we proceed to the past. For some years now, as part of a seminar entitled 'Suicide: the cultural history of a social phenomenon' conducted at the National University of Ireland (NUI) Maynooth, each semester commences with a simple, yet telling exercise based on the most recent suicide data provided by the World Health Organization (WHO). I refer to this exercise as 'Fun with statistics'.

Table 9.1 provides a truncated reproduction of the latest WHO statistics of 2011 on comparative world suicide rates. The chart is divided into units of analysis by country, year in which the census was taken, and a breakdown of the rate of suicide per 100,000 inhabitants by sex. My truncation limits the number of countries from the original 104 to thirty-eight in order to highlight discreet regional blocks convenient for our discussion here; though, as will presently become clear, the original chart could be broken down into any number of other arbitrary patterns.[3] The geographic blocks highlighted here are:

1. Western countries of the so-called First World.
2. Caribbean countries.
3. Middle Eastern countries.
4. Countries of the former Soviet Union.
5. Asian countries, particularly The People's Republic of China and the Special Administrative Region of Hong Kong.

The WHO, a branch of the United Nations, is one of the most highly respected institutions in the world. Its standards for vetting information must be among the most rigorous internationally, with inputs required to meet the most stringent scientific requirements. However, two limitations of the WHO analytic categories leap out – country and year. All the data presented on Table 9.1 result from a limited number of national surveys taken in different years. If one were to examine the

Country	Year	Males	Females
BAHAMAS	2005	1.9	0.6
BARBADOS	2006	7.3	0
BELARUS	2007	48.7	8.8
CHINA (selected rural and urban areas)	1999	13	14.8
CHINA (Hong Kong SAR)	2009	19	10.7
CUBA	2008	19	5.5
DENMARK	2006	17.5	6.4
EGYPT	2009	0.1	0
ESTONIA	2008	30.6	7.3
FINLAND	2009	29	10
FRANCE	2007	24.7	8.5
GERMANY	2006	17.9	6
GRENADA	2008	0	0
HAITI	2003	0	0
HUNGARY	2009	40	10.6
IRELAND	2009	19	4.7
ISRAEL	2007	7	1.5
ITALY	2007	10	2.8
JAMAICA	1990	0.3	0
JAPAN	2009	36.2	13.2
JORDAN	2008	0.2	0
KAZAKHSTAN	2008	43	9.4
KUWAIT	2009	1.9	1.7
LATVIA	2009	40	8.2
LITHUANIA	2009	61.3	10.4
NETHERLANDS	2009	13.1	5.5
NORWAY	2009	17.3	6.5
POLAND	2008	26.4	4.1
PORTUGAL	2009	15.6	4
REPUBLIC OF KOREA	2009	39.9	22.1

Country	Year	Males	Females
RUSSIAN FEDERATION	2006	53.9	9.5
SPAIN	2008	11.9	3.4
SWEDEN	2008	18.7	6.8
SWITZERLAND	2007	24.8	11.4
SYRIAN ARAB REPUBLIC	1885	0.2	0
UKRAINE	2009	37.8	7
UNITED KINGDOM	2009	10.9	3
UNITED STATES OF AMERICA	2005	17.7	4.5

**Table 9.1 Suicide rates per 100,000 by country, year and sex
(at 2011, most recent year available)**

original data, one would find that – with the telling exception of South Africa – the continent of Africa remains in virtual darkness in terms of reported suicides.

Let us turn our gaze to those prosperous industrialized countries of the West, among which Ireland still happily counts itself. Ireland, long considered an anomaly for its low reported rates, weighed in with 19 (per 100,000 males)/4.9 (per 100,000 female) successful suicides (as opposed to parasuicides) in 2009. Let us take Ireland as our norm. How does that stack up against other countries in this group? That same year the United Kingdom reported figures of 10.9/3, while the Netherlands reported 13.1/5.5. In 2006, Germany revealed figures of 17.9/6. In the latter two cases, the proportion of male to female suicides is lower than Ireland; does this indicate greater gender emancipation among those countries with higher rates of female suicide? In 2008, Spain came in at a felicitous 11.9/3.4. France, on the other hand, led Western Europe with 24.7/8.5 in 2007, while in 2005 the USA scored a rather pedestrian 17.7/4.5. Among the Nordic countries of Scandinavia (Denmark, Norway, Sweden, notorious for their bleak Kirkegaardian temperament) rates are, in fact, all lower than the norm in Ireland, though here again, women make greater strides towards gender parity.

Now let us examine the tropical paradise of the Caribbean. Like Western countries, there is a high level of compliance with the WHO request for information, which may be attributed to their heritage of deferential colonial administration. And yet, what a difference!

Students naturally jump to various conclusions to account for the comparatively low rates of 0.3/0.0 in Jamaica; they cite the beneficent effects of climate, beautiful beaches, and, even, the widespread use of cannabis to explain why the inhabitants stopped bothering to report suicide entirely after 1990. While Barbados' outlying rate of 7.3 for men is extremely high for the region, it still compares favourably to the West. On most of the islands, women apparently never kill themselves; perhaps this is a beneficent effect of greater gender emancipation? Meanwhile, on the island of Haiti (as well as Grenada), there appears to be no suicide at all. The one major exception here is Cuba. In the workers' paradise of Fidel and Raul Castro, rates of 19.9/5.5 seem to suggest that relative economic equality, a truly functioning, world-class healthcare system, universal free education, and social welfare are no guarantors of happiness, but rather promoters of *ennui*. Or perhaps the rates simply reflect the bleak realities of life under communism?

From the WHO statistics, one might construe that life in the Middle East is also viewed with much hope and optimism. In Jordan, Kuwait, Syria and Egypt, there is no suicide at all to speak of, while Israel suffers only moderate levels, well below Western norms. One is justifiably left to ponder the status of so-called suicide terrorists in the official figures. Will the recent introduction of democratic liberties in some Middle Eastern states produce a higher or lower numbers of self-killers? Ultimately, we will have to await the long-term results of the Arab Spring to assess accurately the effects of changed political conditions on future rates of suicide.

This brings us to Eastern Europe, the region with the highest rates of suicide in the world. Hungary led the world in recorded suicides for most of the twentieth century.[4] Hungary's position was surpassed after the fall of the Iron Curtain by the successor states of the USSR. The Baltic Republics weigh in far higher than Western Europe; at an astounding rate of 61.3/10.4, Lithuania leads the pack, while the core area of the former USSR, Russia, trails closely at 53.9/9.5, with Kazakhstan in third place at 43/9.4. According to *The Guardian*, suicide rates doubled in Russia following the dissolution of the Soviet Union, a sensational increase blamed by local experts on social dislocation and by the WHO on the excessive consumption of vodka.[5] Perhaps the end of communism was not such a good thing after all?

Problematic here is the fact that suicide statistics were long suppressed and presumably underreported under the Soviet regime for the sake of international appearances, as high rates of suicide might have been interpreted as a failure of the Bolshevik experiment.[6] Certainly, there is little evidence to suggest that vodka consumption increased radically after the fall of the Soviet Union and, indeed, it was already cited as a contributory factor to suicide in nineteenth-century Imperial Russia.[7] Of course, there remains the nagging question of the extent to which death by alcohol poisoning figures in the WHO suicide statistics as an analytic category. Finally, given the historical role of the social sciences in the Union of Soviet Socialist Republics, demographic control played a major role in state-sponsored strategic plans, such as the infamous five-year plans of the Stalinist era. In an alternate reality, suicide simply disappeared for a time, not unlike the equally infamous vanishing image of Leon Trotsky, cosmetically edited out of a picture of Lenin speaking in 1920 in Sverdlov Square after the former's deportation in 1929. From this standpoint, one might deduce that the mania for statistics in other areas of former Soviet life only embraced suicide rates for the first time in a serious way after the end of the paternalistic regime.

Another socialist society, China, has also been the source of rather astounding speculations arising from its suicide statistics. A cursory glance at the gender ratios provided by the WHO indicates that men kill themselves more often than women in all countries except one – the Peoples' Republic of China (13/14.8). This sensational result overturned a century-old statistical truth about gender ratios and was rendered no less remarkable by the demise of a second sociological axiom: for the first time, Chinese national reports also indicated that suicide rates in rural regions surpassed those in industrialized urban areas.

Widely reported throughout the international media, the BBC specifically referred to research on over 250,000 suicides per year, and, because suicide was the third largest cause of death among rural Chinese women, dubbed it a 'blight': the co-leader of the research team cited by the BBC, Canadian psychiatrist Michael R. Phillips remarked that 'in some particular villages, it [female suicide] almost becomes normalized'.[8] In a series of seminal articles in *The Lancet*, Phillips claims suicide is the leading cause of death among young people, especially rural women aged nineteen to thirty-four, with reported rates an astounding 25 per cent higher than men.[9] One contributory factor is the ready availability of toxic chemical fertilizers in the countryside, though method explains very little about cause. Currently, China alone accounts for 49 per cent of all global suicides. Phillips uses a novel, though common method-ology currently employed by psychiatrists known as psychological autopsy (essentially, the psychological profiling of dead people) to determine reasons for suicide, citing specific cultural trends behind high rates of female suicide that challenge Western psychiatric assumptions about depression and other psychiatric illnesses.[10]

Like Phillips, the Harvard medical anthropologist Arthur Kleinman has been researching suicide and mental illness in China for decades. Kleinman too contrasts patterns of suicidal behaviour in China with those of the West.[11] Long an advocate of the relevance of cultural factors in the study of suicide and mental illness, he has even suggested that, historically, female suicide in China often represents an act of resistance to family pressures from husbands and mothers-in-law to accede to enforced marriages or brutal bondage.[12] Kleinman, citing an earlier ethnographer, suggests that:

> In the West we ask of a suicide, 'Why?' In China the question is more commonly 'Who? Who drove her to this? Who is responsible'... for a woman it is the most damning public accusation she can make of her mother-in-law, her husband, or her son.[13]

Kleinman's linkage of the high rates of female suicides and the history of the family is informed by an essay co-authored by Jonathan Spence, which appeared in Kleinman's 1981 collection of essays on deviant behaviour in China.[14] The authors point to a tradition of female suicide dating back to Confucius and identify four stereotypical circumstances that encourage suicidal behaviour: the death of the husband; threats to the laws of propriety by remaining alive; threats to the husband's propriety; and intolerable pressures on the wife due to conflicting familial loyalties.[15] Quite often, the distribution of property and/or heritable assets was involved. Elsewhere, Spence explored the excessive pressures on women in early modern China in his superb micro-historic case study of the murder of Wang, the seventeenth-century wife who left her husband, fell into desperate material and honorific circumstances and was forced to return, only to be murdered by him.[16]

Subsequent historians have also elaborated upon familial issues related to suicide, which culminated in legislation during the Q'ing dynasty to prevent what was viewed as an epidemic of female suicides.[17] Indeed, the Chinese intellectual Mao Tse-tung, future chairman of the Communist Party, commented on this cultural propensity among Chinese women at the beginning of the twentieth century.[18] Today, the one-child policy continues to aggravate the situation in a culture which smiles more favourably upon male offspring.

Shown in this historical and cultural light, the WHO statistics for the People's Republic are far less surprising. Ironically, however, the WHO statistics for Hong Kong evidence a completely different reality. Studies conducted by the Hong Kong Jockey Club Trust Centre for Suicide Research and Prevention consistently reveal that, in the Special Administrative Region (SAR) and former British crown colony, suicide rates conform to Western norms, a phenomenon which Phillips has also addressed with special regard to new immigrants from the mainland and their effects on these traditional patterns.[19] To this extent, one is also left to ponder how Han culture differs from Cantonese, Uighur, Taiwanese aboriginal or any of the other ethnic minorities in China, both today and historically.

Obviously, the assertions arising from our cursory exercise with the WHO statistics are extremely speculative. However, two key points emerge. First, in viewing the WHO statistics, we can hardly help but evaluate them according to one underlying assumption: suicide is a bad thing. Therefore, in this crude Olympic games of international comparative statistics, the quality alone is what counts – less is more. However, as we shall see, this was not always the case and suicide was viewed by many nineteenth-century experts as a positive measure of modernity; to cite Nietzsche, some theorists truly believed that 'what does not kill me, makes me stronger'. Either viewpoint can lead to all sorts of unfounded assertions about quality-of-life issues devoid of significant criteria, such as regional and ethnic differences, socio-economic variations or considerations of human worth. Ultimately, statistics reflect a bureaucratic interest which predicates record keeping. In other words, if one looks for something, one is more likely to find it than if one doesn't. In turn, the chart also reflects comparative levels of bureaucratization, that is the ability as well as the will to collect relevant data.

Secondly, as our last case in point (China) more than adequately illustrates, when we make judgements about any type of behaviour without adequate historical sensitivity, we do so at our peril. Historians may be relative newcomers to suicidology, but history arguably has a central part to play in any meaningful analysis of self-killing. Therefore, in order properly to understand the social phenomenon of suicide, it needs to be properly historicized. Presently, I will examine the historical processes through which suicide came to be measured in the first place. It is an attempt to answer a rhetorical question historically, one we generally take for granted: why bother to study suicide at all? Although the answers emanate from that simple point of departure, those answers are anything but self-evident. They are contextual.

Sociology, System Builders and *Le Suicide*

The nineteenth century, often characterized by numerous social, political and historical processes, is sometimes referred to as the age of the 'isms' and 'izations', e.g. nationalism, republicanism, bureaucratization and professionalization. Processes imply movement and contemporaries interpreted these movements as unidirectional aspects of human progress, subsequently dubbed the modernity thesis. The modernity thesis and its attendant teleology are largely discredited today, owing in no small part to the labours of subaltern historians and their critiques of Euro-centrist master narratives.[20] However, if the Western concept of modernity continued to shape global policy at institutions like the United Nations throughout the twentieth century, its political and social implications categorically obsessed most nineteenth-century European thinkers.[21]

Here, history found itself in the thick of the discussion over modernity. In Hegel's *Philosophy of History* (1837), the Berlin philosopher replaced the Christian soteriological struggle of good versus evil with a secular dialectic (thesis + antithesis = synthesis) and promoted a view of the nation state as the ultimate goal of history. Hegel's ideological and cultural spirit of human progress captured the imagination of the Borussian historians (such as Droysen, Ranke and Mommsen) who favoured a small German solution to the question of national unification, and helped to elevate Martin Luther to the status of a national father-figure as the great man who translated the Bible into German. During the twentieth century, this tradition shaped the anti-positivist modernism of German sociologists like Troeltsch, Sombart and Weber, who championed the spirit of capitalism arising out of the Reformation as the harbinger of modernity. However, here I have chosen three other important system builders of nineteenth-century sociology to illustrate their relationship with suicide and how that subject came to occupy a central place in the nascent discipline.

In 1839, Auguste Comte established sociology as an intellectual endeavour and set out his positivist teleology of modernity as a history of scientific progress. With one caveat: Comte only resorted to 'sociology' as a name for the new discipline after his chief competitor, the Belgian polymath Adolphe Quételet, appropriated his original designation, called 'social physics'. However, the two terms appear interchangeably throughout the corpus of his work and he even favoured the latter for its scientific inferences. Comte, a system builder, developed a strategic and overarching interpretation of historical progress. According to this systemic interpretation, he divided history into three discreet stages or phases: first, the theological (fetishistic); second, the metaphysical; and third, the positive (scientific). The last stage saw modernity initiated by the Renaissance rediscovery of ancient knowledge and copper-fastened by the Scientific Revolution.[22]

As his positive philosophy concentrated chiefly on the contributions of natural science to human advancement, Comte proposed that social physics 'may perhaps convince men worthy of the name of statesmen that there is a real and eminent utility in labours of this kind'. The alarming revolutionary constitution of modern societies (his reference to the perceived anarchy of the French Revolution) led him to contest the utility of social physics in political terms:

> The Ancients used to suppose order and progress to be irreconcilable: but both are indispensible conditions in a state of modern society; and their combination is at once the grand difficulty and the main resource of every genuine political system.[23]

Like other social physicists, Comte touted the utilitarian scientific value of his profession in the service of the state. Unusual among other early practitioners of social physics, however, Comte had relatively little to say about actual social phenomena like suicide, crime or divorce, and limited his observations to the history and advantages of scientific progress. However, Comte did have an early personal experience of suicide, having attempted to take his own life in 1827. He had just recovered from a severe nervous condition the year before, when he was admitted to the clinic of the famous Parisian alienist, Jean Étienne Dominique Esquirol (a *protégé* of Philippe Pinel) and was treated for mania and paranoia. The factors contributing to this condition apparently included his quarrels with the Saint-Simonians, financial difficulties relating to his publishing activities and marital strife with his wife, Massin (whom he suspected of licentious behaviour and is alleged to have been a prostitute).[24] In anticipation of the anniversary of his recovery, Comte feared a relapse and threw himself into the Seine from the Pont des Arts. Had it not been for the chance intervention of a Royal Guard, he may well have succeeded.[25] These events had a profound influence on his positivist philosophy, eventually leading him to found the Religion of Humanity, a secularist movement devoted to altruism which flourished in France and Brazil.

The references highlighted from Comte's writings are consciously rendered here from a translated and condensed version by the English intellectual Harriet Martineau. Just as Hegel and Comte developed their own modernist systems,[26] Martineau, an accomplished writer and social theorist in her own right, engaged in a systematic approach to ethnographic studies in her comprehensive study of *How to Observe Manners and Morals* (1838).[27] One of the earliest 'how-to' manuals for travelling ethnographers, it explored comprehensive methods for the examination of culture. Her chapter on 'religion' included a subsection devoted to the practice of suicide and its observation among foreign peoples.[28] Apart from a brief allusion to cowardly acts ('the remaining suicides (except, of course, the insane) are justified by none'), Martineau concentrated on the positive aspects of suicide among different cultures, which enabled the observer better to understand their character and number, and the prevailing morals and religious sentiments that animate or control the act.[29] Many of her examples were heroic and she explicitly referenced martyrdom as a form of suicide. Several comments arise from her experience of women's rights and slavery during two years in America, the basis for her *Society in America* (1837) and her first novel, *The Hour and the Man* (1841), the story of a French slave-trader. For example, she recounts how an American child who witnessed a sati in India was whipped by her mother for claiming to have seen hell – although one wonders whether her comment is a critique of widow-burning, corporeal punishment for children or violence within the family in general. Her vindication of Africans who preferred to take their own lives rather than serve as slaves on the sugar plantations of Cuba recalls a motif popular among abolitionists at the time; Richard Bell has traced the stylistic development of this literary genre as it progressed from pathetic to heroic stories of Africans who committed suicide in order to escape slavery to suit public tastes during the ante-bellum abolitionist campaign in the United States.[30]

When comparing the French to the Irish, Martineau noted the abundance of suicide among the former, especially young lovers who evoke copycats – a Werther-effect she blamed on press coverage, 'till a sensible physician suggested that suicides should not be noticed in the newspapers, or should be treated with ridicule'. In Ireland, however, she suggests that religious beliefs mitigated high rates of suicide:

> This profusion of self-murders could not have taken place amidst a serious belief of an immediate entrance upon purgatory, such as is held by the majority of the Irish. Only in a state of vague speculation as to another life could the future have operated as so slight a check upon the rash impulses of the present. The Irish,

231

> an impetuous race, like the French, and with a good share of
> vanity, of sympathy, and of sentiment, are probably deterred from
> throwing away life by those religious convictions and sentiments
> which the French once held in an equal degree, but from which
> they are now passing over into another state.[31]

Martineau was not the first English person to connect the irreligiosity
of the French Revolution to an increased propensity for self-killing.
Of course, there is no evidence to suggest that this was, in fact, the
case.[32] In Martineau's scenario for Ireland, the deprecating association
of revolution and suicide was paternalistic and had anti-republican
implications. Similarly, we simply do not know whether the subsequent victory of republicanism in the southern counties had any
demonstrable effect on suicide rates. What evidence we do have
suggests that most suicides in Ireland during the War of Independence
and Civil War continued to arise from more mundane quotidian
circumstances.[33] Throughout Europe, the social and ruling elite
engaged in similarly unflattering condemnations of republican
atheism as an enticement to suicide.

In mid-nineteenth century Russian, for example, suicide preoccupied
many scientists, writers and slavophiles. Dostoevsky deployed it as a
literary trope against Westernizing influences and social revolutionaries.[34] In his novel *Demons* (1872), youthful characters flaunt
godless nihilism and defiant suicide.[35] Apart from a litany of crimes
perpetrated by a bohemian cell of bourgeois idlers and immoral
advocates of violent revolution, two of their number, Kirilov and
Stavrogin, dramatically commit suicide; the former to establish absolute
free will and the non-existence of God, and the latter out of guilt over
murder, as well as the brutal molestation of a young girl – as a
consequence, she too took her own life, though Imperial censors initially
cut this ending to the story.[36] In his condemnation of the immorality
exerted by modernizing influences on Russian society, Dostoevsky
concluded that religious and patriotic values (Eastern Orthodoxy and
Mother Russia) offered the only moral barrier to many unthinkable
crimes permitted by socialist nihilism imported from the West. However,
as noted above, we simply cannot know what sort of effect Bolshevism
and the campaign against religion under Lenin and Stalin had on suicide
rates. To cite Lucien Febvre, perhaps to posit any causal nexus between
social revolution and suicide is simply *une question mal posée*?

Indeed, in nineteenth-century sociology, the proposed relationship
between suicide and religion assumed near law-like status as the so-

called 'One Law of Sociology', that is, Protestants ostensibly kill themselves more often than Catholics and, to a less clear extent, Jews. This 'law' is widely attributed to the arch-system-builder Émile Durkheim, first academic chair of sociology and considered by many to be the founder of the discipline. His most influential work, *Le Suicide* (1897), represents the first sociological case study in history. As suggested in its subtitle (quite bold at the time), the monograph was actually a 'study of sociology' (*Étude de Sociologie*); that is, a demonstration of his sociological method. Durkheim employed suicide as the most viable vehicle of his age to demonstrate and confirm the scientific credentials of the quantitative method for measuring and establishing the existence of social phenomena through demographic analysis. Armed with the scientific positivism of Comte, Durkheim set out to prove the existence of coercive social forces transcending individuals and controlling human behaviour at the strategic level of shared beliefs and moral values. His analyses of collective consciousness rendered sociology quite distinct from psychology and psychiatry, which treated of the individual rather than the group.

Durkheim attributed higher rates of suicide among Protestants to the individualistic nature of their theology, resulting from lower levels of social integration than Catholics.[37] However, like most attempts to interpret causation in suicidal behaviour, the association of greater suicidal proclivities to any one particular Christian sect is fraught with problems. Obviously, in a global sense, Christians make up only a small fraction of the earth's total population and are therefore not an essential example in terms of numbers alone. There have also been serious challenges to the credibility not only of Durkheim's data, but also to the methods he employed to analyse them. A chief difficulty involves the methods used by Durkheim to determine whether a population of a certain region was Catholic or Protestant. In the 1980s several detailed comparative studies from the United States produced inconclusive and, at times, contradictory evidence concerning differential rates between Catholics and Protestants in particular areas.[38] More recently, the model of the 'One Law' has been the object of an extended and direct attack from Rodney Stark and William Sims Bainbridge for its derivative nature, as it was first posited by the German national economist, Adolf Wagner, and, subsequently, taken up by the Italian psychiatrist, Enrico Morselli.[39] This is true and a cursory examination of Durkheim's citations reveals that most of his statistical data were taken from other authors' writing on suicide, primarily Morselli and Wagner. The major critique here, however, is that while both others admitted the limits of their data, Durkheim did not. Stark and Bainbridge's accusations are indeed quite serious:

> While Durkheim is exceedingly vague in citing his sources, Wagner gives precise details about each one of his very many data sources. Where Durkheim sweeps to unsubstantiated conclusions, Wagner carefully weighs alternative explanations. As models for painstaking, rigorous, thorough science, there could hardly be a greater contrast between Wagner and Durkheim, and we fear that the better scientist lost the competition for history's notice ... It seems to us that Wagner was struggling to explain the problem of spuriousness and wishing for multivariate statistical techniques to solve it. Durkheim handled this problem very differently. When the facts refused to fit his argument he either suppressed them or wrapped them in twisted rhetoric. Wagner recognized the problems, worked to the absolute limit of the analytical techniques of his day to find the truth, and expressed honest uncertainty that he had succeeded.[40]

On Durkheim's behalf, it should be noted that this accusation may be based upon a misreading of his intent, since it too hones in on the issues of causality and derivation. Durkheim's contemporaries were well aware of the problems associated with 'the easy inference of causes from differentials revealed in statistical tables ...'.[41] Durkheim's chief purpose lay in positively establishing the capability of a method (quantitative demographics) to prove a theory (the existence of social forces beyond the individual). This leads us to confront the relationship between sociology, statistics and suicide in the emergent quantitative culture of the nineteenth century. Specifically, how did suicide statistics come to form the basis of what is the most influential sociological case study of all time? Durkheim consciously chose suicide as the object of his experiment because of the availability of a large corpus of pre-existing research, as he admitted (albeit not always as readily as he might have). Viewed in this light, the question shifts from the causes of and solutions to suicide onto a far more complex historical question: how did suicide become a significant social phenomenon in the first place?

Suicide Statistics as Moral Statistics
The answer lies buried somewhere in the dusty history of quantitative demography and biometrics – not subjects that usually generate much enthusiasm. Nonetheless, recent historical attention to the Foucauldian

concept of biopower has drawn the scholarly gaze onto population management strategies undertaken by modern states, especially from the Enlightenment onwards, to control, increase and direct human resources for deployment by the ruling elite.[42] In that process, statistics and measurements of all sorts played a crucial role as national bureaucracies and scholars were increasingly involved in their production on behalf of the state, both in the interests of increasing the power of the ruling elite and in legitimizing their own professional credentials as technocractic functionaries in the employ of the state.[43] Etymologically, the Göttingen scholar Gottfried Achenwall first employed the word 'Statistik' in 1749 to describe 'remarkable facts about the state' and it reputedly derives not from the Latin 'status', but from the Italian 'statista' (statesman).[44] By the nineteenth century, the state and statistics were inexorably intertwined.

Reliable demographic statistics certainly require reliable data. Although the Imperial Roman census, and Chinese tax scrolls so efficiently produced by the mandarin administration system, represent early attempts to determine static population size for economic exploitation, the real origins of a modern demography capable of detecting changing population patterns lay with the introduction of parish registers recording baptisms, marriages and deaths. The first regular parish registers were kept by St Sebald's in Free-Imperial Nuremberg in 1524, a measure resulting from the institution of religious reforms; by the 1540s, most Evangelical cities of the Holy Roman Empire regularly recorded such information. They were introduced by order of Thomas Cromwell in England in 1538 and, by 1563, the Council of Trent issued a similar decree, spreading parish record-keeping to Catholic regions as well.

The introduction of parish registers went hand-in-hand with the creation of seminaries, as their administration required a literate clergy to serve in the function of bureaucrats. In Protestant areas, pastors became de facto state functionaries and the registers became records of state available for policy-making decisions. By tying the keeping of demographic records to religious sacraments and sacramentals, the authorities thereby legitimized the procedure and ensured near absolute compliance on the part of the average Christian – unlike inclusion in tax registers, which one might greedily seek to avoid, it was in the best metaphysical interests of the average Christian to engage in baptism, marriage, and the last rights. Initially, parish records were collected by the authorities to provide evidence of confessional allegiance during an age fraught by sectarian strife. They also contributed to a modern sense of identity – for the first time it was possible for a person and for the authorities to know exactly where a person came from, what their full name was, how old they were, etc. Thus routinized, the ecclesiastical procedure was gradually appropriated and, in the wake of the Josephine and revolutionary secularizations of the eighteenth century, formed the unquestioned basis for an ever-expanding state bureaucracy.

We can trace the origins of modern demographic statistics to John Graunt (1620–74) and his *Natural and Political Observations upon the Bills of Mortality* (1662).[45] Graunt, a London haberdasher, employed mortality records in the service of Charles II in an attempt to develop a demographic barometer as an early warning system for outbreaks of plague in London. He obtained his information primarily from 'weekly bills of mortality extant at the Parish-Clerks Hall'.[46] Graunt submitted his statistical results to the Royal Society with humility becoming a commoner, and he deferentially referred to their purpose in the dedication to John Lord Roberts: 'Now having (I know not [by] what accident) engaged my thoughts upon the bills of mortality, and so far succeeded therein as to have reduced several great confused volumes into a few perspicuous tables …'.[47]

Repeatedly, he recommended various courses of action to the magistrates based on data extrapolated from the bills of mortality, expressing especial concern for the health of the British body politic in his demographic critique of the city: 'that London, the metropolis of England, is perhaps a head too big for the body, and possibly too strong: that this head grows three times as fast as the body unto which it belongs, that is, it doubles its people in a third part of the time: that our parishes are now grown madly disproportionable …'.[48] Graunt's primary preoccupations revolved around corporeal issues of Baconian natural history and epidemiology (for example, disease, birth versus death rates, the potential for a male/female population imbalance through war), all with a keen eye to population increase as reason-of-state policy. The groundbreaking nature of his statistical research led Charles II to recommend his co-option to the Royal Society. Nevertheless, his work could prevent neither the horrific plague in 1665 nor the Great Fire of London in 1666, for which he and a good many other Catholics were popularly held responsible.

Apart from his statistical analysis of natural influences (disease, for example) on population growth, Graunt also pioneered considerations of behavioural factors. For example, he engaged in a rhetorical rumination on the pros and cons of polygamy. Here – among a number of examples cited from husbandry, livestock breeding and the herd instinct among animals – Graunt argued that polygamous marriages, such as those practiced by Muslims, did not foster real population growth.[49] From this he inferred both the superiority of Christian morality as well as the influence of human behaviour on demographic growth.

Hence, from its very inception, demographic record-keeping sought to serve the state by measuring behaviour according to Christian values as the conscious arbiter of social norms. As we have seen above in our examples of sociological systems, behaviouralist arguments infused sociological discourse from the start and continue to do so to the present day. However, a few decades before the emergence of sociology as a discreet discipline, one particular form of statistical measurement, exclusively behavioural in its focus, rose to prominence in the early nineteenth century: moral statistics. Nineteenth-century moral statistics represent the lynchpin connecting sociology and suicide, culminating in their Durkheimian nuptials in *Le Suicide: Étude de Sociologie*. It remains to sketch out the development of suicide statistics as the most important branch of moral statistics, though the significance of pre-Durkheimian suicidology is considered elsewhere in greater detail.[50] For the present discussion, we first need to consider the nature of moral statistics as secular expressions of values still deeply rooted in Christian morality.

An exact definition of moral statistics is elusive, not least because many of its early practitioners were amateur polymaths concerned less with terminological specificity than with the extrapolation of recommendations for government policy arising from the assumed self-evident nature of their own statistical research, not unusually in the service of partisan political or religious goals. Three mid-century works on moral statistics from Britain and Scotland illustrate the situation: a printed lecture delivered by minister William Arthur Wesleyan on the moral statistics of the British Empire, which contained no statistics whatsoever, but focussed instead on the sacred blessings bestowed upon the world by all things emanating from Britain, typified by a hearty closing salutation ('God bless London') extended to the presumably enthusiastic membership of the Young Men's Christian Association, which comprised his audience; William Logan's moral statistics of Glasgow, published by the Scottish Temperance League to demonstrate numerically the costs of drink to society in terms of pauperism, prostitution, juvenile delinquency, Sabbath profanation, crime and mental derangement; and the relatively comprehensive survey of moral statistics in England and Wales written by the school inspector Joseph Fletcher, which despite some rather sound reporting of demographics of population, crime, education and social organization was so unsensational that it had to be published privately.[51]

An early case-in-point of professionalization is described by the British historian of statistics, Ian Hacking. Dramatically, Hacking characterizes a squabble between British and French physicians at the end of the Napoleonic Wars (about which race had a greater proclivity to suicide) as '... the beginning of numerical sociology because (a) there were numbers and (b) the numbers of suicide were seen as a moral indicator of the quality of life'.[52]

This incident, he claims, should concern us on two levels. First, the debate assumed overtly nationalist overtones and therefore had propagandistic value beyond the sphere of medicine. Secondly, and far less obviously, it transcended national boundaries and united alienists in their professional struggle to monopolize competence over mental illnesses, not self-evident at the time. The incident concerns us presently for two additional reasons. Not only does it interpret the French Revolution as a failure for its purported turn from traditional religion, but it also involved one of the chief psychiatrists of the age. Specifically, in 1815 the alienist George Burrows opened a debate with his French colleagues by alluding to revolutionary irreligiosity as a possible cause for high rates of suicide in Paris, in an argument similar to that later employed by Harriet Martineau:

> Whether this deplorable propensity by the consequence only of recent political events which, having annihilated religion have deprived the wretched of its resources and consolations in affliction, and by their demoralizing effects dissolved the social compact that alone makes life a blessing, is not easy to determine ... periods of great scarcity and distress, and sudden revolutions, political or religious, are always active and universal agents in originating insanity.[53]

In response, none other than Esquirol (the very alienist who later treated Auguste Comte) 'took up cudgels against the egregious Burrows who had dared to suggest that Parisians are more suicidal than Londoners'.[54] And yet, the overtly nationalist character of the debate (metaphorized by Hacking as an international duel that aroused public interest for baser reasons of patriotism) belied an underlying level of subtle manipulation on both sides. Both Esquirol and Burrows took great pains to explain that suicidality, by extension another form of insanity, was in fact the sole province of alienists and physicians as they were the only persons with the proper qualifications to deal with such persons as patients. In other words, moral statistics could be employed to legitimize the social usufruct of their profession.

At the time, what was considered moral indicated that it was also reasonable. Morality was linked to human reason. Lack of morality implied a lack of reason and, particularly in the treatment of nervous disorders, moral treatment embodied the most progressive form of early nineteenth-century psychiatry, exemplified by the Retreat operated by the Quaker Tukes of York and the methods of Pinel (*traitement moral*), which concentrated on the treatment of emotions and moods. In a rather vague definition of moral statistics, Alexander von Oettingen expressed dissatisfaction with Drobisch's attempts at Germanized renderings of *statistique morale*, preferring instead to adhere closely to the original French meaning, describing morals as customs (*Sitten*), though not in an ethnographic sense.[55] In reference to suicide, the Italian moral statistician Melchiorre Gioia suggested that 'suicides should be considered an integral part of *costumi* [habits of a population] as, in their majority, they depend on moral causes.'[56]

Oettingen noted that moral statistics were usually employed to measure behaviours, given the implications of rationality, free will and choice. Ironically, however, since much of the actionable data available was limited to deviant behaviour, which came to the attention of the authorities, 'one might sooner speak of immoral rather than moral statistics'.[57] One dictionary of sociology defines moral statistics such as the measurements of 'suicide, divorce, mental health, illegitimacy, and abortion' as indicators of social pathology, which is defined, in turn, as 'an early form of deviance theory, no longer in wide use, which drew upon the organic metaphor to suggest that parts of societies, like parts of bodies, could suffer breakdown and disease'.[58] As Ursula Baumann is quick to point out, *moral* statistics tended to focus – far more often than not – on types of behaviour generally recognized as *immoral*.[59] Those values measured remained steeped in Christian moral casuistry and the effects measured 'silently presumed their negative evaluation'.[60]

Often recognized as the first work on moral statistics, André-Michel Guerry's *Essai sur la Statistique Morale de la France* appeared in 1833. However, Guerry's definition of moral statistics too is extremely diffuse:

> Moral statistics, having as its object of investigation the mind of man, studies his capabilities, his morals and customs, his feelings and sentiments, and his passions. Thus it encompasses at once the whole of moral philosophy, politics, religion, legislation, history, literature and the arts.[61]

From the very birth of moral statistics, suicide emerged as the immediate and primary focal point. According to Guerry, 'among the subjects included in moral statistics, suicide is one of those which has attracted the most lively attention and about which there has been the most discussion'.[62] Chosen as Director of Criminal Statistics shortly after the Revolution of 1830, he compiled data for the *Compte Général de l'Administration de la Justice Criminelle en France*, a massive compilation of criminal data commissioned in 1825. He quickly became fascinated by the implications of the *Compte Général*, which formed the basis of his statistical analysis in the *Essai*. Guerry acknowledged the limitations of his sources and the under-reporting of suicide on a large scale. He conducted the first social content analysis to establish motives for self-killing in suicide notes deposited with the Paris police. His method, limited to a basic statistical tabulation of hangings, charcoal, shootings and the like, fell short of any qualitative analysis of the texts themselves. Overall, apart from attempting to establish a link between self-killing and recidivism and to tabulate personal motives for the act, Guerry's study revealed patterns of an inverse relationship of suicide to homicide throughout France; whereas the north of France had higher rates of suicide and lower rates of murder, the south exhibited contrary traits. The question of relative levels of bureaucracy or the extent and reliability of record keeping escaped his attention.

A similar north–south divide later reported for Italy by Morselli was instrumentalized in the national debate over Italian unification to argue for the ostensible backwardness of the south.[63] Along with fellow scholars like his mentor, the psychiatrist Carlo Livi and the eminent criminologist Cesare Lombroso, Morselli represented positivist rationalization against the conservative forces of particularism. They also had a professional agenda. Together, they promoted an evolutionary model based on phrenology to suggest that southern Italians suffered from [physical] anthropological atavisms in order to promote a policy of penal reform which would grant psychiatrists a much larger role in the care and treatment of prisoners.

Furthermore, Morselli turned our presumed notion that high rates of suicide represented an unfavourable condition on its head by developing an evolutionary view of civilization, modernity and progress. Counter-intuitively, he claimed that high rates of suicide actually mirrored higher levels of civilization in the advance towards modernity. He first published interim findings from a phreniatric study of the prisoner population in southern Italy in 1875, and then in his award-winning masterpiece, *Suicide: a Study of Comparative Moral*

Statistics, which appeared in 1879 to international acclaim and quickly went into German and English translations.[64] It was no coincidence, certainly, that Durkheim chose the same title for his own *Le Suicide* eighteen years later. As a psychiatrist, Morselli viewed the pressures of modernity in terms of an internalization of violence. Whereas in less civilized areas (southern Italy, for example) violence was liable to be externalized as murder, in more civilized areas, the internalization of social pressures moved weaker members of society to take their own lives; regrettable and preventable, suicide ultimately represented a positive and natural Darwinian check on deviance in populations, a 'fatal tendency of civilized society'. In this rendering, suicide became a perverse badge of modernity.

In the debate over German unification, suicide too achieved notoriety as a subject of national import. In this regard, the social economist Adolf Wagner rendered a seminal contribution to moral statistics, one to which Morselli frequently recognized his indebtedness. Wagner, a nationalist and an evangelical who vocally favoured German unification under Prussia, had a famously choleric temperament (at one time, he was challenged to a duel by an aristocratic member of the Reichstag for his dogged political opposition) and, initially, was not offered an academic chair in pre-unification Germany.[65] In a typically alternate career trajectory for brilliant but unpopular German academics (not unlike that of the celebrated psychiatrist, Emil Kraepelin), Wagner took a post at the German-speaking Czarist University of Dorpat, largely facultied by Baltic ethnic Germans. Called back to a chair in political science (*Staatswissenschaft*) at the University of Berlin in 1870, he served the unified German state as a chief representative of academic socialism (*Kathedersozialismus*) and principal architect of Bismarck's social welfare program. He is most famous for his law of increase, known today as Wagner's Law. According to Hegelian principles, Wagner posited that after the nation had been achieved, state activity would continually and unceasingly be on the increase, especially in the areas of public expenditure and bureaucratization.

In fact, this law of economy had other origins. Wagner began his career as a statistician and, in 1864, he published a monumental study with an equally monumental title: *The Laws of Regularity in Apparently Arbitrary Human Behaviour from the Viewpoint of Statistics.*[66] In it, he attempted to prove that individual behaviours actually conformed to patterns, which, over time, remained generally constant, but exhibited a tendency to increase. While the work covered many different types of human behaviour using the methods of moral statistics, Wagner focussed overwhelmingly on suicide statistics, with an extended interpretation in volume one of the statistical appendix in volume two. It was in the context of that interpretive discussion of suicide that he laid out the general principles of what later became sociology's 'One Law'; Protestants always suffer higher rates of suicide. As the above critique of Stark and Bainbridge points out, this was indeed Wagner's contribution, though he never expressed any intent to see the supposition drawn from his statistics enshrined into law. However, as an Evangelical Lutheran, Wagner did feel compelled to engage briefly in some soul searching on the nature of the spirit of Protestantism, which might contribute to that condition.

This particular line of argumentation was quickly taken up and taken to its logical extension by Wagner's Dorpat colleague, the evangelical theologian Alexander von Oettingen. In his *Moralstatistik* (1868), Oettingen deployed Wagner's statistics to evaluate social behaviour and to offer his ethical prognosis based upon empirical data; it was, literally, theology become scientific. While he had much to say about suicide in that volume, he devoted a second book *On Acute and Chronic Suicide* (1881) specifically to that subject. Here he developed a full-blown explanation for higher rates of Protestant suicide, which rested upon the premise that the sect represented the spirit of modernity and progress. Unfortunately, too many modern Protestants engaged in the pursuit of worldly matters to the exception of their inner spiritual life. Suicide among modern Protestants he likened to an infectious disease, with the evangelical religion representing the proper anti-septic, like some carbolic acid.[67] As for the duties of being a Protestant, Oettingen could not deny a greater demand for sacrifices than among Catholics, 'with their priestly life-insurance tendencies' (the sacrament of penance, for example) or Greek 'orientalists'. However, it was not only their superstitious religiosity, but also their impure culture, which differentiated them from Protestants:

> Therefore it is understandable that the German, with his high culture and deep inner affective life, with his tendency to self-reflection and self-critique, carries with him a greater danger of suicide than the easy-living, sanguine Roman or the even less developed, less-civilized Slav, who only tends toward suicide, when licked by half-culture or if infected with nihilism.[68]

Note that this (and other depictions) assumes Germans to be Protestant and that nihilism is brought into connection with Russia. Both intimations surely stem from Oettingen's background in the Baltic States of the Russian Empire, where most ethnic Germans were indeed

Evangelical Lutherans, and where Dostoevsky's *Demons*, published in 1872 (nine years earlier), had already sparked a debate on nihilism and anarchism in Russia. Thomas Masaryk's *Suicide and the Meaning of Civilization* only appeared in the same year and it is unclear whether Oettingen was cognizant of the Czech author and his causal theory of half-education.[69] Appearing as it did at the tail end of the *Kulturkampf*, Oettingen's study of suicide manifested the deeply rooted longings of many ultra-nationalist Baltic Germans, who looked to the Prussian state to realize their own yearnings for reintegration into the Fatherland. Viewed from this perspective, therefore, any suggestion that Oettingen somehow represented a moderate voice in the nineteenth-century scholarly discourse over moral statistics and suicide is open to doubt.[70]

Conclusions

The history of nineteenth-century suicidology evidences the pervasiveness of nationalism, bureaucratization, an awareness of republicanism, and a self-awareness of professionalization in contemporary thought. Less expected is the continued importance of religion inherent in the interpretation of moral statistics, which was ubiquitous, from Italy, France, Britain, Russia and even Scandinavia, whereby suicide continued to be viewed pejoratively.[71] Indeed, contemporaries throughout Europe often continued to view the condemnation of the bodies of self-killers to hospitals for anatomical classes as a form of punishment even when suicide had been decriminalized.[72] Richard Bell has recently demonstrated how the topic of suicide was intricately woven into the broader cultural tapestry of the United States as part of political fear-mongering, generational conflict, campaigns for public altruism and criminal reform, and the abolitionist debate from the end of the Revolution until the Civil War.[73] Obviously, there is far more at stake in the topic for historians than a simple empirical analysis along the lines of Durkheimian quantitative method.

Indeed, the present consideration may give some cause to pause and reflect on the development and derivation of this method, coming as it did from within the particular context of a nineteenth-century debate on the nature of the state and its relationship to the nascent discipline of sociology. As we have seen, Durkheim was building on some rather large and solid foundations, and his choice of subject matter for the original sociological case study was hardly arbitrary and perhaps indicative of Wagner's theories about regularity in human behaviour. Durkheim's *Le Suicide* was very much the culmination of an intellectual process. The present overview demonstrates how suicide caught the attention of moral statisticians and, subsequently, sociologists. The question it does not address is why this happened. Unfortunately, the answer to that lies more in the synchronicity and contingency of human political affairs than in immutable laws governing human behaviour.

If the growth in interest in suicide was a ubiquitous European phenomenon that was gradually exported throughout the globe along with the master narrative of modernity, its practitioners nonetheless found reason to quarrel over the nature of their findings. The French (such as Comte, Durkheim, Mauss) and the Italian (such as Morselli, Lombroso, Levi) modernists supported a positivist and scientific approach. Their theories of material progress tended to be highly mechanistic and, more often than not, fatalistic. The German modernists, on the other hand, were more prone to anti-positivism. They developed an ideological interpretation of Hegel's spirit of the times (*Zeitgeist*) as the social dynamic behind progress that found its apotheosis in Weber's Protestant ethic and spirit of capitalism. Werner Sombart, a student of Adolph Wagner who also supported an interpretation of the Renaissance and Reformation as dynamic spiritual forces behind modern processes, once famously derided the pseudo-science of French positivism as 'physics envy'. In the end however, the seminal input to moral statistics by Germans such as Wagner, Oettingen and Drobisch, disappeared from the picture, while Morselli is only slightly more recognized and the theories of Durkheim have been replaced by the bland empiricism of British biometrics. Here, I agree entirely with Stark and Bainbridge, as well as the conclusions of Theodore Porter:

> From our perspective, this German tradition has become almost invisible, and the more mathematical approach developed by English biometricians has become almost obligatory. Within that kind of statistics, the primacy of elemental social facts has, to a degree, been restored. Durkheim was no party to the biometricians' scheme of social explanation.[74]

Apart from that, the history of nineteenth-century suicidology not only demonstrates how the topic came to represent the union of sociology and the state, but also indicates that historicizing that process continues to have lasting and immediate significance. Again, in academic scholarship, one might return to the implications of quality and quantitative control exercises as a form of bibliometric (if not biometric; but what are human resources for if not to be exploited?) trap. And indeed, it seems appropriate, if not outright prophetic, to apply Wagner's Law of Continual Increase to characterize that phenomenon too.

Nonetheless, this situation also has its history, which begins with the adoption of the Northcote–Trevelyan Report of 1853, recommending the implementation of the Chinese mandarin examination system for the civil service, first in India, then in Britain itself. Perhaps, however, in the history of all system building as in the history of the relationship between suicide, sociology and the state, it is, as Andreas Bähr so aptly points out, more a question of semantics than numbers.[75]

NOTES

1 It is argued that this is a misreading of Durkheim, who opposed empiricism and literal factualism: see Theodore K. Porter, 'Statistical and Social Facts: from Quetelet to Durkheim', *Sociological Perspectives*, 38 (1995), pp.15–26.

2 Most recently, in a cogent, well-documented and incisively argued critique of managerial culture at universities, the senior academic Richard Hill finds that: 'The once stereotypical image of an academic – a middle-class, pipe-smoking patriarch with all the time in the world to contemplate lofty ideas – has been replaced by the current reality of workers immersed in the rush of corporate activity, mostly aimed at peddling their institutions' educational wares and maintaining market share. This change has been accompanied by bureaucratic practices and corporate jargon common to other sectors – inputs, outputs, targets, key performance indicators, performance management, unit costs, cost effectiveness, benchmarking, quality assurance and so on – that together form a system dedicated to maintaining corporate discipline, brand distinctiveness and market share.' See *Whackademia: An Insider's Account of the Troubled University* (Sydney: New South Wales University Press, 2012), p.9. For the Irish context, see Brendan Walsh and Roger Scruton (eds), *Degrees of Nonsense: The Demise of the University in Ireland* (Dublin: Glasnevin Publishing, 2012). For a commentary on the situation in Great Britain see Keith Thomas and Martin Rees, 'Fidei defensores', *Times Higher Education*, 8 Nov. 2012: online at http://www.timeshighereducation.co.uk/421722.article (accessed 18 March 2013).

3 The entire chart can be found at: www.who.int/mental_health/prevention/suicide_rates/en/ [accessed 23 June 2012].

4 David Lederer, '*Honfibú*: Nationhood, Manhood, and the Culture Of Self-Sacrifice in Hungary', in Jeffrey R. Watt (ed.), *From Sin to Insanity: Suicide in Early Modern Europe* (Ithaca: Cornell University Press, 2004), pp.116–37.

5 Nick Paton Walsh, 'Russia's suicide rate doubles', *The Guardian* [Online], 9 July 2003, available from: www.guardian.co.uk/world/2003/jul/09/russia.nickpatonwalsh [accessed 23 June 2012].

6 For a more accurate portrayal of suicide under Stalin, see Kenneth M. Pinnow, *Lost to the Collective: Suicide and the Promise of Soviet Socialism, 1921–1929* (Cornell University Press, 2009).

7 Susan K. Morrissey, 'Drinking to Death: Suicide, Vodka and Religious Burial in Russia', *Past and Present*, no. 186 (2005), pp.117–46.

8 'Suicide Blights China's Women', BBC International [Online], 29 Nov. 2002. Available from: http://news.bbc.co.uk/2/hi/asia-pacific/2526079.stm [accessed 23 June 2012]. Phillips is currently the Director of Suicide Research and Prevention Center and Research Methods Consulting Center, Shanghai Mental Health Center, Shanghai Jiaotong University School of Medicine, and the Executive Director of the WHO Collaborating Center for Research and Training in Suicide Prevention, Beijing Huilongguan Hospital.

9 Michael R. Phillips, X. Li, Y. Zhang, 'Suicide Rates in China, 1995–99', *The Lancet*, no. 359 (2002), pp.835–40; Michael R. Phillips, Hui G. Cheng, 'The Changing Global Face of Suicide', *The Lancet*, 379 (2012), pp.2318–9.

10 Michael R. Phillips 'Risk Factors for Suicide in China: A National Case-Control Psychological Autopsy Study', *The Lancet*, 360 (2002), pp.1728–36; Michael R. Phillips, Gonghuan Yang, Shuran Li, Yue Li, 'Suicide and the Unique Prevalence Pattern of Schizophrenia in Mainland China: A Retrospective Observational Study', *The Lancet*, 364 (2004), pp.1062–68; Michael

R. Phillips et al., 'Prevalence, Treatment, and Associated Disability of Mental Disorders in Four Provinces in China during 2001–05: An Epidemiological Survey', *The Lancet*, 373 (2009), pp.2041–53; Michael R. Phillips, 'Rethinking the Role of Mental Illness in Suicide', *American Journal of Psychiatry*, 167 (2010), pp.731–33.

11 Jianlin Ji, Arthur Kleinman, Anne E. Becker, 'Suicide in Contemporary China: A Review of China's Distinctive Suicide Demographics in their Socio-Cultural Context', *Harvard Review of Psychiatry*, 9 (2001), pp.1–12.

12 Sing Lee and Arthur Kleinman, 'Suicide as Resistance in Chinese Society' in Elizabeth J. Perry and Mark Selden, *Chinese Society: Change, Conflict and Resistance* (London: Routledge, 2003), p.296.

13 Margery Wolf, 'Women and Suicide in China' in Margery Wolf, Roxane Witke and Emily Martin (eds), *Women in Chinese Society* (Stanford: Stanford University Press, 1975), p.112.

14 Andre C.K. Hsieh and Jonathan D. Spence, 'Suicide and the Family in Pre-Modern Chinese Society' in Arthur Kleinman and Tsung-Yi Lin (eds), *Normal and Abnormal Behavior in Chinese Culture* (Dordrecht: D. Reidel, 1981), pp.29–47.

15 Ibid., pp.29–31.

16 Jonathan D. Spence, *The Death of Woman Wang* (London: Penguin, 1979).

17 Paul Ropp, Paola Zamperini and Harriet T. Zurndorfer (eds), *Passionate women: Female Suicide in Late Imperial China* (Leiden: Brill, 2001); see also Paola Paderni, 'The Crime of Seduction and Women's Suicide in Eighteenth-Century China', in Hans Medick and Andreas Bähr, *Sterben von Eigener Hand: Selbsttöttung als Kulturelle Praxis* (Cologne: Böhlau Verlag, 2005), pp.241–55.

18 Roxane Witke, 'Mao Tse-Tung, Women and Suicide in the May 4th era', *Chinese Quarterly*, 31 (1967), pp.128-47.

19 Sing Lee et al., 'Attitudes Toward Suicide among Chinese People in Hong Kong', *Suicide and Life-Threatening Behavior*, 37 (2007), pp.565–75.

20 The inadequacies of the modernity thesis were, most recently, a subject of an extensive forum in the *American Historical Review*, 116 (2011); the concluding piece by Richard Wolin, '"Modernity": The Peregrinations of a Contested Historiographical Concept', pp.741–51, provides a useful overview.

21 For example, see Mark Mazower's critical history of the United Nations presented in his 2008 Lawrence Stone lectures at Princeton University and published as *No Enchanted Palace: The End of Empire and the Ideological Origins of the United Nations* (Princeton: Princeton University Press, 2009).

22 Harriet Martineau (trans.), *The Positive Philosophy of Auguste Comte* (2 Volumes, London: John Chapman, 1853). Comte's interpretation of historical stages is introduced from the onset (i, p.2), while the full explication of 'the historical question', that is, each stage and its characteristics appears later (ii, pp.181–483).

23 Ibid., ii, 2ff.

24 Mary Pickering, *Auguste Comte: An Intellectual Biography* (2 Volumes, Cambridge: Cambridge University Press, 1993), i, pp.371–92.

25 Ibid., i, p.394.

26 Comte appears to have read notes from Hegel's lectures on his philosophy of history over a decade before its publication and the pair exchanged views through an intermediary, Adolphe d'Eichtal; Pickering, *Comte*, pp.278, 296–301.

27 Harriet Martineau, *How to Observe Men and Morals* (London: Charles Knight and Co., 1838).

28 Ibid., pp.94–100.

29 Ibid., p.96.

30 Ibid., p.97f. On the usage of this motif more generally in abolitionist literature, see Richard Bell, *We shall be no more: Suicide and Self-Government in the Newly United States* (Cambridge, MA: Harvard University Press, 2012), pp.201–46.

31 Martineau, *Morals and Manners*, p.98. Later, Martineau visited Ireland as well, a visit recounted in her *Letters from Ireland* (London: John Chapman, 1852; republished by Irish Academic Press, Dublin, 2001).

32 See Jeffrey Merrick, 'Death and Life in the Archives: Patterns of and Attitudes to Suicide in Eighteenth-Century Paris', in David Wright and John Weaver (eds), *Histories of Suicide: International Perspectives on Self-Destruction in the Modern World* (Toronto: University of Toronto Press, 2009), pp.73–90; idem, 'Suicide and Politics in Pre-Revolutionary France',

Eighteenth-Century Life, 30 (2006), pp.32–47; idem, 'Suicide in Paris, 1775' in Watt (ed.), *From Sin to Insanity: Suicide in Early Modern Europe*, pp.158–74.

33 See Georgina Laragy, 'Suicide in Ireland, 1831–1921: A Social and Cultural Study' (unpublished Ph.D. Thesis, NUI Maynooth, 2005).

34 On this aspect of Russian literature, see Irina Paperno, *Suicide as a Cultural Institution in Dostoevsky's Russia* (Ithaca: Cornell University Press, 1997), esp. pp.123–61. On suicide in nineteenth-century Russia more broadly, see Susan Morrissey, *Suicide and the Body Politic in Imperial Russia* (Cambridge: Cambridge University Press, 2006).

35 *Бесы* is sometimes translated as *Devils* or *The Possessed*.

36 Originally, this chapter 'At Tikhon's', also known as 'Stavrogin's Confession', was censored, but now appears as an appendix; for example, Fyodor Dostoevsky, *Demons* (London: Penguin, 2008).

37 Émile Durkheim, *Le Suicide: Étude de Sociologie* (Paris: Anienne Librairie Germer Bailliere, 1897), pp.153–60.

38 Charles E. Faupel, Gregory S. Kowalski and Paul D. Starr, 'Sociology's One Law: Religion and Suicide in the Urban Context', *Journal for the Scientific Study of Religion*, 26 (1987), pp.523–34; William B. Bankston, H. David Allen and Daniel S. Cunningham, 'Religion and Suicide: A Research Note on Sociology's "One Law"', *Social Forces*, 62 (1983), pp.521–8; Whitney Pope and Nick Danigelis, 'Sociology's "One Law"', *Social Forces*, 60 (1981), pp.495–516.

39 Rodney Stark and William Sims Bainbridge, *Religion, Deviance, and Social Control* (New York: Routledge, 1996), pp.31–52.

40 Ibid., p.46f.

41 Porter, 'Statistical and Social Facts', p.25.

42 For a recent overview of the concept and its historical applicability, see Majia Holmer Nadesan, *Governmentality, Biopower, and Everyday Life* (New York and London: Routledge, 2008).

43 See, for example, Lars Behrisch, Vermessen, Zählen, Berechnen, *Die Politische Ordnung des Raums im 18. Jahrhundert* (Frankfurt am Main: Campus Verlag, 2006); I. Bernard Cohen, *The Triumph of Numbers: How Counting Shaped Modern Life* (New York: W.W. Norton, 2006).

44 Ian Hacking, *The Taming of Change* (Cambridge: Cambridge University Press, 1990), p.24; Mary Poovey, *A History of the Modern Fact: Problems of Knowledge in the Sciences of Wealth and Society* (Chicago: Chicago University Press, 1998), p.308. On the Italian derivation of the word 'statistics', see Alexander von Oettingen, *Die Moralstatistik in Ihrer Bedeutung für eine Socialethik* (Erlangen: Andreas Deichert Verlag, 1882), p.7.

45 *Natural and political observations mentioned in a following index and made upon the bills of mortality ... with reference to the government, religion, trade, growth, ayre, diseases, and the several changes of the said city* (London, 1662).

46 Ibid., p.4.

47 Ibid., Dedication.

48 Ibid.

49 Ibid., p.48.

50 As a starting point is the highly recommendable overview by Adelaide psychiatrists, Robert D. Goldeney, Johan A. Schioldann and Kirsten I. Dunn, 'Suicide Research Before Durkheim', *Health and History*, 10 (2008), pp.73–93: Pre-Durkheimian suicidology was the subject of a conference, 'The Making of Modern Suicide', held at NUI Maynooth in 2010 supported by a grant from the Wellcome Trust for the History of Medicine. The results of this meeting appear as a special issue in the *Journal of Social History* 46:3 (2013).

51 William Arthur Wesleyan, *The Extent and Moral Statistics of the British Empire: A Lecture Delivered Before the Young Men's Christian Association* (London: B.L. Green, 1848); William Logan, *The Moral Statistics of Glasgow* (Glasgow: Scottish Temperance League, 1849); Joseph Fletcher, *Summary of the Moral Statistics of England and Wales* (London: Privately printed, c.1850).

52 Hacking, *Taming of Chance*, p.64.

53 George Burrows, *Commentaries on the Causes, Forms, Symptoms, and Treatment, Moral and Medical, of Insanity* (London: Thomas and George Underwood, 1828), p.442.

54 Hacking, *Taming of Chance*, p.65ff.

55 Oettingen, *Moralstatistik*, p.11.

56 Melchiorre Gioia, 'Nota dei Suicidj Avvenuti Nelle Provincie Lombarde Negli anni 1817 al 1827', *Annali Universali di Statistica, Economia Pubblica, Storia, Viaggi e Commercio*, 17 (July 1828), pp.67–8; reference and translation from: Maria Teresa Brancaccio, '"The Fatal

Tendency of Civilized Society": Enrico Morselli's Suicide, Moral Statistics and Positivism in Italy', *Journal of Social History*, 46.3 (2013), pp.700–15.

57 'Sodann aber umfassen die aählbaren und registrirbaren Daten fast ausschliesslich böse, unmoralische Handlungen. Man könnte eher von einer Immoralitäts-, als von einer Moralstatistik reden' in Oettingen, *Moralstatistik*, p.12.

58 Gordon Marshall, 'Moral Statistics', *A Dictionary of Sociology* (1998); *Encyclopedia.com*. [Online]. Available from: www.encyclopedia.com/doc/1O88-moralstatistics.html [accessed 4 May 2012].

59 Ursula Baumann, *Vom Recht auf den Eigenen Tod. Die Geschichte des Suizids vom 18. bis 20. Jahrhundert* (Weimar: Böhlaus Nachfolger, 2001), p.220.

60 Ibid., p.220.

61 André-Michel Guerry, 'La Statistique morale (1), ayant pour objet l'homme intellectual, elle étudie ses faculties, ses moeurs, ses sentimens, ses passions; elle embrasse ainsi à-la-fois dans son ensemble, la philosophie morale, la politque, le culte, la legislation, l'histoire, la literature et les art', in idem, *Essai sur la Statistique Morale de la France* (Paris: Chez Crochard, 1833), p.69; Hugh P. Whitt and Victor W. Reinking (eds and trans.), *A Translation of André-Michel Guerry's Essay on the Moral Statistics of France (1833): A Sociological Report to the French Academy of Science* (Lewiston: Edwin Mellon Press, 2002), p.136.

62 André-Michel Guerry, 'Parmi les sujets qu'embrasse la statistique morale, le suicide est un de ceux qui ont le plus vivement attire l'aatention, et sur lesquels on a le plus disserté', in *Essai*, p.61; Whitt and Reinking, *Translation*, p.121.

63 Brancaccio, 'Fatal tendency', pp.703-06.

64 Enrico Morselli, *Il Suicidio: Saggio di Statistica Morale Comparata* (Milan: Dumolard, 1879).

65 This section represents a summation of David Lederer, 'Sociology's "One Law": Moral Statistics, Modernity, Religion and German Nationalism in the Suicide Studies of Adolf Wagner and Alexander von Oettingen', *Journal of Social History*, 46:3 (2013), pp.684-99.

66 Adolph Wagner, *Die Gesetzmässigkeit in den Scheinbar Willkührlichen Menschlichen Handlungen vom Standpunkte der Statistik* (Hamburg: Boyes and Geisler, 1864).

67 Alexander von Oettingen, *Über die Akuten und Chronischen Selbstmord* (E.F. Karow's Universitätsbuchhandlung Dorpat, 1881), p.28.

68 'So erklärt es sich, daß er Germane mit seiner Hochkultur und seinem tief innerlichen Gemüthsleben, mit seiner Neigung zur Selbstbeobachtung und Selbstkritik, auch eine gröre Selbstmordgefahr in sich trägt, als der leichtlebige, sanguinische Romane oder der noch unentwickelte, naturwüchsige Slave, der nur dort zum Selbstmord neigt, wo ihn die Halbkultur beleckt oder der Nihilismus angekränkelt hat': ibid., p.31.

69 Though it seems likely that he did and, occasionally, the theory is also attributed to Adolph Wagner. The habilitation of Tomáš G. Masaryk is *Der Selbstmord als Sociale Massenerscheinung der Modernen Civilisation* (Vienna: Konegen, 1881). Masaryk later became the first President of Czechoslovakia.

70 Indeed, as regards his ability to weave Wagner's interpretation into a persuasively nationalistic sermon, Porter seriously underestimates Oettingen's 'creativity': 'Oettingen, who appears in my trajectory as the most sociological author in this statistical tradition, was rather an ordinary thinker, certainly not a brilliantly creative one' (Porter, 'Statistical and Social Facts', p.25).

71 On religious attitudes toward suicide in Denmark, Finland, Norway and Sweden, see Evelyne Luef, 'Low Morals at a High Latitude? Suicide in Nineteenth-Century Scandinavia', *Journal of Social History*, 46.3 (2013), pp.668–83; and for a discussion of the etymological origins of the term 'suicide' in the Enlightenment, which debates the much acclaimed secularization of suicide, see Andreas Bähr, 'Between "Self-Murder" and "Suicide": The Modern Etymology of Self-Killing', *Journal of Social History*, 46.3 (2013), pp.620–32.

72 This is an area where much research is still needed. For Prussia, see Julia Schreiner, *Jenseits vom Glück. Suizid, Melancholie und Hypochondrie in Deutschsprachigen Texten des Späten 18. Jahrhunderts* (Munich: Oldenbourg Verlag, 2003).

73 Bell's *We shall be no more* is a triumph of historical narrative.

74 Porter, 'Statistical and social facts', p.25.

75 The central thesis of his prize-nominated monograph on self-killing from the Enlightenment to Romanticism, Andreas Bähr, *Der Richter im Ich, Die Semantik der Selbsttötung in der Aufklärung* (Vandenhoeck & Ruprecht, Göttingen, 2002).

10

DEATH NOTICES AND OBITUARIES IN PROVINCIAL IRISH NEWSPAPERS, 1820–1900

CIARA BREATHNACH AND DAVID BUTLER

This essay* explores the nature and function of obituaries and death notices in nineteenth-century Irish provincial newspapers.[1] Employing a database of examples extracted from newspapers, it is argued that the publication of obituaries and death notices served a dual purpose: firstly, it represents an expression of rising middle-class Catholic aspirations, and, secondly, it assisted the Catholic Church to exert control over funerary culture.

The essay is divided into three overlapping thematic sections; it commences by locating obituaries as a writing genre, and argues that while they fall outside the definition of 'ego-documents', or documents of the self, they were crucial to the family of the deceased on a number of levels. Furthermore, they can be interpreted from class, gender and religious perspectives. Through a discussion of prevailing folk customs mainly in southern Irish counties, the second section shows how the placement by Catholics of death notices in newspapers marked a shift away from traditional (oral) modes of communication towards print culture. This mirrors 'the re-emergence of Catholicism as a formal institutional presence' which, Kevin Whelan has pointed out, 'was uneven in temporal and spatial terms'.[2] The final section demonstrates how a sample from the database of 157,005 death notices can be rendered using historical Geographic Information Systems (GIS). It concludes that regional folk identities were undermined over time by the homogenizing impact of print culture, and that this process encountered no opposition from the Catholic Church because it was in keeping with the ultramontane agenda it promoted, which aspired to 'tame' Irish funerary customs.

Contextualizing Obituaries and Death Notices

The terms obituary and death notices are clearly distinguishable and serve the specific purposes of eulogizing in one instance and conveying funeral information in the other. However, the distinction implicit in the manner in which these terms are used in the present cannot be applied neatly to nineteenth-century newspapers. For example, the *Weekly Irish Times* was in no doubt that there were different forms, with different purposes; obituaries were for people of note, such as General Nassau Lees, editor of the *Times of India*, whose lengthy obituary was carried on the news pages in March 1889.[3] Such distinctions were not observed equally by all newspapers; two years previously, the *Freeman's Journal* reported the death of Sir William Hort in the following manner:

> We regret to notice in our obituary columns to-day the death of Sir William Hort, of Hortland House, county Kildare, in the 61st year of his age. The deceased baronet, was formerly a stipendiary magistrate, and his name is still kindly remembered in the districts over which his jurisdiction extended.[4]

Hort's entry resembles what we might now describe as a death notice, which were characteristically brief and were increasingly devoted to recording the fact that someone had died, though the *Freeman's Journal* described that section as an obituary column. Given the variable manner in which newspapers apprised its readers of deaths in their immediate hinterland and elsewhere, we have expanded our terms of reference to embrace all manner of obituary and death notices.

Obituaries are difficult to categorize in literary terms; by some criteria, they can be defined as commissioned journalism. In obvious contrast to diaries and letters – both compiled and intended for private or limited consumption – obituaries and death notices are public forms of writing, written about, but not normally by, an individual. In his examination of North American obituaries, Gary Long calls them '... claims made by others about the dead'. He describes them as 'mediated, abbreviated, stylized biographies', incorporating 'aspects of both "personal identity" and "social identity"'.[5] Ego-documents are clearly problematic as historical sources, not least because of their Freudian echo, though von Greyerz defines them sympathetically as 'historical sources and texts ... [which can] offer us access to an ego'.[6] By this definition, obituaries, which are normally not ego-generated, can be classified as ego-documents, because they offer insights into individual lives. Yet we cannot with confidence comment on the authorship of obituaries and death notices. Many, it is reasonable to assume, were written by family members or by printers according to an agreed formula. However, ego-generated obituaries cannot be ruled out. The evidence of wills attests to the careful consideration some people gave to their demise, and their desire to control how they are remembered. For example, some testators carefully specified how they wished to be memorialized in bequests to various churches.

Obituaries are a distinct genre of writing; unlike other 'morbid' literary forms such as wills and codicils, they belong in the biographical sphere, though their brevity means they rarely offer a substantial life of the individual. Despite their obvious informational limitations, obituaries are an important evidential category for scholars who pursue a prosopographical approach to history; they are a source of personal 'metadata', albeit of a type that is generally used in a supplementary fashion. For example, Fergus Campbell has recently revisited the obituaries Laurence McBride appealed to in the preparation of his influential work on 'the greening of Dublin Castle' to re-evaluate how Irish elites evolved between 1890 and 1914.[7] Both the *Dictionary of National Biography* and the *Dictionary of Irish Biography* made extensive use of obituaries as a primary source, and they are routinely employed by genealogists to assist with the reconstruction of family trees.[8] However, obituaries have not been scrutinized as a category in and of themselves. Indicatively, Charles Lysaght's 2008 compilation of a select number of Irish dignitaries in *The Times* obituaries offers little analysis either of structure or of form of the biographies that are his subject.[9]

In the absence of reliable authorial information (rarely available), obituaries and death notices must be approached with caution. Gary Long's above cited study, which explored the obituaries published in urban, rural and black American newspapers, instances the case of an obituary writer from a north Mississippi Delta town. She claimed her eight-year experience of writing obituaries for black people encouraged her to adopt a creative approach to the truth.[10] The primary thrust of her commissioned work was to portray 'good people'. As a result, indiscretions, even employments that might be deemed embarrassing by relatives, were quietly omitted. 'Whatever remained was embroidered with piety and kinship. Work was ignored unless it was the respectable work of ministers, teachers, and the college-educated.'[11] Racial considerations apart, similar caveats may be entered with respect to obituaries and death notices published in nineteenth-century Ireland.

It is notable in this context that Irish newspapers, which were content to engage in large-scale 'borrowing' from foreign and domestic titles, sometimes reprinted obituaries and death notices verbatim.

Historians of death have paid little attention to obituaries, or death notices as a genre. This may be ascribed, in part at least, to their formulaic character and selective content, but there are other reasons. Julie Marie Strange's examination of the commodification of death by the working classes in Great Britain in the late nineteenth century does not address expenditure on death notices, because the rise and role of the undertaker, the expense associated with giving someone 'a good send off', the notion of buying into the fluidity of 'respectability', and the significance of large monetary outlays took precedence.[12] As a result, Strange had no cause either to engage with or to use obituaries in her study. The situation is little different in the case of Patricia Jalland's studies of middle- and upper-class death in Victorian Britain; she cites only two death notices.[13] It can be suggested, based on these examples, that historians of death who use class as a prism do not believe obituaries to be important. Yet, a contrary case can be made.

For the majority of the Irish population, funerary customs were deeply rooted historically in the vernacular and in a cultural tradition that was primarily oral, so the increased recourse to written obituaries and death notices that can be identified provides a valuable perspective on shifts in customary practices. Significantly, death notices, and to a greater extent obituaries, did not become part of the funerary practice of the Irish urban and rural working classes until well into the twentieth century. This was two centuries after newspapers began selectively to report the death of the socially respectable and locally eminent.[14] For the upper echelons, obituaries were long since commonplace, and were compiled, as Charles Lysaght has pointed out, in some instances when the subject was still young.[15] During the nineteenth century, the placement of obituaries and death notices in the provincial press became more normative, and 'class conscious'. They were part of the ritualization of the funerary process, with the aspiring English-speaking and Catholic middle classes in the vanguard, which partly explains why some nineteenth-century death notices were very detailed: the dead person was named, their full address was given, their lineage was described, and the occupations of named relatives and colleagues identified. Place of death was also indicated, and, less frequently, the cause of death might also be given.

While the increased presence in newspapers of social and personal announcements emanating with the middling orders mirrored their upwards mobility, it was also part of a tradition with historical precedent. The concept of memorializing the dead through inscription has a long history in Ireland. Ogham writing, which etched important lineages on wood and stone, is the earliest known form, though Ogham stones were not concerned with conveying location.[16] In Gaelic Ireland, a defining function of the professional 'file' or bardic poet, was to deliver a formal eulogy on the death of a chieftain. These laments were replete with reference to noble descent, great deeds and geographic location. Some laments survived in the oral tradition for many generations and were eventually transcribed.[17] Another identifiable corpus of memorial records is the 'Funeral Entries', which were assembled by Officers of Arms for heraldic purposes. These have been described by Clodagh Tait as one of the earliest forms of 'death notices'.[18] The legitimacy conferred by print culture was not lost on the rising Catholic elite, which continued to appeal to the 'learned classes' during the eighteenth century, and, as Ó Cíosáin notes, used genealogical tracts to great effect to 'demonstrate noble descent, to be eligible for office, whether civil, military or ecclesiastical, or to arrange suitable marriages'.[19] Ogham, bardic laments and 'Funeral Entries', their divergent cultural origins notwithstanding, all share similar features; they name, claim kinship bonds with, and convey the geographical location of the deceased. Moreover, these practices, once exclusive to the ruling elite, percolated downwards, and were adopted by professionals within military, medical, mercantile and political circles.

The emergence of a mass newspaper readership was central to the popularization of the death notice. Despite the restrictions imposed by taxes on paper and advertising until 1855, Ireland sustained a thriving newspaper sector, which catered for all classes at national and provincial level.[20] Practically all newspapers provided a similar diet of advertisements, political, world and local news. By 1860, social and personal notices formed a distinct part of the national newspaper repertoire. Unfortunately, efforts to establish the costs associated with newspaper obituaries have proven unfruitful, because of the absence of pertinent newspaper records. We know that each word incurred a charge, that the text was generally written by journalists, and that families were asked to contribute towards costs. However, some were used as fillers, as nineteenth-century newspapers bought, or simply appropriated, content from a variety of sources. As Mark O'Brien observes in his study of the *Irish Times*: 'announcements of births, deaths and marriages were initially treated as news, and the paper only began to treat such announcements as chargeable adverts in 1860'.[21]

Until that point, only people of note were included as a matter of course or would contemplate being included in such a process; it was evidently the pursuit of a 'discerning constituency'.[22] The transition to a more modern form of brief notice can be illustrated by the 'deaths' column carried by *The Nation*. In its issue of 2 March 1861 the paper noted three deaths; it accorded nineteen words, and precedence, to Mrs Cambridge who died on 25 February 1861, at Ballymena, aged 23, though it is notable that her husband's full name is recorded but hers is not (see Fig. 10.1). The eighteen-word notice of Robert J. Smith published in the same column delineated his status, his death abroad, his tender age and his residence, while Catherine Lacy, who was only 2 years of age when she died, was allocated a mere ten words that simply conveyed the name, age, and place of death.[23] These early notices marked the passing; they claimed kinship and social status. They did not provide information of a kind commonly present in modern death notices like funeral arrangements or the place of burial; this was communicated by invitation or word of mouth. Figure 10.1 also shows that marriage notices were more informative, though they too followed a distinct pattern, and were concerned to highlight strategic unions between families of equal social standing.

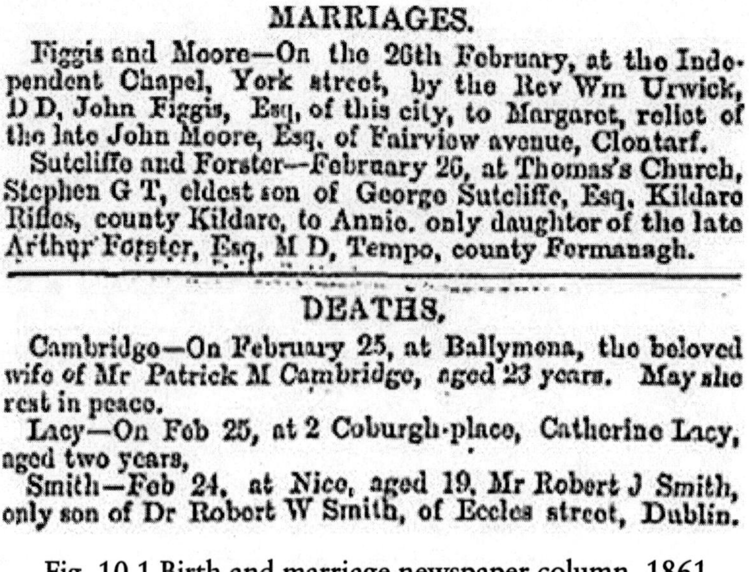

MARRIAGES.

Figgis and Moore—On the 26th February, at the Independent Chapel, York street, by the Rev Wm Urwick, D D, John Figgis, Esq, of this city, to Margaret, relict of the late John Moore, Esq, of Fairview avenue, Clontarf.

Sutcliffe and Forster—February 26, at Thomas's Church, Stephen G T, eldest son of George Sutcliffe, Esq, Kildare Rifles, county Kildare, to Annie, only daughter of the late Arthur Forster, Esq, M D, Tempo, county Fermanagh.

DEATHS,

Cambridge—On February 25, at Ballymena, the beloved wife of Mr Patrick M Cambridge, aged 23 years. May she rest in peace.

Lacy—On Feb 25, at 2 Coburgh-place, Catherine Lacy, aged two years,

Smith—Feb 24, at Nice, aged 19, Mr Robert J Smith, only son of Dr Robert W Smith, of Eccles street, Dublin.

Fig. 10.1 Birth and marriage newspaper column, 1861
Source: *The Nation*, 2 March 1861, p.432.

The database of obituaries, which informs this paper, comprises entries from eighty-three Irish newspapers, journals, and other sources primarily from the southern Irish counties, dating from the seventeenth[24] to the twentieth century.[25] The data was originally extracted by higher education students working under the auspices of Tipperary Clans, a community group based in Tipperary town. The resulting Tipperary Clans Archive was manually transcribed, and arranged into fields according to source, source year, forename/title, surname, place, age, graveyard and county. As the example from *The Nation* (Fig. 10.1) illustrates, it is not always possible to establish either the religion of the deceased or their place of residence. The net result is that 84,039 entries (53.5 per cent of the total) cannot be ascribed geographically to a particular county. A total of 42,487 were extracted, albeit inconsistently, from the *Freeman's Journal*, from 1760 to 1870. These limitations notwithstanding, it was determined that the dataset should be analysed temporally, socially and geo-spatially, with a particular focus on the nineteenth century, which century of origin of formed 87 per cent (137,800 entries) of the overall dataset (see Table 10.1). It is also apparent, in keeping with its geo-spatial origin south of a line from Dundalk to Limerick, that this dataset is disproportionately representative of the Catholic middle classes. Indicatively, it reflects the demographic percentage of professed Catholics living in Ireland from 1861 to 1901, which was between 77.69 and 74.21 per cent, as compared to 11.96 and 13.03 per cent for the Church of Ireland in the same years.[26]

Years	Number
1800–1809	2,129
1810–1819	8,057
1820–1829	23,661
1830–1839	36,496
1840–1849	28,518
1850–1859	21,532
1860–1869	16,264
1870–1879	331
1880–1889	200
1890–1899	612
Total	137,800

Table 10.1 Decennial analysis of the sample of nineteenth-century obituaries and death notices, 1800–99

The 'uneven penetration of the new Tridentine Catholicism' introduced to Ireland in the seventeenth century was, Whelan has pointed out, linked to local power bases and the wealth of the Catholic gentry which managed to retain lands and educate their sons in continental colleges. Whelan argues that the 'unequal conflict' faced by the Catholic Church is revealed by the way in which parishes kept their birth and death registers.[27] While the rise of the Catholic middle class in the nineteenth century was a complex process, it was assisted by the erosion of the administrative hegemony of Protestants in provincial Ireland – the origins of which Butler has traced to the Catholic Relief Acts of 1792–3.[28] By the mid-nineteenth century, as O'Flanagan has shown in his study of urban Munster, higher Catholic birth rates, coupled with an outward flow of the artisan Protestant class, allowed a Catholic middle class to emerge.[29]

The spatial and temporal range of the dataset reflects the rise of a largely urban, Catholic middle class among whom the institutional church found unequivocal support.[30] The dataset cannot be firmly categorized by denominational affiliation because newspaper obituaries do not normally reveal religion, but the persuasions of the chosen newspaper can tell a lot about the readership the families selected to identify with. Marie-Louise Legg has noted the links between newspaper production, newspaper reading and teetotallers in the 1840s.[31] She has drawn particular attention to the *Cork Examiner*, which was founded in August 1841 by John Francis Maguire as 'a teetotal newspaper'. Maguire decided the ordinary (Catholic) people needed a paper to counteract the *Cork Constitution*, which served only landed interests and the southern Unionists. In his opening editorial, Maguire argued the new paper would stand or fall 'mainly upon the honesty with which its columns are devoted, not to private and personal ends, but to the welfare and interests of *the whole community*'. As such, it is a revealing source for the study of death notices of the upwardly mobile across a wide portion of the island of Ireland, and it is discussed in greater detail in the final section.

As Figure 10.2 shows, approximately two-thirds of the database entries date from the three decades 1820 to 1850, and they provide a window on the emergence of a Catholic middle class. It also attests to the displacement by modern funerary practices of vernacular custom; the west as a stronghold of traditional practices is notable by its absence in the dataset, and subsequent renderings in GIS. Although the dataset is not without methodological limitations, the poor representation of towns and townlands in monoglot Irish-speaking regions, where oral

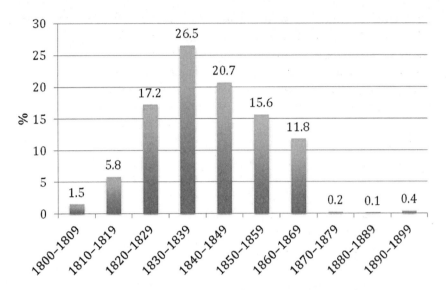

Fig. 10.2 Tipperary Clans Archive, c.1800–99
(decennial percentage breakdown)

traditions survived well into the twentieth century, is evidence of resistance in these areas and among those social groups to print culture.

With respect to the distinction between oral and written sources, Lawrence Taylor advises caution when comparing literary and oral forms: 'It is tempting, and to a limited extent justified, simply to interpret the form and function of the texts from the perspective of class relations.'[32] This raises challenging questions about how we define literacy and how we interpret the flow of information in traditional societies. In temporal terms, literacy is, according to Ó Gráda, inextricably linked with occupational requirements and, by association, class.[33] Furthermore, the dissemination of information is heavily gendered, as it tends predominantly to link women to the oral tradition, when it is in its declining state, and men to the modernizing forces of print culture.[34] Reconciling the space between the oral and the literary form is a cause of disagreement between scholars of literature and folklore. The very nature of the study of folklore embodies a paradox, as the process of evidence collection necessitates the transfer of oral information to a written form to ensure conservation. This transfer is never easy, and the process can corrupt. Sean Ó Tuama, in his discussion of lament poetry, identified the difficulties associated with extricating the oral from the written.[35] Others are less categorical; Gearóid Ó Crualaíoch, for example, is 'reluctant to accept so rigorous a division between oral tradition and written literature'.[36]

Obituaries and death notices pose particular challenges because they draw from both oral and written traditions. Our project highlights the tension between the written and the oral and is illustrative of the eventual supremacy achieved by print over the spoken word. The extent to which newspaper obituaries were used evokes not only class but definite geo-spatial patterns, as the final section of this essay will illustrate. These spatial considerations largely follow socio-economic and cultural trends, as evidenced by the fact that monoglot Irish-speaking areas, were less likely to use newspapers in the earlier period. The west as 'periphery', as Whelan has labelled it, was far removed from the 'core' of upwardly mobile clerics and their faithful in the south-eastern counties.[37] Those who employed obituaries were the same class of people who engaged in orthodox, as opposed to popular, religious practices and writing as opposed to oral transmission. As time progressed, placing a notice in the newspaper became part of the ritual of funerary culture, even in monoglot Irish-speaking areas, albeit after our project timeline. Death was, as Lawrence Taylor argues, an opportunity for furthering social, cultural, and political ends.[38] Nowhere are family ambitions made clearer than in the pageantry of funerary customs.

Funerary Culture

Nineteenth-century Ireland was a society devastated by mass mortality. It has been described, by Witoszek and Sheeran, as a 'funerary culture'.[39] In the nineteenth century, no single orthodoxy in relation to death and burial traditions existed; in fact, plurality was the primary feature of Irish funerary customs. These pluralities are visible in the newspapers, both in how families chose to self-identify and in what they chose to convey; as such, these were very powerful mechanisms in social mobility terms. Theoreticians like Jean Baudrillard and Philippe Ariès have highlighted the power struggles that surrounded the rituals of death, and their approach is relevant here. Baudrillard's *Symbolic Exchange and Death* is particularly important in the study of commodification of death, whereas Philippe Ariès' study of Europe, although controversial, is more useful in locating various tropes in obituary writing.[40] As the associated monetary transaction data pertaining to obituaries used by Baudrillard are not available, this study relies on Ariès' concepts to a greater extent. He used France as a case study and identified different types of death. The first type he explored was the 'tamed death', which was expected and accepted; it was conveyed 'through an inner conviction, rather than through a supernatural, magical premonition'.[41] To exemplify this, Ariès appealed to literature and chose the example of the Knights of the *Chanson de Geste*:[42] noble, aware of their impending demise, it was 'felt' and documented.[43] He cited how Tristan was aware of his impending doom and 'sensed that life was ebbing away'.[44] According to Ariès, tamed death occurred in an orderly way in a domestic space; people lay down and waited for it calmly. This contrasts sharply with the modern societal attitude, which 'banishes death'.[45] Although his assertions with regard to 'banishing death' are not uncontested, parallels with Ariès' summary of trends can be found in the Irish tradition. Examples of the tamed death can be found in Irish epics and *Laoch scéalta*, or hero-cycle stories; later examples from *Amhráin na nDaoine*, crudely translated as the songs of the people, show an acute awareness of death and a sense that people prepared for it. This is similar to the Christian tradition, which allows for fear of death, but emphasizes the necessity of a willingness to receive it.

In terms of international motifs, the way in which people prepared for and accepted death is very important. It is well documented in laments; one of the more popular examples is *Caoineadh Airt Úi Laoghaire*.[46] The *Caoineadh*, which recounts the killing of Art O'Leary by Abraham Morris in May 1773, survived in the oral tradition of counties Cork and Kerry. It was first transcribed from a professional keening woman, Norry Singleton, in 1800. Like devices used in the epic poetry used by Ariès, there is a prophetic moment where the main protagonist makes us aware of his impending demise. Art warns Eibhlín Dubh (Black Eileen) to:

… rise up quickly,
Put your affairs in order,
With speed and with decision.
I am leaving home now,
And there is no telling if I'll return.[47]

Ó Tuama's account of *Caoineadh Airt* is insightful; he classified this lament as a formal act, emanating from a family who 'were living or endeavouring to live as if the old Irish aristocratic order had not collapsed nearly two centuries previously'.[48] This inter-class, inter-cultural existence is not uncommon. *Airt Ó Laoghaire* was waked in what might be described as traditional norms, which retained elements of the old Gaelic order, but instead of a professional male poet, it is the redoubtable Eibhlín, his widow, who takes up the mantle. In the lament his violent death is recounted; the manner in which Eibhlín found him and drank his blood is symbolic of their intimacy, while also highlighting her classical education. The *Caoineadh* is littered with references to class, lineage, wealth and social status. It details to a great degree the way in which he was waked in the family home – a custom that was mimicked by the lower orders and attracted considerable ecclesiastical ire from the mid-seventeenth century.[49]

Connolly shies away from 'emotional or psychological' reasons for wakes; instead he calls attention to superstitions, and Seán Ó Súilleabháin's suggestion that their function was to 'placate the spirit of the deceased person'.[50] The prevalence of excessive drinking and lewd wake games led to various edicts and pastoral letters condemning the festive wake, and in particular keening women, which had very little impact on their occurrence, particularly in rural areas. Connolly locates the Church's efforts to suppress 'merry wakes' in the broader context of changes in work practices, which reduced leisure time, and encouraged cultural shifts that prompted the decline in merry wake practices and patterns.[51] Witoszek and Sheeran's interpretation empowers the peasantry; they see traditional funerary customs not as passive observance but as active resistance to Church hegemony.[52] Ó Crualaíoch is less specific, but he also regards the merry wake as 'a central social mechanism for the articulation of resistance ... on the part of the Irish peasantry to new forms of civil and clerical control'.[53] He adds that indigenous traditions like wakes, patterns and pilgrimages incurred particular Church disapproval because they derived 'as much from a Celtic or pagan cosmological tradition as from a Christian one'.[54] Viewed from this perspective, the endurance of Irish traditional practices served to undermine the Anglicizing power and modernizing intent of the British administration and the Protestant ruling elite. Ó Crualaíoch, like Connolly, draws attention to ritual public mourning and 'merriment and licence, especially of a sexual nature' as flashpoints for the Catholic hierarchy.

Despite poor levels of doctrinal awareness among the lower orders, the hierarchy's dissatisfaction with the role of women in the funerary tradition was pronounced.[55] John Brady identified the 1660 synods of Armagh and Tuam as the earliest efforts to denounce the use of keeners at funerals.[56] Apart from oft-cited seventeenth and eighteenth-century edicts, the *Short Catechism* published following the Synod of Maynooth 1851 had little to say on decorum surrounding death save that 'extreme unction is a sacrament which gives grace to die well' and that it should be preceded by a good confession.[57] The limits of doctrinal knowledge have been explored by historians of religion, but lay interpretations of orthodoxy have received very little attention.[58] Niall Ó Cíosáin has highlighted how hymns from Tadhg Gaelach Ó Súilleabháin's (1715–95) early eighteenth-century *Pious Miscellany* became part of the repertoire of recitals at Munster funerals or wake traditions. Although far from ideal, the Church, as Ó Cíosáin argues, was content that Ó Súilleabháin's piety displaced 'vile compositions' more customary to such occasions.[59] Presumably these 'vile compositions' were akin to the following mock lament, in which a woman rejoices in the death of her brutish husband, but is careful in her mockery to thank 'the Noble Son'.

My treasure and my darling!
You used to club me with branch and root,
And with the stout end of the flail;
And I will praise the Noble Son,
That you died before me,
Johnny, my love! *(thrice)*
My love and my treasure!
You used to give me the hardest side of the bed,
And the smallest portion of food,
And the biggest end of the stick,
Johnny, my love![60]

Vernacular funerary customs were explicitly gendered. Men opened the tombs; men arranged the food, drink and tobacco. The treatment of the body, washing, shrouding or 'laying out', was conducted by women; they lamented the dead; moreover, they were allowed and expected to.[61] Ó Súilleabháin makes little of who announced the death, saying it was mainly by word of mouth via the local trader.[62] Such news invariably travelled quickly.[63] The origins of the allocation of tasks have biblical resonances, for example the role of the women at the cross, for though the roles performed by women are usually associated with rural customs, Clodagh Tait has noted their prevalence in early seventeenth-century Dublin.[64] Despite the female domination of the keening process, which borrowed from the example of the Blessed Virgin Mary in the oral tradition, the Catholic authorities frowned upon the practice.[65] Parallels to the *ochón* or the *ullagón* can be found in many cultures from the Indo-European traditions. The *tangi-hanga*, which is an oral mourning ritual in Maori cultures, was also conducted by women.[66] *An Seabhac* (Pádraig Ó Siochfhradha, 1883–1964) wrote in 1927 how, in County Kerry, it was believed that 'women should not be in a cart in which a corpse is, nor should a mare be yoked to such a cart',[67] but in neighbouring County Cork the keening woman was permitted to ride with the coffin in the horse cart.[68] *Ochón*'s or *caoineadh's* regional variations (whether women walked before or after a coffin) reflected the disorder of traditional ways.[69]

Most accounts of keening women are less than complimentary. Croker observed in 1824 that:

> The Irish funeral howl is notorious, and although this vociferous expression of grief is on the decline, there is still, in the less civilized parts of the country, a strong attachment to the custom, and many may yet be found who are keeners or mourners for the dead by profession.[70]

Keening women were routinely aspersed by the Catholic Church, and by travel writers, probably because they accepted payment for their services and because they commanded a fair degree of power over the order of funerary events. Larkin has highlighted priestly avarice in pre-Famine Ireland, and the extent to which posthumous masses were a main source of income.[71] James O'Shea, in his study of County Tipperary priests, has noted how, in the 1840s, 'corpse masses' were a crucial supplement to curate incomes.[72] Campbell, citing Larkin's statistics, notes in the 1830s that 'a sung mass for dead shopkeepers and farmers would cost as much as 15*s*, while an unsung mass for a dead labourer would cost as little as 5*s*'.[73] While it must be borne in mind that canon law governed when and how priests could conduct funeral masses, the employment of keening women reduced parish revenues, especially those of curates.[74]

In a parallel world of popular belief, laments in the form of hymns like *Caoineadh na dTrí Muire* [the Lament of the three Marys], were allowed to develop in the Catholic tradition. This is an example of how Irish vernacular devices were grafted onto the Catholic tradition, and accepted; indeed, both traditions borrowed heavily from each other. Bourke highlights, for example, the significance of an uneven number of women lamenting.[75] Further mingling of traditions was noted by the Rev. John Seymour, Rector of Donohill in Tipperary: he noted similarities in burial customs for both Catholics and Protestants, where shovels and spades were laid across the opening of the grave 'in the form of a Saint Andrew's Cross'.[76] Inter-denominational boundaries were highly fluid throughout the nineteenth century but by its close, as Angela Bourke has noted, the continued use of the oral traditional exposed the difference between classes:

Oral tradition, as the product of a subaltern class, served a different agenda from that of the courts and newspapers. Decentralized, discontinuous, and unstandardized, its discourse was available in 1895 to women as well as to men, both as tellers and as listeners.[77]

Contrary to Taylor's warnings not to view literary forms in class terms, death notices can profitably be viewed through the class prism. They were the preserve of those who could afford to pay for their publication, or those who had the mindset to prioritize such expenditure. This was a literate class reaching out to their peers, making clear strides away from folk customs.[78] Newspaper accounts could tame even the most violent of deaths so their use did not attract ecclesiastical dissatisfaction. By and large, 'tame deaths' were confined more to older people who passed away peacefully; young adult deaths, by contrast, were described as 'awfully sudden'. Infant deaths, like the earlier cited Lacy, had a sense of inevitability, given the prevailing high mortality rate. Death notices and obituaries usually convey tamed scenarios symbolic of a life lived well. For example 'Theresa Agnes, beloved wife of Mr Thomas Joseph Walsh' from 2, Grattan Place, Merrion Square, who died on 26 April had 'May she Rest in Peace' added to the end of her three-line notice; while 60-year-old Mrs Sophia Ward, whose 'end was at peace' went 'leaning on her saviour'.[79] The latter is the Protestant art of obituary writing that still largely pertains; the former, the Roman Catholic. In ideological terms, the evangelical revival prompted, as Campbell argues, a 'shift away from ritual towards scripturalism ... [that] resulted in greater separation between Protestant and Catholic churches since it emphasized the differences between them'.[80] Strikingly, and in obvious contrast to its vociferous opposition to traditional customs, we have yet to encounter any Church resistance to the use of newspapers to announce death, despite the fact that they were an intrinsically secular form.[81] As Taylor observes, the Catholic Church saw death as an opportunity to 'invoke social units and cultural values'.[82]

Death notices were schematic unless it was someone of note. For example, the *Nenagh Guardian* of 5 December 1860 lamented the loss of Lord Rossmore, who 'departed this life at Rossmore Park, on Saturday night, at eleven o'clock. His Lordship's death was unexpected although for some time declining in health.'[83] Women like 'Susan Taylor', who reached the 'advanced age of 93', were described as 'relict of' their closest male next-of-kin. This was true also of men who did not exceed the status of their father; thus George Lloyd was described as 'formerly high sheriff of the city of Limerick and eldest son of late Alderman Francis Lloyd, of Violet Hill in the same city'.[84] Apart from language, what is remarkable about these obituaries is their geographical spread. Susan Taylor was from Athenry, County Galway, yet her death notice appeared in the *Nenagh Guardian*; the aforementioned George Lloyd was from Richmond, Drumcondra. In Irish national newspapers, British nationals featured regularly, as did Irish expatriates. For example, the passing of Terence Bellew McManus, who died in San Francisco in 1860, was marked in March 1861 by a *Memoriam*, which eulogized his love of Erin and recounted his exile.[85] In a study of Welsh immigrants in North America, Knowles points to rich geographical data:

> Of the several thousand obituaries considered for this study, about half include individuals' home parishes and farm names in Wales and the locality where they settled in the United States, thus making it possible to map immigrant origins and destinations with some precision.[86]

Religiosity also featured prominently in the notices.[87] On 7 September 1867, the *Tuam Herald* noted the death of Alicia, beloved wife of Charles O'Malley esq., of Cloonane, who died aged 90, and concluded the notice with a conscious biblical evocation: 'The sweetness and serenity of such a death! Well might her happy soul cry out "Death where is thy sting"?'.[88] Indicatively, fifteen priests from as far afield as All Hallows (Dublin) officiated at this most tame of Christian obsequies. The procession, we are informed, was 'numerous' and the cortège 'respectable'; it stretched a mile long, bearing witness, to 'the esteem the deceased was held by all classes'. The 606-word obituary, borrowed from the *Mayo Telegraph*, occupied a sizeable portion of the front page.

The place of burial is carefully recorded in this instance as Islandeady, County Mayo, but, apart from mass pauper graveyards used to deal with Famine dead, 'high density' burial grounds or, indeed, commercial cemeteries or burial clubs, never quite achieved the reputation in Ireland that they did in England. The pageantry associated with events staged by 'funeral directors' in urban areas had little purchase in rural Ireland until relatively recently; even then, funeral parlours were more likely to be replete with rosaries rather than the top hats, horse-drawn carriages, and plumes such as were commonly associated in England with the class-conscious proletariat mimicking their social betters.[89] In his comparative analysis of a number of North American newspapers, Gary Long found that:

> Death ceremonies also vary – in price, display, and ceremonial content – by religious, ethnic, and income groups. In American society, groups who have less in life frequently have 'more' in death. Lives un-distinguished by prevailing standards are often made conspicuous, retrospectively, in the rituals that mark their endings. For example, blacks are sometimes compensated in their obituaries by extensive descriptions of funeral ceremonies.[90]

The extent to which people borrowed to pay for funerals (and American wakes) was clearly a problem in rural Ireland. Although the evidence is anecdotal, it is notable that the *Irish Homestead* cautioned smallholders of the dangers associated with using money-lenders to fund lavish wakes and funerals. These 60 per cent philanthropists, the *Irish Homestead* warned, used newspaper adverts to appear legitimate but charged excessive interest rates.[91]

Age, health status and personal habits were important elements of the obituary, as evidenced by the example of John Morgan, age 110, whose death in 1857 was recorded in the *Nenagh Guardian*: 'Up to recently hale and hearty, and able to walk the two miles into Nenagh to attend chapel', Morgan was an eccentric character who would get up in the middle of the night '... and sit by the fire in a state of nudity, while smoking his pipe'.[92] This contrasted with the polite reports of the respectable. The death in 1859 of Mr Hyndman, City Coroner, described as an 'estimable gentleman', was recorded 'at his residence in Wellington Road', Dublin. His death is noted as 'sad' and caused by 'an organic disease of the heart'.[93] Hyndman's occupation is emphasized at the end of his obituary as he 'occupied the position of coroner for the city for many years'.

Geospatial Patterns

Tait has drawn attention to the lapse of time between the burial and the Genealogical Office (GO) Funeral Entry. A chronological analysis could also be applied to our data but we have elected to focus on other distinct patterns.[94] What is most significant in our visualizations is the geospatial range of obituaries. The following GIS maps from various parts of the island for the year 1863 represent the seven best newspaper coverages noted for the 1860 to 1900 period. Of the seven newspapers mapped here, most of them are based in the southern part of the country although – as the maps reveal – this did not prevent the publication of obituaries and notices from all quarters. The newspapers are the: *Cork Examiner*; *Drogheda Argus*; *Freeman's Journal*; *Kilkenny Journal*; *King's County Chronicle*; *Southern Chronicle*; *Waterford Mail*. It is not possible with our dataset to pinpoint statistically when precisely obituaries come into wider use. The focus has been on how they borrow from previous traditions, when they become stylized and come to represent upward mobility, especially for Catholic middle classes. As Curl has argued, 'Lavish expenditure on funerals had its social purpose, for the standards of class had to be maintained in death. Of course the middle and lower classes did not manage to copy the upper classes exactly.'[95]

The Cork Examiner was an evening paper that issued three times a week until 1858, when it changed from a three-day evening to a six-day morning newspaper. Our maps of death notices published in this newspaper over the five years 1859 to 1863 demonstrate that it had an impressive geospatial coverage and remit. In 1859, as Map 10.1 demonstrates, this paper's publication of obituaries focused more-or-less equally on Cork (sixty-one) and Dublin (fifty-eight), with a scattering of coverage throughout Munster (thirty-six), and Leinster (seventeen); Connaught/Ulster (nine) barely featured in the 181 obituaries published in that year, while Munster accounted for 54 per cent of all published obituaries.

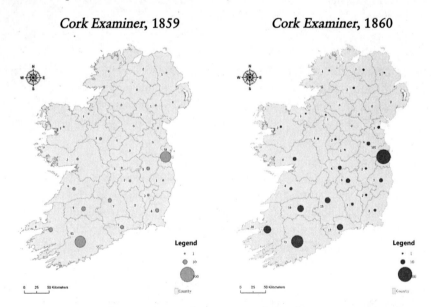

Cork Examiner, 1859   *Cork Examiner, 1860*

Maps 10.1–2 *Cork Examiner*, obituaries and death notices, 1859, 1860

Cork Examiner, 1861   *Cork Examiner,* 1862

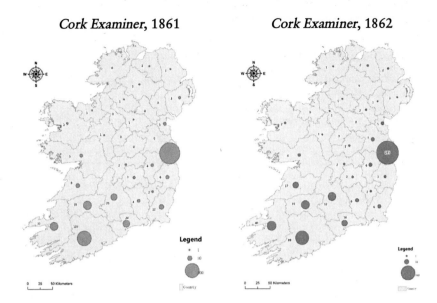

Maps 10.3–4 *Cork Examiner,* obituaries and death notices, 1861–2

The death notices in the *Cork Examiner* increased substantially over the following four years, 1860–3 (see Maps 10.2–10.4), particularly from Cork, Dublin and the interior south of a line drawn from Dundalk to Galway. The number from Dublin particularly manifested a sizeable increase from the fifty-eight in 1859 to 298 in 1863, while the number from County Cork increased, year-on-year, from sixty-one to 111 in the same time period. Munster and the midlands are also well represented. Actual obituary numbers also continued to grow, year-on-year, from 181 in 1859, to nearly double that the following year (318). The number almost doubled again in the early 1860s to 564 in 1863, to register a more than three-fold growth in five years (see Table 10.2).

The map generated for 1863 (see Map 10.5) is particularly useful, being a year in which a direct comparison between the *Cork Examiner* and six other regional newspapers is possible. In that year, 564 death notices were published in the paper, just thirty fewer than the *Freeman's Journal*; intriguingly, the main population centre featured was Dublin: with 298 entries or 53 per cent, it far exceeded the newspaper base of Cork, and its Munster provincial hinterland (195 entries or 34 per cent); Connaught and Ulster (twenty-seven entries) and the eastern province of Leinster (excluding Dublin), with forty-seven entries, comprised 13 per cent of the total (see Table 10.2).

	1859	1860	1861	1862	1863
All Ireland	120	318	481	543	564
Munster (outside Cork)	36	156	221	229	195
Leinster (outside Dublin)	17	44	38	41	47
Dublin	58	101	205	255	298
Connaught/Ulster	9	17	17	18	24

Table 10.2 Provincial dispersion of obituaries, *Cork Examiner*, 1859–63

In 1863, the obituary was sufficiently firmly established as a cultural phenomenon that many newspapers drew death notices from areas far removed from their place of publication. Foremost amongst these was the *Freeman's Journal*, Ireland's earliest and longest running newspaper. With a decidedly national focus, it drew principally on Dublin and Cork (see Map. 10.6); in 1863, these two areas accounted for 47 per cent (280 of 597) of the death notices published – with the remainder coming from fourteen other counties, stretching from

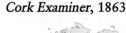

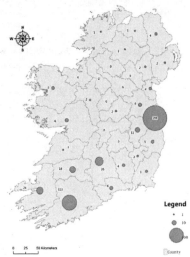

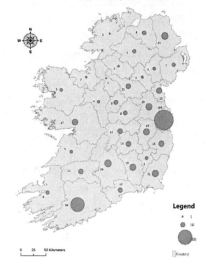

Map 10.5 *Cork Examiner*, obituaries and death notices, 1863

Map 10.6 *Freeman's Journal*, obituaries and death notices, 1863

Drogheda Argus, 1863

Waterford Mail, 1863

Map 10.7 *Drogheda Argus,*
obituaries and death notices, 1863

Map 10.8 *Waterford Mail,*
obituaries and death notices, 1863

Antrim to Limerick and from Wexford to Cavan. It was alone in its penetration of the four provinces in a meaningful way: it was weakest in Connaught (twenty-nine); Ulster (sixty-five) exceeded Munster not including Cork (fifty-seven); Leinster (166), Dublin (186) and Cork (ninety-four entries) were its primary regional catchments.

Other newspapers possessed a definite local and regional focus – none more obviously than the *Drogheda Argus,* which focussed on the county town of Louth and its hinterland. This newspaper commenced publishing in September 1835, and by the year 1863, close to the end of its third decade of circulation, had made little attempt to expand outside that north-eastern region. Just seventy-five death notices were published in the newspaper in this year and, as Map 10.7 highlights, the loyalty of the readership seems to have been quite evenly divided between counties Louth and Meath, with some attention in the direction of Dublin, and the adjacent counties of Down, Armagh, Cavan and Kildare. Distinct regional biases are also in evidence in the *Waterford Mail* (established 1824) and the *Kilkenny Journal* (which had been established as *Finn's Leinster Journal* in 1767). Many of these regional newspapers issued two or three times weekly. In the case of the *Waterford Mail,* which published 111 death notices in 1863, the home base of Waterford city and county is surprisingly small at just ten entries;

the largest geographical sources are Dublin (forty-eight) and Wexford (twenty). Map 10.8 attests to a regional focus on Waterford and adjacent south-eastern and southern counties with a combined fifty-one entries (46 per cent), while Connaught, Ulster and the rest of Leinster furnished just twelve entries that year. The *Kilkenny Journal*, while located in a south-eastern city, seems to have retained much of the Leinster provincial focus in evidence in its original *Leinster Journal* title, and to have a far more cultivated home base; indeed, of the eighty-three notices published during 1863, the spatial distribution of which is displayed in Map 10.9, County Kilkenny accounts for forty-one or just under half, while the addition of its adjoining counties raises that total by a further twenty-three to sixty-four, or 77 per cent of the funerary notices.

In spite of strong conservative unease with the burgeoning provincial press, and various taxes, newspapers established a firm foothold in most strong market towns.[96] For example, the *King's County Chronicle*, which was established in September 1845, focussed on the midland towns of Birr, Tullamore and Roscrea and their hinterlands. As a result, the midland counties of Tipperary and Offaly, and adjacent areas of counties Galway and Laois account for forty of

Kilkenny Journal, 1863   *King's County Chronicle*, 1863

 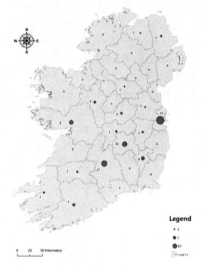

Map. 10.9 *Kilkenny Journal,* obituaries and death notices, 1863

Map 10.10 *King's County Chronicle,* obituaries and death notices, 1863

the ninety-eight death notices published in 1863. As Map 10.10 clearly shows, Dublin was by far the largest single place of origin, with 32 per cent (thirty-one entries) of the total. By contrast, the penetration of the provinces of Ulster (four entries) and Munster beyond Tipperary (eight entries) was decidedly weak.

Southern Chronicle, 1863

Map 10.11 *Southern Chronicle,* obituaries and death notices, 1863

The death notices published in the *Southern Chronicle* (from 1864 known as the *Limerick Southern Chronicle*) in 1863 are mapped on Map 10.11. From its Limerick city base, the newspaper registered a strong presence in the Munster region; indicatively, the regional capital of Cork (eighty-two entries) was responsible for more than double that of Limerick (thirty-one). While its focus was strongly provincial (167 entries, or 57 per cent of the 293 recorded that year), Dublin's eighty-nine entries and a wide scattering of entries from Ulster, Connaught and the rest of Leinster is remarkable for a newspaper in its first year of publication and is, perhaps, indicative of the pattern of migration from Munster – particularly Limerick – across the island of Ireland.

Conclusion

What all of these maps and our wider dataset shows is the widespread and sustained growth in the use of death notices, and the urban bias of this phenomenon. Monoglot Irish-speaking areas are notable by their absence. For this reason, it was necessary in locating our study to pay close attention to other funerary customs, particularly the struggle for control over death rituals between the church, state and the vernacular. For the vast majority of people, obituaries and death notices were neither important nor culturally relevant. Custom, class and landscape are of paramount importance in their explanation.[97] Those who chose to use newspapers to memorialize their dead were making explicit social statements, consistent with their upward mobility on one hand and dissociation from the vernacular on the other. This sets those who used them apart from the peasantry. During the nineteenth century, newspapers offered the rising middle classes the opportunity to self-identify with the practices of those they perceived as social equals or, indeed, their betters. Death notices predominantly tend to say more about their surviving descendants rather than the dead.

The publication of death notices and obituaries possessed manifest cultural significance. Death notices contrasted vividly with the 'merry wake' and shrillness of the keen, and did not offend religious sensibilities. Their publication in newspapers was facilitated by both vanity and modernity. The lack of church opposition is insightful. Newspapers afforded the rising Catholic classes the opportunity to convey social importance in print. The practice of placing a notice in the newspaper was beyond the reach of most in the 1820s but by 1900, it had become part of the pageantry of the funerals of the rising middle classes. The use of newspapers to instil orthodoxy and convey regulated funeral arrangements had far-reaching implications in the process of 'taming death' in the nineteenth century.

NOTES

* These are the preliminary findings of the project *Death and Funerary Practices, 1829–1901*, which is funded by the Irish Research Council for the Humanities and Social Sciences funded. We gratefully acknowledge this funding. We would also like to thank Lorna Moloney for her help with data modelling.
1 The terms obituary and death notices are used loosely throughout this article to mean accounts of death reported in newspapers.
2 Kevin Whelan, 'The Regional Impact of Irish Catholicism 1700–1850', in William J. Smith and Kevin Whelan (eds), *Common Ground: Essays on the Historical Geography of Ireland* (Cork: Cork University Press, 1998), pp.253–77, at p.253.
3 *Weekly Irish Times*, 16 Mar. 1889.
4 *Freeman's Journal*, 20 Sept. 1887.
5 Gary Long, 'Organizations and Identity: Obituaries 1856–1972', *Social Forces*, 65:4 (1987), pp.964–1001, at pp.966–7.
6 Kaspar von Greyerz, 'Ego-Documents: the Last Word?', *German History*, 28:3 (2010), pp.273–282, at p.280.
7 Fergus Campbell, *The Irish Establishment, 1897–1914* (Oxford, 2009), p.322; Lawrence McBride, *The Greening of Dublin Castle: The Transformation of Bureaucratic and Judicial Personnel in Ireland, 1892–1922* (Washington, DC: Catholic University of America Press, 1991).

8 H.D.G. Matthew and Brian Harrison (eds), *Oxford Dictionary of National Biography: from the Earliest Times to the Year* 2000 (60 Volumes, Oxford: Oxford University Press, 2004); James McGuire and James Quinn (eds), *Dictionary of Irish Biography: from the Earliest Times to the Year 2002* (9 Volumes, Cambridge: Cambridge University Press, 2009).

9 Charles Lysaght (ed.), *The Times: Great Irish Lives* (London: Times books, 2008), p.xii. In his overall assessment of the Irish representation, he comments: '[I]n the obituaries columns, as elsewhere, the Irish of all backgrounds got a good show. Just occasionally there was some stereotyping, although it was not unfriendly.'

10 She states she was 'lying a lot': Long, 'Organizations and Identity', p.990.

11 Long, 'Organizations and Identity', p.990.

12 Julie Marie Strange, *Death, Grief and Poverty in Britain, 1870–1914* (Cambridge: Cambridge University Press, 2005).

13 Patricia Jalland, *Death and the Victorian Family* (Oxford: Oxford University Press, 2000), pp.141, 306.

14 See, for example, *Hoey's Publick Journal*, 1772, which regularly carried a short column of deaths.

15 Lysaght, *The Times*, p.x.

16 For an account of the debate surrounding the 'Stone corridor' at University College Cork see Damian McManus, *Ogham Stones at University College Cork* (Cork: Cork University Press, 2004), pp.10–12.

17 Damian MacManus and Eoghan Ó Raghallaigh (eds), *A Bardic Miscellany: Five Hundred Bardic Poems from Manuscripts in Irish and British Libraries* (Dublin: Department of Irish, Trinity College, 2010), p.5 'A dhuine, chuimnigh an bás' and 'A dhuine, féach ar an uaigh' possess overt religious references and both ask us to ponder death. Taking example from other translations in that volume, they translate crudely as 'O man, remember/ponder death' and 'O man look at/observe the grave', respectively. We are grateful to Dr Lesa Ní Mhunghaile for advice on translation; responsibility for errors lies with the authors.

18 Clodagh Tait, *Death, Burial and Commemoration in Ireland, 1550–1650* (Basingstoke: Palgrave, 2002), p.40; NLI, GO MS 64, Funeral Entries Vol. 1, 1588–1617.

19 Niall Ó Cíosáin, *Print and Popular Culture in Ireland, 1750–1850* (Basingstoke: Palgrave/ Macmillan, 1997), pp.174–5.

20 Marie Louise Legg, *Newspapers and Nationalism: The Irish Provincial Press* (Dublin: Four Courts Press, 1999), pp.30–1; *Parliamentary Papers*, HC 1866 (491) xl.113. Advertisement taxes were imposed in 1712 and continued until 1853, news print tax 1757–1861, and from 1712 to 1855 the stamp tax was collected. The stamp tax allowed for free postage. Newspapers were obliged to print 'on stamped paper, which was bulk bought in advance from the Stamp Office in Dublin'. Estimating newspaper circulation is a notoriously tricky enterprise. Legg uses stamped paper as a guide to estimate baseline copies; see also Mark O' Brien, *The Irish Times: A History* (Dublin: Four Courts Press, 2008), p.16.

21 O'Brien, *The Irish Times*, p.17.

22 Ibid.

23 *The Nation*, 2 Mar. 1861.

24 246 records exist for the seventeenth century ranging from c.1603–99, derived from six sources: Burke's *Landed gentry*; *Journal of the Cork Historical and Archaeological Society*; *Memorials of the Dead*, Vol. 4; Funeral Entries Ireland; *Dictionary of American Biography*; and St Patrick's Graveyard, Kilkenny.

25 The transcription work was originally conducted by students on FÁS funded summer employment schemes in the 1990s.

26 W.E. Vaughan and A.J. Fitzpatrick (eds), *Irish Historical Statistics: Population, 1821–1971* (Dublin: Royal Irish Academy, 1978), p.49.

27 Whelan, 'The regional impact of Irish Catholicism', p.254.

28 David J. Butler, *South Tipperary, 1570–1841: Religion, Land and Rivalry* (Dublin: Four Courts Press, 2006), p.238.

29 Patrick O'Flanagan, 'Urban Minorities and Majorities: Catholics and Protestants in Munster Towns c.1659–1850', in Smith and Whelan (eds), *Common Ground: Essays on the Historical Geography of Ireland*, pp.124–45.

30 Whelan, 'The Regional Impact of Irish Catholicism', p.253.

31 Legg, *Newspapers and Nationalism*, p.60.

32 Lawrence J. Taylor, 'The Language of Belief: Nineteenth-Century Religious Discourse in Southwest Donegal', in Marilyn Silverman and P.H. Gulliver (eds), *Approaching the Past: Historical Anthropology Through Irish Case Studies* (New York: Columbia University Press, 1992), pp.142–75, at p.149.

33 Cormac Ó Gráda, 'School Attendance and Literacy Before the Famine: a Simple Baronial Analysis', University College Dublin Centre for Economic Research, Working Paper Series 10/22, 2010.

34 There are several examples of men occupying that role; see for example, Tomás O'Crohan, *Island Cross-Talk: Pages From a Diary*, translated by Tim Enright (Oxford: Oxford University Press, 1986).

35 Sean Ó Tuama, *Repossessions: Selected Essays on the Irish Literary Heritage* (Cork: Cork University Press, 1995), p.78.

36 Gearoid Ó Crualaoích, *The Book of the Cailleach: Stories of the Wise-Woman Healer* (Cork: Cork University Press, 2003), p.15.

37 Whelan, 'The Regional Impact of Irish Catholicism', pp.268–70.

38 Lawrence J. Taylor, *Occasions of Faith: An Anthropology of Irish Catholics* (Philadelphia: University of Pennsylvania Press, 1995); Lawrence J. Taylor, '*Bás in Éirinn*: cultural constructions of death in Ireland', *Anthropological Quarterly*, 62:4 (1989), pp.175–87.

39 Nina Witoszek and Pat Sheeran, *Talking to the Dead: A Study of Irish Funerary Traditions* (Amsterdam: Rodopi, 1998), p.8.

40 Jean Baudrillard, *Symbolic Exchange and Death* (London: Sage Publications, 1993).

41 Philippe Ariès, *Western Attitudes Towards Death: From the Middle Ages to the Present*, translated by Patricia M. Ranum (Baltimore: Johns Hopkins Press, 1974), p.4.

42 *Chanson de Geste* literally translates as 'songs of deeds' and comprises poems describing, for example, the gallant deeds of Frankish defenders of the Christian faith see Michael A. Newth, *Heroes of the French Epic: a Selection of Chansons De Geste* (Woodbridge: Boydell Press, 2005).

43 Ariès, *Western Attitudes*, p.2.

44 Ibid., p.3.

45 Philippe Ariès, *The Hour of our Death*, translated by Helen Weaver (Oxford: Oxford University Press, 1991), p.560.

46 Brendán Ó Buachalla, *An Caoine is an Chaointeoireacht* (Baile Átha Cliath: Cois Life, 1998), p.22 argues that Caoineadh Airt probably receives too much scholarly attention: 'Ni heol dom aon dán Gaeilge eile a bhfuil láimhseáil chroin-eolaíoch mar sin tugtha dó ná míniú mar sin déanta air' crudely translates as: 'I do not know any other poem that has been given such chronological handling or explanatory treatment like that.'

47 Ó Tuama, *Repossessions*, p.93.

48 Ibid., p.83.

49 Gearóid Ó Crualaoích, 'The "Merry Wake"', in James S. Donnelly and Kerby A. Miller (eds), *Irish Popular Culture, 1650–1850* (Dublin: Irish Academic Press, 1998), pp.173–200, at p.173.

50 S.J. Connolly, *Priests and People in Pre-Famine Ireland, 1780–1845* (Dublin: Gill and Macmillan, 1982), p.152.

51 Connolly, *Priests and People*, p.172.

52 Witoszek and Sheeran, *Talking to the Dead*, p.9.

53 Ó Crualaoích, 'The "Merry Wake"', p.173.

54 Ibid.

55 Ibid., p.175. Ó Crualaoích, citing Ó Súilleabháin's *Irish Handbook*, 'lists edicts against the practice of employing the services of keening women at wakes and funerals' over a 170-year period, encompassing virtually the entire seventeenth and eighteenth centuries (from Tuam (1631), Armagh (1660), Dublin 1670), Armagh (1670), Meath (1686), Kildare and Leighin (1748) and Cashel and Emly (1800)).

56 John Brady, 'Funeral Customs of the Past', *Irish Ecclesiastical Record*, 78 (1952), pp.330–9, at p.336.

57 *The short catechism extracted from the catechism ordered by the National Synod of Maynooth and approved by the cardinal, the archbishops, and bishops of Ireland, for general use throughout the Irish Church* (Dublin, M. H. Gill and son, n.d.), p.24 imprimatur: Cardinal McCabe (1816–85). The same catechism warned 'When purchasing prayer books, please

examine the title-page and see that it bears our name, which is a guarantee that the book is orthodox, up-to-date and of Irish manufacture.'

58 Connolly, *Religion and Society*, p.48. Connolly highlights how, in the nineteenth century, 'non-obligatory religious services, such as benediction and Stations of the Cross, were unknown in many parishes and common only in a few'.
59 Ó Cíosáin, *Print and Popular Culture in Ireland, 1750–1850*, p.130.
60 Cited in Patricia Lysaght, '*Caoineadh os Cionn Coirp*: The Lament for the Dead in Ireland', *Folklore*, 108 (1997), pp.65–82, at p.81.
61 Seán Ó Súilleabháin, *Irish Wake Amusements* (Dublin and Cork: Mercier, 1976), p.13.
62 Ibid., p.14.
63 Ó Crualaoích, 'The "Merry Wake"', p.178.
64 Tait, *Death, Burial and Commemoration in Ireland*, p.31. For full transcripts of these depositions, see http://1641.tcd.ie/, accessed 20 July 2011.
65 Angela Partridge, *Caoineadh na dTrí Muire: Téama na Páise I Bhfilíocht Bhéil na Gaeilge* (BAC, An Clóchomhar, 1983), p.94.
66 Karen P. Sinclair, '*Tangi*: Funeral Rituals and the Construction of Maori Identity', in Lyn Poyer (ed.), *Cultural Identity and Ethnicity in the Pacific* (Honolulu: University of Hawaii Press, 1990), pp.219–36.
67 An Seabhac, 'Superstitions, Cures etc.', *Béaloideas*, 1:1 (1927), p.217.
68 Crualaoích, 'The "Merry Wake"', p.182.
69 James Mooney, *Funeral Customs of Ireland* (Philadelphia: MacCalla and Company, 1888), pp.32–3.
70 Lysaght, '*Caoineadh os Cionn Coirp*', p.70.
71 Emmet Larkin, 'The Devotional Revolution in Ireland, 1850–75', *American Historical Review*, 77 (1972), p.633.
72 James O'Shea, *Priests, Politics and Society in Post-Famine Ireland* (Dublin: Wolfhound Press, 1983), p.23.
73 Fergus Campbell, *The Irish Establishment, 1879–1914* (Oxford: Oxford University Press, 2009), p.252.
74 *Irish Ecclesiastical Record* (1917), p.328. Clearly such rules perplexed priests and one letter to the *Irish Ecclesiastical Record* in 1917 queried: 'In our *Ordo* (page xii) regarding Masses for the Dead it is laid out that a Low Mass can be said for the deceased poor person whose body is present, on the same days and under the same conditions in which a Mass *cum cantu* is permitted. Then in section (4) a more restricted concession *ob inopiam sacerdotum* is granted to Ireland (SCR 9 Mai, 1899). Now, does the wider and later concession apply to Ireland also in the case of a deceased poor person?' The respondent explained that 'If the family is able to bear the expenses a Low Mass cannot be celebrated' and that these provisions were made to circumvent the problem of priest shortages, which by 1917 was no longer a problem.
75 Angela Bourke, 'More in Anger Than in Sorrow: Irish Women's Lament Poetry', in Joan Newlon Radner, *Feminist Messages: Coding in Women's Folk Culture* (Illinois: University of Illinois Press, 1993), pp.160–184, at p.178 n.12.
76 Rev. John D. Seymour, 'Funeral Customs', *Béaloideas*, 1:1 (1927), p.315.
77 Angela Bourke, 'Reading a Woman's Death: Colonial Text and Oral Tradition in Nineteenth-Century Ireland', *Feminist Studies*, 21:3 (Autumn 1995), pp.553–86 at p.555.
78 Ó Crualaoích, *The Book of the Cailleach*, p.9.
79 *Freeman's Journal*, 1 May 1860.
80 Campbell, *The Irish Establishment*, pp.243–4.
81 Rev. William Moser, 'Use and Abuse of Flowers at funerals', *Irish Ecclesiastical Record*, 3rd ser.16 (1895), pp.806–12. It lamented how the pagan practices of 'flower-worship' had permeated funeral traditions and traces its origins to post-revolution France and later America. It encouraged people to donate proceeds to the poor.
82 Taylor, *Bás in Éirinn*, p.182.
83 *Nenagh Guardian*, 5 Dec. 1860.
84 Ibid.
85 *The Nation*, 2 Mar. 1861.
86 Anne Kelly Knowles, 'Immigrant Trajectories Through the Rural-Industrial Transition in Wales and the United States, 1795–1850', *Annals of the Association of American Geographers*, 85:2 (1995), pp.246–66, at p.247.

87 *Freeman's Journal*, 1 May 1860.
88 *Tuam Herald*, 7 Sept. 1867.
89 James Stevens Curl, *The Victorian Celebration of Death* (Stroud: Sutton, 2001), p.121.
90 Long, 'Organizations and Identity', p.986.
91 Ciara Breathnach, *The Congested Districts Board of Ireland, 1891–1923: Poverty and Development in the West of Ireland* (Dublin: Four Courts Press, 2005).
92 *Nenagh Guardian*, 31 Mar. 1857.
93 *The Irish Times*, 21 Apr. 1859.
94 Tait, *Death, Burial and Commemoration*, p.38.
95 Curl, *The Victorian Celebration of Death*, p.195.
96 Legg, *Newspapers and Nationalism*, pp.32–3.
97 Witoszek and Sheeran, *Talking to the Dead*, p.9.

11

WANDERING GRAVEYARDS, JUMPING CHURCHES AND ROGUE-CORPSES: TOLERANCE AND INTOLERANCE IN IRISH FOLKLORE

CLODAGH TAIT

In 1939, Eileen Fitzgibbon of Castletown, Killeagh, County Cork, reported a tale told to her by a Mrs Fitzgibbon about a graveyard near Clonmult, which 'is said to have moved from its former place which was Clonmult village'. 'Many years ago', a man was on his way home late at night when he heard a lot of commotion in the graveyard:

> He looked over the fence, and was greatly astonished at the scene, which met his eyes. He saw hundreds of men, women, and children coming out of the graveyard, and crossing over the hill going in the direction of where it now stands. When he went over the hill they vanished out of his sight. Next day the people wondered when they saw that [the graveyard] had vanished when they were asleep …All had vanished except the graves in which some Protestants were buried. It is believed that the Protestants were buried amongst the Catholics during the trouble in Ireland.[1]

With some notable exceptions, the extensive folklore heritage of Ireland has been underused in social or cultural historical enquiry. Despite calls, in particular by Guy Beiner, for historians to reconsider their attitude to 'vernacular source materials (both written and oral)', few have risen to the challenge.[2] On one level, it is possible to see why this is the case. The stories told by contributors to the folklore collections held in the Irish Folklore Commission Archive, and published by a myriad amateur and professional compilers from the nineteenth century, are often similar in form to the short tale above from the Schools Folklore Collection. Wonders and marvels are commonplace, and accounts are deeply embedded in local landscapes. How, sceptics might ask, can such material ever transcend its 'local' origins, and how can a satisfactory methodology be arrived at to deal with sources that are 'inherently polyphonic', regularly fantastic, contradictory, partial and, when it comes to accounts of historical events, demonstrably at odds with the documentary record? Yet these are concerns that have already been extensively addressed in other contexts. One example is the large group of historians of early modern Europe who have used the oral traditions of the sixteenth and seventeenth centuries to reveal the mental worlds of people from all sections of society and from all walks of life. Significantly, it has assisted with the excavation of their understandings of the past; their beliefs (broadly defined), and constructions of the sacred; how they defended the perceived interests of their communities; and how they policed the norms of gender relations.[3] What has become particularly clear is that we should not make the mistake when writing history 'from below', of assuming that 'local' people's concerns were not national, or, indeed, universal in their nature. Neither should we assume that tales of marvels and wonders reflect mere frivolity or credulity. Henry Glassie has observed that stories of experiences of the supernatural 'are true, true because they happened or true because … they are fictions set in fact. They tell the truth about the other world or the little world of the community.'[4] This study is based on stories told about the dead and their burial places that cannot ever have happened – at least, not in the way the stories said they did – but through them we are given glimpses of pressing social concerns. Accounts of unwise burial choices identify symbolic boundaries between different religious communities, and, since they guided people's actions, they assist us to establish the influences that informed their decisions. After all, oral tradition not only reflects how communities understand their own pasts but also actively shapes human actions and interactions in different presents. And, as will emerge as we move from cases of supernatural ejections from graves to literary accounts and real incidents of disinterment by human actors, folklore is also an imaginative resource, both for writers facing up to the challenge of social change, and activists seeking to drive political agendas.

I

As prominent sacred sites on the landscape, graveyards feature regularly in narratives about the local past. Graveyards are viewed as repositories of local notables: museums of the celebrated dead. Parish histories and folklore often focus on the antics of their founder saints and the famous and infamous people buried within them. In the past, graveyards even served as storehouses of materials that were of practical assistance to local communities. Parts of dead bodies and the consecrated clay itself might be deemed to possess curative powers. The spiritual benefits of burial in or pilgrimage to certain graveyards were regularly lauded – burial at Clonmacnoise, for example, is still perceived as a certain path to heaven.[5]

Graveyards were also associated closely with the dead themselves. Irish ghost belief has barely been studied, so generalizations are difficult, but it seems that the spirits of the dead had a relatively limited role in folk belief, in keeping with the fact that many activities that in other parts of Europe were attributed to ghosts and witches, in Ireland were instead largely associated with the fairies.[6] Mostly, the dead returned and were seen by the living because they had been stolen by the 'good people'. They were not the unquiet dead, were not usually even dead at all in fact, since they could often be rescued by the prompt action of the living.[7] Elsewhere, the dead returned to reveal secret knowledge or hidden treasure, but in Ireland such knowledge or treasure generally belonged to the fairies. The human ghosts that turn up in nineteenth and early twentieth-century tradition seem to be highly corporeal. In contrast to their English counterparts in particular, they also seem unusually attached to their graves. Those stolen by the fairies turned up in the houses where they had lived. Except at specific times of the year, such as Halloween, ghosts generally stayed close to their own corpses. When they left the graveyard the spirits of the dead usually returned to it.[8]

Folk ghosts have increasingly been recognized as highly politicized entities: as revealers of hidden truths, the information they brought might be used to discomfit or accuse. Confounding expectations that predominantly Catholic ghosts should be concerned with chronicling the horrors of Purgatory, Ireland's graveyard-ghosts seem actively to have shared the preoccupations of the living – evincing in particular a peculiar obsession with the defence of property. They are often described as being highly protective of the sacred ground on which they were buried, and of their own burial plots. Annie Flood, an informant of the Schools Folklore initiative from Oldcastle, County

Meath, for example, reported a tale, told to her by her mother, which echoes many others:

> Three years ago, there were three men living in a house in Moylough. They had an earthen floor[. O]ne night one of them went to the castle of Moylough and broug[h]t the headstones that were on the graves. He went home with them and put them in the kitchen for a floor. That night the two brothers were in bed, and he was sitting at the fire. The headstones stood up on one end and the people that were buried, were sitting on them. The man sitting at the fire went to the bed room, and they cried after him to leave them back, so he left them back that night.
> The two brothers are living yet and the man that brought the headstones, died in three days after bringin[g] them. Gibney was the name of the family, to whom it happened.

Such tales clearly served to protect sacred ground from disturbance, as well as cautioning those who sought to profit at the expense of their neighbours by taking away undefended property such as gravestones.

One common reaction on the part of churches and graveyards and their inhabitants to disturbance or sacrilege was simply to move. The most usual reason for graveyards moving in the middle of the night was desecration by the burial of Protestants within them. As with the example of Castletown in Killeagh, County Cork, Kilsarcon graveyard, County Kerry, also allegedly moved from its original site. Bartholomew Hickey, a farmer, relayed the story about Kilsarcon:

> Over a hundred years ago the churchyard, now situated at Kilsarcon ... , was situated at Dromultan. It was a Catholic churchyard. It is said that a Protestant was buried there once. This was against the usual practice and the burial aroused great anger in the people of the locality. On the night after the burial the church removed itself about a distance of two miles across to Kilsarcon. It brought all the graves with it except the Protestant one, which it left behind in the place where it was dug. It brought the walls that were around it and the ruins of an old chapel, which were in the centre of the churchyard. When the church-yard was on its way from Dromultan to Kilsarcon one huge stone fell into the river Flesk. It may be seen there ever since and no flood, of all the big floods that swelled the river since that time,

could move that stone an inch from the spot where it fell in. It is said that the man who owned the land to which the churchyard moved got a great surprise one morning when he saw it placed in one of his fields.[9]

Meanwhile, one of the informants of a pupil at Presentation Convent, Drogheda, told the story of the 'jumping church of Millextown' (Millockstown, the church of the old parish of Kildemock), a ruin standing two miles outside Ardee, County Louth:

The old church stands in a very ancient graveyard and when it was in use it was a Catholic church, and also a Catholic burying place. Now there lived in the locality a Protestant family and one of this family died, and the relatives wanted the remains buried inside the walls of the old church but those in authority would not allow this, but in spite of all the objections the Protestant parties succeeded in having the remains buried inside the walls where they desired. The day after the funeral some of the local people were passing the old ruins, they noticed that something strange had happened during the night, and going into the churchyard they found that the old end-wall of the church had actually jumped over the grave, and left it outside, and this can be seen to this present day, and that is how it got the name of the Jumping Church of Millextown.[10]

The Ordnance Survey letters of the mid-nineteenth century confirm that the church may have been seen as a Catholic burial site, but not the graveyard:

The people say that a man, who was excommunicated, having died, was by force of arms interred within this church immediately at the western gable, and that gable miraculously moved from its foundation so far inward as to leave the grave outside the wall of the church ... The people say it was never used as a Protestant church. The churchyard is used as a burial ground common to Protestants and Catholics.[11]

A more recent version of the story suggests that the wall jumped over the burial of an 'unworthy corpse', implied to be that of a freemason, a society Catholics were forbidden to join after 1737:

a man, who was (appropriately) a mason by trade, abandoned the Catholic faith and turned Protestant. He was working on the building of Stabannon Church when he fell to his death from scaffolding. After attempts to bury the remains elsewhere proved fruitless, the body was brought to Kildemock and laid to rest within the ruined church, inside the west wall. The very next day, the wall was discovered to have jumped inwards, leaving the remains outside the sacred enclosure of the one-time building.

A plaque on the site gives both natural and supernatural explanations, which encourages readers make up their own minds about the cause of the phenomenon:

> This wall by its pitch, tilt and position can be seen to have moved three feet from its foundation. Contemporary accounts mention a severe storm in 1715 when the wall was lifted and deposited as it now stands but local tradition states that the wall jumped inwards to exclude the grave of an excommunicated person.[12]

Robert Chapple has recently identified a gravestone outside the west wall of the church commemorating a Mr Morgan and dating to 1791 that bears both Catholic and masonic symbolism, which may have given rise to or become entangled with the story of the 'jumping church'.[13]

Given the evident preoccupation with maintaining denominational (Catholic) purity, it is not surprising perhaps that some of the tales of moving churches and churchyards were tied up with the recurring theme in Irish folklore of Protestant persecution of Catholics. The church at Matehy, County Cork, had supposedly originally been in the nearby townland of Loughane:

> One Sunday as the priest was celebrating Mass ... an officer of the 'Yeos' [Yeomanry] entered ... Before the terror-stricken people could move he cut off the arms of the priest as he raised them after the elevation. The horrified congregation saw him mount his horse, and, followed by his soldiers, ride down the hill towards Fox's Bridge. Near the bridge the horse stumbled throwing its rider to the ground and breaking his neck. The soldiers buried him in the graveyard and went on their way. In the morning the graveyard [had] moved to the other side of the river.[14]

The informant added: 'The tale is told with variations but all agree on the shifting of the burial ground.' In 1861 Richard Caulfield provided one of these variations to *Notes and Queries*. According to his version, the church was removed across the river Shournagh by angels when an evil landlord was buried in it (priests had forbidden his burial). The gable of the church apparently fell into the river in transit, and an impression of angelic footprints was left on a rock. The site was so highly-regarded locally that when an antiquarian of Caulfield's acquaintance proposed to dig there, he was dissuaded by a tenant who believed his pregnant wife would be endangered by the supernatural 'influences' that would be released.[15] A further version of the legend graveyard, compiled by Shane Lehane from various tales, has recently been published online. In this vivid account, following the death of the 'yeoman', Captain Fox:

> at the stroke of midnight, the very ground of Loughane Graveyard ... began to quiver and move and the dead themselves awoke ... One by one they slid out of their coffins and graves, until the entire graveyard was awakened ... They took their headstones upon their backs and the dead of Loughane crawled and slithered their way across the field to the Shournagh and up the hill to the Matehy cemetery. They lost some of the headstones en route and a number can still be seen in the riverbed. When they reached the top of the hill, the sun was rising in the east and a cock crew to announce the day and as he did, all occupants of Loughane graveyard had re-interred themselves, headstones and all ... Back in Loughane, a solitary, large, flagstone marks the original position of the graveyard and according to legend the burial place of Fox.

The name of the townland in this account is attributed to the incident, being rendered as 'Magh Teithe', 'the place of the fleeing [from the priest hunter]', and the author suggests that the story of the moving graveyard continues to resonate locally: 'this legend, folklore and story is deep within the psyche of my neighbours and the inhabitants of the extended hinterland.'[16]

In other cases, the bodies of individual Protestants might be magically disinterred from their graves. Brendan Sheridan of Roebuck, County Cavan described how:

One time about fifty years ago a Catholic girl from this place got married to a Protestant man. They went to live in Granard. There was a burial ground near where they went to live, and the girl's father and uncle had [been] buried there. When the Protestant died he was buried in the same grave as the other two men. That night the two dead men arose out of the grave and dug up the Protestant. There was a lake near and the dead men put the coffin in that lake. Next day the people put the Protestant back in the grave and they watched it. To their horror the same thing happened that night. So the people buried the man in a Protestant graveyard and the man was left there.

Such tropes had precedents in the early modern period. For example, in the early seventeenth century, Philip O'Sullivan Beare told the legend of an Elizabethan Protestant Bishop of Ferns who had dropped dead while destroying a church at Castle Ellis, County Wexford:

His body, buried in the church by his brother and comrades, was found the next day outside the church, thrown up on the walk. The English, thinking the Irish had done this, again buried the body and put guards, but again the second night the grave was opened, and the body was nowhere to be found.[17]

A similar story was told in the twentieth century about a Protestant minister named Kennedy based in a parish near Abingdon Abbey in County Limerick who refused to allow locals access to a holy well. When he died he was buried by his son, a Captain John Kennedy, 'but no sooner was the grave closed than it began to stir'. The grave kept filling with water, forcing the family to disinter the minister and bury him with another man. However, the same thing happened again, as a result of which 'The coffin was taken out and put in a concrete grave. Captain John knocked the wall around the well and it was found to be full of worms and other things and couldn't be cleaned up. Soon after the dead minister's ghost was seen walking around looking for a drink of water and he haunts the place to this day.'[18] This account combines a graveyard story with the common theme of the desecration of holy wells. These and other sacred sites were equally as sensitive to insult as graveyards. Wells and objects credited with supernatural power regularly responded decisively to mistreatment. A standing stone in a field in Bere Island, County Cork, carted off for use as a lintel reappeared in the field from which it had been taken the next morning; a stone holy water font from Allihies taken by a priest for use at a new church at Cahermore returned more than once to its original site; while a flagstone at Portlick, County Longford that would magically carry the bodies of the dead to the cemetery on Inchcleraun, or Saint's Island, sank into Lough Ree when a women washed clothes on it.[19]

II

In their accounts of desecration and retribution, stories of moving graveyards are revealing of the negotiation of interdenominational relationships in local communities in the past. They certainly seem to highlight quite clearly a strong sense of difference between the Catholic and Protestant communities, and a preference for mutual exclusivity in burial practice. However, such inferences need to be interrogated carefully. We know for a fact that in most parts of Ireland the co-interment of Catholics and Protestants was a regular practice and, by extension, a fairly stable feature of interdenominational interactions, particularly in rural areas. Evidence from continental Europe dating from the early modern period has comprehensively demonstrated that religious toleration was not an invention of the Enlightenment, but a lived reality in most communities from the sixteenth and seventeenth centuries. Given that all-out sectarian conflict is not really sustainable over long periods of time, communities containing both Catholics and Protestants tended to organize themselves practically, in the interests of avoiding or at least reducing conflict. Scribner talks about 'tolerance of practical rationality', while other writers have indicated ways in which boundaries between religious groups might be asserted by means of symbol, custom and law rather than violence.[20] Yet compromise was often hard-won, and high levels of discrimination and sectarian distaste might merely be pushed aside in order to allow communities to live 'apart and together'. The 'tactics of toleration' deployed by religiously-mixed communities varied according to local circumstances (note that the deployment of violence could also be tactical). Generally, however, they implicitly acknowledged that neighbours of different confessions were mutually concerned to ensure the orderly running of society, and their own standing within it, and that such communities were bound by friendship, kinship and economic interests.

Crucially, they often had to share the same spaces.[21] There is a growing literature on how conflicting claims to control public thoroughfares and squares, buildings such as churches, and sacred sites in the rural landscape, were expressed and resolved in the post-Reformation period as 'confessionalized space'[22] carved out of 'sacralized' landscapes.[23] As Maurice Halbwachs has pointed out, 'religions are rooted in the land, not merely because men and groups must live on land but because the community of believers distributes its richest ideas and images throughout space. There are the holy places and other spots that evoke religious remembrances, as well as the profane sites inhabited by enemies of God.'[24] Disputes over burial grounds were particularly fraught, since these were not only places for the disposal of the dead, but also sites entwined with notions of personal identity and family and community histories. People strongly favoured burial with spouses, children, ancestors, kin, colleagues, and neighbours in the graveyard of the parish church, and social location was demonstrated via the spatial location of burials (some parts of graveyards were seen as more prestigious than others) and the display of heraldry and accomplishments on funerary monuments. Places of burial were therefore particularly evocative sites of different types of collective memory. It was not easy to throw over such a weight of accumulated meaning.

Even when confessional conflicts over the ownership of church buildings were settled in favour of a particular group, contests over graveyards were more likely to lapse into uneasy truce.[25] Just as in France, the Holy Roman Empire and central Europe, compromise in Ireland might mean confessional groups choosing to (or being obliged to) bury their dead on different sites; to bury on the same site and ignore reasons theoretically precluding this; or to bury in separate parts of the same site.[26] Though Catholic burial within church buildings used for Protestant worship may have declined rapidly from the 1650s, Irish Catholics preferably continued to bury in existing parish burial grounds. A variety of kinds of understandings on the allocation of burial space ensued. Patrick Kennedy noted that at the churchyard of Kilranelagh, near Baltinglass, County Wicklow, 'no corpse of Protestant man or woman has ever been allowed to rest', though an exception was clearly made for Sam MacAllister, a Presbyterian killed in 1798.[27]

Custom and material culture might distinguish certain sections of graveyards as Catholic or Protestant: Harold Mytum's work on Ulster has shown that in cemeteries like Aghalurcher, County Fermanagh and Kileevan, County Monaghan, Protestant and Catholic graves might cluster in certain areas. Different monumental traditions indicate that different sets of craftsmen were used by the two communities – Mytum points out, for example, that Catholics tended to use headstones, and Protestants ledger slabs.[28] Similar patterns elsewhere are revealed in folklore and other accounts. Caesar Otway explained in the nineteenth century that the old graveyard in Schull, County Cork, was divided into Protestant and Catholic plots (he felt it was 'unseemly thus to carry division into the grave'), though the expanded graveyard on the site is now multi-denominational.[29]

Everyday negotiations over such arrangements are all but invisible to history. A possible exception occurs in Patrick Kennedy's *Legends of Mount Leinster* (1855) – a collection of folklore cast in the form of a novel. Four Palatines (members of a Protestant community descended from eighteenth-century refugees from the Palatinate in present-day Germany) called at Duffrey Hall, County Wexford, seat of the landlord character, Mr Colcough, and were invited to stay for dinner. One explained that they were 'returning home to Ballinlugg from the church-yard of Templeshambo, after interring, for the third time, the deceased aunt of these boys'. He described how:

> The poor old lady was first interred about a month since: a few days after, there was a funeral which came from beyond the Slaney; and, next morning, the coffin in which the remains of my poor sister lay, was found perched up against the church door. Word was sent to us, and we laid it in the earth again, and set a night watch. All was useless, and now this…is the third time of performing the sorrowful duty. What can be the cause? We cannot suspect Protestants for doing it.

A poet present during dinner told the story of Templeshambo churchyard, which was believed to have been founded by a monk who built both a monastery and a convent of nuns. '[T]he nuns' burying place was on one side of the stream, and the monks kept to the side next the rising of the sun.' Even in later times 'no woman ever attempted to bury herself on the men's side', and in the seventeenth century the cemetery had been further honoured by the interment of Daniel Jordan, 'who fought under the brave Sarsfield, at Aughrim, and Limerick', and who was 'buried before the church door, with his sword by his side, his cuirass on his breast, and the crested helmet on his head'. On hearing this, one of the Palatines diagnosed the problem:

> My aunt is laid close beside the tomb of this famous warrior, and as sure as you live, some one or other, taking offence that a

woman should be buried on the men's side, and so near this great
trooper, and she a Protestant too, has got her removed.

The Palatines were greatly mortified at their inadvertent violation of
the custom, and the party resolved to 'remove the body from its
inhospitable neighbourhood'. The procession to the graveyard was
joined by local people and the parish priest, and the coffin was 'borne
across the brook and … lowered into its never-more-to-be-disturbed
resting place'. Kennedy, who had a keen ear for the folklore of his local
area, is likely to have based his story on a real occurrence, and used the
opportunity to disseminate a message of religious tolerance – in his
publications he was consistent on the theme of coexistence between
different denominations. The account emphasized that the incident had
proceeded from an honest mistake on the part of the Palatines, and the
character of Colcough, in his impromptu oration at the graveside
'expressed his hopes, that the only strife among the Protestants and
Catholics under his jurisdiction would still consist in the emulation of
friendly and good-natured offices towards each other'.[30]

Such 'good-natured' accommodations were not always forthcoming.
At times of heightened religious and political tension it was always
possible that suppressed grievances over burial might be revisited. Luria
notes how periodic drives by church and community leaders to
emphasize confessional differences and educate their flocks in belief
and practice might break 'the bonds between neighbours of different
faiths by invoking fears of social contamination'. Carefully built
community relationships might collapse abruptly and wholly, with a
knock-on impact on the dead. In the early modern period, collapses of
community, as occurred, for example, in the 1640s, resulted in multiple
incidents of refusal of burial to Protestants, or their disinterment from
their graves.[31] Some modern-day graveyards in Belfast likewise
exemplify such impulses. Since the onset of the Troubles, there has been
a rapid increase in separation of burial. Protestant graves in the City
Cemetery off the Falls Road have largely been abandoned, and it has
even been rumoured (wrongly) that 'the Catholic church insisted that
the wall dividing Catholic graves from Protestant ones should be
extended by a full 9ft under the ground, presumably to guard against
any unwarranted fraternization with religious rivals in the afterlife.'[32]

Given the example of what can happen in times of heightened
sectarian tension, narratives of moving churches and graveyards and
their guardian-ghosts indicate most strongly the degree to which the

negotiation and defence of 'confessionalized space' was an ongoing exercise. Tales of Protestants miraculously disinterred from their graves expressed concerns about misappropriation of property and pollution in a vivid and memorable way, and delineated the limits of tolerance, by setting aside certain graveyards, or parts of graveyards, for Catholic use only. The context of this defence has changed over time of course, and this is reflected in the fact that the accounts have themselves altered, sometimes in the course of merely a few decades. This is seen clearly in the cases of Kildemock's jumping church, and Matehy's flying graveyard, and it exemplifies the process of what Guy Beiner calls the 'regeneration of recollections, which are adapted or reinvented to suit changing contexts'.[33] Folk history does not tell an unchanging story of a fixed past, but amends the past to meet the needs and attitudes of present communities.

The theme of moving graveyards has been adopted and adapted by 'serious' authors as well. In 1885, George Bernard Shaw, then a relatively unsuccessful novelist trying to make ends meet in London, published a satirical short story called 'The Miraculous Revenge'.[34] It told the tale of Zeno Legge,[35] a young drunkard with a high opinion of what he felt were his own underappreciated talents, sent by his despairing family to stay with his uncle, the Cardinal Archbishop of Dublin. The Cardinal, keen to get rid of his irritating guest, sent Zeno to a village called Four Mile Water in County Wicklow to investigate a reported miracle. The local priest, Father Hickey, had reported that one 'Brimstone Billy' Wolfe Tone Fitzgerald, 'a dirty, drunken, blasphemous, blackguard', an admirer of rebels, and, 'worse again … an atheist,' had died 'in a fit brought on by drink' and had been buried in the local burial ground, the first non-Catholic ever to be placed there. The burial had gone ahead in the face of Fr Hickey's protestations, and was held late in the evening of 14 July (in 1880 Bastille Day had become a public holiday in France) to prevent the body 'being stolen and buried at the cross-roads'.[36] Next morning, to the surprise of all, 'the graveyard was found moved to the south side of the water, with the one newly-filled grave left behind on the north side'. The priest expressed his opinion that 'the departed saints would not lie with the reprobate'; the cardinal wished to ascertain whether this was 'a strange manifestation of God's power', or some sort of fraud. On arriving in Four Mile Water, Zeno inspected the sites, looked at maps and interviewed the locals, Protestant and Catholic. He was inclined to believe that a miracle had indeed occurred. However, he fell out with a local girl, was punched by her boyfriend, and called an informer and spy when he revealed his mission. Enraged by the recalcitrant attitude of Fr Hickey and the local people, Zeno vowed to 'undo the visible work of God's hand'. That night, he dug up the coffin of Brimstone Billy, rowed it across the river, and reinterred it in the runaway graveyard, which promptly removed itself to its original position, once again leaving behind the man 'with whom the blessed would not rest'.

It is unknown how Shaw came up with the plot of this story, but it is probable that it was inspired by some of the folklore he came across in south Dublin in his younger years. Shaw may have been the source of a pertinent passage in W.B. Yeats' *Fairy and Folk Tales of the Irish Peasantry* (1888), or they may have had a common progenitor:

> The bodies of saints are fastidious things. At a place called Four-Mile-Water, in Wexford, there is an old graveyard full of saints. Once it was on the other side of the river, but they buried a rogue there and the whole graveyard moved across in the night, leaving the rogue-corpse in solitude. It would have been easier to move merely the rogue-corpse, but they were saints, and had to do things in style.[37]

Both Shaw's Four Mile Walter and Yeats' Four-Mile-Water may be based on the seventh-century Old Threemilewater church and graveyard, near Brittas Bay, County Wicklow – there is no place of that name in Wexford.[38] There are signs also that some moving graveyard traditions were current in the area: Patrick O'Toole, of Hacketstown, County Carlow reported to Folklore Commission collectors in the 1930s a graveyard that 'I heard the old people say went from one side of the river to the other at Arklow.'[39]

Some tales of disinterred Protestants and rogues had rather more prosaic explanations. In 1942, Laurence McIntyre of Kilcrossduff, County Cavan, told the folklore collector P.J. Gaynor:

> There was an old lassie called Sheridan lived at Moybologue [cemetery], and she would take the name of every corpse that would be buried in it. A man called Cox, a Protestant, was buried in it, and when she told about the burial his body was lifted. His people got word that if the body wasn't removed it would be burned, so they came and took it away. No Protestants are buried in Moybologue Graveyard.[40]

On 15 September 1936, the *Irish Independent* newspaper reported what was termed an 'extraordinary affair' being investigated by Gardaí in Pallaskenry, County Limerick.

> Mr John Sheehy was driving along the road near Ballysteen, county Limerick, when he came across a coffin lying in a ditch by the side of the road. The casket was obviously new and fresh clay adhered to it. The coffin contained the body of John McGivern, son of a farmer at Ballymartin. The remains had been interred in Beigh [Beagh] Catholic churchyard the previous day and were disinterred during the night. The coffin was found about 100 yards from the churchyard. It is understood that McGivern was not a Catholic and the occurrence is attributed to religious feelings. The coffin was removed and later reinterred at Dunmanway, county Cork, from where the McGivern family came to live in county Limerick about ten years ago.[41]

The Irish Times described him as 'the son of an extensive farmer living in Ballymahon [recte Ballymartin], who came from Cork and settled in the district about ten years ago'.[42] Later reports name the dead man as Henry rather than John McGivern, and in November one Michael Doran of Pallaskenry was charged at Askeaton District Court 'with disinterring a coffin containing the dead body of Henry McGivern'. The case was withdrawn after 'Inspector Brazil asked that informations be refused'.[43] Judging from the 1911 census, the McGivern family, headed by John McGivern and including his then five-year-old son Henry, originally lived near Castlelyons in County Cork. They were members of a Church of Christ, probably an independent congregation along the lines of the Churches of Christ that became widespread in the United States in the nineteenth century – it is notable that the same or a related group had adherents in the Pallaskenry area where members of the Coyne and Neazor families were described in 1911 as of the Church of Christ and 'Church of God'.[44] Despite their membership of a minority religious group, there are indications in the newspapers' reports that something more than 'religious feelings' may have been involved in this case. McGivern was a newcomer to the area, with no claims on an ancestral burial site. Perhaps his family's claims to their lands were also contested in a time of widespread agrarian disaffection.

During a previous outbreak of strife over land, one of the people focussed on in north County Kerry was George Sandes, a landowner in his own right and agent for Trinity College and a number of significant absentee landlords in the county. Known in the local area for his ruthlessness, Sandes attracted the attentions of the Land League for running a regime of rack-renting and evictions. He was involved in several cases of sexual harassment, and may even have been a rapist. He needed extensive police protection in the last years of his life, was removed from his position as a magistrate for perjury, lost his position as High Sheriff of County Kerry, and antagonized the local Church of Ireland community to the extent that when he was appointed to the Listowel Select Vestry, the majority of the members walked out. When Sandes died, there was jubilation in the local area, and his son was the sole mourner at his funeral.[45] Sandes was buried in the family tomb in the medieval churchyard of Aghavallen, which was the last resting place of a mixed population of Catholics and Protestants.[46] Shortly afterwards, some of the local Land League members broke into the tomb at night, and removed Sandes' body, which was thrown into the Shannon. Apparently in homage to local belief that the Sandes family was subject to a curse, the 'Curse of the Crows', which meant that no crow would nest in their woods, the grave robbers scratched up the ground, and scattered crow feathers around the hole they had made.[47] When Sandes' body was recovered, it was buried in Listowel and the grave put under an armed guard.[48]

Conclusion

In the story of Sandes' disinterment, the experience of Henry McGivern, and the case in County Cavan that justified the statement that 'No Protestants are buried in Moybologue Graveyard', we can see how the burial and disinterment of bodies combined with folkloric ideas to be used as a resource in local politics. We may also surmise that our earlier tales of ejected and rejected Protestants and rogue-corpses may derive from real incidents that were smoothed by the deletion or omission ('forgetting') of inconvenient details as they passed from fact into legend, and as they settled into a pattern of purveying universal rather than specific truths. Graveyards, then, were not quiet places of the slumbering dead, but sacred sites in which past generations of the community were present in a very real way. The tales told about them assisted in the construction of local and confessional identities, while their use by all religious communities, or just one, impressed on sacred space the map of human relationships within parishes.

NOTES

1 National Folklore Collection (henceforth NFC), Schools Folklore Collection [S]397, pp.38–9.
2 Guy Beiner, 'Recycling the Dustbin of Irish History: The Radical Challenge of "Folk Memory"', *History Ireland*, 14:1 (2006), p.43.
3 One may instance, for the British and Irish Isles, Raymond Gillespie, Alexandra Walsham, Peter Marshall, Adam Fox, Daniel Woolf, Ronald Hutton, David Cressy, Diane Purkiss, Lizanne Henderson and Edward Cowen, Alison Shell, Darren Oldridge, Keith Thomas, among others.
4 Henry Glassie, *Passing the Time in Ballymenone: Folklore and History of an Ulster Community* (Bloomington: University of Indiana Press, 1995), p.69.
5 See Clodagh Tait, 'The Ghosts of Lislaughtin Abbey and Other Stories: The Folklore of Irish Graveyards', forthcoming.
6 Though there are many collections of 'Irish ghost stories', there are few academic treatments, the main exception being brief accounts in Linda Ballard, 'Before Death and Beyond: Death and Ghost Traditions with Particular Reference to Ulster', in H.R. Ellis Davidson and W.M.S. Russell, *The Folklore of Ghosts* (Cambridge: D.S. Brewer, 1982), pp.13–42; eadem, 'Fairies and the Supernatural on Reachrai', in Peter Narváez (ed.), *The Good People: New Fairylore Essays* (Lexington: University Press of Kentucky, 1991), pp.63–71. On British ghost belief, see Owen Davies, *The Haunted: A Social History of Ghosts* (Basingstoke: Palgrave, 2009); R.C. Finucane, *Ghosts: Appearances of the Dead and Cultural Transformation* (Amherst: Prometheus Books, 1996); Jean-Claude Schmitt, *Ghosts in the Middle Ages* (Chicago: University of Chicago Press, 1998); Peter Marshall, *Mother Leakey and the Bishop: A Ghost Story* (Oxford: Oxford University Press, 2007); Peter Marshall, *Beliefs and the Dead in Reformation England* (Oxford: Oxford University Press, 2002); P.G. Maxwell-Stuart, *Ghosts: A History of Phantoms, Ghouls and Other Spirits of the Dead* (Stroud: Alan Sutton, 2007); Jo Bath and John Newton, '"Sensible Proof of Spirits": Ghost Belief During the Later Seventeenth Century', *Folklore*, 117 (2006), pp.1–14; Sasha Handley, *Visions of an Unseen World: Ghost Beliefs and Ghost Stories in Eighteenth-Century England* (London: Pickering and Chatto, 2007); Shane MacCorristine, *Spectres of the Self: Thinking About Ghosts and Ghost-Seeing in England, 1750–1920* (Cambridge: Cambridge University Press, 2010); John Newton (ed.), *Early Modern Ghosts* (Durham: Centre for Seventeenth Century Studies, 2002).
7 On fairies, see especially Narváez, *The Good People*; K.M. Briggs, 'The Fairies and the Realms of the Dead', *Folklore*, 81 (1970), pp.81–96; eadem, *The Fairies in Tradition and Literature* (Oxford: Butler Publishing, 1991).
8 Tait, 'The Ghosts of Lislaughtin Abbey'. Davies suggests that as late as the seventeenth century, ghosts were regularly associated with graveyards in England – in Shakespeare's *A Midsummer Night's Dream*, spirits wandering by night are described as trooping 'home to churchyards', while the ghosts of the damned return to their 'wormy beds' in 'cross-ways and floods' – but this connection has been lost in more recent times (Davies, *The Haunted*, pp.49–50). Brown has noted some English ghosts associated with churchyards in the south-west of England, though it seems that for those ghosts, the churchyard is not their chosen place of habitation. However, churchyard earth was frequently employed as a means of confounding or 'laying' troublesome ghosts: Theo Brown, *The Fate of the Dead: A Study in Folk-Eschatology in the West Country after the Reformation* (Ipswich: D.S. Brewer, 1979), pp.29, 36, 58–9.
9 NFC, S50, pp.111–2.
10 NFC, S679, pp.7–8.
11 'Louth Ordnance Survey Letters', *Journal of the County Louth Archaeological Society*, 7 (1929), p.83.
12 'The mystery of Kildemock's jumping church' [Online]. Available from: www.irishidentity.com/extras/supernat/stories/kildemock.htm [accessed 26 June 2012]. See also Frank McNally, 'An Irishman's Diary', *Irish Times*, 23 July 2011. Image of plaque (and church) at: www.geolocation.ws/v/W/File:Trinity%20Green,%20Paughanstown,%20Co.%20Louth%20-%20geograph.org.uk%20-%201343759.jpg/-/en [accessed 28 June 2012]. J.B. Leslie comments of the 'natural' explanation that '[this] strange accident though greatly

enquired into has no way yet been accounted for in a satisfactory manner': J.B. Leslie, *Armagh Clergy and Parishes* (Dundalk: William Tempest, 1911), p.323.

13 R.M. Chapple, 'The Jumping Church of Kildemock: Speculations on Catholics and Freemasons in 18th-Century County Louth' [Online]. Available from: http://rmchapple.blogspot.ie/2011/09/jumping-church-of-kildemock.html [accessed 8 June 2012].

14 NFC, S347, pp.352–3; see also pp.287, 351–2, where some standing stones in Loughane were pointed to as the original site of the church.

15 R.C., 'A Church Removed by Holy Angels', *Notes and Queries*, 2nd ser. 12 (1861), pp.498–9.

16 S. Lehane, 'Matehy Graveyard in County Cork – Spelling And Lore (How did Headstones end up in a Riverbed)' [Online]. Available from: http://historicgraves.ie/blog/places/matehy-graveyard-county-cork-spelling-and-lore-how-did-headstones-end-riverbed [accessed June 2012].

17 Clodagh Tait, *Death, Burial and Commemoration in Ireland, 1550–1650* (Basingstoke: Palgrave Macmillan, 2003), p.92.

18 NFC, S524, p.185.

19 Allihies Folklore Group, *The Beara Book of Wonders* (Allihies: Allihies Folklore Group, 1991), pp.4, 22; Anne Ridge, *Death Customs in Rural Ireland: Traditional Funerary Rites in the Irish Midlands* (Galway: Arlen House, 2009), p.101.

20 Keith Luria, *Sacred Boundaries: Religious Coexistence and Conflict in Early Modern France* (Washington: Catholic University of America Press, 2005); O.P. Grell and Robert Scribner (eds), *Tolerance and Intolerance in the European Reformation* (Cambridge: Cambridge University Press, 1996); Vincent Carey (ed.), *Voices for Tolerance in an Age of Persecution* (Washington: University of Washington Press, 2004); C. Scott Dixon, Dagmar Freist and Mark Greengrass (eds), *Living with Religious Diversity in Early Modern Europe* (Farnham: Ashgate 2009); T.A. Brady, 'Limits of Religious Violence in Early Modern Europe', in Kaspar-Von Greyerz and Kim Siebenhüner (eds), *Religion und Gewalt: Konflikte, Rituale, Deutungen (1500–1800)* (Gottingen: Vandenhoeck and Ruprecht, 2006), pp.125–54; B.J. Kaplan, *Divided by Faith: Religious Conflict and the Practice of Toleration in Early Modern Europe* (Cambridge, MA: Belknap Press, 2007); Alexandra Walsham, *Charitable Hatred: Tolerance and Intolerance in England, 1500–1700* (Manchester: Manchester University Press, 2006); Howard Louthan, G.B. Cohen and F.A.J. Szabo (eds), *Diversity and Dissent: Negotiating Religious Difference in Central Europe, 1500–1800* (Oxford: Berghahn Books, 2011); Jesse Spohnholz, *The Tactics of Toleration: a Refugee Community in the Age of Religious Wars* (Lanham: University of Delaware Press, 2011). Such negotiations were an ongoing project: see, for example, H.W. Smith (ed.), *Protestants, Catholics, and Jews in Germany, 1800–1914* (Oxford: Berg, 2001) which deals with communities in the 'new confessional age' of the nineteenth century.

21 Will Coster and Andrew Spicer (eds), *Sacred space in early modern Europe* (Cambridge: Cambridge University Press, 2005); Andrew Spicer and Sarah Hamilton (eds), *Defining the Holy: Sacred Space in Late Medieval and Early Modern Europe* (Aldershot: Ashgate, 2005); Alexandra Walsham, *The Reformation of the Landscape: Religion, Identity and Memory in Early Modern Britain and Ireland* (Oxford: Oxford University Press, 2011).

22 D.J. Corpis, 'Space and urban religious life in Augsburg, 1648–1750', in Coster and Spicer (eds), *Sacred Space in Early Modern Europe*, pp.302–25.

23 Walsham, *Reformation of the Landscape*, p.23. Walsham notes that despite the impression that Protestants desacralized the landscape, there is evidence of significant 'resacralization' as well.

24 Maurice Halbwachs, *The Collective Memory* [Online] (1950), p.6. Available from: http://web.mit.edu/allanmc/www/hawlbachsspace.pdf [accessed 3 June 2012].

25 See Tait, *Death, Burial and Commemoration*, pp.59–96.

26 See, especially, Luria, *Sacred boundaries*; Tait, *Death, Burial and Commemoration*; Corpis, 'Space and Urban Religious Life'; also Penny Roberts, 'Contesting Sacred Space: Burial Disputes in Sixteenth-Century France', in Bruce Gordon and Peter Marshall, *The Place of the Dead: Death and Remembrance in Late Medieval and Early Modern Europe* (Cambridge: Cambridge University Press, 2000), pp.131–48; Amanda Eurich, 'Between the Living and the

Dead: Preserving Confessional Identity and Community in Early Modern France', in M.L. Halvorson and K.E. Spierling, *Defining Community in Early Modern Europe* (Aldershot: Ashgate, 2008), pp.43–60; D.M. Luebke, 'Customs of Confession: Managing Religious Diversity in Late Sixteenth-Century Westphalia', in Louthan et al. (eds), *Diversity and Dissent*, pp.53–72; Craig Koslofsky, *Reformation of the Dead: Death and Ritual in Early Modern Germany, 1450–1700* (Basingstoke: Palgrave, 2000).

27 Patrick Kennedy, *Legendary Fictions of the Irish Celts* (London: Macmillan, 1891), p.162.
28 H.C. Mytum, 'The Eighteenth and Nineteenth Century Graveyard Monuments of Killeevan, Co. Monaghan and Galloon, Co. Fermanagh', *Clogher Record*, 18 (2003), pp.1–31; idem, 'Archaeological Perspectives on External Mortuary Monuments of Plantation Ireland', in James Lyttleton and Colin Rynne (eds), *Settlement and Material Culture in Early Modern Ireland* (Dublin: Four Courts Press, 2009), pp.165–81.
29 'Sketches in the South of Ireland', in Cesar Otway, *Sketches in Ireland* (Dublin, 1827), p.258.
30 H. Whitney (Patrick Kennedy), *Legends of Mount Leinster: Tales and Sketches* (London and Dublin, 1855), pp.102–108; R. Garnett, 'Kennedy, Patrick (1800–1873)', rev. by W.J. McCormack, *Oxford Dictionary of National Biography* (60 Volumes, Oxford: Oxford University Press, 2004).
31 Tait, *Death, Burial and Commemoration*, pp.82–3.
32 M. Fealty, 'United in mourning', *The Guardian*, 10 Dec. 2005.
33 Guy Beiner, *Remembering the Year of the French: Irish Folk History and Social Memory* (Madison, WI.: University of Wisconsin Press 2006); idem, 'The Decline and Rebirth of "Folk Memory": Remembering "The Year of the French" in the Late Twentieth Century', *Éire-Ireland*, 38 (2003), pp.7–32.
34 G.B. Shaw, 'The Miraculous Revenge', *Time* (Mar. 1885), pp.315–30; republished in B. Shaw, *The Black Girl in Search of God and Some Lesser Tales* (Harmondsworth: Penguin, 1966), pp.119–45. A novel by the Scottish Catholic writer Bruce Marshall takes a related theme. In *Father Malachy's Miracle* (London: Heinemann, 1962 [1931]) a Benedictine, Fr Malachy, is so unhappy with activities at a dance hall situated near a Catholic church in Edinburgh, that he calls on God to transport it to a rock in the sea in the hope that the miracle would be the cause of widespread spiritual renewal: when the miracle occurs, the dancehall only increases its fame and clientele, so Fr Malachy causes it to be returned to its original location. The book was later adapted as a play and film.
35 Possibly a reference to the Stoic philosopher, Zeno of Citium.
36 The crossroads was a regular place of burial for suicides, excommunicates, and other malefactors. See, for example, Robert Halliday, 'The Roadside Burial of Suicides', *Folklore* 121 (2010), pp.81–93.
37 W.B. Yeats, *Fairy and Folk Tales of the Irish Peasantry* (1888), p.214.
38 Shaw lived for a time in Dalkey, County Dublin: Brittas Bay, then as now, was a popular holiday spot for people from Dublin. The church at Threemilewater/Ennisboyne is dedicated to St Baothin: Archibald Henderson, *George Bernard Shaw: Man of the Century* (New York: Appleton-Century-Crofts, 1956); A.M. Gibbs, *A Bernard Shaw Chronology* (Basingstoke: Palgrave, 2001), p.26.
39 NFC, 265, p.453.
40 NFC, 815, p.292.
41 *The Irish Independent*, 15 Sept. 1936.
42 *The Irish Times*, 15 Sept. 1936.
43 *The Irish Times*, 17, 21 Nov. 1936.
44 There has been no history of Churches of Christ in Ireland. The movement in the US was strongly influenced by Thomas Campbell, of County Down, and his son, Alexander: R.T. Hughes and R.L. Roberts, *The Churches of Christ* (Westport, CT: Greenwood Publishing, 2001).
45 B. MacMahon, 'George Sandes of Listowel: Land Agent, Magistrate and Terror of North Kerry', *Journal of the Kerry Archaeological and Historical Society*, 3 (2003), pp.5–56. Thanks to Mr MacMahon and Mike Sandes for discussing this case with me. Mr MacMahon had heard of the disinterment incident, but had no specific details and did not know of the

subsequent burial in Listowel.

46 There is a photograph of the vault at http://sandesancestry.net/0320-george-sandes [accessed 26 June 2012].

47 'The curse of the crows' is a common trope in Irish tradition, usually deployed against bad landlords, and often in the context of the desecration of graveyards. Rookeries were seen by many to be a sign of good luck and prosperity. In Rostellan, County Cork, for example, a landlord who took the gravestone of an old woman's son to pave his scullery floor was cursed by the woman 'and from that day crows never built their nests in Rostellan': NFC, S393, pp.248–9.

48 Thanks to Dr Declan Downey for this account of Sandes' disinterment: in turn, it was told to him by a man whose grandfather was involved in the Land League in Kerry in the late nineteenth century.

12

DYING, DEATH AND HUNGER STRIKE: CORK AND BRIXTON, 1920

WILLIAM MURPHY

In *This Republic of Suffering: Death and the American Civil War*, Drew Gilpin Faust has reconstructed the ways in which the soldiers, their families and wider society prepared for death. She argues that it remained important, perhaps more important given the then novel, terrible and aberrant conditions of modern war, that each man's story be a story of a good death.[1] The hunger strike conditions of Brixton and Cork in 1920, though very different from those of the battlefields of Antietam or Gettysburg, were also aberrant. The hunger strikers faced death in novel circumstances, yet they and those around them shared the near universal desire that if it came, even or maybe especially as a consequence of hunger strike, that the story of their deaths should be told in ways that offered meaning and solace, and in ways that evoked admiration rather than condemnation. This essay will explore the prolonged and very public deaths of Terence MacSwiney, Michael Fitzgerald and Joseph Murphy, focussing on the manner in which this impulse toward a good death manifested itself in the environments of Cork and Brixton prison, Ireland and Britain, during the Irish War of Independence.

On 6 November 1920, the *Anglo-Celt* newspaper reported that an elderly nun, who lay dying at a convent at Weybridge, England, had heard the banshee on three successive nights in late October. The nun assumed that the banshee had travelled to Weybridge to herald her death, but, according to the *Anglo-Celt*, she (the nun that is) was not fully informed of the circumstances of her family. Specifically, she did not know that her nephew, Terence MacSwiney, also lay dying in

Brixton prison and it was only upon receipt of news of his death that she realized that the banshee's cries were not for her, but him.[2] This elderly nun must have been one of the few people in Britain and Ireland who was unaware that Terence MacSwiney was dying. In the course of a seventy-four day hunger strike (from his arrest on the evening of the 12 August to his death at 5.40am on 25 October 1920), the fate of the Lord Mayor of Cork had attracted extraordinary public attention that was not confined to these islands.[3]

MacSwiney's strike ended in Brixton with a heart attack during delirium, but it began at Cork prison.[4] There he joined a hunger-striking group of prisoners who had embarked on their protest on the morning of 11 August, following the authorities' failure to respond to an ultimatum, demanding their 'unconditional release'.[5] In the initial stages, the number of men on strike at Cork varied somewhat, peaking at sixty-five on 12 August. Although the first strikers were occasionally joined by newly arrested suspects, such as MacSwiney, the general trend was downward as the authorities released some who were young or had been recently arrested, and transferred two large cohorts of convicted prisoners to English prisons, twenty-five on 12 August and eighteen more on 18 August.[6] In each instance the transfer prompted these groups to give up their strike. On the occasion of the second transfer, Mark Sturgis, a senior official at Dublin Castle, expressed the hope that this 'means a real break-up of the rotten hunger striking business'.[7] Such optimism soon receded and by the second half of August a core of eleven determined strikers – Michael Fitzgerald, Joseph Murphy, Joseph Kenny, Thomas Donovan, John Crowley, Christopher Upton, Peter Crowley, Michael O'Reilly, John Hennessy, Michael Burke and John Power – remained at Cork. Ten had been on the strike from the beginning, while Kenny had joined on 15 August. Ten of the men, including Kenny, had not yet been charged with a specific offence, but were held under the orders of the competent military authority. The exception was the generally recognized leader of the group, Michael Fitzgerald. He had been a trade union official and was officer commanding the Fermoy Battalion of the IRA when he was arrested in September 1919 in the aftermath of an attack on a group of Shropshire Light Infantry that had been on its way to Sunday service in Fermoy.[8] Nearly a year later Fitzgerald was still awaiting trial on charges of murdering Private William Jones who had died as a consequence of that attack.

Shortly after his imprisonment Fitzgerald had participated in a brief hunger strike at Cork prison, involving forty-six prisoners. Then the chief warder, Denis O'Donoghue, had described most of the untried prisoners involved as 'soft country young fellows' who would soon give in, but excepted Fitzgerald from this characterization.[9] On 10 August 1920, Fitzgerald was one of three prisoners to sign the ultimatum that signalled the beginning of the fatal hunger strike and he would be the first to die at 9.45pm on Sunday, 17 October. Next morning, the medical officers recorded the cause of death as 'gradual cessation of the vital functions due to prolonged abstention from all forms of nourishment'.[10] Joseph Murphy, they reported on the same day, 'can now be only described as just alive'.[11] Murphy had been an active, though not leading, volunteer based in Cork city and, on 15 July 1920, he was arrested on suspicion of possession of a bomb. Reports as to his age varied but he was in his early twenties and had been born in the United States.[12] He lasted a further gruelling week, dying at 8.35pm on 25 October, fourteen hours after MacSwiney's death at Brixton. The medical officers recorded the same cause of death as they had for Fitzgerald.[13] Extraordinarily, there were no further fatalities although the remaining nine men continued to strike until 12 November. They then stopped in response to a letter issued by Arthur Griffith that encouraged (though expressly did not order) them off their protest. He wrote that they had 'sufficiently demonstrated their devotion and fidelity' and had proven that 'those whom England advertises … as criminals are Irishmen whose patriotism is proof against torture and death'.[14]

Griffith's intervention saved the men's lives. Ninety-four days earlier, when embarking on their hunger strike, it is unlikely that they anticipated death. Prisons and internment camps of Ireland were key sites of Irish revolution, and frequently witnessed conflict, but they were not especially dangerous places. Indeed, by the summer of 1920 some felt it was safer to be in prison than outside. In the aftermath of the 1916 Rising there had been sixteen executions, but there had been none since. Two so-called German plot internees had died of influenza while in prison: Richard Coleman at Usk in December 1918 and Pierce McCan at Gloucester in March 1919.[15] That was one more than had to date died on hunger strike. This was Thomas Ashe, who had not died after prolonged self-starvation; he succumbed to a heart attack that was probably a consequence of his forcible feeding at Mountjoy prison on 25 September 1917, just five days after he had embarked on his protest.[16]

In the aftermath of Ashe's death, the prison authorities abandoned forcible feeding in the case of Irish political prisoners to all practical purposes (there were rare exceptions). This exposed the authorities to what the press described as 'hunger-strike mania',[17] and cohort after cohort of Irish Volunteers achieved improved prison conditions or their release using the tactic. In late February 1918, facing the collapse of the Irish prison system, the then Chief Secretary for Ireland, H.E. Duke, informed the House of Commons – and prison governors all over Ireland informed individual prisoners – that those who embarked upon a hunger strike would not be forcibly fed nor released but would be allowed to starve themselves and the state would regard their action as suicide.[18] In the spring of 1918, this strategy, combined with the concession of an agreed privileged regime for most political prisoners, resulted in the effective stifling of the hunger strike threat.[19] By late 1919, however, as violence in the country escalated, Irish Volunteers inside the prisons returned to the hunger strike with a vengeance. The government failed to maintain their hard-line stance, and the most significant consequence of this failure came in April and May of 1920 when, after mass hunger strikes, they released two large groups of men, one consisting of some ninety prisoners (both convicted and awaiting trial) at Mountjoy and the other consisting of some 200 internees held at Wormwood Scrubs. Prison, as it had two years earlier, appeared to be on the verge of worthlessness as a weapon against the IRA. The hunger strikers of Cork, including Terence MacSwiney, therefore had good reason to believe that they would not be obliged to choose between abandoning their strike and death.

That is not to say that they embarked upon their action without a consciousness of danger, including the danger of death. Since the modern hunger strike's arrival in Ireland in 1912, conducted first by suffragettes, it had been accompanied by a rhetoric of death. Mary Leigh, one of the first group of suffragettes to go on hunger strike in an Irish prison, told the governor of Mountjoy in August 1912, 'if the Government will undertake to give votes to women, I will take my food, and I will gladly do my sentence of 5 years or longer, but under no other circumstances. You can kill me if you like, and I will gladly die, but I won't give in.'[20] In an action that MacSwiney would echo, in June 1915, Francis Sheehy Skeffington responded to a sentence of six months' hard labour under the Defence of the Realm Act by telling the court: 'I'll serve no such sentence. I'll eat no food from this moment and long before the expiration of the sentence I shall be out of prison, either alive or dead.'[21] In the early stages of the strike that would result in Thomas Ashe's death, Constance Markievicz told a large protest at Smithfield, Dublin, that the men in Mountjoy were carrying on the 'fight for love of Ireland in long drawn sighs of agony, from hour to hour, from day to day, from moment to moment, seeing that grim spectre, death, coming nearer and nearer'.[22] Most infamously perhaps, Laurence O'Neill, the Lord Mayor of Dublin, told the inquest into Ashe's death that when the prison doctor, Raymond G. Dowdall, warned him that forcible feeding might be fatal, Ashe expressed his determination to persist, stating 'even if I do die I die in a good cause'.[23]

Although no death had been directly attributable to hunger strike since Ashe's, each strike generated terrible anxiety among family and friends, if not always the prisoners. While participating in a strike at Dundalk in early March 1918 (one of the last during that phase of hunger strikes), Michael Brennan wrote to Madge Daly: 'A wire has just come from my mother asking if it is true that I am dead. Well, to the best of my knowledge its [sic] not true yet anyway & I only wish I could lay my hands on the disturbing gossipers who spread such yarns ... For God's sake pay no heed to those damned rumours!'[24] Michael Brennan, along with his brothers, Paddy and Austin, was a pioneer of the hunger strike among the Irish Volunteers, and their activities in this regard regularly elicited intuitions of death from their mother, Mary.[25] She sent a telegram to one prison governor, warning 'if my boys are dead by return I leave their deaths at your door'.[26] In nationalist propaganda and elsewhere during these years, participation in hunger strike was cited as a contributing factor to the subsequent ill-health or death of former prisoners. An example is the death of Francis Gleeson on 9 May 1920. The immediate cause of Gleeson's demise was appendicitis, but the medical evidence at his inquest prompted the jury (at the coroner's suggestion) to note that it had been 'accelerated' by the affects of hunger strike: Gleeson had been released from Mountjoy on 14 April as a consequence of the mass hunger strike of that month. Unsurprisingly, the nationalist press afforded the jury's finding extensive coverage.[27] This was part of a wider pattern of blaming various forms of imprisonment for the subsequent deaths of Irish nationalists. For example, four former inhabitants of Frongoch internment camp died in 1917, within a year of their release from that camp. On each occasion, and with varying degrees of credibility, the nationalist press ascribed their death to the effects of their incarceration.[28]

Four days after his arrest Terence MacSwiney was tried by court martial, found guilty of three charges – including possession of an RIC cipher – and sentenced to two years' imprisonment. He informed the court that he would 'be free, alive or dead, within a month'.[29] He did not return to Cork prison, but was transferred to London.[30] Unlike other convicts transferred from Cork, MacSwiney did not abandon his protest at that point. He persisted in the belief, as his comments in court suggest, that there would be a speedy resolution to the contest of wills between him and the authorities. Most likely, MacSwiney and the other strikers anticipated, based on previous experience, that they would be released.[31] Should the alternative scenario transpire, no one believed that a hunger striker would survive more than a few weeks.

The authorities came under enormous pressure to release Mac Swiney and the other men, and not only from nationalist Ireland. As Edward Shortt, the Home Secretary, noted at cabinet, on 25 August, 'practically the whole [British] press' and moderate unionist opinion in Ireland favoured MacSwiney's release.[32] In late August, among those to intervene on behalf of MacSwiney alone, or all the hunger-striking prisoners, was a self-appointed group calling itself 'the Peace Conference' (led by Sir Nugent Everard and Sir Horace Plunkett[33]), King George V,[34] and the elderly Mrs Georgina Bowen-Colthurst. Mrs Bowen-Colthurst was the mother of Colonel John Bowen-Colthurst who had shot Francis Sheehy Skeffington, Thomas Dickson and Patrick James McIntyre in cold blood at Portobello Barracks during the 1916 Rising. In making her representations, she visited both Scotland Yard and the Home Office where an official noted:

> She was a rambling old lady, but she had a perfectly clear story to tell. Her story was that when the family property suffered depredation [as a consequence of her son's actions] she appealed to the Lord Mayor of Cork, and the Lord Mayor apparently, as head of the local Sinn Fein organisation, secured her some measure of redress and protection. Mrs Colthurst felt that, although she was not a sympathiser with Sinn Fein, it was her duty to say that the Lord Mayor had behaved well to her.

The official's surprise at this intercession is indicated by his comment 'I understand that all the Bowen-Colthursts are rather eccentric, but I think this lady is quite *compos mentis*.'[35] Despite the wave of representations, ministers refused to change their position at meetings on 25 August and 2 September. The implication was clear; MacSwiney would either stop or starve.[36]

As early as 20 August the leadership of Sinn Féin began to realize that this time the government would not submit to the threat of hunger strike. Art O'Brien, the leader of the Irish Self-Determination League, based in London, informed Michael Collins that his contacts at the Home Office believed that the government had 'definitely and finally decided that if any of the Irish prisoners persisted in the hunger strike, they were to be allowed to die in prison. If this decision really is adhered to, and I am afraid, from present appearances, that it will be, the situation will be very serious.'[37] On the afternoon of the same day, O'Brien's report appeared to acquire substance when he and Mary MacSwiney, Terence's sister, met Sir Ernley Blackwell, Under-Secretary of State at the Home Office. Blackwell insisted that they would not release Terence, while Mary was adamant that she would not encourage her brother to give up 'his principles'.[38] Meanwhile, at the prison, on the orders of Edward Shortt, the governor warned MacSwiney that he would not be released and that he alone would be responsible for the consequences if he persisted in hunger-striking.[39] MacSwiney's immediate reply was a letter to the Home Secretary in which he argued that Shortt would be responsible in the event of his death and 'knowing the revolution of opinion that will be thereby caused throughout the civilised world and the consequent accession of support to Ireland in her hour of trial, I am reconciled to a premature grave. I am prepared to die.'[40] Although MacSwiney and the strikers in Cork continued to hope for a change in the government's position, by early September the realization that the government was determined to stand firm caused them to accept the likelihood that they would die. On 8 September, one of the medical officers at Cork reported the prisoners' refusal to receive medical treatment, stating 'all wish to die and are prepared to die and have asked to be left alone'.[41] On the same day his colleague recorded in his diary: 'I now consider that the desire for Death is strongly marked in all.'[42]

It is important to remember that at this stage, almost a month in, the strikers had exceeded their doctors', their own, their families' and the press' estimations of their capacity to survive. As early as 19 August, Dr W.D. Higson, then medical officer at Brixton prison, described MacSwiney as seriously ill. On 29 August, Annie MacSwiney, Terence's other sister, sent a telegram to a friend in Cork, stating 'doctor says end may come any time'.[43] The Times reported on 30 August, and the Home Office recorded on 4 September, that he might 'die at any moment',[44] while the Freeman's Journal, on 3 September, reported that 'there are all the indications of death about the exhausted, helpless, heroic figure that lies on the prison bed'.[45] In Cork, D.J. Flynn, the medical officer, began describing the prisoners as in danger and recommending their release as early as 16 August; however, it should be acknowledged that Flynn's desire to relieve himself of the responsibility for these men probably influenced this judgement. C.J. MacCormack, the medical member of the General Prisons Board of Ireland, on the other hand, was certainly sincere in his assessment on 25 August when he reported that 'they are all in a decidedly critical state and have in my opinion reached the danger zone'.[46] The Freeman's Journal again reported on 31 August that four of the men – Burke, O'Reilly, Hennessy and Kenny – were 'on the point of death', and on 3 September. that for O'Reilly and Hennessy 'the end ... is at hand'.[47] Art O'Brien wrote to Collins from London on 4 September, describing MacSwiney's body as 'practically lifeless' although his mind was 'thoroughly alive and alert'. In recording that MacSwiney believed it would all be over within a week, O'Brien commented 'it seems extraordinary that he should have hope of lasting another week'.[48] Sir Edward Troup, Permanent Under-Secretary at the Home Office, initiated discussions on the disposal of MacSwiney's body on 8 September.[49] All continued to believe that his death was imminent right through September and into October,[50] but he did not die nor did his colleagues in Cork, transfixing their friends, family, supporters, the authorities, and the wider public in a gruesome 'death watch'.[51] Annie MacSwiney wrote to a friend on 21 September that Terence had commented: 'I never thought it could drag on so long – I am just dying by inches.'[52]

By September then, the question had changed from whether the men would die to what would be the manner and meaning of their deaths? Or to put it another way; the prisoners and their supporters were by then deeply concerned that their protest and likely deaths should be presented as good, honourable, and heroic – and if nothing else, death by inches gave them time to make their case – while the authorities were anxious to minimize any legitimization or glorification of the prisoners' fatal protest and the consequent propaganda impact.

A question which seemed to offer an immediate threat to the prospect of an honourable death, and it was a question that gained more and more currency as the strike persisted, was this: how are these men still alive? Surely some slight of hand must be involved. Especially, but not only, in the British press an element of incredulity and of the freak show crept into some of the coverage.[53] This was probably the result of a degree of boredom and, perhaps, some press management by the British government. In August, Dublin Castle had sought to improve its capacity to influence the press by establishing a Public Information Branch.[54] The *Globe*'s comments on 4 October were probably the most cynical:

> Mr McSwiney [*sic*], you understand, has had no food, no food at all, for fifty-two days – seven weeks and a half – and is still, if we may be allowed to use the expression, going strong. Nothing but pure cold water, or at any rate water as pure as they can get it in Brixton prison, has passed his resolute lips since the day when he fell into the hands of the base, bloody, brutal Saxon, and was clapped in gaol … If he can go, miraculously, without food for fifty-two days there does not seem to be any good for saying he cannot go the whole two years of his sentence, and it would be a pity if the British Government were to deprive him of the glory attending to a manifestation so remarkable.[55]

The MacSwiney family, never a clan to shy away from inferring dishonourable intent on the part of the British, first complained of English papers that 'deliberately misconstrue the truth'[56] and later alleged that there existed a 'deliberate campaign of misrepresentation and falsehood engineered by the English Government'. They cut contact with the English press in late September (rarely a tactic that pays dividends), but continued, of course, to communicate with the Irish and international press.[57]

This issue had also arisen in Cork. On 13 September, the *Freeman's Journal* took a report from Hugh Martin, a correspondent for the English newspaper the *Daily News*. Martin was regarded as critical of British policy in Ireland and knowledgeable about Sinn Féin.[58] He had just been to Cork prison where he had interviewed Alan C. Pearson and E.A. Battiscombe, the two Home Office doctors then 'in charge'. Pearson and Battiscombe, worried by death threats from the IRA, had one key message that they wanted to communicate. Martin wrote: 'they assured me on their professional honour that no nourishment or stimulant of any sort is being administered to the prisoners' and continued, 'Four nuns of the Bon Secours are in constant attendance, and near relatives are also admitted, but close observation by the doctors has convinced them that the men are taking nothing but pure water. I emphasise this fact because of the rumours that the prisoners are being secretly fed.'[59] Two days later the medical officers reiterated this in a report to the General Prisons Board, stating that the Reverend Mother of the assisting nuns had expressed 'extreme annoyance' at the 'unjust innuendos', and asked that they be publicly contradicted.[60] When the rumours persisted, the hunger strikers and their relatives requested that an independent medical man might be allowed to examine them. Pearson and Battiscombe 'welcomed' this proposal,[61] but the request was refused, renewed, and refused on a number of occasions.[62] It was these rumours that Griffith implicitly addressed when he asserted in his letter that signalled the end of the strike that 'those whom England advertises as criminals ... are Irishmen whose patriotism is proof against torture and death'.[63]

If the government had denied the allegation of secret feeding when asked to do so in mid-September, then the denial would probably have been true. However, such a denial would not have been true at all times during the strikes. There is no evidence that the strikers' families or supporters, either in Brixton or in Cork, secretly fed them. In the middle of September, the day nurse at Brixton did report that MacSwiney's personal chaplain, Fr Dominic, dissolved a tablet in a spoon of water and administered this to him each morning and the authorities did begin to suspect that MacSwiney's relatives were secretly feeding him.[64] When they found a substance in the glass in which MacSwiney washed his teeth, the Home Office had it tested (it was soap) and they tested his faeces on 19 October, but again the results revealed 'nothing'.[65] The authorities themselves did, however, contemplate secretly feeding the prisoners. In the first days of MacSwiney's strike, Andrew Bonar Law raised the possibility of surreptitiously introducing vitamins into his water, but Higson rejected the strategy as too high risk. Anything that was likely to be of use in sustaining MacSwiney would carry a taste and if MacSwiney suspected he was being fed, Higson believed, he would stop drinking as well as eating.[66] In early October, Dr O.F.N. Treadwell, the medical inspector of prisons, affirmed this position.[67] Cork was a different matter. On 26 August, Mark Sturgis noted in his diary: 'The Cork boys are getting albumen in their water – they don't know it but they should not die just yet.'[68] Two days later he recorded that 'the Amazing Ass who is RAMC doctor at Cork has put into his report that the hungry there were having albumen in their water – as all these things leak of course it has got round to them and they have now "waterstruck" too, so it had to be discontinued as it was done only on the quiet – damn him!'[69] This obviously informed the Cork prisoners' subsequent reluctance to receive any treatment from medical officers, and their plea to be left alone to die.

For MacSwiney, the fear that his integrity, the authenticity of his good death, would be sullied by the consumption of any sustenance became a pressing issue at the very end. In August, officials at the Home Office and English Prison Commission had decided that their best hope of sustaining MacSwiney was that he 'reached a state of mind [by which they meant delirium] at which he would swallow liquid food under persuasion'.[70] At this time, Higson mentioned to MacSwiney and his relatives that he would consider feeding MacSwiney if the point arrived that 'the prisoner was too weak to resist'. This called forth what Higson characterized as 'an hysterical outburst' from Mary who 'regarded it as merely a way of prolonging life'.[71] In the last week of MacSwiney's protest relations between the authorities and the family deteriorated as these issues arose. He developed scurvy, prompting his doctors to urge him to take some lime or orange juice. He refused, stating that if he did 'the scurrilous Press egged on by the Government' would say he was taking food, and he was supported in this by Mary who argued that his taking juice would be misrepresented because 'you English all tell lies from the Government downwards'.[72]

On the next day, 19 October, G.B. Griffiths, the doctor then in charge, reported that MacSwiney became 'black angry' with him when he tried to persuade him to take juice. According to Annie MacSwiney, Griffiths had threatened to make Terence take the juice and MacSwiney had responded by threatening to 'give up swallowing everything'. In her view, this incident was fatal as it excited her brother to such an extent that it pushed him towards delirium.[73] In the succeeding days relations between the family and the doctors collapsed entirely because when MacSwiney slipped into unconsciousness the doctors began to give him food. Griffiths recorded that the family accused him of 'only prolonging the torture' whereas he explained that they were acting as they had informed MacSwiney they would weeks earlier.[74] According to Annie, Terence became extraordinarily agitated when, in lucid moments, he realized that he had been fed:

> 'They tricked me, they tricked me, how did they do it? How did they do it?' And then he went off again into delirium striking out again with his hands at both sides of the bed. As a result all the stuff they gave him came up again, and it was agonizing to see the added pain and struggle it all meant to him.[75]

The doctors came to believe that Annie was inciting this resistance, while they consistently felt the lash of Mary's tongue. This was Shortt's experience also; when he commented on the matter in parliament, Mary accused him of misrepresenting MacSwiney's action as the voluntary consumption of food, alleging: 'of all the infamies possible to an individual, or a government, that of lying about an unconscious victim, who for the time being, is in their power, is the most vile'.[76]

The doctors' final role in the cases of the hunger strikers was to give evidence at the inquest or, as was the case for Fitzgerald and Murphy, at the military inquiries held *in lieu* of inquests after their deaths. These were fora where the authorities attempted to disrupt the narrative of a good death that the men and their supporters wished to construct. It was at these inquiries that the cause of the strikers' death was officially established and in each case the authorities were determined that a verdict of suicide should be returned. The courts of military inquiry obliged – in both instances returning the verdict that the striker had 'feloniously kill[ed] himself'.[77] In the case of MacSwiney, the authorities had an extra motivation to secure a verdict of suicide. Under English prison law this would have allowed them to bury the body, thus depriving the family and Sinn Féin of an enormous propaganda funeral. The jury did not oblige, simply finding, in accordance with the medical evidence, that MacSwiney 'died from heart failure and acute delirium following scurvy, due to exhaustion from prolonged refusal to take food'.[78]

If the authorities were anxious to present these deaths as suicide then the hunger strikers and their supporters presented them as exemplary Christian deaths. In the nationalist newspapers the reports of the men's final hours emphasized their faith and piety in their last moments. The *Irish Independent*'s account of Fitzgerald's *hors mori* was particularly comprehensive in this regard. It told that as death approached, four priests and four nuns gathered around his bed. Friends and families of the prisoners assembled within the prison, and hundreds more gathered outside. The following passage gives a clear sense of the occasion, of the impression they sought to create, and of its impact:

> In the bare whitewashed apartment the priests and nuns knelt about the bed. From a table close by two candles lit on either side of the Crucifix threw their light across the pallid form breathing painfully in the last hour of life. Outside in the passage and at the door friends murmured the responses to the prayers for the dying.
>
> At 9.15 pm the voices of the many hundreds outside the prison gates answering their Rosary could be faintly heard. At about 9.30 the singing of the hymns could be heard more clearly still. There was a silence and the crowds without could be heard moving away. Then Fr Fitzgerald [the prison chaplain] began the recital of the third Rosary within the cell.
>
> One of the Bon Secour Sisters, who had been as angels of mercy and comfort to the dying man, took the Crucifix, and held it to the poor sufferer's lips. He seemed to know, and kissed it devoutly.
>
> The Rosary continued and as it did it was noticed the breathing was becoming more and more laboured, the face twitched somewhat, and when the second decade had been reached a look of repose came over the pale, worn face, and everything ceased.
>
> The Sister turned around to the kneeling group. She did not speak. There was a quiet resigned look on her face. Everyone understood. They knew the end had come. The Rosary begun for one in his last moments concluded for the peace and happiness of a noble soul now beyond the reach of pain and suffering.[79]

It seems clear that the piety ascribed here to the striker and his supporters was genuine, but it is also evident that the public projection of this image through the press was calculated, and that it was crucial to the overall portrayal of the hunger strikers as men of deep faith, and the strike as a quasi-religious act. In the case of Murphy the *Irish Independent* reported that 'while the Litany of the Sacred Heart, to which the intrepid prisoner had a great devotion, was being recited by Father Fitzgerald another soul left its earthly tenement to join the spirits of those who died that their country might be free'.[80] Similarly, MacSwiney's final hour, as described by Fr Dominic and recorded by various newspapers, constituted an unmistakable version of a good, Christian death. Having completed the prayers for the dying and the rosary, Dominic stated that 'I again approached the bedside and continued the prayers from the ritual, "Subvenite Sanotia Dei. [Subvenite, Sancti Dei, – Saints of God, come to his aid]". Just as I had finished the Antiphon the Lord Mayor breathed his last.'[81]

Having achieved such a death, it was desirable that the presiding priest should be a willing public advocate for the deceased. MacSwiney certainly had such a priest in Fr Dominic, while Fr Fitzgerald, at Cork prison, also appears to have been supportive of the prisoners. The press reported that Fitzgerald and the assistant chaplain, Fr Duggan, were prominent when Murphy's remains were transferred from the prison to his local church.[82] Such support could not be taken for granted. During the strike at Wormwood Scrubs in May 1920, the Catholic chaplain in Wormwood Scrubs, Fr Musgrave, had experienced 'qualms of conscience with reference to giving the sacraments to the men who were on hunger strike', but he was persuaded to relent.[83] During the hunger strike at Mountjoy in April 1920 the authority figures within the prison who were most consistent in their opposition to the strike were the prison chaplains, led by Fr John Waters. As a consequence of the chaplains' efforts to persuade the men off the strike, using the threat of damnation, Liam Gogan, a prisoner in Mountjoy at the time though not on hunger strike, described them as a 'rotten lot', 'false shepards', and 'only the hirelings of Dublin Castle'. Todd Andrews, who was on that strike, remembered that the 'chaplain was the only one of the prison staff who kept his nerve and did his duty, although in our estimation "doing his duty" was merely doing the dirty work required by his British employers'. According to Andrews, the prisoners were sufficiently bolstered against this by the knowledge that the wider Irish public felt that their actions were morally justified.[84]

As the differing approaches of the priests implies, before, during and after the Cork and Brixton strike, the morality of the hunger strike was contested publicly. On 9 September, the Irish press carried Mary MacSwiney's vigorous defence of the morality of her brother's actions. This was a direct response to the public suggestions of a well-known English Jesuit, Father Bernard Vaughan, that the sacraments should be denied to the hunger strikers, and it was characteristically trenchant.[85] MacSwiney made a brief, blunt theological defence of hunger strike and asked 'how then, can any one be so stupid, or so malicious, as to suggest that the Lord Mayor of Cork, or any other man in a similar state, for the sake of a great principle is guilty of self-murder'.[86] This was not an isolated incident. There was a good deal of diplomatic activity in Rome as some senior English diplomats and ecclesiastics sought a 'condemnation of hunger-striking by the Holy See', which sparked a determined and successful defensive campaign by sympathizers with the Irish cause.[87] Extensive contemporary debates on the morality of hunger strike took place in theological and clerical journals (to which John Waters regularly contributed), in the press, and beyond.[88] Although many Catholic churches facilitated masses and vigils for the strikers, this was not always so.[89] Archbishop William Walsh of Dublin received complaints when Monsignor Dunne, the parish priest of Donnybrook, refused to make his church available for regular Masses in support of MacSwiney.[90] As a Quaker, Rosamond Jacob was perhaps not as susceptible to the already burgeoning martyr cult as others, but her diary entry on the news of MacSwiney's death probably reflected the private thoughts of many Irish nationalists: 'I can hardly think of anything braver that was ever done, but I'm not sure about the rightness of hunger strikes always.'[91]

So it was not just the arguments of the British authorities that the prisoners and their supporters aimed to counteract as they sought to set at rest their own minds and those of others. On 9 September at Cork prison, one of the strikers, Thomas Donovan, sought reassurance, asking 'that the Pope should be communicated with in regard to giving him his blessing'.[92] In his statement to the Bureau of Military History, Michael V. O'Donoghue recalled that the crowds that gathered outside Cork prison in this period developed a nightly habit of singing the hymn 'Faith of Our Fathers'. This had the purpose, in O'Donoghue's opinion, of banishing 'any conscientious scruples or theological misgivings which the hunger strikers within may have had about their deliberate abstention from food even to death'.[93] Throughout, MacSwiney appears to have been confident of the morality of his actions, but many of the statements attributed to him during the course of the strike seem designed to emphasize his piety and thereby reassure any doubters.[94] On 1 September, Father Dominic told the press that MacSwiney had asked him to convey a message: 'I wish that those who are praying for my release would include in their intentions an appeal to Almighty God to grant me the grace of a happy death and the strength to endure my sufferings in the final hour.' The *Irish Independent*'s report concluded that MacSwiney's 'only interests now are preparation for death and news from his fellow-sufferers in Cork Jail'.[95]

Just as it was important to demonstrate that the strikers' actions were honest and that they were pious, it was crucial that their deaths should be presented as patriotic and manly. Consequently, very often, piety and patriotism were wedded in the presentation of events. This is true of a statement released to mark the fortieth day of the strike – a moment of obvious significance to those religiously minded. MacSwiney, speaking on behalf of his colleagues at Cork also, included the paragraph: 'we forgive all those who are encompassing our death. This battle is fought with a clean pure heart purely for our country. We have made our peace with God, and bear illwill to no man.'[96] The fifty-seventh day of the strike was the occasion of another statement; this one took the form of a message to his colleagues in Cork asking them to join him in prayer, a prayer that concluded:

I offer everything Thou askest for Ireland's resurrection; it is Thy Will. Accept our willing sacrifice for our people. May we in dying bring glory to Thy Name, and honour to our Country that has always been faithful to Thee. We rely on Thy Mercy to sustain us in the last moment for the constancy of our martyred people, and the redemption of our Country. God Save Ireland! God save, bless, and guard the Irish Republic to live and flourish and be a model of Government of Truth and Justice to all Nations. May the liberty of the Irish People shine with Thy Glory, oh my God! for ever and ever. Amen.[97]

Dying in a prison hospital was not, however, an obvious example of soldierly patriotism: indeed it may seem to offer all of the downside with none of the glory. In response, sympathizers sought to present MacSwiney's death as an exemplary patriotic death. On 3 September, while MacSwiney was still alive, the *Freeman's Journal* printed a poem by A.E. in which he became a model for all of how to 'go to death alone, slowly and unafraid'.[98] Francis P. Donnelly, a Jesuit, also addressed this concern in 'He Taught us how to Die', which emerged soon after the events. In the ballad, Donnelly took various archetypes of patriotic death, beginning with death in battle, and found them all wanting when compared to MacSwiney's:

In flaming fight when man his man is facing
And down the line ten thousand madly cheer

311

When through his veins the blood goes hotly racing
Then, death forgotten loses all its fear.
But let the strife through months of anguish lengthen
And all be silence save our lonely sigh,
Be with us God, our frightened soul to strengthen
'Twas so MacSwiney taught us how to die.

Oh! all too swift was Barry's sacred scaffold
And swift the guns their gifts to Plunkett sped
And hurried graves have often tyrants baffled
When Ireland calls to fame her patriot dead
But here was one who clung to death's embraces,
Who, drop by drop, let all his life go by;
Dark Rosaleen, how queenly are thy graces,
For thee, he dared death's longest death to die.[99]

In the cases of both MacSwiney and Murphy, former colleagues have suggested that these men's determination in pursuing their hunger strikes derived, at least in part, from a desire to make amends for past failings or to 'purge' alleged misdemeanours that might have sullied their reputations as patriots.[100]

In emphasizing MacSwiney's patriotism his family and supporters brought another element of the good death into play: the last words. Writing about the importance of last words to the families and communities of those soldiers who died during the American Civil War, Gilpin Faust has noted that great weight was placed on these because it was believed that the dying used this opportunity to tell the truth and because last words 'imposed meaning on the life narrative they concluded and communicated invaluable lessons' to those left behind.[101] MacSwiney's final words, as regularly recounted in the press, were 'I am dying as a soldier of the Irish Republic. God Save Ireland.'[102] Given that his death had been long anticipated and closely watched, he had had a number of rehearsals. Under the headline 'Patriot's Dying Message', the *Freeman's Journal* of 31 August recounted how MacSwiney expressed the hope that 'my death may be of greater service to the Irish Republic than the whole of my life's work'.[103]

Reports of Fitzgerald's and Murphy's deaths were also decorated with manly, martial adjectives and phrases. Upon Fitzgerald's death the *Irish Independent* described him as one of 'the gallant band of hunger strikers in Cork jail', but more than that he was an IRA officer and as such, the *Independent* continued, he had 'acted the part of leader with extraordinary courage and fortitude ... A man of brave and robust physique, he battled bravely for the first seven weeks of the strike, and when the strength of some of the other and more youthful prisoners gave way he still held up and encouraged by his word and example.'[104] Instead of last words from Murphy, the *Meath Chronicle* quoted his father: 'I am proud that my son Joseph died for Ireland … If he had been a criminal I would hang my head … but now I can walk with my head erect through Cork.'[105]

Gilpin Faust begins her book by acknowledging the shared human experience of death, before warning that 'death has its discontinuities as well. Men and women approach death in ways shaped by history, by their culture, by conditions that vary over time and across space. Even though "we all have our dead", and even though we all die, we do so differently from generation to generation and from place to place.'[106] Terence MacSwiney, Michael Fitzgerald and Joseph Murphy died in a certain way at a certain time, and they, their families, their friends and their supporters were conscious of this. The manner in which MacSwiney has dominated this story for posterity to the exclusion of the other strikers is bound up with the unmistakably successful efforts made by him, those around him at the time, and others since, to use these circumstances to create a martyr. The representation of his death was obviously an important element in this. On the day after he died, a cartoon in the *Freeman's Journal* by Shemus depicted Lloyd George and a figure – perhaps Hibernia, perhaps death – standing at the door of MacSwiney's prison cell as the figure tells Lloyd George: 'Hush, little man. You know how to live, but my concern is with one greater than you – one who knows how to die.'[107]

It would be a mistake, however, to focus on the work of martyr creation to the exclusion of the other, more immediate, purposes that the hunger strikers, their families and the nationalist movement had as they attempted to shape perceptions of the deaths. In seeking to ensure that these deaths were seen as good deaths, they attempted to influence how these men would be remembered. And, indeed, to influence what would be forgotten. But in returning to these men's efforts to achieve a good death and by placing these efforts in detailed context, it becomes clear that their primary audiences were contemporaries. They wanted to establish that the strikers' protest was honest because it was suggested otherwise. They trumpeted the Christian character of the deaths because the strikers faced the charge that their deaths were not Christian deaths, and emphasized that dying on hunger strike was a manly, patriotic manifestation of death precisely because it did not conform to the contemporary models for such a death. As they did this, the manner in which future generations of nationalists, never mind how historians, might regard them, mattered a whole lot less than their worries about how the doctors were treating the strikers, whether priests would minister to them, whether the strikers could reconcile themselves to the death that faced them, and whether their families and communities would approve, or at least not disapprove publicly, of their actions. Those who have been created martyrs eventually come to exist outside of time, part of an ahistorical tradition or elite. It is important to remember, however, that these men died but once and in very particular circumstances.

NOTES

1 Drew Gilpin Faust, *This Republic of Suffering: Death and the American Civil War* (New York, 2008), pp.3–31.
2 *Anglo-Celt*, 6 Nov. 1920.
3 Report of Publicity Department to Dáil Éireann, 18 Jan. 1921 (NLI, Kathleen McKenna Napoli papers, MS 22609).
4 Report of Dr G.B. Griffiths, Medical Officer (MO) at Brixton prison, 25 Oct. 1920 (TNA, HO144/10308).
5 Joseph King, governor of Cork prison, to Max S. Green, chairman of the General Prisons Board of Ireland (GPB), 10 Aug. 1920 (NAI, GPB1920/6651).
6 Phone call from Cork prison, 13 Aug. 1920 (NAI, GPB1920/6639); Weekly survey of the state of Ireland, 23 Aug. 1920 (TNA, CAB27/108); *Irish Times*, 16, 18 Aug. 1920.
7 Michael Hopkinson (ed.), *The Last Days of Dublin Castle: the Diaries of Mark Sturgis* (Dublin: Irish Academic Press, 1999), p.24.
8 For biographical information on Fitzgerald, see Peter Hart, *The I.R.A. and its Enemies: Violence and Community in Cork, 1916–1923* (Oxford: Oxford University Press, 1998), pp.248–9.
9 D. O'Donoghue, chief warder Cork prison, to Green, 29, 30 Sept. 1919 (NAI, GPBHS folder 1920/207–286).
10 Medical Officers' report (Alan C. Pearson and E.A. Battiscombe), 18 Oct. 1920 (NAI, GPB1920/9001).
11 Medical Officers' Report (Alan C. Pearson and E.A. Battiscombe), 18 Oct. 1920 (NAI, GPB1920/9002).
12 *Irish Independent*, 26 Oct. 1920; *Freeman's Journal*, 26 Oct. 1920.
13 GPB minute of phone call from Pearson and Battiscombe, 25 Oct.1920 (NAI, GPB1920/9378).
14 *Irish Independent*, 13 Nov. 1920.
15 Seán McConville, *Irish Political Prisoners, 1848–1922: Theatres Of War* (London: Routledge, 2003), pp.650–1.
16 Seán Ó Lúing, *I Die in a Good Cause* (Tralee, 1970).
17 *Daily Express*, 28 Feb. 1918.
18 *Hansard 5 (House of Commons)*, ciii, pp.746–7, 20 Feb. 1918; Sir William Byrne, Under-Secretary of State for Ireland, to Green, 22, 23, 27 Feb. 1918, 'File (F) re Hunger Striking' (NAI, GPBDORA Box 2).
19 Memorandum by Chief Secretary on the condition of Ireland, 22 Mar. 1918 (Bodleian, Library, H.E. Duke papers, Dep c.717).
20 Major A.F. Owen Lewis to Green, 17 Aug. 1912 (NAI, GPB Suffragette files, folder 17, Box 3).
21 *Irish Times*, 10 June 1915.
22 Police Intelligence Report (TNA, CO904/23 Part 3B); *Irish Independent*, 24 Sept. 1917.
23 Evidence of Laurence O'Neill, 27 Sept. 1917 in Minutes of the inquest of Thomas Ashe (NAI, DE 2/507).
24 Michael Brennan to Madge Daly, 5 Mar. 1918 (University of Limerick, Daly papers, P2/8(3)).
25 David Fitzpatrick, *Politics and Irish life, 1913–1921: Provincial Experience of War and Revolution* (Cork: Cork University Press, 1998), pp.124–5.

26 Mary Brennan, to governor of Mountjoy, 26 Sept. 1917, 'File (A) re Prison Treatment of DORA prisoners, June to Oct 1917' (NAI, GPBDORA Box 1).
27 *Freeman's Journal*, 11 May 1920; *Irish Independent*, 12, 13 May 1920.
28 These were William Thomas Halpin, Christopher Brady, Jack O'Reilly, and Thomas Stokes: see Seán O'Mahony, *Frongoch: University of Revolution* (Dublin: FDR Teoranta, 1987), pp.110–1.
29 Francis J. Costello, *Enduring the Most: The Life and Death of Terence MacSwiney* (Dingle: Brandon Books, 1995), p.149.
30 GPB minute of phone call from Cork prison, 17 Aug. 1920 (NAI, GPB1920/6720).
31 Mark Sturgis acknowledged on 20 August that this probably was the hunger strikers' belief: Hopkinson, *The Last Days of Dublin Castle*, p.25.
32 Minutes of Cabinet, 25 Aug. 1920 (TNA, CAB23/22).
33 Hopkinson, *The Last Days of Dublin Castle*, p.31.
34 George V to Home Office, 25 Aug. 1920, Shortt to George V, 26 Aug. 1920 (TNA, HO144/10308).
35 Home Office minute to Sir Basil Thomson, 30 Aug. 1920 (TNA, HO144/10308).
36 Minutes of Cabinet, 2 Sept. 1920 (TNA, CAB23/22).
37 Art O'Brien to Michael Collins, 20 Aug. 1920 (TNA, DE2/4).
38 Minute of meeting between Sir Ernley Blackwell, and O'Brien and Mary MacSwiney, 20 Aug. 1920 (TNA, HO144/10308).
39 Note by Blackwell, 20 Aug. 1920 (TNA, HO144/10308).
40 Terence MacSwiney to Edward Shortt, 20 Aug. 1920 (TNA, HO144/10308).
41 E.A. Battiscombe to Dr O.F.N. Treadwell, Medical Inspector of Prisons, 8 Sept. 1920 (TNA, HO144/1633/408763).
42 Diary of A.C. Pearson, 8 Sept. 1920 (TCD, MS 4043).
43 Annie MacSwiney, Belgrave Place, London, to Pauline Henley, Cork, 29 Aug. 1920 (CAI, MacSwiney-Henley correspondence, U207).
44 *Times*, 30 Aug. 1921; Home Office minute, 4 Sept. 1920 (TNA, HO144/10308).
45 *Freeman's Journal*, 3 Sept. 1920.
46 C.J. MacCormack, medical member of the GPB, to Sir John Anderson, Under-Secretary of State for Ireland, 25 Aug. 1920 (NAI, GPB1920/7037).
47 *Freeman's Journal*, 31 Aug., 3 Sept. 1920.
48 O'Brien to Collins, 4 Sept. 1920 (NAI, DE2/4).
49 Sir Edward Troup to Sir John P. Mellor, solicitor, Department of H.M. Prosecutor General and of the Solicitor to the Treasury, 8 Sept. 1920 (TNA, HO144/10308).
50 See daily medical reports on MacSwiney's condition (TNA, HO144/10308).
51 Peter Hart, *Mick: the Real Michael Collins* (London: Macmillan, 2005), p.222.
52 Annie MacSwiney to Pauline Henley, 21, 25 Sept. 1920 (CAI, MacSwiney-Henley correspondence, U207).
53 *Morning Post*, 13 Oct. 1920.
54 Maurice Walsh, *The News from Ireland: Foreign Correspondents and the Irish Revolution* (London: I.B. Tauris, 2008), pp.122–3.
55 *Globe*, 4 Oct. 1920.
56 *Freeman's Journal*, 10 Sept. 1920.
57 Statement to the press by Muriel, Mary, Annie and John MacSwiney, 24 Sept. 1920 (CPM, Terence MacSwiney material, L1955:8).
58 Walsh, *The News from Ireland*, pp.63–5, 73–5.
59 *Freeman's Journal*, 13 Sept. 1920.
60 Pearson and Battiscombe, 15 Sept. 1920, and C. J. MacCormack to Sir John Anderson, 15 Sept. 1920 (NAI, GPB1920/7800).
61 King to Green, 5 Oct. 1920 (NAI, GPB1920/8487); GPB minute of phone call from Cork prison, 5 Oct. 1920 (NAI, GPB1920/8490).
62 GPB minute of phone call from Cork prison, 7 Oct. 1920 (NAI, GPB1920/8569); GPB minute of phone call from Cork prison, 12 Oct. 1920 (NAI, GPB1920/8772).
63 *Irish Independent*, 13 Nov. 1920.
64 Griffiths to the Prison Commissioners, 20 Sept. 1920, and Treadwell to Troup, 4 Oct. 1920 (TNA, PCOM8/349).
65 John Webster (senior official analyst to the Home Office) to Troup, 13, 19 Oct. 1920 (TNA, HO144/10308).

66 Davidson to Maxwell, 20 Aug. 1920 (TNA, HO 144/10308); Maxwell to Davidson, 23 Aug. 1920 (TNA, HO144/10308).
67 Treadwell to Troup, 4 Oct. 1920 (TNA, PCOM8/349).
68 Hopkinson, *The Last Days of Dublin Castle*, p.29.
69 Ibid., p.30.
70 Minute of meeting attended by Shortt, Blackwell, Troup, Treadwell, Higson, Dr Maurice Craig and Dr Beddard, 26 Aug. 1920 (TNA, HO144/10308).
71 Minute of meeting between Higson, Treadwell, and Blackwell, 24 Aug.1920 (TNA, HO144/10308).
72 Report of Griffiths on condition of Terence MacSwiney, 18 Oct. 1920 (TNA, HO144/10308).
73 Ibid.; 'Outside Brixton Prison' by Annie MacSwiney (CPM, Terence MacSwiney material, L.1955:118).
74 Report of Griffiths on condition of Terence MacSwiney, 21 Oct. 1920 (TNA, HO144/10308).
75 'Outside Brixton Prison' by Annie MacSwiney (CPM, Terence MacSwiney material, L.1955:118).
76 Mary MacSwiney to Edward Shortt, 22 Oct. 1920 (TNA, HO144/10308).
77 *Irish Times*, 20, 28 Oct. 1920.
78 *Freeman's Journal*, 28 Oct. 1920.
79 *Irish Independent*, 19 Oct. 1920.
80 *Irish Independent*, 26 Oct. 1920.
81 *Nenagh Guardian*, 30 Oct. 1920.
82 *Freeman's Journal*, 27 Oct. 1920. For further evidence of Fr Duggan's sympathies during the strike, see NAI, BMH WS 435 (Tadhg Crowley).
83 Initialled memo from London, 17 May 1920 (NAI, DE2/135).
84 Notebook titled 'The Affair of the Ashtown Ballad', and Notebooks 6 and 7, 'An Account of the Hunger Strike in Mountjoy, Easter 1920' (NLI, W. J. Gogan papers, MSS 41,633–4); C.S. Andrews, *Dublin Made Me* (Dublin: Lilliput Press, 2001), p.154.
85 *Irish Independent*, 9 Sept. 1920.
86 Press release (UCDA, MacSwiney papers, P48b/436).
87 NAI, BMH, WS 687: iii (Monsignor Michael Curran).
88 P.J. Gannon, 'The Ethical Aspect of the Hunger Strike', *Studies*, 9 (1920), pp.448–54; J. Kelleher, 'The Lawfulness of the Hunger Strike', *The Irish Theological Quarterly*, 16:61 (Jan. 1921), pp.47–64; John Waters, 'The Lawfulness of the Hunger Strike: a Reply', *The Irish Theological Quarterly*, 16:62 (Apr. 1921), pp.130–46.
89 *Weekly Irish Times*, 28 Aug. 1920; *Freeman's Journal*, 3 Sept. 1920.
90 Committee of parishioners, Donnybrook, to Archbishop William Walsh, 10 Sept. 1920 (DDA, Walsh papers, 380/4 (1920, laity)).
91 Rosamond Jacob diaries, 25 Oct. 1920 (NLI, Rosamond Jacob papers, MS 32582 (37)).
92 GPB minute of phone call from Cork prison, 9 Sept. 1920 (NAI, GPB1920/7616); Medical notes on T. Donovan in diary of A.C. Pearson, Cork, 1920 (TCD, MS 4043).
93 NAI, BMH, WS 1741 (Michael V. O'Donoghue).
94 Report of Dr W.D. Higson on condition of Terence MacSwiney, 29 Aug. 1920 (TNA, PCOM8/349).
95 *Irish Independent*, 1 Sept. 1920.
96 Press Release (UCDA, MacSwiney papers, P48b/435).
97 Press Release (UCDA, MacSwiney papers, P48B/437).
98 *Freeman's Journal*, 3 Sept. 1920.
99 *Irish Monthly*, 50:585 (Mar. 1922), p.93.
100 NAI, BMH, WS 939 (Ernest Blythe); WS 1741 (Michael V. O'Donoghue). In MacSwiney's case, it has been suggested he sought to make amends for a number of misjudgements in 1916 including not rising in rebellion.
101 Gilpin Faust, *This Republic of Suffering*, p.10.
102 *Freeman's Journal*, 26 Oct. 1920.
103 *Freeman's Journal*, 31 Aug. 1920.
104 *Irish Independent*, 19 Oct. 1920.
105 *Meath Chronicle*, 30 Oct. 1920.
106 Gilpin Faust, *This Republic of Suffering*, p.xi.
107 *Freeman's Journal*, 26 Oct. 1920.

13

PROBLEMATIC KILLING DURING THE WAR OF INDEPENDENCE AND ITS AFTERMATH: CIVILIAN SPIES AND INFORMERS

EUNAN O'HALPIN

Introduction

This essay discusses IRA killing of alleged civilian spies and informers during the War of Independence and its aftermath. Such deaths form a discrete category in Irish political conflict in these years. The data were initially gathered as part of the Irish Research Council for the Humanities and Social Sciences-funded project *The Dead of the Irish Revolution* (DOIR). The DOIR project aims were, first, to ascertain how many people died and by whose hand; and, second, to establish the pattern of deaths during the independence struggle and the succeeding months up to December 1921.

The sources used for DOIR, and their limitations, have recently been outlined in some detail.[1] Here I will add only that political killing did not stop on the day of the Anglo-Irish Truce, 11 July 1921. It continued at a reduced pace, often barely noticed at national level, until the outbreak of civil war at the end of June 1922; fatalities, civilian as well as combatant, then grew very considerably. The DOIR research is ongoing, and the data up to 31 December 1921, while reasonably accurate, are still provisional. This is particularly so as regards attribution of responsibility for the deaths of alleged spies. Some killers left no calling cards; others masqueraded as their opponents in order to disguise their own responsibility for murder.

Counties are treated as equals irrespective of population numbers and physical scale. The Irish county, rather than smaller or larger units such as towns or provinces, remains the default focus of popular loyalty and local history. Note the titles of the first major tranche of local histories that the Irish revolution produced – the 'Fighting Stories' series published by *The Kerryman* newspaper in the 1940s.[2] The same approach is reflected in more recent published local studies, even where their coverage sensibly breaches county boundaries to reflect IRA brigade theatres of operation.[3]

The IRA's treatment of alleged spies must be considered in terms of the fact that republicans saw the War of Independence as one where British forces engaged in a campaign of systematic terror, murder and despoliation. We also have empirical evidence on how the British military and police operated. We know that Crown forces were definitely responsible for more civilian deaths (381) than were the IRA (281); and further, we know that, quite apart from additional killings by disguised police or military 'murder gangs' in areas such as east County Cork, and counties Galway, Limerick, Louth, Roscommon and Tipperary, a large number of civilians died at Crown hands in very dubious circumstances. In 1922, the War Office calculated that from September 1920 onwards just over three hundred people had been lawfully killed by Crown forces either for refusing to halt when ordered to do so (249), or while 'attempting to escape' (fifty-seven). Just fifty-six of these killings arose in ambushes, and the great majority of those civilians killed by Crown forces were acknowledged to have been non-combatants.[4]

Reservations and remorse about the killing of civilian spies were sometimes expressed in the individual recollections and testimonies of IRA veterans interviewed by the Bureau of Military History (BMH), quietly challenging the public orthodoxy that anyone killed by the IRA had received their just desserts after due process. This is less so in County Cork, where far more civilians were killed as spies by the IRA, than elsewhere. During the Truce, the IRA's Cork No. 1 Brigade responded very strongly to efforts made to establish the whereabouts of various members of British forces and civilians believed to have been abducted and killed: 'Those shot during the war [are] not to be inquired into as they are all spies in this area.'[5] Perhaps not coincidentally, that brigade killed by far the largest number of alleged civilian spies, as well as some captured Crown forces. Cork No. 1 Brigade also secretly killed and buried an unascertainable number of people whose identities remain unknown and who are not included in the figures for fatalities under analysis here, both before and after the Truce.[6] The general problem presented by such as yet unverifiable killings is discussed separately towards the end of this essay.

The Bureau of Military History, established in 1947 to collect documentary and oral evidence about the period from 1913 to 1921, prepared a rough chronology of events, based largely on newspaper reports, as a guide for its investigators as they went about their business. The introduction to the chronology observed:

> Among the civilians who were killed there were a number whose bodies were found bearing a label with the word 'spy' or similar inscription. It is understood that the implication in many such cases was unfounded.[7]

This was an early and courageous official acknowledgement that on occasion civilians had been killed as spies by the IRA, either in error or through malice during the independence struggle. It deserves more consideration than it has received. It not only touched an ethical and moral sore point for the republican movement, but challenged one of the key foundations of the traditional revolutionary narrative: that, other than through accidents and mishaps, the IRA, in contrast to its British military, Ulster loyalist, and police enemies, had conducted a campaign which was law-bound, targeted and proportionate.

Historians mownust approach accounts of individual deaths with care. As has been powerfully illustrated by Anne Dolan and Jane Leonard in discussing the shooting of alleged British intelligence officers in Dublin on the morning of Bloody Sunday, 21 November 1920, any individual violent death is brutal and arbitrary. Dead men leave behind them traumatized families, unpaid bills, unanswered letters, and their futures. Blood, brain matter, torn flesh, remorse or the lack of it, are everywhere. The killers are marked forever, whether they realize it or not, by the horror they wrought. The same is true of the murders that same night of Dick McKee and Peadar Clancy, of which I have published a gruesome account.[8] But we must remember that some of those British officers who died defenceless in the hallways or bedrooms of Georgian Dublin were, like McKee and Clancy who had helped to plan their deaths, at war. The same is true for some of those civilians who died as spies and informers. The pathos of their personal circumstances or the horror of their individual deaths has nothing to do with whether they were spies or not.

Determining who was responsible for killing civilians branded as spies is not straightforward. Members of Crown forces who murdered civilians sometimes attempted to conceal responsibility by leaving notices saying 'Spies beware: IRA' or the like. IRA GHQ (General Headquarters) alluded to this practice in a circular to units in April 1921. One such case was probably that of Thomas McKeever, pulled from his lodgings in Dunmore, County Galway on the night of 21 May 1921, and shot by men who left a card stating 'Convicted Spy. Traitors beware. Executed by order of the IRA'. He is commemorated as a victim of a police murder gang.[9] Crown forces also spread rumours that people whom they had murdered anonymously had been killed by former IRA associates.

Consequently, this discussion only covers killings where there is clear evidence that the IRA was responsible. Thus it excludes a number of civilian fatalities that bear all the hallmarks of IRA killings, such as that of an unidentified man found shot dead in Dundrum, County Dublin, in February 1921: 'his black hair ... oiled and neatly parted', he 'wore woollen drawers with the marks "2nd Welsh Regiment" ... printed on them ... A 10/- note was found inside one sock'. No direct evidence of IRA involvement has been found in this or in a number of similar cases, where there is always the possibility that Crown forces, either on or off-duty, or freelance criminals were the perpetrators. An instance of the latter is probably that of Bridget Walpole of County Kerry, labelled a spy, apparently killed by relations over land.[10]

Who Killed Whom and Why

The term 'informer', used interchangeably with 'spy', has a particular resonance in Irish nationalist memory. Spies featured extensively in Irish separatist discourse, these 'human bloodhounds' and 'vampires' being blamed for successive failures to throw off the British yoke. Their masters were the British authorities in Dublin Castle, accorded an almost superhuman capacity for thwarting nationalist conspiracies through subtle penetration of rebel circles: – what the ablest republican historian Dorothy Macardle termed an 'almost flawless system of espionage', which had held Ireland down despite the rebel heroics of 1798, 1803, 1848 and 1867.[11] The terms have been applied variously to individuals within communities or movements coerced into giving secret information to the authorities; to people who volunteered information in return for payments, favours or concessions; to people who defied the authority of the republican movement and separatist institutions; and to people acting as penetration agents, employed by the authorities to join political conspiracies and to report on their activities.

The term 'spy' has an additional meaning in the Irish revolutionary canon, as it was sometimes applied to serving policemen and soldiers who the IRA killed or tried to kill. Such deaths of serving personnel are excluded from this analysis. Thus I do not discuss Bloody Sunday, nor the killing of other soldiers or police alleged to be engaged in intelligence work such as Lieutenant S.L. Vincent, captured, shot and buried by the Cork IRA in May 1921, or Constable Michael Dennehy, tied to a stone and thrown into the River Shannon after being captured near Rooskey in County Roscommon while out walking with a girl (GHQ were concerned about aspects of this killing).[12]

The Hardinge Commission on the causes of the 1916 Rising disclosed that both the Dublin Metropolitan Police (DMP) and the Royal Irish Constabulary (RIC) had quite good low-level local intelligence on preparations for an uprising in 1916, though their sources were in the dark about the inner workings of the conspiracy. Yet no one who came through the Rising, not even Michael Collins, devoted energy to a witch-hunt at any level to uncover informers in or around the separatist movement such as the DMP's 'Chalk' and 'Granite'.[13] That was to change in 1919–21, though the IRA remained comparatively dilatory in weeding out and punishing spies within its own ranks.

The basic IRA rationale for killing and attempting to kill civilians branded as spies was that they had deliberately provided information to the British authorities. Such spying did not have to be a *sub rosa* activity: people who publicly defied the IRA and republican authority generally, such as the spirited Carlow pharmacist William Kennedy and his solicitor Michael O'Dempsey, shot in March 1921 after initiating court action over intimidation, were coyly categorized as 'suspected spies' by the Carlow IRA who killed them.[14] Equally, the Flemings father and son in County Monaghan, the Pearson brothers in King's County, and John Harrison in County Leitrim, were apparently killed not because they were giving information, or because they were Protestants, or because locals coveted their land, but because they had previously clashed with IRA parties on their property. Similarly, two Protestant farmers in west County Cork, Mathew Sweetnam and William Connell, were killed in February 1921 after giving evidence in open court about an IRA attempt to force them to contribute to an arms levy. Sweetnam received an anonymous warning to flee, but was advised by a solicitor not to worry as there had been no killings in the locality.[15] After Tom Barry's Cork No. 3 Brigade Flying Column abandoned a plan to do the job, they were killed by the local IRA battalion. Barry argued quite coherently in *Guerrilla Days in Ireland* that what was primarily at issue in such cases was not the religion or the status of those attacked, nor their land and assets, but their unwillingness to comply with republican authority. Yet in ordering the killings of Sweetnam and Connell, the brigade added that 'their lands [be] forfeited'.[16] Giving evidence against the IRA automatically conferred the status of spy, with risk of the attendant death penalty. Thus Bridget Noble (*née* Neill) was killed as a spy in Cork. In Dublin, the IRA targeted a shopkeeper who had been a witness in an unsuccessful prosecution for armed robbery against the IRA's Bill Corri and his girlfriend; an IRA unit tersely reported 'Execution of spy [Henry] McMahon Bolton St carried out this afternoon, 8 rounds .45 used', although, remarkably, McMahon survived.[17]

At the other end of the spectrum of civilian spies attacked were two who died in Dublin in March 1920. 'John Jameson' (Joseph Byrne) was an English ex-soldier and paid intelligence operative recruited in England; Alan Bell was a retired magistrate.[18] Bell was engaged essentially in forensic intelligence-gathering rather than spying, but was also acting as the undeclared head of intelligence for Dublin Castle. The IRA consequently got the right man, if for the wrong reason: 'Mick McDonnell caught Bell by the shoulder and said: "We want you". I know he resisted', as he was dragged off a tram in Ballsbridge and shot.[19] Almost 180 other civilians were killed who gave, or were thought to be attempting to collect and give, information to the authorities. Many – about 47 per cent – were ex-servicemen or ex-policemen, including the unfortunate Godfrey Jasper, who was kidnapped in County Kerry shortly after he left the RIC, held prisoner for some weeks, and killed. In the case of at least a few civilian deaths, the term 'spy' was a flag of convenience used to conceal personal animosities, local grievances and disputes.[20]

There is ample evidence, as Peter Hart argued, that tramps, drifters and ex-servicemen were particularly liable to fall under suspicion and to face IRA sanctions. This is explicit in republican veterans' recollections of how ne'er do wells and down-at-heel strangers were automatically suspected. We can learn something from the story of one such 'spy' who survived the IRA's attention. John McCabe, an ex-soldier, was an itinerant pedlar of religious trinkets. In April 1921, he was abducted by the IRA outside Carrickmacross, County Monaghan. Accused 'of coming from Belfast to spy on them', he was imprisoned in a derelict house, court-martialled, and sentenced to death. When McCabe appealed for help to a priest who had come to hear his confession, this latter day Pontius Pilate blithely 'replied that he could not interfere, and he then left through the broken window'. McCabe, shot a number of times in the back and head, was left for dead. He features in IRA veterans' recollections as an 'enemy espionage agent' who somehow got away, but the RIC in Monaghan reported to Dublin Castle that they knew nothing of him.[21]

The key points of McCabe's case are, firstly, that had he disappeared, it is unlikely that anyone would have missed him or actively sought him; and secondly, it illustrates how a stranger looking suspicious, or to being found wandering in a sensitive area, was sufficient reason for them to be targeted. IRA accounts of its activities in the Knockraha company area in east Cork lay particular stress on the need to protect two concealed munitions factories from discovery, and hence people such as British deserters or tramps who strayed into the area were captured and killed out of hand.[22]

Administration of Republican Justice and IRA Procedures
In principle, even spies and informers were entitled to republican justice. They were to be brought before an IRA court martial, which would determine guilt and impose penalties ranging from fines and confiscation of property to exile and death. In most cases, a handful of officers would decide on someone's fate, whether or not the person was present to defend themselves or was even aware of proceedings. If not already in custody, the guilty party would then be captured and the penalty enforced. Sometimes the brigade Officer Commanding (O/C) was consulted before an execution, but often he was not. In Kerry, one Brigade O/C refused to permit the killing of fisheries inspector James Kane in Listowel, but gave retrospective sanction after the man had been shot.'[23]

Sentences for spying were not uniform across the country; nor was enforcement of the penalties imposed. These factors have to be borne in mind in reflecting on the number of spies actually killed in each county. In County Limerick, for example, it appears that many more spies were convicted than were ever shot (including one IRA officer, who had his death sentence reduced at GHQ's insistence to a fine of £100, the destruction of his home, and his expulsion from Ireland). It may well be that some brigade O/Cs were much more severe than others in dealing with spies. Sean O'Hegarty of Cork No. 1 Brigade was known to be ruthless; so too, in the very different climate of County Monaghan, was Eoin O'Duffy, at whose feet his own men later laid responsibility for a number of the more problematic shootings in the county.[24]

Occasionally convicted spies got lucky: Michael 'Mickeroo' Walsh and a Mrs Marshall, 'a woman of easy virtue', who had separately been sentenced to death by IRA courts martial, were rescued from detention in Cork Female Asylum during a search by the British military. They both left the country, but Walsh soon returned to Cork, scarcely the act of a guilty man. In February 1921, he was taken from his sick bed in Cork Workhouse Infirmary – the Cork IRA's Mick Murphy said that 'this low type' had venereal disease – and shot dead on the road outside.[25] In County Tipperary, an IRA party which included my grandfather's brother Captain Paddy Moloney were about to shoot an alleged spy, a one-eyed plaster from Tipperary town. Impressed with the man's demeanour, a member of the party persuaded the battalion O/C Seán Duffy that GHQ should be consulted about the case. The prisoner was released. The following day Duffy and Moloney died in an engagement with Crown forces near Limerick Junction; ironically, an RIC report shows that the police were acting 'on reliable information' from an unidentified source.[26]

Occasionally convicted spies were offered the consolation of a clergyman, but often the IRA had neither the time nor the inclination to fetch one. There was always the danger that a priest would intercede to save lives. This happened at Banteer in County Cork in 1921, when an IRA group decided to shoot three RIC policemen who had surrendered: 'Prisoners were placed on the Bridge as we were going to act [following words excised from the document: probably something like 'as a firing squad' or 'as a court martial']. This was frustrated owing to the Rev Fr Kavanagh CC coming on and intervening, so [they] were let off on promising to resign.'[27]

It is clear from Bureau of Military History and Military Service Pensions records that many IRA men involved in killing spies drew moral comfort as well as a sense of legitimacy from using the language of due process to describe the steps by which civilian spies were killed.[28] Sometimes, as in the notorious case of Kate Carroll of County Monaghan, obeying orders was the only fig leaf of honour available. What was crucial to salve a conscience was the belief that a spy had received the fairest treatment available in the circumstances, and that the killers were simply doing their duty. Contemporary accounts of IRA courts martial indicate that they were generally cursory affairs, the judges being the IRA officers holding the prisoner (if the defendant was even present or aware of proceedings). A rare exception was the case of William Gordon, an ex-soldier and authentic reprobate, responsible for a contract killing related to a land dispute in Meath in June 1920. Thanks to GHQ, Gordon actually received two trials, in the second of which he was defended by an IRA officer specially sent from Dublin, before being convicted and shot, after receiving the ministrations of a Protestant clergyman. The RIC also came to the conclusion that Gordon's killing arose from what was fundamentally an agrarian crime.[29]

There is evidence of growing GHQ unease at the fate of spies in some areas. In February 1921, the Chief of Staff warned Tipperary No. 2 Brigade that 'you must be very careful that where there is any doubt about the correctness of any evidence against spies the matter is referred to GHQ before any action is taken against them' – by then just two civilians had been shot as spies in the county.[30] The IRA's General Order No. 20 issued by GHQ on 20 April 1921 stipulated that all death sentences on spies had to be ratified by the brigade commandant, and that each execution must be reported to GHQ. These attempts to tighten procedures reflect GHQ's concern about this aspect of the military campaign. Such instructions were resented at local level, nowhere more so than in Cork. When Tom Hales of the West Cork IRA went up to Dublin to express dissatisfaction with the higher command's attitude towards Cork's conduct of the war, the Director of Intelligence Michael Collins cheerily advised him to ignore GHQ fussing: 'Shoot first and ask questions afterwards.'[31] Cork's Seán Culhane insisted that 'we were careful that before a spy was shot it had to be a definite case of spying', but the surviving records suggest otherwise.[32]

In June 1921, the intelligence officer of the newly-created 1st Southern Division forwarded reports which in his view demonstrated that spies whom the Cork No. 1 Brigade had tracked down and killed had been primarily responsible for the disasters at Mourneabbey and Clonmult in early 1921:

> I think GHQ has somehow got the idea that in the Cork Brigades, and especially in Cork No. 1, men are being shot as spies more or less on suspicion. Instead of this, as I am aware myself, the greatest care is taken in every instance to have the case fully proved and beyond all doubt. As a matter of fact, the men shot have in most cases admitted their guilt before being executed.

Yet the new division's commander, Liam Lynch, who had barely escaped capture at Mourneabbey, dismissed the argument that the calamity could be blamed simply on a spy. He knew about one informer, a drunkard ex-soldier named Shields, who had been retained in the Flying Column despite warnings about his character. Despite this, Lynch ascribed the *débâcle* squarely to poor local leadership and inefficient scouting.[33] Similarly, when an Active Service Unit (ASU) in a farmhouse at Clonmult in east County Cork was caught unprepared by British forces who killed twelve of them, some after surrender, the fact that senior officers were absent because they had gone to 'bid farewells ... to some people at whose fire they used to sit and chat & have a drink' was downplayed.[34] The IRA instead blamed a shell-shocked ex-soldier named David Walsh whom they captured and killed, allegedly after he admitted that 'I met a party of military in February last and told them I knew where Volunteers were in Clonmult and afterwards led them to the house. I was getting £1 per week and a lump sum for information.' Research in British records indicates that Clonmult was attributable to an enterprising Hampshire Regiment intelligence officer, while on 19 July 1924, General Strickland, who had commanded the British 6th Division in Munster in 1921, wrote to Walsh's brother Andrew that he had ascertained that Walsh 'gave us no information, and he was not known to us'. Andrew Walsh stated that his brother's erratic behaviour 'has given me a good deal of trouble. I have had to give up my situations in search of him.' David was 'sent home from hospital' in March 1921 – that is a month after the Clonmult massacre for which he was allegedly the informant – still 'suffering from gas posion [*sic*] and shell shock', and had been impossible to control. Andrew Walsh continued to press his brother's case for vindication, writing on 9 April 1925: 'I think it a very wrong thing' to treat 'in such a manner a man that lost his position through not being capable of himself ... he was tried and sent to his doom wrongly'. The IRA's search for a scapegoat for Clonmult was, as some veterans later acknowledged, just that, and it led to the gratuitous killing of a damaged and probably innocent man.[35]

The County Distribution of IRA Killing of Civilian Spies and Informers

The figures in Table 13.1 require careful analysis. They are drawn from the DOIR database as it stood in 2012.[36] They record 181 deaths of civilians killed as spies, which represents 64 per cent of the total number of civilian fatalities (282) for which the IRA was definitely responsible. The first of these, that of the paid agent Harry Quinlisk, took place in Cork in February 1920. Mick Murphy recalled shooting him: 'He was a tall, fair, athletic-looking lad who had a good Irish accent.'[37]

In the remaining months of 1920, twenty-five more killings took place. In the following seven months, 155, or 86 per cent of all civilian spies, were killed by the IRA. In the same period, the overall number of deaths arising from the conflict grew by 43 per cent. This and other evidence indicates that the growth in the killing of civilian spies in 1921 was not simply the *pro rata* result of the escalation of violence generally: rather, civilian spies were singled out largely on the basis that they were soft targets as the IRA found it increasingly difficult to confront Crown forces.[38] Overall, alleged spies constituted 64 per cent of all civilians definitely killed by the IRA.

The killing of civilian spies was very unevenly distributed across the thirty-two counties (plus one killing in Surrey). In six Ulster counties – Antrim, Donegal, Down, Fermanagh, Londonderry, and Tyrone – there were no deaths at all. In Cavan (two), one of the killings was an unplanned act of indiscipline by an IRA guard who struck his former employer, the elderly Canon Finlay of Bawnmore, on the back of his head with a metal object while escorting him from his house (this killing was ferociously condemned by three local parish priests, who walked in the funeral procession). No one inside or outside the IRA appears to have credited the official republican story that this was a planned and legitimate execution of an informer.[39]

The first striking feature of the data is the absence of consistent proportionality across the six most violent Irish counties between the overall number of fatalities per county, and the number of civilians killed as spies and informers. In County Cork, which saw the most recorded fatalities (495), civilian spies constituted 14 per cent of these. Cork is followed by County Dublin (309 fatalities, but with only 5 per cent civilian spies). Then comes County Antrim (224 fatalities, no civilian spies), County Tipperary (152 fatalities, 7 per cent civilian spies), County Kerry (136 fatalities, 7 per cent civilian spies), and County Limerick (121 fatalities, 4 per cent civilian spies). County Cork therefore stands out among these six counties not only for being the most violent overall, and for having the largest absolute number of civilian spies killed by the IRA, but also for having the largest proportion of civilian spies in the overall total of deaths. In addition, County Cork is striking for the high proportion of ex-servicemen (twenty-nine, or 41 per cent) in the total of seventy civilians definitely killed as spies up to July 1921. Only in a few counties with very small numbers of fatalities overall do ex-servicemen constitute a higher percentage of civilian spies killed. The Cork figures cannot be compared directly with those provided by Peter

Counties	Actual numbers				Percentages				
	Total Deaths	Civilian Fatalities by IRA	Civilian Spies	Ex-serviceman Spies	Spies as % of Civilians killed by IRA	Spies as % of total spies killed overall	Ex-servicemen as % of Spies	Ex-Servicemen as % of Civilians killed by IRA	Civilian spies as % of total deaths in conflict
Antrim	224	9	0	0	0%	0%	0%	0%	0%
Armagh	28	3	2	0	67%	1%	0%	0%	7%
Cavan	9	3	2	1	67%	1%	50%	33%	22%
Carlow	13	4	4	1	100%	2%	25%	25%	31%
Clare	95	5	3	1	60%	2%	33%	20%	3%
Cork	495	89	70	29	79%	39%	41%	33%	14%
Donegal	20	2	0	0	0%	0%	0%	0%	0%
Down	28	1	0	0	0%	0%	0%	0%	0%
Dublin	309	37	15	9	41%	8%	60%	24%	5%
Fermanagh	9	2	0	0	0%	0%	0%	0%	0%
Galway	58	7	4	1	57%	2%	25%	14%	7%
Kerry	136	15	10	4	67%	6%	40%	27%	7%
Kildare	12	5	1	1	20%	1%	100%	20%	8%
Kilkenny	19	5	4	3	80%	2%	75%	60%	21%
King's (Offaly)	21	8	8	6	100%	4%	75%	75%	38%

County									
Leitrim	15	2	2	0	100%	1%	0%	0%	13%
Limerick	121	7	7	4	71%	3%	80%	57%	4%
Londonderry	41	0	0	0	0%	0%	0%	0%	0%
Longford	26	5	5	1	100%	3%	20%	20%	19%
Louth	26	2	1	1	50%	1%	100%	50%	4%
Mayo	43	2	0	0	0%	0%	0%	0%	0%
Meath	17	7	5	4	71%	3%	80%	57%	29%
Monaghan	25	7	7	1	100%	4%	14%	14%	28%
Queen's (Laois)	10	4	2	0	50%	1%	0%	0%	20%
Roscommon	58	10	7	3	70%	4%	43%	30%	12%
Sligo	18	1	1	0	100%	1%	0%	0%	6%
Tipperary	152	16	11	7	69%	6%	64%	44%	7%
Tyrone	16	1	0	0	0%	0%	0%	0%	0%
Waterford	35	3	2	2	67%	1%	100%	67%	6%
Westmeath	18	6	5	3	83%	3%	60%	50%	28%
Wexford	23	6	4	3	67%	2%	75%	50%	17%
Wicklow	7	0	0	0	0%	0%	0%	0%	0%
Great Britain	11	3	1	0	33%	1%	0%	0%	9%
Total	2138	277	183	85	65%	65%	47%	31%	8%

Table 13.1 Civilian spies and informers killed by IRA, by county, 1920–1 (as a percentage of total fatalities)

329

Hart – 'at least 204 civilians were deliberately shot by the IRA in the course of the revolution, the vast majority of whom were alleged to be spies and informers' – because he engaged with the longer period of 1919 to 1923, and because he included people shot for offences other than straightforward spying, such as applying to join the police or refusing to pay a republican fine.[40]

County Antrim – effectively Belfast city – stands out for the opposite reason: while third in the list of overall fatalities, it produced no known cases of IRA killing of civilian informers. This reflects a key factor which differentiates it (and on a smaller scale, Londonderry (forty-one fatalities, 0 per cent civilian spies)) from the rest of Ireland: most civilians whose death may be attributed to political violence in these counties between 1919 and 1921 died as a result of sectarian street violence in which the IRA, the RIC and British army, the Special Constabulary and organized loyalist and nationalist groups were variously involved.

The Dublin figures merit attention. They indicate that fifteen civilians were killed as spies, constituting just 5 per cent of all fatalities, of which nine (60 per cent) were ex-servicemen. Furthermore, whereas in the case of County Cork we know there were more civilians and military killed and disposed of as spies than we can account for in hard data, and that many of these died uncounted and unnamed, in County Dublin there is no trace of any organized process for the secret killing and disposal of people killed by the IRA. Apart from those included in our data, there are unconfirmed reports of just one anonymous spy possibly killed in County Dublin, in the peaceful district of Howth on the day of the Truce.[41] Yet County Dublin was the political and administrative epicentre of the revolution, the home of 'the Squad', and the place where one of the most celebrated and/or infamous set of targeted assassinations of all time was mounted against alleged British agents on Bloody Sunday in November 1920. Why did Dublin not experience a comparable percentage of civilian spy fatalities? The answer surely lies in the frame of mind of the local IRA leadership, particularly in the Cork No. 1 Brigade.

We also need to consider the figures for civilian spies in those counties where very few fatalities occurred. In King's County (Offaly), a generally quiet area, there was a flurry of killings of ex-servicemen (six) in the last two months of the conflict. Two ex-servicemen were killed in May 1921, three in June, and one, Eric Steadman, in July just two days before the Truce. At least three of these six had ignored warnings by the IRA to leave the area, which hardly suggests that they had been particularly dangerous or effective spies. The last to die was Steadman. An IRA veteran recalled an English drifter and ex-soldier who had been hanging around for some time with 'a billy-can ... he used to work for himself, going from house to house ... a trampish look'. Steadman foolishly returned to Tullamore despite being warned off. He was captured and condemned as a spy:

> ... we had a conscience about it. The brother, Jimmy, pointed out to him how nice it would be if he could die in the state of Grace ... and Seamus explained the Catholic Church situation to him. We sent into Tullamore parochial house for a clergyman as there was a spy to be shot, but no one came out to him. So begob Seamus then got the water and we had him baptized. Then he was shot afterwards.

The Birmingham police could find no relatives or other traces of this 'low, stout block of a man', so he was buried in Tullamore. Dr Philip McConway attributes the upsurge in killing of spies in the county to the galvanizing influence of a new organizer sent by GHQ.[42]

In the neighbouring and even more peaceful Queen's County (Laois), the decision to execute spies may have arisen partly from a desire to fire a fatal shot for Ireland while there was still time to do so. The IRA killed Peter Keyes, a father of ten who was secretary of the Land and Labour Association, on 5 July.[43] John Poynton, who had briefly served in the RIC before resigning for family reasons, was also shot at 4am on the morning of the Truce. These were the only spies killed in that county during the War of Independence.[44]

In counties Kilkenny, Meath, Westmeath and Wexford, much the same pattern is present: a high proportion of the very few civilians killed by the IRA were shot as spies. Furthermore, in these four counties the majority of such spies were ex-servicemen (respectively 75 per cent, 80 per cent, 60 per cent, and 75 per cent).

Who Died as Spies, and Why?
Crown forces across Ireland evidently received a good deal of information about IRA activities, even in – perhaps more in – a county like Cork where the conflict was very intense, than elsewhere where things were far quieter, and IRA and Crown forces could for the most part lead virtually parallel lives, each overawing the general population

but seldom coming into direct conflict. Yet memory of the conflict, and often the identities of those believed to be informers, appears as strong in quiet counties as in violent ones. I have met people in quiet counties such as Cavan and Down, as well as in violent ones like Tipperary, who stated that they know but would not disclose who was the informer responsible for some IRA setback or other in 1920 or 1921 – in Cavan, the detection and destruction of an ill-prepared Active Service Unit by British forces at Lappanduff; in Down, the discovery of arms dumps around Loughinisland; in Tipperary, the death of Paddy Moloney and his battalion O/C.[45]

Of the 165 civilians killed as spies whose religion is known, forty-five were Protestant and 120 Catholic. The data show that ex-servicemen constitute almost half (47 per cent) of those civilians killed as spies. This bears out Hart's conclusion that ex-servicemen were disproportionately targeted by the IRA, particularly in Cork.[46] The reasons are not hard to find. Firstly, ex-servicemen were people who had volunteered to fight for the Crown, albeit very often as much because of poverty as of conscious patriotism. Secondly, their military experience meant they had something in common with serving soldiers, and made them more inclined to casual social contact in pubs and the like. Thirdly, many were unemployed, hanging around the towns or walking the roads seeking casual work – one Cork IRA officer dismissively classified '3 or 4 spies' he shot and buried as 'mainly of the ex-soldier type', despised as destitute and lacking moral fibre. In 1922, in a valedictory report the British 5th Division observed that 'probably almost the only cases in which there has been want during this winter have been among unemployed ex-soldiers and their families'.[47] Fourthly, because of their war service, ex-servicemen were in receipt of official letters and the like. Depending on their circumstances they had occasion to visit military premises in the course of managing their affairs. Take the case of Eugene Swanton, a farm labourer of Ballinacurra, Midleton, County Cork and formerly of the Canadian army. He had had to postpone his assisted passage to the United States because of recurring bouts of malaria following service in the Middle East, and was in regular correspondence with the War Office about his condition and revised travel arrangements. This may have been what aroused the IRA's suspicions: on 5 June 1921, they abducted and killed him. His remains were never found.[48]

The issue of the fairness of treatment meted out to alleged spies is a recurring theme in veterans' recollections in the Bureau of Military

History, and in their dealings with the Military Service Pensions Board.[49] In County Clare, John O'Reilly, a labourer who ran the local ex-servicemen's association in Newmarket-on-Fergus, was shot as a spy. The officer in charge always maintained that he was guilty. But another officer disagreed, saying O'Reilly, who met his end 'in a brave and quiet manner', was 'framed by the postman ... who was himself the real spy'.[50] Such contradictions arise in veterans' accounts of the killing of another County Clare spy, Patrick Darcy, whose last words were reportedly: 'I forgive ye, boys. You are shooting me in the wrong.' Some came to believe that a local publican had avoided exposure as an informer by framing him and when, at the Taoiseach Éamon de Valera's personal request the army Director of Intelligence investigated the case in 1945/6, he reported that the man most closely involved in the killing now believed him innocent.[51] In County Monaghan, many veterans were uneasy at the executions of Patrick Larmour, a young Volunteer who had given information under British interrogation, but had then told his officers everything as soon as he was released, and of Arthur Treanor, a prominent member of the Ancient Order of Hibernians (AOH) who had been ordered out of the district, but who had returned briefly under an IRA safe conduct to tidy up his affairs.[52] Other killings of supposed spies in County Monaghan were also attributed by veterans to bitter local rivalry with the AOH. In County Leitrim, where just two spies (both Protestants) were killed, veterans also differed about the circumstances and the justification. Even one relatively orthodox narrative of the killing of John Harrison – the culmination of a long dispute about an IRA arms levy on which at one point a deal had been brokered by a local Protestant clergyman, whereby Harrison paid £1 and also handed over a gun, recovering his 'best cow' in return – conveys a sense of regret: 'he begged us not to kill him [but] I said we had to carry out our orders, we told him he had to come with us, we also told [him] that he needed no coat'.[53] The other County Leitrim killing, that of William Latimer, is also widely recalled. After an IRA ASU under Seán Connolly had been surrounded and destroyed by Crown forces at Selton Hill outside Mohill in March 1921, suspicion fell on Latimer because he had gone into Mohill that morning 'to get the coutraments' for his mother's wake and funeral. By all accounts Latimer apparently mentioned something to the dispensary doctor Dr Pentland, with whom he would have registered his mother's death, and it was Pentland who alerted the RIC. The first IRA party detailed to kill Latimer 'were four fellows ... from the locality and when they had a look at the house and the poor man that was there and the children ... they turned back anyway, they wouldn't do it'. The task was reassigned to outsiders. After an exchange of fire, the fight ended when an unprimed grenade was thrown into his house. In order to save his wife and children, Latimer shouted: 'I'm going out that will do ya, I'm going out.'[54]

Such individual stories do not prove anything, save to indicate that even amongst people directly involved in the killing of civilian spies, there were frequently doubts about the guilt of individuals and the penalties imposed upon them. Such doubts often intensified as the years passed. It can generally be said that expressions of remorse for informers are disproportionately to be found amongst veterans and communities in counties where the absolute number of killings was low. Where civilian spies were killed on a much larger scale, as in County Cork, most veterans who touched on the topic did so only in passing, or unapologetically like Mick Leahy, or in the cases of a handful such as Frank Busteed of Blarney, Mick Murphy of Cork city and Martin Corry of Knockraha, boastfully.

One obvious potential source of spies was the IRA itself. William Shields and 'Cruxie' Connors in Cork have already been mentioned. Another and probably more significant figure was Paddy Egan, intelligence officer of the IRA's South Roscommon Brigade, who left the country before his treachery was uncovered.[55] There must surely have been others in the IRA across Ireland and abroad. Yet most seem to have gone undetected, or at any rate unpunished. Major A.E. Percival, a vigorous and imaginative intelligence officer of the Essex Regiment based in Bandon in west Cork in 1920–1, whose dashing and brutal conduct marks him out as the Orde Wingate of the Irish campaign, wrote shortly afterwards that while information from IRA sources 'was very rare', he did secure one good agent, a company officer captured and 'turned' after the Dripsey ambush. In return for leniency, this man supplied him with weekly reports. His information led to the large-scale search operation in March 1921 which resulted in the killing of the Cork No. 3 Brigade O/C Charlie Hurley, and which culminated in the clash with Tom Barry at Crossbarry.[56]

The IRA and Women Spies

British records indicate that women were considered 'particularly useful' sources of information.[57] One very striking feature of the data above is the disparity between the number of male civilians (178) and women (3) definitely killed by the IRA as spies. This underlines the point that different rules, assumptions and practices applied to men and women. Women spies posed particular problems, yet even in the most violent counties they were not treated in the same way as male informers.

In November 1920, GHQ attempted to address the question: 'Where there is evidence that a woman is a spy or is doing petty spy work, the Brigade Commandant ... will set up a Court of Inquiry ... If convicted, except in the case of an Irishwoman, [she should] be ordered to leave the country within 7 days. It shall be intimated to her that only consideration of her sex prevents the infliction of the statutory punishment of death.' The order continued: 'Ordinarily it is not proposed to deport Irishwomen, it being hoped that the bringing of publicity on the actions of such will neutralise them. In dangerous and insistent cases of the kind, however, full particulars should be placed before GHQ and instructions sought.'[58] Such instructions were not always followed: in June 1921, in Rosscarbery, County Cork, the 'dwelling house of Miss Whitley loyalist was destroyed by fire ... Miss Whitley was also suspected of giving information and has been ordered to leave the country'. That the sixty-year old Beatrice Whitley was Protestant, and thus not quite 'an Irishwoman' in west Cork IRA eyes, may have had something to do with this outcome (for good measure the IRA also killed Frank Sullivan, who had worked for the Whitleys for over twenty years).[59] More typical was a case in County Donegal in April 1921, where a 'woman informer had her hair clipped'. The homes of alleged women spies were occasionally destroyed – this certainly happened in counties Roscommon and Cork. Women were sometimes driven out of the district. But they were almost never killed.[60]

Fraternization between women and soldiers or policemen was feared for security reasons. In some instances, perhaps partly to appeal to local opinion, moral considerations were also adduced to justify punitive action such as 'bobbing' a woman's hair; in others, jealousy may have been a complicating factor.[61] One instance may be that of Nellie Carey of Fermoy, shot dead while out walking with two soldiers who were slightly wounded. The IRA claimed that her death was accidental and that the soldiers were the target, but Fermoy town was generally safe for military personnel, and there were no other serious attacks on off-duty soldiers there in 1920 or 1921.[62] During the Truce, IRA units were instructed to monitor liaisons between Irish girls and Crown forces, with a view to action should hostilities be resumed: thus the Limerick IRA solemnly reported to the IRA's 1st Southern Division headquarters in August 1921 that 'Bridget Casey is going with the RIC Int[elligence] Officer in Newcastle … a Black and Tan named Stafford.'[63]

Just three women were definitely killed by the IRA as spies: Kate Carroll in County Monaghan, and Mary Lindsay and Bridget Noble in County Cork. The first two cases caused great embarrassment for GHQ. Kate Carroll was an impoverished, slow-witted woman in her forties who supported her mother and her disabled brother by the sale of 'poteen to soldiers & anyone who would buy it'. One Monaghan IRA man recalled that she 'was often seen around the barracks', but was considered harmless. She resented IRA interference in her distilling, and wrote chaotic letters to the RIC in Scotstown denouncing their inaction against the IRA and rival illicit distillers. Some of these were intercepted by an IRA informant in Monaghan Post Office. She was warned off, but wrote another letter. Versions differ as to what happened next. One Monaghan veteran wrote that 'the proof … was very strong. She was scarcely normal and was not sufficiently intelligent to cloak her activities', whereas the man who investigated the letters wrote an apologetic and incomplete account emphasizing that the unwelcome execution order came from the Brigade O/C Eoin O'Duffy, a man always happy to have others pull the trigger on supposed informers. Charlie O'Neill, in jail when she was killed, was less reticent:

> … it is now thought that one of the Volunteers himself was an informer but deliberately shifted the blame on to Kate Carroll who was condemned to death by a secret court-martial. Seven men were sent out to execute Kate Carroll. Nobody thought in their wildest dreams they would have to do this as a lot of them didn't agree with the decision. Most of the seven cried the whole way out [to] the mountain where Kate Carroll died. This brought a wave of revulsion against the IRA.

Charlie's family blamed him for his father's sudden death the following year, believing that this was a judgement on them for allowing their son to be in an organization which had killed a hapless neighbour. It and other cases, such as the killing, already mentioned, of Canon Finlay in County Cavan, caused GHQ considerable unease because they provided the British with atrocity stories to counter rebel propaganda.[64]

The case of Bridget Noble (née Neill) attracted little attention at the time or since. Abducted early in March 1921 from her home near Ardgroom on the Beara peninsula, she was killed some days later. She was deemed a spy because, on her release from hospital, she had named local IRA men who had assaulted her, bobbed her hair and robbed her of £35. After the Truce, her husband Alexander wrote piteously to de Valera that 'it is not clean work to take away my lone & defenceless wife', and GHQ sought information on her death. Liam O'Dwyer, the O/C of the Castletownbere battalion, replied that at her court martial 'she admitted guilt on all the charges'. His account hinted that the IRA disapproved of what they saw as her improper friendships with a number of RIC men in Castletownbere. Her remains were never recovered. O'Dwyer made no reference to Bridget Noble whatsoever in his melodramatic and self-serving BMH witness statement.[65]

The third woman definitely executed by the IRA was Mary Lindsay, an elderly Protestant landowner from Coachford in County Cork. Her fate became a *cause célèbre* even before her death, because she and her driver were kidnapped and held for three weeks as hostages for the lives of five IRA men sentenced to death after capture at the Dripsey ambush. Mrs Lindsay had warned the British authorities about the ambush, but she had also advised the local priest to tell the IRA to clear out in good time. The IRA O/C foolishly decided to ignore the priest's warning – 'Fr Shinnick was not taken seriously as he was always preaching from the Altar against ambushes.' The IRA group was consequently taken by surprise by British forces, having one man fatally wounded and seven men captured, of whom five were executed. Responsibility for this disaster lay squarely with the O/C, who strove to make Mrs Lindsay a scapegoat, arresting her as a spy. The Dáil Minister for Defence actually ordered her release on 9 July, unaware that she and her driver had been killed four months earlier. In subsequent years, her killers twice moved her remains to prevent their recovery. In the weeks after her capture, her house was burned down and her farm stripped of everything: 'stable fittings, iron gates, donkey and cart, and 11 cows were taken', indicating an undercurrent of agrarian feeling against large landowners.[66]

There are indications that one or possibly two other women in Carrigtwohill were killed and their remains hidden by the Cork No. 1 Brigade, though this has not been confirmed. They belong in the disturbingly large number of probable IRA killings in Cork for which no further information is available at present.[67]

Finding Dead Spies

IRA GHQ provided no guidance on how the remains of executed spies were to be disposed of. In many cases, bodies were left to be found, often with a card proclaiming the deceased to have been a spy, coupled with a warning to 'Spies and Informers beware'. This intimidatory dimension was well understood: during the civil war, the Sligo IRA was commended for 'the good effect' the 'execution of spies' in Tubbercurry in November 1922 had on the locality.[68] But many other people killed by the IRA simply disappeared; they were buried secretly or their bodies weighed down and cast into lakes, rivers or the sea.

During the Truce period, GHQ made some efforts to list and investigate IRA killings of civilian spies and of missing military and police, and to locate their remains. But inquiries encountered much local obfuscation, and with the outbreak of the civil war in June 1922 they seem largely to have ceased. Most of the army's records on these matters were most likely either transferred to the Garda Síochána in 1926, or burned during the post-election interregnum in March 1932, when Minister for Defence Desmond FitzGerald directed the incineration of:

a) Intelligence reports – including reports and particulars supplied by agents and other persons.
b) Secret Service vouchers, etc.
c) Proceedings of Military Courts, including Committee of Officers; Reports on and details of executions, 1922–1923 period.

This destruction was carried out because material in such records 'may lead, if disclosed to unauthorised persons – to loss of life'.[69] There was irony in this incendiary exercise: it was Desmond FitzGerald's son Garret who, as Taoiseach introduced robust legislation protecting state archives in the National Archives Act 1986, while Dan Bryan and Niall Harrington, who oversaw the destruction of the records in 1932, were very active in retirement in encouraging the serious study of the War of Independence and Civil War.[70]

Material transferred from the army to the Garda Síochána in 1926–7 remains inaccessible, if it still exists. The most complete surviving record of an army investigation into an executed civilian is probably that on Mrs Lindsay. It survives in photocopy in a private collection in the National Library. Accompanying material indicates, amongst other things, that as recently as the early 1970s, Moss Twomey, Chief of Staff of the IRA from 1926 to 1936 and himself a Cork man, attempted to secure the help of the Provisional IRA to prevent the publication of Sean O'Callaghan's *Execution* because he feared it would disclose that in 1921 the IRA had poisoned Mrs Lindsay, because they had not wanted to shoot a woman.[71]

There were often practical reasons for the IRA to conceal the remains of those whom they killed. Their discovery by Crown forces might lead to local repercussions or – or as the Carlow IRA claimed in respect of one spy whose remains they concealed – the uncovering of one dead spy might alert others in a locality, causing them to flee before they could be dealt with.[72] Stan Barry of Cork recalled how one spy, 'an Irishman ... was between tears and acts of contrition when we shot him ... Nobody knew where he was buried and nobody but ourselves knew that he had been shot ... not being found created uncertainty among the British and it prevented their reprisals in a particular area.'[73] (This killing is not included in my data as no supporting documentary source has been found.) The Cork No. 1 Brigade adopted the practice, where possible, of the secret killing and burial of spies and other prisoners. The assumed deterrent effect on the general population of publicly killing an informer was traded for increased security. Secrecy also meant that GHQ remained unaware of the sheer scale of killings.

Occasionally concealment failed. A few bodies disposed of in water courses floated up and were recovered: examples are Thomas Smith, an ex-serviceman who was bound with wire and weights and drowned in the River Boyne in County Meath; and John Coughlan of Cobh, who killed himself in August 1920 while in IRA detention for 'using his two daughters as prostitutes for the British'.[74] The Cobh IRA tied his body to the axle of a cart, which they sank in the sea, but this was washed up shortly afterwards. Mick Leahy broke into the morgue to see if the body was Coughlan's:

We moved along from corpse to corpse with a flash lamp ... when we pulled back the cloth we found that the crabs had got hold of his face and that there was nothing left of it. A month later we got evidence that this man had been a spy, and that's why he hanged himself.[75]

After the Truce, IRA units were occasionally willing to provide information about the fate of people whom they had killed and hidden. Sometimes bodies could no longer be found: the Longford Brigade explained, charitably if perhaps disingenuously, that when they killed the informer John McNamee in April 1921 'his body was thrown into the Shannon with the object of saving his children from any disgrace that might arise'.[76] In cases in County Cork, no information about the whereabouts of remains of spies was offered. Take the case of Patrick Ray, who 'came out of the train [and] he met his little boy and told him to go home. But he never turned in home since'. The IRA killed him two days later. His distraught wife Catherine sought information: 'I am heartbroken, and only ask you ... to let me know is he a prisoner or is he dead or alive. I have 4 young children and am destitute.' His sister Agnes wrote that 'he was an ex-serviceman but I know him not to be doing any harm ... one would be satisfied to know if he was dead ... but living in suspense is awful'. The Dáil Minister for Defence wrote on 25 January 1922 that Ray was executed after conviction by 'a duly authorised authority'. The family then sought a death certificate, as Ray was 'insured in the Royal Liver Friendly Society ... it is 31 pounds that is coming' to Catherine Ray 'and her 4 young children almost starving and with no one to turn to. May be you could get it done in Dublin ... also for Christian Charity's sake.' After further representations, Catherine Ray was assured that her husband had 'received the ministrations of a priest' from Passage West. It is not known if she secured the insurance money, but her husband's body was never returned.[77] Similarly, the Cork IRA agreed during the Truce that the fact of James Herlihy's killing in July 1920 could be revealed 'as this man's relatives are all right', but not the location of his remains.[78] Perhaps out of a misplaced sense of decency, the Carlow IRA dissimulated about the fate of Michael Hackett, sending assurances that after receiving 'the rites of the Catholic Church' he was shot and 'buried in consecrated grounds'. His mother Julia was so informed. She subsequently identified her son's remains at Coolnasaughta: 'I cannot see how the consecration comes in on top of a mountain four miles from a churchyard.' Caught out in a lie, the local IRA O/C resorted to spite: Hackett had 'had half an hours' audience with a priest. I believe that he did not avail himself of this opportunity to go to confession.'[79]

The remains of some people killed and secretly buried by the IRA before the Truce, mainly British soldiers, were recovered after the Civil War, with priests often acting as intermediaries. Executed soldiers were in IRA eyes of a higher moral standing than policemen and spies, and the return of their remains after the conflict was in accordance with international military norms. In addition, there was often considerable public sympathy: as one Cork farmer wrote in pressing for action to rebury an unidentifiable British soldier whose corpse he had discovered on his land, 'He is surely somebody's boy.'[80] To disclose the burial place of spies, on the other hand, would be to accord the lowest of the low more respect than they deserved; in addition, such action might reopen the awkward issue of the guilt of individuals, as well as casting unwelcome light on their treatment at IRA hands. There were also potential legal hazards in disclosing the burial places of people killed after the Truce came into effect on 11 July 1921. Take the case of the ex-RIC man Michael Williams, who was kidnapped in Queen's County (Laois) in June 1922 and brought down to Cork. He was questioned about the murder in March 1920 of Lord Mayor Tómas MacCurtain, court martialled, and killed on Martin Corry's land, his corpse buried close to that of another man killed a fortnight earlier. Despite the fact that this was plainly murder, after the Civil War the Gardai were unwilling to search Corry's farm, reputed to house many corpses, for fear of stirring up the neighbourhood.[81] Such sensitivities may partly explain why so few concealed remains of civilians killed by the IRA as spies or for other reasons were ever uncovered.[82]

The Missing Dead of the Irish Revolution

In addition to the problems of defining what constituted a spy, other issues arise from exploration of detailed republican accounts of the killing and disposal of civilians. The most significant problem is that accounts of spies in County Cork, where far more were killed than anywhere else, indicate a considerably greater number of fatalities than have been individually traced. Stan Barry (Cork No. 1 Brigade), who operated to the west of Cork city, spoke of killing and burying '3 or 4 spies' at Clogheen. Frank Busteed and others have maintained that fifteen or so spies were executed and buried at 'the Cottage' in Rylane, north-west of Cork city.[83] Martin Corry, Captain of E company, 4th Battalion, Cork No. 1 Brigade, operated a brigade prison, 'Sing Sing', in Kilquane graveyard near Knockraha. A Military Service Pensions document says that up to the Truce, 'twenty seven ennemies [sic]' went through Sing Sing and were executed by Corry's company and buried in a nearby bog, 'the Ray'. Corry, an unusually loquacious veteran, spoke of thirty-five secret killings and burials carried out by his company (which may include people killed on his farm after the Truce).[84] Those who died were British soldiers, RIC men and Auxiliaries, and civilians, but the numbers involved and the identities of most of these people cannot be confirmed. Furthermore, Corry and others indicated that other IRA units also used the Ray as an execution and burial ground. On this, Mick Leahy, O/C of the 4th Battalion, Cork

No. 1 Brigade, and later the brigade Vice-Commandant, is a significant witness. Regarded as an able and level-headed man, Leahy described killing his first spy at Knockraha towards the end of 1920. The victim asked for a clergyman: "'Sorry we can't", I said, so I had to say the act of contrition for him and he had to repeat it after me. Then we all knelt down and said the Rosary before we shot him. I was a bit worried about it then, but I have felt no remorse since.' Leahy set up a dedicated squad to detect and deal with informers – there were 'a bloody pile of spies' in Carrigtwohill in his battalion area – some of whom were brought up to Knockraha to be killed. He told Ernie O'Malley that '90 spies were buried near Knockraha ... an excellent place'.[85] Military Service Pensions records should shed some more light on Knockraha, the Ray, the Cottage, and other sites of killing and concealment. In the process, they will prompt further questions about how many people could disappear and not be missed in one part of a single county.[86]

Gerard Murphy's exploration of *The Year of Disappearances: Cork, 1921–1922* encountered considerable critical hostility on foot of its necessarily speculative attempt to address the question of who might have been abducted and killed by the IRA's Cork No. 1 Brigade in Cork city and surrounding areas in the year after the Truce. Much of the academic criticism of Murphy's work hinged on reviewers' disdain for his writing style and his speculative approach, and on relatively minor points of fact. Such critics may also have been unfamiliar with important sources including the Martin Corry recordings and the Florence O'Donoghue papers, with their chilling and meticulous post-Truce codification and listing of different classes of potential enemies from ex-RIC men to Freemasons to loyalists, 'Enemy Agents (Special)', 'Enemy Post Offices', 'Enemy Social Institutions (to include County Clubs, Golf Clubs, Tennis Clubs, etc.)' suggestive of preparations for a once and for all clear-out of inimical elements of the population if hostilities resumed.[87] Few of Murphy's critics have attempted to address the wider question he raises, which is that Cork IRA testimonies about the abduction and secret killing of civilians in 1921–2 indicate that far more people were secretly killed and buried than has hitherto been acknowledged, and that in 1921–2, there appears to be a sectarian, or at any rate anti-Protestant, subtext to these killings which may help explain the particular secrecy surrounding them. It is very likely that material in crucial sources such as the Military Service Pensions records – of which I briefly had limited sight in 2010 – will bear out the thrust of Murphy's research as regards the scale of secret killing, if not its

342

explicitly sectarian dimension, more than it will his critics, be they ultramontane anti-revisionists, fastidious academics, or hybrids with a foot in both camps.[88]

Conclusion

The data in Table 13.1 show that proportionately far more civilians were definitely killed as spies and informers in Cork than in any other of the six most violent Irish counties as measured by fatalities. They also show, however, that in some relatively quiet counties – Monaghan, Meath, Kings County – the killing of civilians as spies constituted a very significant element of IRA activity. In eight of the nine Ulster counties, there were just four killings of alleged spies, and in at least three of those counties the killings seem to have been due to factors other than giving information to the authorities. The figures also show that most civilian spies (155 or 86 per cent) died in the last seven months of the War of Independence, whereas the overall number of deaths in that period was 954 (43 per cent of the total reported fatalities of 2,138). This bears out the view that many supposed civilian spies were killed not for what they had done or the real threat which they posed to the independence campaign, but because they were convenient and soft targets.

This is supported by other evidence. British records seldom yield up names of informants, but they do show that a good deal of information came to the police and military from 'respectable' sources within communities who were seldom suspected. They repeatedly indicate that, with the exception of a number of farmers around Bandon who paid with their lives for their attachment to the Crown, Protestant communities were of little use as sources of intelligence.[89] Equally, British and other evidence suggests that one of the safest places for an informer to be was within the IRA. Across Ireland, almost no IRA officers or Volunteers were ever charged with spying or informing, and only a handful – perhaps as few as half a dozen – were killed up to December 1921.

Finally, it is clear from IRA testimonies that while the execution of individual civilians as spies lay on the consciences of many republicans and communities, in the most violent county of Cork there persisted a marked triumphalism about the killing of spies generally. The uniqueness of Cork's experience in the War of Independence is also reflected in the emerging questions of how many more people than can yet be counted were secretly killed and buried in the killing fields of

Knockraha, 'the Cottage', and elsewhere; of why and when such killings occurred; and of why they happened on such a scale only in the Cork No. 1 Brigade area before and after the Truce. These are matters which only meticulous and dispassionate scholarship will answer.

NOTES

1 Eunan O'Halpin, 'Counting Terror', in David Fitzpatrick (ed.), *Terror in Ireland, 1916–1923* (Dublin: Trinity History Workshop, 2012), pp.145–8. The assistance of the Irish Research Council for the Humanities and Social Sciences is gratefully acknowledged, as is the invaluable work of Dr Daithí Ó Corráin as a postdoctoral fellow from 2003 to 2007, Dr Ciarán Wallace and, especially, Dr Eve Morrison.

2 *Dublin's Fighting Story* (Tralee: The Kerryman, 1948); *Kerry's Fighting Story* (Tralee: The Kerryman, 1947); *Limerick's Fighting Story* (Tralee: The Kerryman, 1948); *Rebel Cork's Fighting Story* (Tralee: The Kerryman, 1947).

3 For a more scientific approach to mapping political violence, see 'The social geography of revolution' in Peter Hart, *The IRA at War, 1916–1923* (Oxford: Oxford University Press, 2003), pp.30–61; Thomas Toomey, *The War of Independence in Limerick, 1912–1921* (Limerick: O'Brien-Twoomey publishers, 2010). The cover of the latter states: 'also covering actions in the border areas of Tipperary, Cork, Kerry and Clare'. I am very grateful to Dr Philip McConway for observations on this and other issues.

4 Courts of Inquiry in lieu of inquests held in Ireland, 7/9/1920 to 11/1/22 (TNA, WO35/162).

5 Note by Brigade Police Officer, Cork 1st Brigade [1921] (MAI, A/0649, Group I).

6 John Borgonovo, *Spies, Informers and the 'Anti-Sinn Féin Society': The Intelligence War in Cork City, 1920–1921* (Dublin: Irish Academic Press, 2006), argues that in general the Cork city IRA's activities against civilians were justified on intelligence grounds up to July 1921. By contrast, Gerard Murphy, *The Year of Disappearances: Political Killings in Cork, 1921–1922* (Dublin: Gill and Macmillan, 2010) argues that many secret killings of civilians by the Cork No. 1 Brigade in the last months of the conflict appear to have been based on flimsy or non-existent evidence, and that such killings, particularly of Protestants, did not stop with the Truce.

7 *Chronology: Parts I to III* (Dublin, 1947). This can be found in MAI.

8 Anne Dolan, 'Killing and Bloody Sunday, November 1920', *The Historical Journal*, 49:3 (2006), pp.789–810; Jane Leonard, '"English Dos" or "Poor Devils": the Dead of Bloody Sunday Morning', and O'Halpin, 'Counting Terror', in Fitzpatrick (ed.), *Terror in Ireland*, pp.102–40 and 142–3.

9 RIC Inspector General's Monthly Report, May 1921 (TNA, CO 904/115); MAI, BMH, WS 1408 (Thomas Mannion), pp.15–16; *Cork Examiner*, 23 May 1921.

10 Court of inquiry, 7 Feb. 1921 (TNA, WO35/161A); MAI, BMH, WS 1079 (Patrick Fitzgerald); WS 1167 (Michael O'Leary). Bridget Walpole's case is discussed in O'Halpin, 'Counting Terror', p.149.

11 MAI, BMH, WS 1643 (Seán Healy), p.23; WS 1092 (Michael J. Kehoe), p.24; Dorothy Macardle, *The Irish Republic* (1st edn., London: Victor Gollancz, 1937; New York, 1965), p.144.

12 NAI, JUS/H/257/13 contains details of the recovery of Vincent's remains and their reburial in Glenville, County Cork, on 20 Oct. 1926. On Dennehy, see TNA, HO 184/35; MAI, BMH, WS 479 (Michael Murphy); WS 1121 (Martin Fallon); Ernie O'Malley notebooks (UCDA, P17b/131, p.45 (Jim Fehily).

13 Eunan O'Halpin, *The Decline of the Union: British Government in Ireland, 1891–1920* (Dublin: Gill and Macmillan, 1987), p.109.

14 County Inspector's Monthly Report for Carlow, Feb. 1921 (TNA, CO 904/114); TNA, WO 35/157A; MAI, BMH, WS 1442 (Thomas Ryan), pp.4–5; WS 1496 (John Hynes), pp.5–14; *Cork Examiner*, 18 Mar. 1921.

15 Jasper Ungoed Thomas, *Jasper Wolfe of Skibbereen* (Cork: Collins Press, 2009), pp.115–16.

16 Thomas Earls Fitzgerald, 'The Execution of "Spies" and "Informers" in West Cork, 1921', in Fitzpatrick (ed.), *Terror in Ireland, 1916–1923*, pp.185–6; Tom Barry, *Guerrilla Days in Ireland* (Tralee: Anvil, 1947; Dublin, 1981), pp.113–4; MAI, BMH WS1471 (Patrick O'Sullivan).

17 Report by H Company, 1st Battalion, 16 June 1921 (UCDA, Mulcahy papers, P7/A/19); *Irish Independent*, 17 June 1921.

18 Peter Hart, *The IRA and its Enemies: Violence and Community in Cork, 1916–1923* (Oxford: Oxford University Press, 1998), p.303.

19 MAI, BMH, WS 380 (David Neligan); WS 387 (Paddy Daly); WS 615 (Frank Thornton); WS 663 (Joseph Dolan); WS 735 (Charles J. MacAuley); Lecture by Joe Leonard, 9 Mar. 1948 (UCDA, Mulcahy papers, P7/D/101); Eunan O'Halpin, 'British Intelligence in Ireland, 1914–1921', in Christopher Andrew and David Dilks (eds), *The Missing Dimension: Governments and Intelligence Communities in the Twentieth Century* (Basingstoke: Palgrave, 1984), p.73.

20 TNA, HO 184/37; MAI, BMH, WS 1205 (Patrick McKenna); WS 1413 (Tadhg Kennedy).

21 Fearghal McGarry, *Eoin O'Duffy: A Self-Made Hero* (Oxford: Oxford University Press, 2005), p.65; *Irish Times*, 10 Oct. 1921. McCabe was awarded over £4,000 compensation.

22 Martin Corry recordings, 1976, courtesy of Jim Fitzgerald, Knockraha Historical Society.

23 MAI, BMH, WS 1030 (Patrick McElligott).

24 McGarry, *Eoin O'Duffy*, pp.63–72.

25 Text of British military correspondence re Mrs Marshall, 21, 26 Feb. 1921 (NLI, O'Donoghue papers, MS 31223(1)); UCDA, O'Malley notebooks, P17b/112 (Mick Murphy).

26 TNA, CO 906/19, entry dated 2 May 1921; extracts from notes of an interview with Brian Shanahan, [late 1960s], courtesy of Jim Maher; *The Anglo-Celt*, 7 May 1921; Summary of Police Reports, May 1921 (TNA, CO 904/145); TNA, WO 35/155A; County Inspector's Report for Tipperary South Riding, 31 May 1921 (TNA, CO904/115); MAI, BMH, WS 1433 (Michael Fitzpatrick), p.16; WS 1658 (Tadhg Crowe), p.20; 'IRA Casualties' (MAI, A/0612); UCDA, O'Malley notebooks, P17/b/95 (Seán Fitzpatrick), p.59; *Cork Examiner*, 3 May 1921. Paddy Moloney was the son of P.J. Moloney TD; his brothers James (my grandfather) and Con were also IRA officers.

27 Report from 5th Battalion, Cork No. 2 Brigade, 25 Mar. 1921 (UCDA, Mulcahy papers, P7/A/38).

28 For a discussion of the Military Service Pensions records, see Eunan O'Halpin, 'The Military Service Pensions Project and Irish History: A Personal Perspective', in Caitriona Crowe and P. Brennan (eds), *A Guide to the Military Service Pensions Records* (Dublin, forthcoming).

29 Summary of Police Reports, May 1920 (TNA, CO 904/139); TNA, CO 905/009; MAI, BMH, WS 1060 (Séamus Finn); WS 1622 (Michael Hilliard); WS 1624 (Patrick Loughran); WS 1625 (Michael Govern); WS 1659 (Peter O'Connell); WS 1715 (Seán Boylan).

30 UCDA, Mulcahy papers, P7/A/17, 23 Feb. 1921.

31 UCDA, O'Malley notebooks, P17/b/112 (Connie Neenan).

32 UCDA, O'Malley notebooks, P17/b/108 (Seán Culhane).

33 1st Southern Division to GHQ, 23 July 1921 (UCDA, Mulcahy papers, P7/A/22, O/C). On Connors and on Cork city generally, see Borgonovo, *Spies, Informers and the 'Anti-Sinn Féin Society'*, pp.89–91.

34 UCDA, O'Malley notebooks, P17/b/108 (Mick Burke).

35 Hart, *The IRA and its Enemies*, p.97; MAI, BMH, WS 1009 (William Buckley), p.21; WS 1065 (James Coss), p.11; MAI, BMH, CD 230/5 (Liam McKenna Collection); 'Casualties – British Military & Police' (MAI, A/0614); 'Executions by IRA' (MAI, A/0649 II).

36 O'Halpin, 'Counting Terror', p.152. Further research has yielded over fifty additional fatalities that have not been included in these calculations. Note also that fatalities in India (three) have been excluded from this table.

37 UCDA, O'Malley notebooks, P17/B/112 (Mick Murphy).

38 William Sheehan, *A Hard Local War: The British Army and the Guerrilla War in Cork, 1919–1921* (Dublin: The History Press, 2011), pp.158–9.

39 County Inspector's report for Cavan, June 1921 (TNA, CO 904/115); TNA, WO 35/149B; 'Casualties – British Agents' (MAI, A/0614); *Anglo-Celt*, 18, 25 June 1921.

40 Hart, *The IRA and its Enemies*, pp.295–6, 298.
41 Listed without comment or elaboration in MAI, A/0694, Group IX.
42 UCDA, O'Malley notebooks, P17/b/120 (Seán McGuinness); observation by Dr McConway at the weekly Research Seminar in Contemporary Irish History, Trinity College Dublin, 26 Sept. 2012.
43 MAI, BMH, WS 1514 (Edward Brennan); Summary of Police Reports, July 1921 (TNA, CO 904/146); *Leinster Express*, 9 July 1921; *Irish Independent*, 21 Oct. 1921.
44 MS. list of spies executed, undated (MAI, A/0649, Group IX); *Offaly Chronicle*, 14 July 1921.
45 The IRA's Sam McCartney of Belfast, the only fatality at Lappanduff on 7 May 1921, is commemorated in a Belfast republican song, 'The Ballad of Sam McCartney'.
46 Hart, *The IRA and its Enemies, 1916–1923*, p.49.
47 'History of the 5th Division in Ireland, Nov. 1919–Mar. 1922', Appendix XIV, p.2 (Imperial War Museum, London, Jeudwine papers).
48 Summary of police reports June 1921 (TNA, CO 904/146); TNA, WO 35/89; *Irish Independent*, 8 June 1920; *Irish Times*, 22 Aug. 1921; Borgonovo, *Spies, Informers and the 'Anti-Sinn Féin Society'*, p.100; Murphy, *The Year of Disappearances*, pp.34–5. Swanton's service records were consulted at www.ancestry.co.uk.
49 The records of the Military Service Pensions Board, constituting about 260,000 individual and subject files, are due for phased release: see O'Halpin, 'The Military Service Pensions Project', forthcoming.
50 Summary of Police Reports, Apr. 1921 (TNA, CO 904/145); MAI, BMH, WS 976 (Séamus Connolly); WS 1073 (James Quinn); WS 1112 (Patrick Reidy).
51 Summary of Police Reports June 1921 (TNA, CO 904/146); West Clare Brigade Activities Report for June 1921 (UCDA, Mulcahy papers, A/20); MAI, BMH, WS 1149 (J.M. McCarthy), including Colonel Bryan to the Taoiseach, 8 Mar. 1946; WS 1226 (Michael Russell).
52 Summary of Police Reports, June 1921 (TNA, CO 904/146); TNA, WO 35/159B; MAI, BMH, WS 574 (John McGonnell), p.6; WS 575 (Joseph McKenna), p.5; WS 1028 (James McKenna), p.7; Statement of Paddy Moran, Paddy McCluskey, Harry Lavery and Francie McKenna, Statement of Patrick McGrory (Monaghan County Museum, Marron papers, 3F, 2G1); McGarry, *Eoin O'Duffy*, pp.68–9.
53 Quoted in O'Halpin, 'The Military Service Pensions Project'.
54 Leitrim County Library, Ballinamore Oral History Collection, Pat Moran (5 Mar. 1991) and Larry Moran (12 Sept. 1991); UCDA, O'Malley notebooks, P17/b/113 (Frank Davis; Paddy Morrissey); MAI, BMH, WS 496 (Frank Davis); WS 1146 (Eugene Kilkenny); WS 1195 (Patrick Doherty); WS 1263 (Charles Pinkman); WS 1268 (Patrick Joseph Hargaden).
55 MAI, BMH, WS 718 (Tom Crawley).
56 A.E. Perceval, Text of two undated [1923?] lectures on Ireland (Imperial War Museum, Perceval papers, P18). Perceval, who won a DSO and an MC in the First World War, regarded the British losses of a dozen men and two trucks at Crossbarry as trifling in terms of the yield – the killing of Hurley, and the shock which near-encirclement gave the IRA, which never again attempted large-scale Flying Column operations. For a very different interpretation, see Barry, *Guerrilla Days in Ireland*, pp.122–31.
57 Peter Hart (ed.), *British Intelligence in Ireland, 1920–21: The Final Reports* (Cork: Cork University Press, 2002), p.47.
58 GHQ circular no. 13, 9 Nov. 1920 (UCDA, Mulcahy papers, P/7/A45).
59 Report for June by Cork No. 3 Brigade, 6 July 1921 (UCDA, Mulcahy papers, P/7/A/19); Hart, *The IRA and its Enemies*, p.299; *Cork Examiner*, 4 July 1921.
60 West Donegal Brigade report for April 1921 (UCDA, Mulcahy papers, P/7/A/20).
61 Joost Augusteijn, *From Public Defiance to Guerrilla Warfare: The Experience of Ordinary Volunteers in the Irish War of Independence, 1916–1923* (Dublin: Irish Academic Press, 1996), p.314.
62 TNA, WO 35/147A; *Cork Examiner*, 21, 25 Mar. 1921. I am grateful to Dr Eve Morrison for this reference.

63 Report for July 1921 by Intelligence Officer, West Limerick Brigade (NLI, O'Donoghue papers, MS 32215).

64 Director of Publicity to Minister for Defence, 23 June 1921 (UCDA, Mulcahy papers, P/7/A/19); Undated notebook marked 'IRA', c.1935 (Thomas Brennan papers (private collection)); Undated notes by Nuala O'Neill (daughter), 1960s (NLI, O'Mahony papers, MS 44064).

65 Alexander Noble to de Valera, 8 Sept. 1921, and other papers (MAI, A/0649, Group IX).

66 Summary of Police Reports, Feb. 1921(TNA, CO 904/144); Mrs Benson to de Valera, Director of Publicity to Minister for Defence, 7 July, and O/C Cork No. 1 Brigade to GHQ, 11 July 1921 (UCDA, Mulcahy papers, P7/A/21); MAI, BMH, WS 713 (Denis Dwyer), p.10; WS 1457 (Daniel McCarthy), pp.7–8; WS 1597 (Thomas P. Waters), p.8; WS 1720 (John Manning), p.24; 'Casualties – British Military & Police' (MAI, A/0614); Report forwarded by O/C Cork No. 1 Brigade, 19 July 1921 (NLI, O'Mahony papers, MS 44045/1 and 2).

67 Martin Corry recordings, 1976, courtesy of Jim Fitzgerald of the Knockraha Historical Society.

68 Chief of Staff (Liam Lynch) to Officer Commanding 4th Western Brigade, 28 Jan. 1923 (NUI Galway, Frank Carty papers, POL7/2).

69 Military Service Pensions project, unmarked file, copy of Minister for Defence to Secretary, Department of Defence, 7 Mar. 1932, and certificate confirming destruction signed by Commandant Dan Bryan and Captain Niall Harrington, 9 Mar. 1932.

70 On Bryan, see DIB sub nom. His papers are in UCDA. Niall Harrington's papers are in the NLI.

71 See the papers in MAI, A/0649, Group IX; Note by Sean O'Mahony, 7 Oct. 1999 (NLI, O'Mahony MS 44045/1); Seán O'Callaghan, Execution (London: Muller, 1974). It is said that after being dug up a second time, Mrs Lindsay's remains were incinerated. On the transfer of records, see Eunan O'Halpin, Defending Ireland: The Irish State and its Enemies Since 1922 (Oxford: Oxford University Press, 1999), pp.60–3.

72 MAI, A/0649, Group IX, correspondence re Michael Hackett.

73 UCDA, O'Malley notebooks, P17/A/111 (Stan Barry).

74 Summary of police reports, July 1921 (TNA, CO 904/146); Dundalk Democrat, 9 July 1921.

75 UCDA, O'Malley notebooks, P17/A/108 (Mick Leahy); Murphy, The Year of Disappearances, p.41; Irish Times, 7 Sept. 1920; Freeman's Journal, 8 Sept. 1920.

76 O/C Longford Brigade to O/C 1st Midland Division, 1 June 1922 (MAI, A/0649, Group IX); UCDA, Mac Eoin Papers, P151/1209 (10).

77 Catherine Ray to Minister for Defence, 11 Dec. 1921, Agnes Ray to Minister for Defence, 15, 22 Jan. 1922, and undated, Command Adjutant, Cork, to Commander in Chief, 11 Apr. 1923, and Minister for Defence to Catherine Ray, 17 Apr. 1923 (MAI, A/0649, Group IX).

78 UCDA, Mulcahy Papers, P7/A/24, John Herlihy to President de Valera, 30 Aug. and 16 Sept., and Adjutant 1st Southern Division to GHQ, 14 Sept. 1921.

79 MAI, A/0649, O/C Carlow Brigade to GHQ, 28 Feb. 1922, Julia Hackett to GHQ, 1 Sept. 1922, and Adjutant (Carlow Brigade) to Divisional Adjutant, 18 Oct. 1922.

80 Jeremiah McCarthy to Officer Commanding, Spike Island (NAI, JUS/H/227/7).

81 Deputy Garda Commissioner to Department of Justice, 16 Dec. 1924 (NAI, JUS 2007/257/11). The Gardai also reported that Private J.A.W. Anderson of the Cameron Highlanders, abducted in Cobh on 26 Oct. 1921, had been killed at Knockraha (NAI, JUS/H/257/13).

82 Borgonovo, Spies, Informers and the 'Anti-Sinn Féin Society', p.181, makes the case for the effectiveness of IRA measures against civilian informers in Cork city. His argument is marked by a circumspect attitude towards British records as compared with Irish ones.

83 UCDA, O'Malley notebooks, P17/A/111 (Stan Barry).

84 Martin Corry recordings, courtesy of Jim Fitzgerald of the Knockraha Historical Society.

85 UCDA, O'Malley notebooks, P17/A/108.

86 Under 'Unknown', the indices to the death registers in the General Register Office record 116 men and forty-seven women between 1918 and 1921.

87 These are among the discrete categories in the printed forms that the Cork 1st Southern Division issued to brigades during the Truce period (NLI, O'Donoghue papers, MS 31203).

88 Murphy, *The Year of Disappearances*. See the review by Eugenio Biaggini, and Murphy's rejoinder, at www.history.ac.uk/reviews/review/1053; David Fitzpatrick, 'History in a hurry', *Dublin Review of Books* [Online], no. 17 (Spring 2011). Available from: www.drb.ie/essays/history-in-a-hurry; and Caoimhe Nic Dháibheid, *The Irish Times*, 11 Dec. 2010. For a less measured review by a current Ph.D researcher, see that by Padraig Óg Ó Ruairc in *History-Ireland*, Mar. 2011, and subsequent clashes with Murphy on www.theirishstory.com/2011/03/09/book-review-the-year-of-disappearances-political-killings-in-cork-1921-1922/ [accessed September 2012].

89 Hart (ed.), *British Intelligence in Ireland*, p.49.

14

THE MUTATIONS OF MARTYRDOM IN BRITAIN AND IRELAND
c. 1850–2005

JOHN WOLFFE

Kilmainham Gaol on the outskirts of Dublin – between 1966, when it was restored and opened to the public to mark the fiftieth anniversary of the Easter Rising and 1986, when it was taken over by Heritage Ireland – was a focus for 'proud and unapologetic' Irish nationalism and republicanism. Voluntary guides would stand on the spot where the leaders of the 1916 Rising were shot by the British, and speak with quasi-religious earnestness of how these men sacrificed their lives for the cause of Irish freedom and should inspire later generations to continue their struggle until the six counties were reunited with the twenty-six. By the 1980s, such language had become alienating for Irish people with less confrontational political attitudes, let alone the occasional British visitor.[1] It was, however, a striking and persistent example of how the language and rhetoric of martyrdom, with its Christian roots, could be seamlessly translated into a secular and contested nationalist context.

This essay explores something of that historical process, weaving together an analysis that spans the Irish Sea. The underlying hypothesis is the paradoxical one that the very way in which the 'terrible beauty' of martyrdom divided Protestant and Catholic, British and Irish, reveals substantial underlying cultural and religious commonalities. Obviously this took on a new form at Easter 1916, but pace W.B. Yeats, this was not so much a birth as a mutation.[2]

The place of political martyrdom and redemptive sacrifice in the nationalist and republican traditions in Ireland has been explored with reference to periods extending from the death of Wolfe Tone in 1798, through the Fenian martyrs of 1867, and the leaders of the Easter Rising in 1916, to the deaths of the IRA hunger strikers in 1981.[3] Guy Beiner has pointed out significant parallels between Protestant and loyalist traditions, especially in the folk memory of the 'sufferings' of Protestants in the 1641, 1689 and 1798 rebellions, and the trauma of the massive losses suffered by the Ulster Division at the Battle of the Somme in July 1916, just two months after the suppression of the Easter Rising.[4] The purpose of this essay, however, is to set these specifically Irish and in part secularized traditions in the wider context both of evolving religious interest in martyrdom and of the parallel experience in Britain. Research on this broader framework remains relatively undeveloped: while early modernists have carried out significant work on martyrdom, coverage of periods since the seventeenth century is much more limited.[5] Church historians have offered suggestive case studies rather than overall analysis;[6] conversely, while historians such as Jay Winter and Adrian Gregory have interested themselves in the cult of the dead of the First World War, they have made little attempt to relate it to a longer tradition of Christian martyrdom.[7] Most recently, in the aftermath of the suicide terrorist attacks on 11 September 2001, considerable journalistic and scholarly attention has been directed towards the analysis of Islamic concepts of martyrdom, but comparable Christian ideas have received little attention.[8]

The *Oxford English Dictionary* usefully encapsulates transitions in the meaning of martyrdom by defining a martyr as 'One who undergoes penalty of death for persistence in Christian faith or obedience to law of the Church, or undergoes death or suffering for any great cause'. Clearly, as David Loades points out, 'the definition of martyrdom … depends not upon the fact or manner of death, but upon the cause died for'.[9] That cause has to be articulated and advocated by the martyr's posthumous apologists and devotees, although sometimes individuals such as Patrick Pearse and Thomas MacDonagh in 1916 could leave behind them emotive utterances and writings that facilitated that task. In the long term, the persistence of a martyr's reputation was dependent on the success, or at least the continued vitality, of the cause for which he or she was perceived to have given their life. Moreover, the revival of a cause could lead to a renewal of interest in the sacrifice of long-dead martyrs.

Following an overview of Protestant and then Catholic views of martyrdom during the nineteenth century, this essay will explore how the initially Christian concept of martyrdom became more broadly applied to sacrificial death for nationalist as well as specifically religious causes. Christian traditions of martyrdom can obviously be traced back to the early Church, but the chronological starting point for the present analysis is the mid-nineteenth century, which saw the Catholic revival in England, the so-called 'devotional revolution' in Ireland, and an associated upsurge in anti-Catholicism on both sides of the Irish sea.

As Protestant polemicists looked for material to sustain arguments against Rome, they naturally turned to the *Acts and Monuments* or 'Book of Martyrs' first published by John Foxe in 1563. Foxe focused particularly on commemorating the Protestants executed in the then recent past, but located them in the long sweep of church history and the persecution of perceived true Christians since the early Church. Copies of Foxe's work were kept in churches, and so became part of religious and national culture and were readily accessible to those who wished to consult them.[10]

The later eighteenth century had seen something of a lull in republications of Foxe, but interest in the text revived in the early nineteenth century in the context of controversy over Catholic Emancipation that followed the conclusion of the Anglo-Irish Union of 1800. In 1807, the journalist Francis William Blagdon published a new edition under the pseudonym of 'Rev J. Milner' thus mischievously identifying himself both with the recently deceased evangelical historian Joseph Milner, and the contemporary Catholic Bishop John Milner. Blagdon added material to Foxe's text including a chapter 'concerning further attempts of the Roman Catholics to overthrow the Protestant government; with the sufferings of martyrs from the reign of James First to the present time'.[11] He was open about his objective of turning public opinion against Emancipation, which would, he alleged, leave the country exposed to 'that accursed bigotry, which, by employing torture and extermination as the means of conversion, has affixed eternal disgrace and infamy on the sixteenth century'.[12] Blagdon claimed that when it first appeared his edition 'was eagerly sought after in all parts of the country', and it was reprinted at least half a dozen times later in the century.[13]

Foxe also heavily influenced other early nineteenth-century interpretations of church history, such as Legh Richmond's *Fathers of the English Church* (1807–12) and Robert Southey's *Book of the Church* (1824).[14] From the 1830s, a renewed sense of conflict with Catholicism, both in its Roman and Oxford Tractarian forms, led to an upsurge in republication. The British Library catalogue lists no less than ten editions of Foxe between the late 1830s and the 1870s, ranging from a massive eight-volume scholarly text edited by Stephen Cattley and George Townsend to pocket-sized abridgements.[15] In 1851, the leading Methodist William Harris Rule published his *Martyrs of the Reformation*, drawing substantially on Foxe, but also extending his narrative to include extensive accounts of persecution of continental Protestants in the seventeenth and eighteenth centuries. He included coverage of the revocation of the Edict of Nantes in 1685, and the enforced migration of Protestant Salzburgers in 1731. Rule acknowledged that 'few persons, indeed, have been solemnly martyred, for the sake of Christ, within the present century'. However, against the background of the Oxford Movement and the restoration of the Catholic hierarchy, he believed that while Roman Catholic methods might have changed, their objective of suppressing the true Christian gospel remained. Clearly during these decades publishers as well as authors were confident that the Protestant martyrs had a substantial appeal to a wide range of different markets.[16]

One widespread feature of these books was the dramatic woodcuts of burnings. The Protestant polemicist Charlotte Elizabeth Tonna, who published an abridgement of Foxe in 1837, recalled that during her childhood in the 1790s her father gave her an old folio edition of Foxe:

> I could not, it is true, decipher the black letter, but ... every wood-cut was examined with aching eyes and a palpitating heart. Assuredly I took in more of the spirit of John Foxe, even by that imperfect mode of acquaintance, than many do by reading his book through; and when my father next found me at what became my darling study, I looked up at him with burning cheeks and asked, 'Papa, may I be a martyr?'[17]

Charlotte Elizabeth was an unusual child and her reaction to the images was a characteristically extreme one. Nevertheless, the incident is revealing evidence of the readiness of parents to regard Foxe as appropriate reading for their offspring, and of the lasting impression that it could make on children. Moreover, her staunchly Protestant father responded to her childishly naïve question, by observing 'if the government ever gives power to the Papists again ... you may very probably live to be a martyr'.

From the mid-nineteenth century onwards, monuments were erected to Protestant martyrs, most famously in Oxford between 1838 and 1843, to commemorate the burning of Thomas Cranmer, Hugh Latimer and Nicholas Ridley. As Andrew Atherstone has demonstrated, the Oxford Martyrs Memorial was in its origins as much a reflection of resurgent antagonism to Roman Catholicism as a protest against the Anglo-Catholic Oxford Movement.[18] Exactly contemporary with it was the martyr's memorial on the Scores in St Andrews, which commemorated George Wishart and other pioneers of the Scottish Reformation. Monuments to commemorate local burnings of Protestants continued to appear as late as the first decade of the twentieth century: in Exeter in 1908 and in Coventry in 1910.

Also at the beginning of the twentieth century militant Protestantism rather unexpectedly acquired a contemporary martyr in the person of John Kensit, a leading anti-Catholic agitator and founder of the Protestant Truth Society. He died on 8 October 1902 as a result of an injury sustained when he was attacked by Roman Catholics in Liverpool a fortnight before. His followers hailed Kensit as 'the first Protestant martyr of the twentieth century' and he too inspired the building of monuments, most notably the Kensit Memorial College in north London, which continues to this day to train ministers for conservative evangelical churches.[19]

It was natural that such celebration of Protestant martyrs should give rise to a Catholic reaction. Early nineteenth-century Catholic apologists, such as Bishop John Milner and the historian John Lingard, tended to concentrate on correcting the bias and partiality in Protestant accounts, but as the century wore on there was increasing enthusiasm for promoting a counter-narrative of Catholic martyrdom in the modern era.[20] Such was the vision of the leading convert George Spencer in a sermon in 1838, when he appealed to the memory of Catholic martyrs whose blood, he believed, has 'been indeed abundantly poured forth' to nourish the eventual renewal of the English church. Spencer's rhetoric was intensely patriotic, characterizing the martyrs' self-sacrifice for the cause of the faith in England as one for 'the Land they loved, the Land for which they suffered and died'.[21]

Nineteenth-century English Catholic writers were slow to provide new detailed accounts of their martyrs and continued to rely on Richard Challoner's *Memoirs of Missionary Priests* (1741–2). However, the absence of any comparable account of post-Reformation Irish Catholic martyrs prompted Patrick Francis Moran, then vice-rector of the Irish College in Rome and later Archbishop of Sydney, to publish in 1861 a memoir of Archbishop Oliver Plunkett, executed in London in 1681 for alleged treason. Moran followed this the next year, with a *Historical sketch of the persecutions suffered by the Catholics of Ireland under the rule of Cromwell and the Puritans.*[22] Then, in 1868, Myles O'Reilly, who had formerly gallantly commanded Irish troops in the service of Pope Pius IX, published *Memorials of those who suffered for the Catholic faith in Ireland in the 16th, 17th and 18th centuries.*[23] O'Reilly attributed the lack of published accounts of the modern Irish martyrs to the extent to which 'the devastation of the Cromwellian persecution annihilated the life of the Irish race'.[24] He was careful to limit himself to those who suffered specifically for their Catholicism rather than for political causes, but still traced a record of overt violence against the faith down to 1745. Moreover in much more recent times, he claimed that many victims of the Great Famine had been 'faithful even unto death' insofar as they had spurned the offer of food from Protestant soupers. Nevertheless, he professed eirenical intent now that 'strife and religious persecution is past' and 'the descendants of the persecutors and the persecuted are ... citizens of a common country'.[25] A substantially expanded edition was published in New York a decade later, where it competed with the *Lives of the Irish Martyrs* published by the Irish-American D.P. Conyngham in 1872.[26]

Meanwhile, in 1859, the English Catholic bishops commenced petitioning Rome for recognition of the English martyrs, but the initial response was discouraging. In the 1870s, however, the cause was advanced through more detailed historical work, notably by the Jesuit John Morris, whose *Troubles of our Catholic Forefathers* was published in three volumes between 1872 and 1877. In 1874, an ecclesiastical tribunal at Westminster gathered extensive evidence, which was then forwarded to Rome. The slow wheels of Vatican process were somewhat speeded up by the observation that portraits of a substantial number of martyrs had been painted on the walls of the church of the English College in the late sixteenth century, thus providing evidence that they were already then objects of devotion. Hence Leo XIII beatified fifty-four martyrs in 1886. A further nine beatifications followed in 1895, and 136 more in 1926. Meanwhile, the Irish hierarchy secured the beatification of Oliver Plunkett in 1920. Subsequently a more select group proceeded to canonization; Thomas More and John Fisher were the first in 1935, and another forty followed in 1970.[27]

The process of gathering evidence followed by the beatifications themselves helped to inspire a growth of devotion to martyr cults in England. In 1884, a nun at the Bar Convent in York published *Short Memoirs* of the Yorkshire martyrs, specifically as an aid to devotion. She reflected that 'Many of our fellow-Catholics have yet to learn the love of those valiant champions of Christ, whose blood watered the roots of the tree of our holy Faith.'[28] In early 1887, a few weeks after the beatifications, Morris himself addressed the boys of Stonyhurst, stressing the religious rather than political reasons for the martyrs' deaths and treating them to lurid accounts of their sufferings. They were, he maintained in language calculated to appeal to impressionable teenage boys, 'the bravest of the brave' who 'nobly teach us that our faith is worth suffering for; yes, and that our faith is worth dying for'.[29] For Austin J. King, speaking on the beatifications at St Mary's School, Bath, the context was avowedly patriotic:

> We Englishmen are deservedly proud of our ancestry. We love to look back upon the history of men who have spent themselves and died in suffering, that others of their countrymen might live, or that the rushing stream of England's greatness and freedom might be unobstructed and unpolluted ... No body of Her Majesty's subjects are more loyal than are we Catholics.[30]

Thus the standard Protestant polemic against the Elizabethan martyrs was turned on its head with the claim that far from being traitors, they were the truest patriots. A few years later, Luke Rivington, preaching at the Church of the English Martyrs in London, associated the cult, and the associated aspirations for the conversion of England, with a robust rebuttal of the claim of the Church of England to continuity with the pre-Reformation church. 'Now', Rivington affirmed 'it was for the opposite of this contention that our Holy Martyrs shed their English and Catholic blood.'[31]

The most notable historian and propagandist for the English Catholic martyrs was Dom Bede Camm, who in 1904 published his compilation of *Lives of the English Martyrs*, providing accounts of those beatified in 1886 and 1895. Indeed, Camm later wrote that having been brought up and ordained as an Anglican, it was the beatifications that led to the collapse of his belief in the continuity of the Church of England with the ancient English church. It was the martyrs, he now believed, who 'held dearer than life the old Faith of old England' and he believed that 'devotion to these heroes of ours will do more than anything else to keep our own faith fervent'.[32] Camm's work benefited from effective popularizers, notably Robert Hugh Benson in his successful novel *Come Rack, Come Rope*, first published in 1912, and the children's writer Ethel Mary Wilmot-Buxton, whose *Book of English Martyrs*, which appeared in 1915, sought to 'breathe a spirit of fervent faith and high adventure that should appeal to every right-minded boy and girl of to-day'.[33]

Thus in both Protestant and Catholic contexts, martyrdom had strong patriotic as well as religious resonances. However, in the earlier part of the nineteenth century, at least in Britain, a clear discrimination had been made between Christian martyrs and secular heroes. Thus a preacher on Lord Nelson's death at the Battle of Trafalgar in 1805 chose a text from Acts relating to the burial of Stephen, but was careful to distinguish Stephen who 'became a martyr to his zeal for the cause of Christianity' from Nelson who sacrificed himself 'to his zeal for his country'.[34] Charles Wolfe's famous lines on the burial of Sir John Moore at Corunna portrayed the deceased as a hero, but stopped well short of the language of martyrdom:

> Slowly and sadly we laid him down,
> From the field of his fame fresh and gory:
> We carved not a line, and we raised not a stone,
> But we left him alone with his glory.

The language of 'glory' rather than sacrifice or martyrdom remained the dominant theme of Alfred Tennyson's 'Charge of the Light Brigade' in 1856:

> When can their glory fade?
> O the wild charge they made!
> All the world wondered.
> Honour the charge they made!
> Honour the Light Brigade,
> Noble six hundred!

In a different context, the Dorset labourers condemned and transported to Australia in 1834 for forming a trade union were not initially known as 'The Tolpuddle Martyrs'. While the contemporary pamphlet account of their experiences by George Loveless describes them as 'persecutions', the word 'martyr' does not feature, and appears only to have obtained general currency with the celebrations of the centenary of the event in 1934.[35]

By contrast, it is possible to find occasional more secular applications of the word 'martyr' in Ireland in the same period. In 1831, Thomas Moore referred to Robert Emmet as a 'martyr' to the cause of Irish freedom, and in 1847, Richard Robert Madden attributed to Emmet himself in his speech from the dock in 1803 a self-characterization as one of a 'band of martyred heroes who have shed their blood … in defence of their country'.[36] Significantly, however, that phrase does not occur in a contemporary account of Emmet's trial.[37] A ballad on the death of Daniel O'Connell, also in 1847, included the following stanza:

> With Christian beauty he did his duty,
> For forty years if I say more
> His precious heart he has bequeath'd
> In his dying moments to the Church of Rome
> He lived a Christian and died a Marter (sic),
> I may well say for sweet Erin's shore,
> Through meditation and contem[p]lation
> His days were ende[d] – he is no more.[38]

Here, however, O'Connell's perceived status as a martyr was founded in his piety as well as his patriotism, and his funeral in Dublin was an intensely Catholic as well as nationalist demonstration. Given that he died from natural causes at the age of seventy-one, the claim that he was literally a martyr, either to his faith or to his country, was hardly a plausible one.

Nevertheless, the stanza was symptomatic of an increasing elision between religious and national language that was also shortly to become apparent in Britain. Here the roots of the trend lay in the military conflicts of the 1850s in the Crimea and in India, when in contrast to prevalent attitudes in the Napoleonic Wars, a soldier's calling came to be seen as more readily compatible with strong Christian commitment. Thus in 'Brave Words for Brave Soldiers and Sailors', sent out to the army besieging Sebastopol in the winter of 1855, the Anglican clergyman and popular novelist Charles Kingsley assured them that 'he who fights for Queen and country in a just cause, is fighting not only in the Queen's army, but in Christ's army, and that he shall in no wise lose his reward'.[39] It followed that death in war began to be perceived in more explicitly Christian terms, increasingly approaching to the language of martyrdom. When the evangelical writer Catherine Marsh penned her widely read tribute to her friend Captain Hedley Vicars, who was killed in action at Sebastopol early in 1855, she did not explicitly describe him as a martyr, but her construction of an exemplary life of Christian devotion, military gallantry and sacrificial death naturally tended in that direction.[40] Two years later, however, the Rev. Robert Meek boldly titled his memoir of Ensign Marcus Cheek, killed during the Indian Mutiny, 'The Martyr of Allahabad'. It is true that young Cheek's claim to the status of a martyr rested not on his military gallantry, but on his courageous explicit profession of Christ while in the hands of Muslim captors; however, Meek's tract represented a further blurring of distinctions that had previously been clear-cut.[41] Subsequently in the early 1860s, the language of martyrdom in relation to military conflict was to become quite widespread in the American Civil War.[42]

A further British instance occurred in 1866 when Francis Hastings Doyle, later professor of poetry at Oxford, published his poem on the wreck of the troopship HMS *Birkenhead* off the coast of South Africa in 1852, an event that became famous for the reported courageous behaviour of the soldiers under extreme circumstances, and the establishment of the principle of 'women and children first'. Doyle perceived those who drowned as 'joint heirs with Christ, because they bled to save /His weak ones, not in vain'. They were 'left His martyrs in the bay'.[43]

The following year, on 23 November 1867, the Fenians William Allen, Michael Larkin and Michael O'Brien were hanged outside Salford Gaol for the alleged murder of a policeman, and the language of martyrdom was immediately widespread and resonant in Ireland. For example, John Martin concluded his address at the gates of Glasnevin Cemetery as follows:

> You will join with me now in repeating the prayer of the three martyrs whom we mourn – 'God save Ireland!' And all of you, men, women, and boys and girls that are to be men and women of holy Ireland, will ever keep the sentiment of that prayer in your heart of hearts.

The Manchester Martyrs might have achieved less for Ireland in life than O'Connell had done, but by the manner of their deaths they ensured a powerfully emotive legacy for the nationalist cause. More-over, despite the earlier ambivalences in the Catholic hierarchy's attitude to Fenianism, the popular response to the executions was suffused with religious as well as nationalist devotion.[44]

This trend also continued in Britain over the next two decades, and reached an initial culmination in the response to the death of General Gordon at Khartoum in 1885. In that year, the novelist Elizabeth Rundle Charles published her account of 'three martyrs of the nineteenth century', eulogizing Gordon, alongside two other recent perceived martyrdoms, that of the missionary Bishop John Coleridge Patteson in Melanesia in 1871, and of David Livingstone in central

Africa in 1873. Charles perceived all three as glowing both with Christian passion and patriotic zeal for the noblest traditions of 'Greater Britain'.[45]

The realities of their deaths were, of course, rather more ambivalent than Charles implied. Patteson, the missionary, had the strongest claim to be regarded as a Christian martyr in the traditional sense, but even he died, as David Hilliard puts it, 'because he was a white man in the wrong place at the wrong time, not in defence of the Christian faith'.[46] Livingstone died of natural causes aggravated by his own obsessive search for the source of the Nile. While Gordon's death has been constructed in both art and literature as a heroic confrontation with the Muslim forces of the Mahdi, this image is not supported by the evidence, and it is very possible that he was actually shot by accident.[47] Nevertheless, discordant facts did little to hamper the development of the legend, which was reinforced by the portrayal of Patteson alongside the martyrs St Alban and St Boniface on the pulpit of Exeter Cathedral; by Livingstone's public funeral and interment in the nave of Westminster Abbey; and by the ongoing cult of Gordon as the model Christian soldier.[48] The blending of the Christian and the national, and the view of Gordon as a martyred, even Christ-like figure, was also very much apparent in verses written on his death, notably by Doyle:

He who for England, helped by none,
So long his crushing burdens bore,
As grand and lonely as the sun,
Set yesterday to rise no more ...

We shall press forward to our goal,
Sustained by echoes from the Past,
Sustained by Him – whose Death-notes toll
Sublime as any, though the last;
Yes! We must follow on his track,
Like those who coming from afar,
To Bethlehem, never looking back,
Followed in faith that sudden star.[49]

Such were some of the religious and cultural traditions of martyrdom that surfaced with renewed intensity in the second decade of the twentieth century. Early in 1913, news of the deaths of Captain Scott and his companions in the Antarctic the previous year reached Britain, and was marked by a memorial service at St Paul's attended by the King, and by widespread national mourning. The casualties were quite widely described as 'martyrs' although this was manifestly a much more secular and ambiguous martyrdom even than that of Livingstone and Gordon. While the courage with which they faced their fate was admirable, their primary enemy was no persecuting or hostile human power but the savagery of the polar weather. Lawrence Oates' apparent readiness – with the famous words 'I am just going outside and may be some time' – to sacrifice his own life in order to give his companions a better prospect of reaching safety gave him the strongest claim to martyr status, but Scott himself was, in the words of his patron Clements Markham, a 'martyr in the cause of science' rather than of any more tangible ideology.[50] Nevertheless, on the eve of the First World War, they provided a very high-profile example of perceived self-sacrificial death. An account of it was read to at least 1.5 million children in elementary schools on the day of the memorial service. It concluded with the words 'they laid down their lives bravely and calmly like true Christian gentlemen'.[51]

After the First World War broke out, Arthur Winnington-Ingram, the Anglican Bishop of London, was prominent in his characterization of the war dead as martyrs, because they stood against the unchristian doctrine that 'might is right', allegedly being advanced by Germany. Early in the war, in an apparent endeavour to console bereaved parents he spoke as follows:

> You have lost your boys, but what are they? Martyrs – martyrs as really as St Stephen was a martyr – martyrs dying for their faith as really as St Stephen, the first martyr, died for his. They looked up when they died in the trenches, or in the little cottage where they were carried, they looked up and saw JESUS standing on the right hand of GOD. And He is keeping them safe for you there when your time comes. Covered with imperishable glory they pass to deathless life.[52]

Winnington-Ingram later acknowledged that some had thought it not 'quite right' to refer to the war dead as martyrs, but in 1917 he reaffirmed his own view in the context of a war that he believed to be clearly a fight for the freedom of the world against a 'remorseless tyranny'.[53] Even if others were more cautious than him about explicit use of the word 'martyr', the concept was still implicit in the language of countless war memorials, with their equation of 'For God, for King and Country'. A further illustration of this frame of mind comes in the language of the fifth stanza of John Arkwright's popular hymn, 'O valiant hearts' written in 1919, in commemoration of the war dead:

> These were His servants, in His steps they trod,
> Following through death the martyred Son of God:
> Victor, He rose; victorious too shall rise
> They who have drunk His cup of sacrifice.

While in London Winnington-Ingram portrayed the British war dead as Christian martyrs and Camm and Wilmot-Buxton were busy popularizing narratives of the English Catholic martyrs, in Dublin Patrick Pearse was developing his ideas regarding blood sacrifice and the religion of nationhood, famously articulated at the graveside of O'Donovan Rossa on 1 August 1915: 'Life springs from death; and from the graves of patriot men and women spring living nations.'[54] This is familiar ground to historians of modern Ireland, but the key point to emphasize here is that although Pearse's thinking had distinctively Irish roots in a reinterpretation both of the nationalist tradition and of the Cuchulain legend, it also needs to be seen in the context of wider currents of interest in both Christian and secular forms of martyrdom that were by no means unique to Ireland.[55] It is one of the many cruel ironies of the months and years following April 1916 that the British authorities initially failed to understand how the very ideology of self-sacrificial death that enabled them to discern some meaning and purpose in the slaughter of thousands of young men in France was also to give an irresistible boost to the cause of the Irish nationalism. The valedictory courtroom speech attributed to Thomas MacDonagh eloquently reaffirmed the connection to the historic tradition of nationalist and Christian martyrdom:

> Gentlemen, you have sentenced me to death, and I accept your sentence with joy and pride, since it is for Ireland I am to die. I go to join the goodly company of the men who died for Ireland, the least of whom was worthier far than I can claim to be, and that noble band are, themselves, but a small section of the great un-numbered army of martyrs, whose Captain is the Christ who died on Calvary … Take me away, and let my blood bedew the sacred soil of Ireland. I die in the certainty that once more the seed will fructify.[56]

In the autumn of 1920, the competing applications of martyrdom came sharply into focus. On 6 October, a service was held at Downside Abbey near Bath to mark the deposit of the relics of Oliver Plunkett, who had been beatified by Pope Benedict XV earlier in the year. In his sermon, Cardinal Bourne 'said that the supreme object of all acts of supplication associated with the martyred Irish Archbishop was the bettering and ultimate settling of the relations between England and Ireland'.[57] Meanwhile, however, in Brixton Prison, Terence MacSwiney, the Lord Mayor of Cork, was nearing the end of his hunger strike protesting against his imprisonment for sedition.[58] MacSwiney's death on 25 October was followed by widespread use of the language of martyrdom in nationalist circles, in which sympathetic Catholic bishops joined. Daniel Cohalan, the Bishop of Cork wrote that 'Terence MacSwiney takes his place amongst the martyrs in the sacred cause of Ireland'; Archbishop Mannix of Melbourne proclaimed that 'Standing over the dead body of her martyred son, Ireland appeals to the whole world to judge between her and her oppressors.'[59] However, MacSwiney's massive funeral in Cork on 31 October was followed less that a fortnight later by a very different but equally impressive funeral in London, when on Armistice Day, the Unknown Warrior was interred in Westminster Abbey. Although, unlike MacSwiney, the Unknown and those he represented were not explicitly described as martyrs, the language used, notably in the inscription subsequently placed on the grave, was redolent of self-sacrificial death:

> THUS ARE COMMEMORATED THE MANY
> MULTITUDES WHO DURING THE GREAT
> WAR OF 1914 – 1918 GAVE THE MOST THAT
> MAN CAN GIVE LIFE ITSELF
> FOR GOD
> FOR KING AND COUNTRY
> FOR LOVED ONES HOME AND EMPIRE
> FOR THE SACRED CAUSE OF JUSTICE AND
> THE FREEDOM OF THE WORLD

Moreover there was a comparable convergence of church and nation, in the active promotion of the idea of burying an Unknown Warrior by leading ecclesiastics – notably Herbert Ryle, the Dean of Westminster, and Randall Davidson, the Archbishop of Canterbury – in the face of the initial preference of the government and the King for a simpler secular ceremony. The wording of the inscription also owed much to Archbishop Davidson.[60]

1920 marked the highpoint of linkages that thereafter began to decline, albeit more rapidly in Britain than in Ireland. In Britain, as the immediate trauma of the First World War began to pass and the cultural ascendancy of Christianity began to weaken, the application of the language of martyrdom in national rather than religious contexts became less common. It is striking that in the Second World War, despite underlying moral issues in the confrontation with Nazism that seemed clearer cut than in the First World War, there was less talk of dead British combatants as martyrs.[61] The iconic Protestant martyr of the Second World War was not an unknown British soldier, but a German pastor, Dietrich Bonhoeffer. In Ireland on the other hand, as Padraig O'Malley has put it, 'Central to the myth on which the ... state is built ... is the idea of heroic sacrifice.'[62] This 'myth', as noted above, continued to have its active promoters at least until the 1980s. Nevertheless, as the struggle for independence passed from living memory into history, alternative constructions of martyrdom began to resurface. A notable example was the cult of Maria Goretti, an Italian teenager murdered in 1902 by a would-be rapist and thus hailed as a martyr to virginity, who was canonized in 1950 and became a popular saint in Ireland in the 1950s and 1960s.[63] On the Protestant side of the coin, Ian Paisley's new Free Presbyterian Church in Belfast was named 'The Martyrs Memorial', but despite the heated political climate at the time of its opening on 4 October 1969, religious rather than political associations predominated.[64]

The early 1980s proved to be something of a further watershed. In 1981, the IRA hunger-strikers at the Maze sought to locate themselves in the tradition of heroic sacrifice, looking back not only to the sacrifices of the Easter Rising, but also to earlier use of the hunger strike as a nationalist strategy, notably by Terence MacSwiney. O'Malley judges, however, that:

> In the Republic the hunger strikes exposed the ambivalence of the country's attitudes towards the North, its less than enthusiastic adherence to the myths of the past, [and] its unwillingness to acknowledge essential elements of those myths.[65]

The response to the hunger strikes further revealed that the merging of the secular and the religious no longer represented a widespread consensus, and was vulnerable to challenge on two fronts, even from within the broad Catholic and nationalist constituency. On the one hand, Bishop Cahal Daly appealed to the prisoners to cease to court martyrdom: 'You can do more for Ireland by living for it than by dying for it ... Let your endurance be dedicated to the service of life, not the work of death.'[66] On the other hand, from the secular nationalist perspective, Bernadette McAliskey in a recent interview saw the hunger strikes as grounds for a critique of Christianity itself:

> ... where the undercurrent of religion comes in 'that God so loved the world' that he sent his only son to be crucified, and so Bobby Sands so loved his country that he crucified himself. The blood sacrifice, the martyrdom, 'greater love does not exist than that a man lay down his life for his friend'. It is that thinking, it is that religious, faith-based enormity that enables people to live with killing and being killed because why would you not? Didn't God send his only son down here and say 'Get yourself killed lad for the forgiveness of sins' so why would people in the community whose understanding of life is around that [not get themselves killed], if they can justify the action within that grand scheme.[67]

Such controversies in Ireland had their more muted counterpart in Britain in July 1982, when the St Paul's Cathedral service to mark the end of the Falklands War gave rise to contentions between the churches and members of the Conservative Party, notably Sir John Biggs-Davison MP, who said that 'it was revolting for cringing clergy to misuse St Paul's to throw doubt upon the sacrifices of our fighting men'. No longer, unlike their predecessors in 1920, were the ecclesiastical authorities prepared uncritically to sacralize a nationalistic under-standing of military sacrifice.[68]

Meanwhile, an alternative construction of 'martyrs for peace' began to gather ground in later twentieth-century Ireland. Its origins can be seen as lying in the response to the Niemba Ambush in the Congo in 1960, when for the first time since independence the Republic sustained significant military casualties not in fighting fellow Irishmen or the British but in seeking to keep the peace in a distant part of the world.[69] It was powerfully reinforced when, on Remembrance Sunday 1987, the whole country was profoundly shocked by the IRA bombing of the Protestant crowd gathered for a service at the war memorial in Enniskillen, an event that turned public opinion in the Republic decisively against the IRA. It also propelled Gordon Wilson, whose daughter Marie was killed in the bombing, into the limelight as an advocate of peace and reconciliation. While the importance of Enniskillen for the subsequent peace process is open to debate, the extent to which it led to bridge-building rather than further confrontation is nevertheless significant in relation to the historical context surveyed in this essay. Had ideas of patriotic martyrdom and blood sacrifice held their former ascendancy, there would have been stronger polarized narratives of Protestant victims perpetuating the sacrifice of the war dead they had met to commemorate, and of Catholic perpetrators securing legitimate revenge for historic atrocities. The reality, however, was that Marie Wilson and her fellow victims emerged primarily as martyrs to peace rather than to Unionism and Protestantism, as was indicated by a notable increase in the wearing of poppies in the Republic in the years after 1987.[70]

Events since the turn of the millennium suggest potential for comparison with the case of Islamist suicide bombers and their attacks in the United States in September 2001 and in London in July 2005. These, however, represent a significant contrast insofar as unlike any of the instances discussed hitherto, they deliberately planned for inevitable death, rather than dying as a result of their obstinacy or convinced principle. Even though the sixteenth-century martyrs knew they were risking their lives by their religious activities, and Patrick Pearse could foresee the likely consequences of his actions on Easter Monday 1916, they could still hope for more positive outcomes. Moreover, the suicide bomber who aggressively seeks to kill others, rather than passively to demonstrate by his death the power of his own convictions or commitments, represents a further significant mutation of martyrdom.[71] Furthermore, the contemporary suicide bomber often constructs the narrative of his own martyrdom, by for example making a video before the event, whereas in the historic cases surveyed in this paper, narratives of martyrdom were normally constructed by others after the event, sometimes decades or even centuries after it.

A *longue durée* perspective is especially important in considering the history of death, where attitudes change slowly but the changes that do gradually occur are particularly indicative of significant underlying cultural shifts. This essay has served to highlight an era from the mid-nineteenth century to the early twentieth in which martyrdom was popular, relative to both the preceding and succeeding periods. This does not necessarily mean that there was a greater readiness than in other eras to seek out or to expect violent sacrificial death, but it does point to a culture in which a narrative of martyrdom was widely drawn upon to give sense and purpose to such events when they did occur. Such narratives were originally stimulated by the intense mid-nineteenth-century rivalry of Protestants and Catholics, and their consequent felt need to celebrate past martyrs who were held to enhance the spiritual legitimacy of the causes for which they died. In the context of the continuing strong cultural influence of religion, of British missionary and imperial expansion, and of the Irish national struggle, it was natural that such motifs should also permeate into more secular spheres. Such models of martyrdom declined in influence in the mid-twentieth century, but other variants of the concept have been prominent in recent years. The 'terrible beauty' of martyrdom in all its permutations merits more attention than it has yet received from historians.

NOTES

1 Personal observation during a visit to Kilmainham Gaol in July 1983; Pat Cooke, 'Kilmainham Gaol: Interpreting Irish Nationalism and Republicanism', *Open Museum Journal* [Online], 2 (2000), pp.1–3. Available from: http://hosting.collectionsaustralia.net/omj/vol2/cooke.html [accessed 2 February 2012].
2 W.B. Yeats, 'Easter 1916': 'MacDonagh and MacBride/And Connolly and Pearse/Now and in time to be/Wherever green is worn/Are changed, changed utterly:/A terrible beauty is born.' *W.B. Yeats: the poems*, Daniel Albright (ed.) (London: Dent, 1990), p.230.
3 Alan Ford, 'Martyrdom, History and Memory in Early Modern Ireland', in Ian McBride (ed.), *History and Memory in Modern Ireland* (Cambridge: Cambridge University Press, 2001), p.43.
4 Guy Beiner, 'Between Trauma and Triumphalism: The Easter Rising, the Somme and the Crux of Deep Memory in Modern Ireland', *Journal of British Studies*, 46:2 (2007), pp.366–89.
5 Ford, 'Martyrdom, History and Memory', passim; Thomas S. Freeman and Thomas F. Mayer (eds), *Martyrs and Martyrdom in England c.1400–1700* (Woodbridge: Boydell and Brewer, 2007).
6 Diana Wood (ed.), *Martyrs and Martyrologies: Studies in Church History 30* (Oxford: Blackwell/Ecclesiastical History Society, 1993).
7 Adrian Gregory, *The Silence of Memory: Armistice Day, 1919–1946* (Oxford: Berg, 1994); Jay Winter, *Sites of Memory, Sites of Mourning: The Great War in European Cultural History* (Cambridge: Cambridge University Press, 1995).
8 For example, M. Al-Rasheed and M. Shterin, *Dying for Faith: Religiously Motivated Violence in the Contemporary World* (London: I.B. Tauris, 2009); Jon and Benjamin Cole, *Martyrdom* (London: Pennant, 2009). Brian Wicker (ed.), *Witnesses to Faith? Martyrdom in Christianity and Islam* (Aldershot: Ashgate, 2006) is the only recent publication to explore the comparative dimension in any detail.
9 'Introduction', in Wood (ed.), *Martyrs and Martyrologies*, p.xv.
10 William Haller, *Foxe's Book of Martyrs and the Elect Nation* (London: Jonathan Cape, 1963).
11 'J. Milner', *An Universal History of Christian Martyrdom* (London: B. Crosby, 1807), p.974.
12 Ibid., Advertisement.
13 Ibid., p.vii; British Library Catalogue.
14 Peter Nockles, 'The Reformation Revised? The Changing Legacy and Reception of John Foxe's *Book Of Martyrs* and Other Protestant Texts in the Nineteenth Century', *Bulletin of the John Rylands Library*, forthcoming, 2014.
15 British Library online catalogue; John Wolffe, *The Protestant Crusade in Great Britain, 1829–1860* (Oxford: Clarendon Press, 1991), p.112.
16 W.H. Rule, *Martyrs of the Reformation* (London: John Mason, 1851), p.vi.
17 Charlotte Elizabeth, *Personal Recollections* (3rd edn., London: Seeley, 1847), pp.14–15. I am indebted to Peter Nockles for this reference.

18 Andrew Atherstone, 'The Martyrs Memorial at Oxford', *Journal of Ecclesiastical History*, 54 (2003), pp.278–301.

19 Martin Wellings, 'The First Protestant Martyr of the Twentieth Century: The Life and Significance of John Kensit (1853–1902)', in Wood (ed.), *Martyrs and Martyrologies*, pp.347–58.

20 Nockles, 'Reformation Revised?', passim.

21 George Spencer, *Our Hope that the Light of Truth Will Yet Shine Forth in England, Encouraged by a Recollection of the Virtues and Sufferings of her Catholic Martyrs* (Birmingham: R.P. Stone, 1838), pp.18–19.

22 P.F. Moran, *Historical Sketch of the Persecutions Suffered by the Catholics of Ireland Under the Rule of Cromwell and the Puritans* (Dublin: Duffy, 1861).

23 Myles O'Reilly, *Memorials of those who Suffered for the Catholic Faith in Ireland in the 16th, 17th and 18th Centuries* (London: Burns, Oates and Co., 1868).

24 Ibid., p.x.

25 Ibid., pp.xi, xv–xvi.

26 Myles O'Reilly and Richard Brennan, *Lives of the Irish Martyrs and Confessors with Additions Including a History of the Penal Laws* (New York: James Sheehy, 1878); D.P. Conyngham, *Lives of the Irish Martyrs* (1872), bound up with Thomas Walsh and D.P. Conyngham, *The Church of Erin: Her History, her Saints, her Martyrs, her Monasteries and Shrines* (New York: D. & J. Sadleir, 1885).

27 *The Canonization of the Forty English and Welsh Martyrs: A Commemoration Presented by the Postulators of the Cause* (London: Office of the Vice-Postulation, 1970), pp.23–9.

28 *Short Memoirs of the English Martyrs* (Leeds: Whitehead, 1884), p.v.

29 John Morris, *The English Martyrs: Why they Died, what they Suffered, what Sort of Men They Were* (Stonyhurst College, 1887), p.3 and passim.

30 Austin J. King, *The English Martyrs* (Bath: Charles Hallett, 1887), pp.3–4.

31 Luke Rivington, *The English Martyrs or Where is Continuity?* (London: Kegan Paul, 1892), p.10.

32 E.M. Wilmot-Buxton, *A Book of English Martyrs* (London: Burns & Oates, 1915), pp.v–vi (preface by Camm); Dominic Aidan Bellenger, 'Dom Bede Camm (1864–1942) Monastic Martyrologist', in Wood (ed.), *Martyrs and Martyrologies*, pp.371–81.

33 Bellenger, 'Camm', p.378; Wilmot-Buxton, *English Martyrs*, p.xi.

34 John Townsend, *Lord Nelson's Funeral Improved* (London, 1806).

35 George Loveless, *The Victims of Whiggery* (London, 1837).

36 Thomas Moore, *The Life and Death of Lord Edward FitzGerald* (2 Volumes, London: Longman, 1831), i, p.304; R.R. Madden, *The Life and Times of Robert Emmet, esq.* (Dublin: Duffy, 1847), p.242.

37 William Ridgeway, *A Report of the Trial of Robert Emmet Upon a Charge of High Treason* (London [1803]).

38 *Lines on the Death of the Glorious Liberator, Daniel O'Connell, esq. MP* [Dublin, 1847]: Trinity College Dublin Library, Irish Ballads Collection.

39 Charles Kingsley, *True Words for Brave Men* (London, 1878), p.205.

40 *Memorials of Captain Hedley Vicars* (London: Nisbet, 1856); Olive Anderson, 'The Growth of Christian Militarism in mid-Victorian Britain', *EHR*, 86 (1971), pp.47–9.

41 Robert Meek, *The Martyr of Allahabad: Memoirs of Arthur Marcus Hill Cheek* (London: Nisbet, 1856), p.3.

42 David Rolfs, *No Peace for the Wicked: Northern Protestant Soldiers and the American Civil War* (Knoxville: University of Tennessee Press, 2009), pp.76, 82–3; Harry S. Stout, *Upon the Altar of the Nation: A Moral History of the American Civil War* (New York: Viking, 2006) pp.82–3.

43 F.H. Doyle, *The Return of the Guards and Other Poems* (London: Macmillan, 1866), p.276. It may be noted that these lines were not included in a later shorter version of the poem: A.C. Addison and C. Matthews, *A Deathless Story; or the 'Birkenhead' and its Heroes* (London: Hutchinson, 1906).

44 A.M. Sullivan, '*The Wearing of the Green*', or the Persecuted Funeral Procession (Dublin: A.M. Sullivan, 1868); *The Irish Times*, 9 Dec. 1867; Gary Owens, 'Constructing the Martyrs: The Manchester Executions and the Nationalist Imagination', in Lawrence W. McBride (ed.), *Images, Icons and the Irish Nationalist Imagination* (Dublin: Four Courts Press, 1999), pp.18–36.

45 Elizabeth Rundle Charles, *Three Martyrs of the Nineteenth Century* (London: SPCK, 1885).

46 David Hilliard, 'The Making of an Anglican Martyr: Bishop John Coleridge Patteson of Melanesia', in Wood (ed.), *Martyrs and Martyrologies*, p.344.

47 Douglas H. Johnson, 'The Death of Gordon: A Victorian Myth', *Journal of Imperial and Commonwealth History*, 10 (1982), pp.285–310.

48 John Wolffe, *Great Deaths: Grieving, Religion and Nationhood in Victorian and Edwardian Britain* (Oxford: British Academy/Oxford University Press, 2000), pp.136–53.

49 Francis Hastings Doyle, *To the Memory of General Gordon* (n.p., 1885).

50 Quoted in Max Jones, *The Last Great Quest: Captain Scott's Antarctic Sacrifice* (Oxford: Oxford University Press, 2003), p.165.

51 Ibid., pp.200–1.

52 A.F. Winnington-Ingram, *A Day of God, Being Five Addresses on the Subject of the Present War* (London, 1914), pp.74–5.

53 A.F. Winnington-Ingram, *Easter the Victory of Freedom* (London, 1917), p.4.

54 Quoted in Ruth Dudley-Edwards, *Patrick Pearse: The Triumph of Failure* (London: Victor Gollancz, 1977), p.236.

55 Sheridan Gilley, 'Pearse's Sacrifice: Christ and Cuchulain Crucified and Risen in the Easter Rising, 1916', in Jim Obelkevich, Lyndal Roper and Raphael Samuel (eds), *Disciplines of Faith: Studies in Religion, Politics and Patriarchy* (London: Routledge, 1987), pp.479–97.

56 Quoted in Maurice Joy (ed.), *The Irish Rebellion of 1916 and its Martyrs* (New York: Devin-Adair, 1916), pp.339–40.

57 *Irish Independent*, 7 Oct. 1920, p.4.

58 Stuart Mews, 'The Hunger-Strike of the Lord Mayor of Cork, 1920: Irish, English and Vatican Attitudes', in W.J. Sheils and Diana Woods (eds), *The Churches, Ireland and the Irish: Studies in Church History 25* (Oxford: Blackwell/Ecclesiastical History Society, 1989), pp.385–99: see also Murphy, Chapter 12 in this volume.

59 *Irish Independent*, 27 Oct. 1920, p.5; 30 Oct. 1920, p.5.

60 Wolffe, *Great Deaths*, pp.262–4.

61 A crude but suggestive indicator is that whereas a search of *The Times* Online for occurrences of the word 'martyr' in the six years commencing 4 August 1914 yields 350 hits, the comparable figure for the six-year period commencing on 3 September 1939 is only 209.

62 Padraig O'Malley, *Biting at the Grave: The Irish Hunger Strikes and the Politics of Despair* (Belfast: Blackstaff, 1990), p.138.

63 Maria Cecilia Buerhle, *Maria Goretti: Saint and Martyr* (Dublin: Clonmore and Reynolds, 1952). I am indebted to Professor Sean Connolly for information on this point.

64 *The Irish Times*, 6 Oct. 1969, p.8.

65 Ibid., p.4.

66 Cahal Daly, 'Addresses on Peace in Northern Ireland', Vol. 2, p.277, 6 Sept. 1981 (Linen Hall Library, Belfast).

67 Interview with Bernadette McAliskey (formerly Devlin) by John Wolffe and John Bell, 28 Mar. 2011.

68 John Wolffe, 'National Occasions at St Paul's Since 1800', in *St Paul's: the Cathedral Church of London, 604–2004* (New Haven and London: Yale University Press, 2004), p.390.

69 David O'Donoghue, 'Army's Congo Mission Casts a Long Shadow', *Irish Studies in International Affairs*, 17 (2006), pp.43–59.

70 Jane Leonard, 'Remembrance Sunday in Dublin since 1919', in Richard English and Graham Walker (eds), *Unionism in Modern Ireland: New Perspectives on Politics and Culture* (Basingstoke: Macmillan, 1986), pp.109–11; O'Malley, *Biting at the Grave*, pp.251–9; Gordon Wilson, *Marie: A Story from Enniskillen* (London: Collins, 1990).

71 See Farhad Khosrokhavar, *Suicide Bombers: Islam's New Martyrs* (London: Pluto Press, 2005), pp.9–10, 13.

INDEX